# THE HOME FRONT

*Essie Mae Thompson  1926  age 23*

# THE HOME FRONT IN WORLD WAR II

## From the Letters of Essie Mae Hill to Field Director Gerald L. Hill

By

### George J. Hill, M.D., M.A., D.Litt.
Captain, Medical Corps, USNR (ret)

HERITAGE BOOKS
2020

# HERITAGE BOOKS

*AN IMPRINT OF HERITAGE BOOKS, INC.*

## Books, CDs, and more—Worldwide

For our listing of thousands of titles see our website
at
www.HeritageBooks.com

Published 2020 by
HERITAGE BOOKS, INC.
Publishing Division
5810 Ruatan Street
Berwyn Heights, Md. 20740

The American Red Cross requests that all authors prominently display the following language in their book or other literary work: This book is not sponsored, endorsed or authorized by the American Red Cross.

### Illustrations

Front cover: The photographs of Essie Mae Hill on the cover and frontispiece are from the Hill family collection. Other images are from the drawings made by Essie Mae Hill and the Hill children, and anonymous Google images. The photo story of Essie Mae in uniform was published in the *Cedar Rapids* [Iowa] *Gazette* in January 1944. A recent picture of the exterior of the Hill family home in Mount Vernon, Iowa, is from Caldwell Bankers' website.

Cover designed by Debbie Riley

International Standard Book Numbers
Paperbound: 978-0-7884-3304-7

To Mom


With eyes brimming tears she ran to him,
Throwing her arms around his neck,
        and kissed him.
                – Homer, *The Odyssey*, XXIII, 206-7

*Essie Mae Hill in 1977*

*Essie Mae Thompson*
*Lisbon, Iowa, High School*
*Graduation photo – 1920*

# Contents

# Prologue
## "Floozy," the B-17

One noon in the late fall of 1942, we heard the roar of a plane overhead. Because the "big ones" were still somewhat of a novelty in our quiet little village in eastern Iowa, the whole family dashed out into the back yard to see it. "Oh Daddy, it's a B17," cried nine-year old George, proud of his ability to identify aircraft. "And it's flying so low, I can see the pilot in it!" he added triumphantly. At this point, not wanting to be outdone by his older brother, seven-year old Tommy danced up and down and exclaimed, "Why I believe it's going to land!" The gap made by those recently pulled front teeth made him lisp just a little in his excitement. "No, son, B17's don't land around here. You know it takes a lot of room for them to maneuver around in," replied Daddy. Nevertheless, there was ill-concealed excitement in his voice too, for he had recently joined the Civil Air Patrol, had been doing a little flying himself, and the sight of that big bomber flying so low was really beautiful. As the plane disappeared into the west beyond the treetops, we all sighed a little, and went back into the house to finish lunch, and take up the humdrum existence of school, housecleaning, and the bank cashier's cage. The episode was over, but it had been nice while it lasted. Little did we know! [1]

A couple of hours later, the phone rang. It was Daddy. "Say, Honey, that plane did land, after all – Emergency. They were out of gas, and came down in the country northwest of town about a mile and a half. Bye," and he hung up, without giving me a chance to caution him to get his heavy coat, for the wind had turned bitter cold. A few minutes later the boys rushed into the house, both talking at once almost incoherently, wanting their bicycles to "go and see the plane." I was left stranded at home, having neither car nor bicycle, and I saw nothing of the family for hours. The unaccustomed quiet of the house made the waiting seem endless. Then suddenly, everything began to happen. A great stamping and doorbell ringing on the front porch – many voices – I rushed to the door and when I opened it and looked out, it seemed to me that there were multitudes of smiling strangers, all dressed in helmets, and heavy fur-lined flying suits. Behind them I saw one tall civilian and a couple of youngsters – my family. "Come on in," boomed Daddy, and in they trooped. It was the crew of the B17 – "Floozy" as she was called. Introductions were made and then Daddy told me, "Do you think you could find places for six of these fellows to sleep here tonight? I took a hasty inventory of my resources, and said, "Of course." Explanations followed. The plane was out of gas and by the time the high octane gas which was needed was trucked from Moline, the tires refilled, the batteries regenerated, and the whole plane ready, it would take several hours, so the crew were to stay all night with various townspeople and be all set for the take-off the next morning. "Floozy" had gotten off course when a cold front had suddenly moved in across their line of flight and with just fifteen minutes of gas left, the pilot had made a beautiful three-point emergency landing in a recently mowed soybean field.

Six of the boys slept at our house that night – twelve for breakfast the next morning at five o'clock! Daddy went back to the plane after all the arrangements were made, and spent the cold, bleak hours of the night as a Civil Air Patrol guard. We were all out there at six o'clock the next morning, after breakfast, to see it take off, but we were doomed to disappointment, for it was nearly two weeks before the plane got into the air again. Engine trouble developed and finally a ground crew and a new engine had to be sent out from the Base, before the final repairs could be made. In the meantime, the news spread. People drove literally hundreds of miles to get their first close-up view of a big bomber. When it was evident that first morning that we wouldn't see it take off right away, I drove the children back to school. A few minutes later, a couple of the crew came to the house and said, "Do you suppose we could find something around here that we could use to keep the people back from the plane with?" The first guard fence was my clothes line stretched around bean poles which were hastily pulled up out of the garden. It was midnight lunches for the fellows who were just finishing the "early watch," and five o'clock breakfasts for those on the "graveyard shift" – telephone calls to girl friends who waited back at the Base for dates which never appeared.

My last supply of pre-war tooth brushes went into the "war effort" – just nine of them, so it happened. But what fun! And what wonderful guests those boys were! So appreciative, and so helpful. A timid knock on the kitchen door, after I'd shooed the last reluctant latecomer to bed. "What is it?" I asked, thinking maybe I should have put an extra cover on the bed in the north room. "I just didn't like to think of you doing those dishes all alone, so I thought maybe you'd let me help. The rest of the fellows are all asleep," he added apologetically, for that had been my instructions. He was the only married man in the group – the co-pilot – and I've always thought that accounted

---

[1] The Prologue is excerpted from "The Floozy Story" in Essie Mae Thompson Hill, *Prairie Daughter* (2e), 104-6.

for his offer.  I was touched by their thoughtfulness – they were all wonderful, but the bombardier, 2nd Lieutenant Marc Pitts, is the one who has a place all his own in our hearts.

"This is Marc Pitts, the bombardier," Daddy said that first morning when I went with the others for my first, and what I thought would be my last, view of "Floozy."  "He stayed to guard his bombsight last night while the others were in town.  As a matter of fact, I was about to pull a gun on him about two o'clock last night.  I saw someone running toward the plane in the dim light, and I challenged him a couple of times before I recognized him.  He had gotten cold, and was just sprinting around for some exercise to warm up a little.  I recognized him just in time."  Daddy grinned rather sheepishly at the recollection.  Until officials came from a nearby military school to take the bombsight into protective custody, Marc stayed close to the plane, as his oath as a bombardier required him to do, but as soon as he was released from his responsibility, he came into town to claim his toothbrush, freshen up, and become a member of our household.  Later we learned that he had a little brother at home, just Tommy's age, but at the time, all we knew was that, left to his own devices, he went out into the back yard where Tommy was building a "Floozy Jr." out of orange crates.

Those two boys, one just past twenty-one, the other only seven, talked over that conglomeration of string and rough boards, bent nails, and rusty wire, like a couple of test pilots discussing a new dive bomber.  Tommy, ordinarily shy and reluctant to talk to strangers, opened his little heart and poured out all his dreams to his new friend, who listened and commented quietly in a "man to man" way.  Tommy even drank his milk with relish when he found that Marc would really rather have milk than a cup of coffee, or even a coke.  Finally, word came that repairs on "Floozy" would be such an extensive job that a B17 would be flown from the Base in Kansas bringing a ground crew, and taking back the crew from "Floozy."  My two boys and I were "elected" to take them to the airport about twenty-five miles away, where the incoming plane would land and take off.  We arrived at the airport about seven o'clock in the evening, all set to see the takeoff.

Tommy, accustomed to early bedtime hours, grew restless and impatient.  Marc took him on his lap, inconvenient as it was, trying to balance himself with his cumbersome gear on a high stool at the counter, and visited with Tommy about his own little brother and sister at home in Delaware.  He showed him the ring his father had given him when he went into the Air Force, and told him how he hoped someday he could learn to be a pilot like his father had been in the other war.  Finally, even that palled, and Tommy said with a sigh, "I'll be glad when I finally see that plane take off."  Marc smiled understandingly, and then stiffened as a thought occurred to him.  "Why, Tommy, it has gotten so dark, and the plane is parked so far out on the field, you won't be able to see it take off after all."  Tommy slumped in Marc's arms, in unspoken disappointment.  "But, I tell you," Marc said, sensing intuitively the little boy's disappointment, "I'll be out in the Bombardier's bay, and I'll flip my lights to you to tell you good bye."  We never saw Marc again, although he wrote to Tommy many times.  His first letter, telling of the details of a practice flight was so interesting and Tommy was so thrilled that he took it to school, and the teacher let him read it aloud to all the children.  The teacher wanted to give her pupils some practical training in letter writing, so she suggested that they each write a letter to Marc, as a Language assignment.  She sent them all in a big envelope, with a note of explanation.  Marc tried to get leave long enough to come back to Iowa and meet the teacher and the friends that he had come to know through letters, but he didn't quite make it.  He was sent overseas.  On June 15, Marc's plane was shot down over Germany.  Nine parachutes were counted as they fluttered down.  Marc and the co-pilot never got out.

**B-17E**
*"Floozy" was this model of the B-17,*
*A four-engine bomber that landed near*
*Lisbon, Iowa in October 1942.*

*Google Image*

# Introduction

This is a true story of an American family on the Home Front in World War II – a mother and two boys – with a father in service. It is the story of the family of Gerald and Essie Mae Hill and their sons George and Tommy. It is largely told in their own words, in the many letters that they wrote over a period of 21 months. During this period, from November 1943 until August 1945, Dad was "away" in uniform with the American Red Cross, and Mom was coping on the "Home Front." They knew that this was an important moment in history, and they intended to make a record that could be preserved for their children and their grandchildren. He wrote a long letter to his family at least once a week, and it was usually typed. She tried to write a letter every day, on a scrap of note paper, whenever she found a free moment. In in the fall of 1945, their letters, photographs, and other documents from World War II were placed in his footlockers, which were then closed, clasped shut, and not opened again for seventy-five years. His letters have been edited and annotated; that book is entitled *Rolling with Patton.*[2]

Very few letters exchanged between husband and wife have been preserved from World War II. I know of no other collection than the letters of Gerald and Essie Mae Hill that has been published; and at this late date, I doubt if any more will be found. Only a few books have been published based on letters from men in service in World War II to his wife or sweetheart.[3]

I can find only one book about the letters that millions of women wrote in World War II to their men in service. This book, *Since You Went Away*, takes its title from a work of fiction published by Margaret Buell Wilder in 1943. Wilder's novel was imagined from a group of letters that she had published in a column for a local newspaper. David O. Selznick transformed Wilder's novel into a movie starring Claudette Colbert, also with the same title, *Since You Went Away*, which was released in 1944.[4]

## The Origins

Gerald and Essie Mae Hill lived in the small town of Lisbon, near Cedar Rapids, at the start of the war. They were both born in farmhouses – his family farmed near Clarion, in Wright County, and her father's farm was near Central City, in Linn County. Gerald, known by his nickname as "Toot" Hill, and Essie Mae (née Thompson), were younger than their siblings, and they had advantages that were unique: they went to college. Gerald, born in 1905, was the first man in his family to go to college, and Essie Mae, born in 1903, was the first woman in her family to attend college. They were doted on by their parents and their older siblings, who had little to offer except guidance and encouragement. Both of them were raised as obedient Methodists; they were taught to read the Bible, sing the hymns, and behave themselves. They met at Cornell College in Mount Vernon, Iowa. Gerald did various jobs for the college during the

---

[2] For the history of American Red Cross in World War II, see: Foster Rhea Dulles, *The American Red Cross* (New York: Harper and Brothers, 1950); this book is copyrighted by the American Red Cross. Also, Patrick F. Gilbo, *The American Red Cross: The First Century* (New York: Harper and Row, 1981).

[3] Three excellent books of letters from Army men to their wives are Laura Cantor Zelman, *In My Father's Words: The World War II Letters of an Army Doctor* (Potomac Falls, Va.: Laura Cantor Zelman, 2016); Roberta Lesner Bernstein and Judy Lesner Holstein, eds., *Somewhere in Europe: The World War II Letters of Sam Lesner* (n.p.: Bernstein and Holstein, 2016); and William M. Kays, *Letters from a Soldier: A Memoir of World War II* (n.p.: Wimke Press, 2010), which includes his letters and a personal narrative of the war. All three men served in Europe; and Cantor and Kays were in Czechoslovakia on VE-Day, as was Hill. Two fine anthologies of letters from American men and women in World War II are Andrew Carroll, ed., *War Letters: Extraordinary Correspondence from American Wars* (New York: Scribner, 2005), 179-319; and Bill Adler (ed.) with Tracy Quinn McLennan, *World War II Letters* (New York: St. Martin's Press, 2002).

[4] Judy Barrett Litoff and David C. Smith (eds.), *Since You Went Away: World War II Letters from American Women on the Home Front* (Lawrence, Kansas: University Press of Kansas, 1991); and Margaret Buell Wilder, *Since You Went Away: Letters to a Soldier from His Wife* (New York: Whittlesey House, McGraw-Hill Book Co., 1943); and movie, *Since You Went Away* (1944).

school years, and he did manual labor every summer. Essie Mae earned money as a grammar school teacher after her freshman and sophomore years, and she was a teaching assistant during her last two years of college. Essie Mae entered Cornell three years before Gerald, and she was teaching in the geology department at the college when he was a senior; he took one of her courses. She graduated in 1926, and was elected to Phi Beta Kappa. After Gerald graduated in 1927, he became publicity director for the college's 75th anniversary. They had each separately spent a summer working at Yellowstone Park, and they enjoyed talking about their wonderful experiences at the park. Three years after his graduation, and after careful scrutiny by her father, they were married on Christmas Day, 1930. She continued to teach geology at the college, and he began a career in business, in an entry level position with Iowa Power and Light Co.

Their first child, George, was born in 1932, and the second, Tommy, in 1935. The Cornell College president reluctantly allowed Essie Mae to continue on the faculty after she was married, but she was not allowed to continue teaching after she became visibly pregnant. She then devoted her life to bringing up her boys, and Gerald began his life's work as a small-town banker. Each of them had additional skills: Essie Mae was an accomplished vocalist and lecturer, and Gerald was a sports writer and publicist. His experience as a journalist would later be cited with approval by his supervisor in the Red Cross. They had a wide circle of friends, and they loved to entertain, to dance, and to travel. Their Methodist upbringing was never forgotten, but after the war, they moved to a larger city and became Episcopalians. They never stopped caring for, helping, and admiring their boys.

## The Book

I have silently edited Essie Mae' letters, correcting typographical and spelling errors, and eliminating some letters, redundancies, and idiomatic expressions. I have converted most of the punctuation in Essie Mae's letters to current usage. However, I have transcribed the quaint correspondence written by the boys as faithfully as I could. Her letters are transcribed in 9 font Paladino Linotype; brief quotations are inserted in 11 font Times New Roman; longer quotations are in TNR 10, or Paladino Linotype 9. I have combined many short paragraphs to save space, and I indented to show paragraphing instead of double spacing between paragraphs, as she usually did. I have also preserved her writing style, in which she often used dashes (–) between phrases and sentences, and her occasional use of quotation marks (").

The important themes in Essie Mae's letters were her love and concern for Gerald and for their sons; for her extended family and for his family; for Cornell College, its faculty and alumni; for the little towns of Mount Vernon and Lisbon, Iowa; for managing, alone, their family's finances; and for the Civil Air Patrol (CAP). She was certain that the U.S. would be victorious in this terrible war, and that a good outcome would finally be the result of America's hard work and suffering. Her letters were usually handwritten, often on scraps of paper. She was frequently pressed for time, and she jotted notes to him when she had a few spare minutes. During the first year of his absence, she was beset with anxiety and loneliness, while working full time as a teacher, parent, and landlady. She had periods of personal illness, and her boys were sometimes difficult and disobedient. She learned to literally keep the home fires burning, shoveling coal and ashes. By the second year, she had learned to balance her various obligations. Her children were then doing well in school and at home, and she was doing more things that she enjoyed. She was able to learn new things, and her health was also better.

Essie Mae's letters also show the change that occurred late in 1944, as Gerald began training to enter the war – perhaps in the Pacific, but then in Europe. He was increasingly excited during training, and more so as he survived close encounters in combat, and he was thrilled at the moment of victory. On the other hand, she could only wait, worry, and pray that he would be safe, and that they could move forward together, as a family, after the war.

*Gerald "Toot" Hill and Essie Mae Thompson     ca. 1930*
*She is wearing his Cornell College letter sweater*

# Glossary of Principal Names
### See Full Listing in Abbreviations and All Names. Frequently occurring names are underscored.

## Hill and Thompson Families

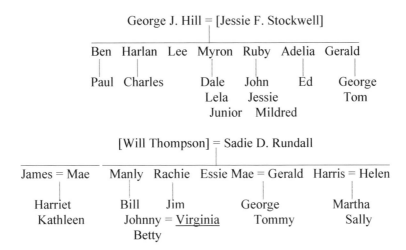

George J. Hill = [Jessie F. Stockwell]

Ben   Harlan   Lee   Myron   Ruby   Adelia   Gerald

Paul   Charles      Dale   John   Ed   George
               Lela   Jessie      Tom
               Junior   Mildred

[Will Thompson] = Sadie D. Rundall

James = Mae    Manly   Rachie   Essie Mae = Gerald   Harris = Helen

Harriet      Bill   Jim      George      Martha
Kathleen   Johnny = Virginia   Tommy      Sally
           Betty

| Hill Family | Thompson Family | |
|---|---|---|
| George J. Hill – "Dad" "Grandpa" | Sadie (Rundall) Thompson – "Mother" "Grandma" | |
| Paul and Marie Hill | James and Mae Thompson | "Runk" Lester Runkle |
| Charles Hill | Manly Thompson | Helene (Black) Runkle |
| Myron and Julia (Woodin) Hill | Bill Thompson | Bob Runkle |
| Dale, Lela, Junior Hill | Johnny Thompson | "Dottie" Runkle |
| Ruby (Hill) Woodin | Betty Thompson | |
| John Howard Woodin | Rachie (Thompson) High | |
| Jessie Woodin | Jim High | |
| Adelia (Hill) Hemenway | Essie Mae (Thompson) Hill + family | |
| Ed Hemenway | Harris Thompson | |
| Gerald "Toot" "Jerry" Hill | Helen (McKune) Thompson | |
| George James Hill "George" | Martha Thompson | |
| Thomas David Hill "Tommy" | Sally Thompson | |

## Others Mentioned in Letters by First Name or Nickname

Al & Bertha Johnson
Charles Arnold, Rev.
"Denny" Denis DeNio
Dick Barker
"Dode" Dorothy Johnson, RN
Doug and Mary Van Metre
Eloise (Stuckslager) Thomas
Gordon Andre, MD
Harold Baltz

Harry and Faye Sizer
Judd Dean, Lt. Col.
"Judge" Claire Littell
Morley Slaght, Lt. Col.
Neil Miner
"Packy" Lanning McFarland
Rowena "Rowie Stuckslager
"Shack" Ruth Shackleford
"Toppy" Clyde Tull

1

# IOWA

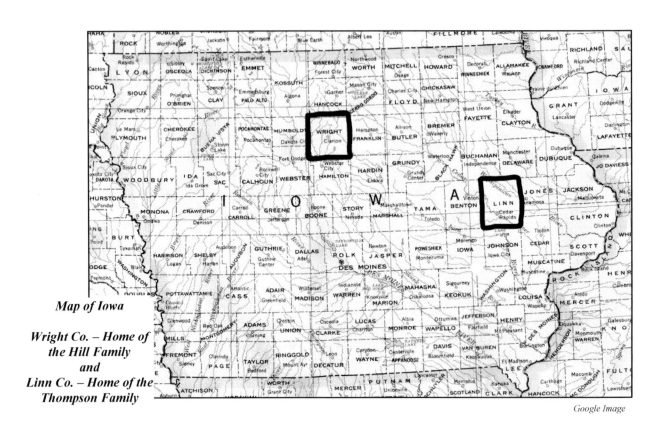

*Map of Iowa*

*Wright Co. – Home of the Hill Family and Linn Co. – Home of the Thompson Family*

*Google Image*

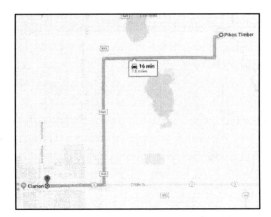

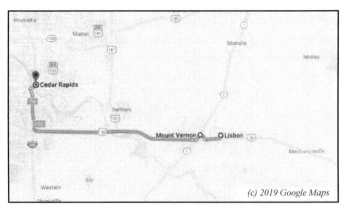

*(c) 2019 Google Maps*

*Wright County, detail showing Clarion and the Hill family farm at Pikes Timber*

*Linn County, detail showing Cedar Rapids, Mount Vernon, and Lisbon. Note Mechanicsville, in Jones County, at right*

# Chapter One

# Before the War

## The Early Years

### Gerald L. Hill and His Family

Gerald Leslie Hill was born 18 September 1905 in a farmhouse in Wright County, Iowa, the last of nine children of George J. Hill and Jessie Fidelia Stockwell. Seven of George and Jessie's children survived to adulthood, but two of their daughters died of diphtheria. Gerald's two older sisters, Ruby and Adelia, were born two years apart after the girls died. They were intended to be replacements for the little girls. But Gerald's birth – five years after Adelia – was unexpected. He was treated with love by his parents and his sisters, and with respect (if not always affection) by his four older brothers, Ben, Harland, Lee, and Myron. We could say that he was spoiled. He was especially close to Ruby and Myron, who always gave him good advice.

He soon showed that he was an independent, precocious young man – indeed, a smarty. He was a good athlete and he was fairly good looking, and he thought he was better than average at everything. He received and preserved his certificates for perfect attendance at school – never tardy – for eight years. His family always called him Gerald (with a hard "g" as in "goat"), but his schoolmates called him "Toot." The reason for the nickname is unknown – there are various stories about it. But he was proud of it. Some say it was because he mispronounced the word "toothless" when he had lost his front teeth; some say it was because he passed gas noisily; but it was more likely a recognition of his talkativeness. Beside his graduation picture in the 1923 Clarion High School Yearbook is written: "Gerald Hill 'Toot' (King Tut), *'And when he talks – Ye Gods! How he does talk!'*."

Gerald's father's parents, Charles "C.W." Hill and Adelia (née Riley), came to Iowa in March 1861 with two little children, George J. (age 4) and Billy (age 1). The Hill family had lived in rural Steuben Co., N.Y., for about 50 years, and land was getting scarce there. Iowa had recently become a state, and Adelia's brother James traveled out there to see what it looked like. James Riley returned with good news about what he found in Wright County. He went back to Iowa with another bachelor brother. C.W. and his small family went with the two Riley boys, and also with them went C.W.'s younger brother, Harlow, known as Harley. C.W. was then 29 and Adelia was 24. It was a hard trip. After traveling on a boat down the Ohio River, they passed through Illinois and most of the way across northern Iowa in a covered wagon, with farm implements, their household goods – including a dropleaf cherry-wood table that C.W. had made – and with a horse and two cows trailing behind them. There were no roads at that time, and it was still Indian country. C.W. purchased forty acres of partially timbered land on the west bank of the Iowa River, six miles northeast of the county seat – the village of Clarion. The piece was called "Pikes Timber." Tragedy struck the family eight years later, when a wagon driven by Harley overturned in the flooded river; Harley and Billy drowned and George just barely survived. The horses' harness was hung in their barn, and the boys were buried on the family farm. They were later re-buried with other members of the family in a cemetery on the other side of the river.

C.W. was industrious and lucky at farming, and he soon bought 240 more acres of good farmland. Eventually, his sons would own three more farms in Wright County, and his grandchildren would own several more. Two of these large farms are still worked by the descendants of his grandson, Myron Hill; one of them is Myron's own "Century Farm." At C.W.'s death in 1923, Pikes Timber passed to his son George. However, unpaid taxes accumulated on the land, and George found it necessary to sell it to his son Gerald, who paid the back taxes. Ten years later, in May 1942, Gerald offered it to Myron for the same reason, but Myron reluctantly declined to accept it, and it passed out of the family. Timberland is not good farmland, but it doesn't produce a yearly income. "Pike's Timber" is now a heavily wooded 46-acre Wright County park and wildlife area on the west bank of the Iowa River.[*] Graceland Cemetery is nearby, a half-mile east of the Iowa River. It was created to be the burial site for the two Hill boys who drowned in 1869, and for the daughters of George and Jessie Stockwell, Nellie and Grace, who died in 1894. The graves of George and Jessie Hill are there, and also others in the Hill family, including C.W.'s spinster sister, Sarah Hill. Many of Jessie's Stockwell family are buried there, too.

Gerald's mother, Jessie Fidelia Stockwell, was the eldest of six children of Benajah Stockwell and Emma Hyde. She and George were married in 1882 on her nineteenth birthday; he was five years older than his bride. Her father, Benajah, brought his family from Vermont to Iowa, after failing in an earlier effort to settle in Illinois. The Stockwell and Hyde families had lived near Lake Champlain for several generations. Benajah was a devout, dour Methodist lay preacher with a long unkempt beard and piercing eyes. He was better as a preacher than as a farmer. After having three more children in Iowa, his wife died, and Benajah married again and moved to Oklahoma.

Jessie's first child was born 10 months after she married George, and within ten years she had a total of six. The first two, Ben and Harlan, decided not to farm, and left their brother Lee to work with their father. Lee failed at farming and he moved away, leaving Myron to take care of his parents and the family farm. Lee's farm was purchased at auction by Ruby and her husband (who was Myron's brother-in-law), and it served as a good source of income for many years. Meanwhile, George and Jessie moved to town, where Jessie was the local midwife and a pillar of the Methodist Church. Gerald was born on the family farm in Grant township when his father was president of the township's School Board, but he attended school in Clarion after his parents moved to town.

Gerald Hill was never curious about his ancestry, although as a young man, he received a copy of "Genealogy of the Hill Family in America." The "Genealogy" is a 14-page mimeographed typescript which was prepared in 1921 by William Edwin Hill, Secretary of the Hill Family Association. Gerald is shown as #153 in this genealogy, in a line that goes back to his great-great-great grandfather, #1 Isaac Hill, said to be "a soldier in the Revolutionary War." Unknown then, but now known, #1 Isaac Hill [Jr.] is the great-grandson of Luke Hill, Sr., and his wife, Mary Hout, who were married in Windsor, Connecticut, in 1651. It is also now known that the ancestors of Gerald's father, George J. Hill, include Edward Fuller, who arrived in Massachusetts in 1620 on the *Mayflower*; Thomas Trowbridge of New Haven, Connecticut, and Taunton, England, who is of Royal Descent; and Edward Howell, of Salem and Long Island, who was a Lord of the Manor in England, and also of Royal Descent.

The ancestors of Gerald's mother, Jessie Stockwell, include the famous Puritan, Samuel Chapin, whose statue stands in Springfield, Mass.; and the Rev. Obadiah Holmes, of Rhode Island, who was publicly whipped by the Puritans in Boston for preaching as a Baptist. Jessie's ancestors also included a Loyalist, John Saxe, who was expelled to Canada after the Revolutionary War; and Jemima Allen, a cousin of the famous Vermont Patriot, Ethan Allen, commander of the Green Mountain Boys. William Stockwell first appeared in eastern Massachusetts in the 1680s, but the Stockwells were part of the diaspora that left Essex County after the witchcraft trials in Salem in 1692. William Stockwell and his sons moved to Sutton, near Worcester, Mass., and William's great-grandson moved to Highgate, Vermont. George's mother, Emma Lodiweska Hyde, descended from men who founded several other towns in Massachusetts, such as Captain Roger Clapp, of Dorchester; Jonathan Hyde, of Cambridge; Obadiah Ward, of Marlboro; and Robert Potter, of Portsmouth, Rhode Island.

Gerald Hill would probably have found these things to be of little interest.[†]

---

[*] For Pike's Timber, map and photos, see: https://www.wrightcounty.org/visitors/outdoor_recreation.php (accessed 6/21/19).
[†] For references to the Hill and Stockwell family genealogies, see Bibliography.

# Essie Mae Thompson and Her Family

Essie Mae Thompson was the fourth child and second daughter of William H. Thompson and his wife Sadie D. Rundall. Essie Mae was born in a farmhouse in northern Linn County, Iowa, on land that had been first settled by Will's father, James Thompson, who came to Iowa shortly before the Civil War began. When he was young, Will Thompson learned to make butter at a creamery in a small town nearby. He loved the work, and was good at it. He married Sadie in 1889, when he was 27 and she was 24. She was born in a small town across the border in the adjacent county, twelve days before Lincoln was shot. Sadie's parents were then living in Lisbon, in the southern part of Linn county. Will and Sadie lived on his father's farm, and then near her parents' house, and he established a small creamery in Lisbon. As they began to have a family, his creamery prospered, and he sold butter to wholesale buyers in Chicago and New York City. The market for his butter collapsed when tariff protections were removed by the Cleveland administration, and cheaper butter could be imported from Europe. Will Thompson never recovered from the failure of his creamery, and he never forgave the Democrats for eliminating the tariff which had protected his butter. He sold cream separators for several years, traveling throughout northwestern Iowa, Nebraska, and South Dakota. Weary of traveling, he spent the rest of his life doing odd jobs, owning a café in Lisbon, farming for a while, and finally working as custodian of the Lisbon school and his son-in-law's bank.

As a young woman, Sadie Rundall passed the rigorous Iowa state examination to become a school teacher. She was working as a grammar school teacher when she married Will. Her father, Reuben Rundall, was a Methodist layman, and her mother, Rachel Manly, was of Pennsylvania Quaker ancestry. Reuben came from a long line of farmers, but he was skilled at carpentry and preferred cabinet making to agriculture. He built an inn for travelers on the old Military Road, now Iowa State Route No. 1, north of Mount Vernon. Before they were married, Rachel was a student in Mount Vernon at the Iowa Seminary, which became Cornell College. They adopted a baby, Pallie, who was left behind after a wagon train stopped at their inn. They then had two daughters – Sadie and her sister Mattie – and they also raised three more orphaned children. They were able to help Pallie to graduate from Cornell College.

Will and Sadie Thompson's first child, James, was born a little over 9 months after the marriage, and they had two more, two years apart – Manly and Rachel, "Rachie." Then a pause, and two more – Essie Mae and Harris, born in 1903 and 1907. Sadie's sister Mattie had a son, Lester Runkle, born in 1904. The three youngsters – Essie Mae, Lester, and Harris – played together. It was a troubled threesome at times when they were young, but they were great friends as they grew older. Essie Mae's older brothers moved out of her parents' home and out of Iowa when she was young. Her sister married when Essie Mae was 11, and she moved to a farm about 10 miles from Lisbon. Rachie's marriage broke up, and as a single parent, she lived on the farm with her son, Jim. She and Essie Mae often visited each other, and Jim was somewhat like an older brother for Essie Mae's sons.

The Thompsons' home in Lisbon was a block north of the school, and Essie Mae remembered her twelve years of school there with fondness. She was a good student. She recalled that "The school day always started with opening exercises – Bible reading and the Lord's Prayer. Then we had some singing, or the teacher read out loud from a book she thought we ought to become familiar with. ... No whispering or communication was allowed after we 'took our seats' and very emphatically there was no gum chewing. ... At the end of the day, the teacher waited to dismiss the children until everyone was sitting 'in position' with desks cleared, hands clasped, backs straight. Then she would say, 'Turn,' pause, 'Stand,' pause again, then 'Pass'; and the children, one row at a time, would make their exit down the stairs in single file. ... After two years of Latin, our class of seven, including two future Phi Beta Kappas, elected to study Virgil's *Aeneid*, instead of the usual third year Latin study of Cicero's *Orations*.[*]

Essie Mae's father's family – the Thompsons – had come to Massachusetts from Nova Scotia in the 1850's. She was told that they had gone to Canada as Loyalists when the British evacuated from Boston in 1776. That was a shameful "family secret," not to be discussed. The truth was not revealed until the 1980s: The first of the family in North America – Archibald Thompson – was not a Loyalist. He was a Presbyterian who had emigrated from Northern Ireland. He was a skilled weaver who came to Plymouth County, Massachusetts, and died there in 1776. His son, Archibald II, served in Nova Scotia during the French and Indian War, and he returned there after the war, believing that it would be a land of opportunity. James Thompson, son of Archibald II, married Hannah Scott, daughter of the sheriff of Colchester County, and his son, Joseph Scott Thompson, married Ruth Archibald – no relation, just a coincidence of names.

---

[*] *Prairie Daughter*, 32-3.

Ruth Archibald's ancestors included many of the early leaders of northern Nova Scotia; the Archibalds are said to be the "first family" of the county. Ruth's ancestors also include John Prescott of Hampton, N.H., John Putnam of Salem, and the most famous of all: Rebecca (Towne) Nurse, known as "Goody" Nurse, who was hanged as a witch in Salem in 1692. For reasons unknown, Joseph and Ruth decided to come back to Massachusetts. Their son James married another Scots woman – Jane Grant, whose grandparents were from the Loch of Inverness. They left Massachusetts for what they believed would be a better place: to the rich black soil of the Iowa prairieland. They arrived in Iowa shortly before the Civil War began, with their four-year old daughter and James' younger brother. They had seven more children on their farm in northern Linn County, including Will, born in 1862.

The ancestry of the Rundall family – Essie Mae's maternal grandfather's – was a mystery to her. All she knew was that her Rundall great-grandparents were buried in a country cemetery near where her grandparents' inn had been located. The reason for the mystery was another "family secret" which was not discovered until late in Essie Mae's life. Martha Tompkins Rundall – her great-grandmother – was a "love child" – from an out-of-wedlock affair. Martha Tompkins' father, Bartholomew Tompkins, a farmer in Putnam Co., N.Y., was already the father of six children, and his wife, Rachel, was still alive. Martha Tompkins was raised by Rachel, her step-mother, which was not unusual in those days. When Martha and Reuben Rundall were married, they moved west to Ohio, and then on to Iowa. A vague and inaccurate story was told that the Rundalls had been ship carpenters in New York. In fact, William Rundle, the first of the family in America, was one of the wealthy founders of Greenwich, Conn., and he was buried there in 1714. The family name has been spelled many ways; Randall's Island in New York City is named for one of them. Essie Mae's ancestors in the Rundall family also include Simon Hoyt and Abraham Pierson.

Rachel Manly, who married Rueben Rundall, descended from of one of William Penn's Pennsylvania Quakers – John Sharples – whose descendants have usually spelled the family name as Sharpless; and from John Townsend, a founder of the Quaker settlement of Oyster Bay, Long Island. Her earliest ancestor in the Manly family is John Manley, a plantation owner in Cecil Co., Maryland, who is probably the same man as John Manly, pirate of the Chesapeake. In that line, her ancestors include many early Irish Quakers in Pennsylvania.

## Gerald Hill and Essie Mae Thompson
## Cornell College

Cornell College in Mount Vernon, Iowa, was founded in 1853 as Iowa Conference Seminary. It provided an opportunity for young men and women, usually Methodists, to become public school teachers in Iowa. In 1857, it became a four-year college, named for a distant relative of Ezra Cornell, for whom Cornell University is named. The names of Cornell College and Cornell University have since been unendingly conflated.

Both the Hill family and the Thompson family were devout members of the Methodist Church.

----------

Essie Mae's mother wanted to have her children go to college, so she refused to leave Lisbon when her husband wanted to move the family to South Dakota. Three of Sadie Thompson's five children went to Cornell, and another "read law" and became a lawyer. Essie Mae graduated from college with honors, walking the five-mile round trip from her home in Lisbon to the college campus in Mount Vernon. She had to work for two years to earn enough money to finish. After her freshman year, she taught grades one to eight in a country school, and after her sophomore year, she taught third grade in another town. It was good experience. It enabled her to become certified as an Iowa public school teacher, as her mother and grandmother had been. Essie Mae soon settled on a major in geology and a minor in vocal music, and she was elected to Phi Beta Kappa at graduation in 1926. She had been a successful teaching assistant in the Geology Department, and she was immediately offered a junior faculty appointment in that department. She endured, and sometimes enjoyed, several summers of field work in geology as an undergraduate and graduate student. She tried to move up in her field, and she had good references, but there were few openings for women in higher education. She saved the sweet, bitter, letters of regret that she received from Washington University in St. Louis, the University of Iowa, and Columbia University. Essie Mae wondered what she would be doing for the rest of her life. If she didn't find a man pretty soon, she would become an old maid. And then in 1929, three things happened which suggested that a change might happen in her life: First, Clark University offered her a fellowship. Clark was one of the few universities that accepted women candidates for the Ph.D., and this would be the step up that she needed. But then in October 1929, the stock market crashed. It was not felt immediately in Iowa, but the Wall Street crash was an ominous warning – the "flapper era" was about to end. The third event in that year was a good one. By chance, she had a conversation with "Toot" Hill, one of the students that she had taught in her first year on the faculty at Cornell. "Toot" Hill had graduated from Cornell College in 1927, and in 1929, he was working at several jobs in Mount Vernon.

Gerald Hill came to Cornell College with great expectations. He was confident, talkative, athletic, and reasonably good looking. His high school experiences had led him to believe that he would do well in college. He was a member of his high school's championship debate team and he played a grim-visage center on his high school's championship varsity football team. He composed his papers quickly and did a rapid re-read for a final draft, so he believed that he could become a journalist. Although he had only turned eighteen at the beginning of his freshman year, Toot Hill looked and acted mature enough to be the paid "father" at Bowman Hall – the girls' dormitory. In this position, he was the man of the house, taking care of the furnace, and mowing the lawn. He presided at the head of the table at each meal, and offered the blessing. The blessings were typed on a card. For dinner, he was to say:

> "We thank Thee for this day and all that it has meant to us.
> "May Thy richest blessing be upon us, as we partake of this evening meal."

Gerald enjoyed being called "Toot," and he would let others wonder what that nickname might mean. He was well groomed, always in a shirt and tie, wearing wire-rimmed glasses. His shirt was usually white, with a stiff collar, and his necktie was very conservative. He had clean hands and well-trimmed fingernails with nicely rounded cuticles. Even then, he looked like a banker. In spite of his good record in high school, he wasn't a strong athlete at the college level. But he wasn't dismayed, and he became the manager of the varsity teams. He earned his "C" letter in that way, with a distinctive "M" on it. His connection with sports led him to be invited to join a secret Cornell fraternity, "the Delts," (Delta Phi Rho), which was usually only for athletes. By the time he was a senior, he was in charge of the college's publicity office, and he was poised to continue that after he graduated. He began to work as a part-time sports writer, rapidly typing feed for the *Cedar Rapids Gazette* and the *Des Moines Register*. He learned that a successful newspaper man can't have writer's block. Toot Hill could type a story as a game progressed, describing its progress. He would finish the piece and send it immediately to the Western Union office when the game ended. He was an avid reader of the daily papers, and he became a friend of the key staff members at both the *Gazette* and *Register*. In fact, he was so gregarious that his circle of friends became wider and wider with each passing year. He would soon find someone in common in conversation with any one that he met. He graduated in 1927 with majors in economics and political science, and he appeared to be on a course to success. Toot soon joined the Lion's Club – a men's service club – and became its secretary. He became the graduate advisor for the Delts, and he passed the tests to become a 3rd degree member of the Masons – the so-called "Blue Lodge." Soon after graduation, he was accepted by the Iowa Electric Light and Power Co. to become its office manager in Mount Vernon. By 1929, Gerald "Toot" Hill had three jobs: He was part-time director of publicity for Cornell College; a part-time newspaper sports writer "stringer"; and a full-time salesman for the power company.

----------

Essie Mae tells what happened next:
"One thing leads to another, and the aftermath of the summer of 1929 in Yellowstone will continue to the end of time. After I came home from Yellowstone, I used to go to Lisbon on the interurban every weekend to visit Mom and Dad, and the ticket office was in the Iowa Railway and Light office at the east end of Main Street in Mount Vernon. Toot Hill worked there and sold me the tickets. He had been a 'Savage' at Lake Camp three years before, and we found we had lots of mutual experiences to laugh about and talk over, in that fall of 1929, while I waited for the car to come. In fact, there was so much to talk about that we began dating. The big date was December 25, 1930, when we were married in the Methodist Church in Mount Vernon. Call it 'The Saga of Yellowstone Park'."*

---

* Essie Mae Thompson Hill, *Prairie Daughter*, 84.

# Marriage, Work, and a Growing Family

## Gerald "Toot" Hill and Essie Mae (Thompson) Hill

Of their courtship, from the fall of 1929 until their marriage on Christmas Day in 1930, little has been preserved. However, one of the souvenirs that Essie Mae saved in her scrapbook is a pair of matching tickets for an airplane ride in Washington, D.C., on August 9, 1930. It appears likely that she traveled to Washington with her fiancé, and they went to places that she seen with her brother Manly seven years earlier, in the summer before her second year at Cornell College. In 1922, Manly was a young lawyer working for the U.S. Forest Service.

Manly's father-in-law, a distinguished Southern gentleman, also worked for the government in some capacity. Perhaps it was the Secret Service. Essie Mae wrote about how he opened doors to many strange and unusual places. Their ride in a single engine plane over Washington was probably their first experience in flying, and it must have whetted their appetite for more of this.

Gerald and Essie Mae complemented each other in some ways, and – like many couples – they differed in other ways. Both of them were unfailingly honest, and they followed an unwritten code of conduct that included dressing "properly"; loyalty, patriotism, and obedience; a cheerful countenance; being kind to others; family values; helpful to those in need; humility; and thrift. Indeed, the principles of the Boy Scouts of America, which Gerald had learned as a child, and which both of them knew of as members of the Methodist Church. They were students of the Bible. Gerald read a short passage in it every day, and he always carried a small leather-bound King James Version and a New Testament with him; they are still with the objects he saved from the war. Essie Mae's growing library included several translations of the Bible, books about its history and literature, and about gems and minerals in the Bible. They believed in the principle of tithing, and they donated regularly to charitable organizations. They made gifts to people in need of help, especially those who had worked hard, but had bad luck.

Gerald and Essie Mae loved outdoor adventure, especially flying in small planes and hiking in the mountains. They couldn't abide cheaters or lazy people. Gerald would later view prospective candidates for bank loans by visiting their farms to see how they managed them, and how well they took care of their animals. After he went into the banking profession, Gerald discovered the importance of personal insurance – especially of life insurance, and health care insurance. He believed life insurance was a good investment, and health care insurance reduced the risk and cost of unplanned but unavoidable expenses. As a result of these beliefs, and acting with permission from his employers at the bank, he was a successful insurance salesman. Gerald often spoke of "other people's money," saying that, "it's more important than my own." His values were what a small-town banker needs – to be absolutely honest and completely respectable – free of sin – in the eyes of the community. He and his employees could not go home after the bank closed every day until all of the accounts were perfectly reconciled. "Every penny must be accounted for." At times, when provoked, he had an explosive temper, but he was also famous for telling jokes on himself. Essie Mae had a good sense of humor, but she usually smiled instead of laughing aloud, and was easily embarrassed.

Essie Mae and Gerald and both of their families were Republicans. They believed in what was then the basic Republican principle: small government – that the federal government was responsible for little else than delivering the mail and defending the nation. And that debt was bad, for the government, or for individuals. They would probably have agreed that roles for the federal government should also include law enforcement, defense of the Constitution and federal courts, and National Parks and National Forests. Some aspects of FDR's "New Deal" were grudgingly acknowledged as being useful, such as the Civilian Conservation Corps (CCC). Although both Gerald and Essie Mae were good with numbers, her skill extended into science, while his was that of the business world. She often thought as a poet, with words in rhyme and rhythm, while he had narrative thoughts that he could rapidly transform into writing. He would respond rapidly to an emergency, rushing to help without thought of personal danger; on the other hand, she was brave, but would pause for a moment to think of the best way to respond. They shared a hobby: an interest in "collections." He was a collector of coins and postage stamps, and she had a collection of bells.

Essie Mae's values also included those of her Quaker ancestors. She wouldn't use "bad language" or say bad things about anyone. From her mother, she learned that silence was the best way to respond to an offense. She taught her children not to fight, or to hurt anyone, and not to hurt any living creature unless it was absolutely necessary. Her boys didn't always behave as they were taught, but when they didn't, they sheepishly remembered her admonitions.

Gerald and Essie Mae's parents believed that good Methodists would not consume alcohol or use tobacco, or dance, or gamble. And sex out of wedlock or before marriage was inconceivable. But Gerald and Essie Mae were of a new generation. They enjoyed dancing, especially foxtrot, swing, and waltz – although not seductive or sexually suggestive Latin dances such as the tango and samba. They enjoyed a cigarette once in a while, and they sometimes played cards with their friends – Gerald enjoyed poker and blackjack, while Essie Mae became a competent bridge player. And they could take an illicit sip of alcohol once in a while, usually of a typical "American" beverage such as bourbon or rye, or a cordial, or perhaps scotch (because it was Scottish); but never gin, beer, or wine – all of the latter had "foreign" or "low class" connotations. Both of them were loyal supporters of Cornell College and they were frequently involved in alumni affairs. Essie Mae enjoyed meetings of her chapter of the American Association of University Women, and she was proud to be there, representing Phi Beta Kappa. Both of them were members of Masonic organizations, including the Order of the Eastern Star.

Before and after they were married, both Gerald and Essie Mae continued to work as they had been doing: He worked for the Iowa Power and Light Co., and she continued to teach in the Geology Department at Cornell College. No woman had been allowed to teach at the college after she was married, but the president made an exception for her. They lived in the Rev. S. W. Williams' "Faculty Apartments" near the campus until after their first child, George, was born in October 1932. By that time, the college had responded to Essie Mae's visible pregnancy by terminating her employment. In the late fall of 1932, they moved to a small house on the north side of Mount Vernon, and they were living there when their second child, Tommy, was born in May 1935. Gerald became a banker at the Mount Vernon Bank in 1931, and he recalled going to work at the bank in March 1933, on the day that Roosevelt closed the banks. He was assistant cashier of the bank in Mount Vernon for five years.

In the summer of 1936, Gerald accepted a promotion to be cashier and executive officer of the Lisbon Bank and Trust Co. The family of four moved two miles east, to a much bigger house in Essie Mae's home town. They purchased their new home with a bank loan and a loan from his sister, Ruby (Hill) Woodin. It was a grand house, three stories high, with a fireplace in the living room, a tile roof, a large yard, a barn with a haymow and stalls for horses, and a row of stately elm trees along the front curb. It would be the largest and most wonderful house that they ever lived in. The Lisbon and Mount Vernon banks had close financial relationships and overlapping boards of directors, so Gerald continued to have reporting responsibilities to the owners of both banks. Essie Mae enjoyed returning to Lisbon and to her friends there, especially in the Methodist Church. She became director of the choir at the church, and she gave vocal lessons at her home, accompanied with a piano in the front parlor of their house. She was often asked to sing at weddings and funerals. She was deservedly admired for her calm composure at times when everyone else, including her husband, was weeping. Gerald was increasingly involved in community affairs, serving on the Town Council and secretary/treasurer of the Lion's Club. He learned to play golf, and the Hills became members of the Mount Vernon Country Club. The club had a nine-hole course which was carved out of a farm field north of the town. Its small clubhouse had a screened porch to keep the flies away. He also joined a social club, the Benevolent and Protective Order of Elks – the B.P.O.E. – in Cedar Rapids. The family enjoyed dinners there on special occasions, such as Thanksgiving, and the network of Elks Clubs gave him a place to stay when he was in other cities.[1]

War broke out in Europe in September 1939. The Hill boys had a happy childhood in a small rural town, far from the war in Europe, and they had no idea of what war would mean to them. Many Americans expected the war in Europe, because Hitler made no secret of Germany's intentions. In the Midwest, there was uneasiness about the situation, but few feared that the U.S. would be drawn into it. We had done enough of that two decades earlier in the Great War. Looking back, after the war was over, the author of the *Centennial History of Mount Vernon* wrote,

World War II came upon Mount Vernon as it did upon the country. Through the late Thirties feeling had swung between a high of hope that the conflict could be avoided and a low of certainty that its coming was inevitable. Editorials and radio eloquence urging defense were accepted and forgotten, but each issue of the local paper carried an advertisement urging young men to enlist in the Navy. In August 1941 the much criticized Rugg textbooks that were thought to undermine Americanism were replaced in the Mount Vernon schools and in November the local school board "was considering a course in defense in. the high school." A new flag pole was dedicated on the Cornell campus that same fall and a sober-faced group of young men watched the flag flutter to the top of it.[*]

Everything changed on December 7, 1941, although on the home front, especially to young children, it was a gradual change at first. George had started school in September 1938; skipping second grade, he was in fifth grade in the fall of 1941. Tommy was in second grade in December 1941. On Monday, December 8, students in grades 1-6 in the Lisbon school were crowded into one room to listen to President Roosevelt speak of "a date which will live in infamy."

----------

Tommy Hill was seven years old on 3 May 1942. He wrote this to his mother on Mother's Day, a week later:

> *Dear Mother*
> *I an Glad it is your day. But*
> *if you wanted to cell it – Mothers day*
> *you can.*
> *your sun Tommy*

_____

[*] *Centennial History of Mount Vernon*, 176.

# Chapter Two

## Pearl Harbor Is Attacked, and Everything Changes
## 1941-1943

### Gerald And Essie Mae Hill Do Their Part in Lisbon

The bombing of Pearl Harbor stirred the country to action, and it was felt in Linn County, Iowa. The Mount Vernon *Hawkeye-Record* of the following week contained a quarter column list of persons and homes whose thoughts flew to someone in the danger area. The issue for January 15, 1942, contained an eye witness account of the bombing. The *Centennial History of Mount Vernon* summarized the first year of the war in Mount Vernon:[*]

> Cornell students were advised by Dean J. B. MacGregor to sit tight and await the orderly procedures of induction into service. Carl Travis was named head of the committee for civilian defense; courses in first aid were planned, and a class of 36 completed the course ... Red Cross plans for sewing and knitting emerged at once and remained active forms of service for the duration of the war.
>
> Food became a matter of concern with sugar the first commodity to be affected. On January 15, 1942 sales were limited to five pounds per person "if the dealer had it to sell" which precipitated a hoarding rush. In April it was rationed with extra stamps issued in May for canning purposes. Gasoline was rationed in November 1942 and fuel oil in the following December. These restrictions became subjects of conversation wherever two or more were gathered together. On January 7, 1943 the schools were closed and on that day the teachers under Superintendent Ostergaard assisted by women of the town registered for general rationing books the 1,389 applicants who appeared at the high school building. Thereafter the housewife budgeted her points and the merchants counted stamps.
>
> In order to meet shortages in essential materials it became necessary to organize nation-wide salvage drives in every community, adding another load to the burdened business man. ... the Boy Scouts collected 347 pounds of aluminum. A box was placed in Heasty's drug store to receive old toothpaste tubes, a source of pure tin. Old silk and rayon hose, needed in the manufacture of war materials, were collected in the Variety Store. ... A Scrap Drive in October 1942 was a community activity of major importance. ... Old furs were rolled out to make aviator's jackets; old rubber filled another need; children in the country schools collected 10,480 pounds of milkweed pods for life preservers and the call for waste fats was never out of the advertisements. A sign of the times was the appearance of "want ads" looking for rides to Cedar Rapids by some of the estimated one hundred who went daily from Mount Vernon to work at Collins Radio or Wilson Packing plant or other plants engaged in war work. A real housing shortage developed as the overflow from Cedar Rapids found homes in Mount Vernon. ...
>
> The work of the Red Cross, well organized before the war, became effective at once. Under Mrs. Cordia Bauman, chairman of the local chapter, war activities were quickly organized. ... In 1943 the local chapter was reorganized and Mrs. H. C. Lane was made chairman. ... In every national drive for Red Cross funds Mount Vernon more than met its quota. Gift packages were prepared by local women's organizations which Mrs. Lane personally delivered on Christmas day to the men in Schick Hospital. ...
>
> In October 1942 thousands of people of the town and country side had their first view of one of the powerful new instruments of war, which our boys were being trained to operate, when a Boeing B-17 on routine mission out of Topeka, Kansas, made an emergency landing on a Fred Sargent farm north of town. Weather and engine trouble kept the big plane grounded for twelve days and for the time of its stay all roads seemed to lead to the Sargent bean field. The local Civilian Air Patrol gave interested assistance to the crew and some members of

---

[*] *Centennial History of Mount Vernon*, 176-8.

11

the CAP were privileged to ride in the Flying Fortress after it was made ready to return to the base. The best of Iowa hospitality was offered to the stranded crew and homes where they were entertained were saddened later to hear that two of them had been killed in action. As a result of this visit from the skies Miss Bernice Gill of Mount Vernon was married the following year to Sgt. J. C. Farrell of Washington, D.C., top gunner on "The Floozy."

----------

Before the attack on Pearl Harbor, Gerald Hill and some of his friends had bought a small airplane, a Piper Cub, to fly as a hobby. They constructed a small building to use as a hanger, adjacent to a field a few miles from Lisbon. Gerald and the others were members of a flying club that was based at Hunter Field in Cedar Rapids. He had soloed but he had not passed the required test to carry a passenger. After the U.S. entered the war, the Civil Air Patrol, established in 1936, became an auxiliary of the Army Air Force. The Cedar Rapids flying club became a Squadron of the Iowa Wing of the C.A.P., and Gerald's small group became the Lisbon Flight – commanded by him as Flight Officer with the rank of First Sergeant. He began to wonder if he could become an officer in the Air Force, as had his friends from Cornell College, Judd Dean and Morley Slaght. Judd was his classmate and was his best man at his wedding, and Morley had been in the Army for many years. Now a lieutenant colonel, he had been sent to China as an adviser to Chiang Kai-Shek.

Essie Mae joined the C.A.P., too, and with her background in teaching and science, she became a certified instructor in Civil Air Regulations, and then in Meteorology and Navigation. Her skills were soon put to use teaching Air Force cadets at Coe College in Cedar Rapids. During the first months of 1942, her brother Manly returned to Army service as a captain in the Military Police, and his sons Bill and John both enlisted as officer candidates in the Navy. Essie Mae's oldest niece, Harriet Thompson, became a Naval Officer in the WAVEs, and was assigned to duties with Naval Intelligence in Washington, D.C. By coincidence, John Thompson was sent to Iowa City – ten miles from Lisbon – for pre-flight training at the State University of Iowa. Essie Mae's boys thus had the opportunity to see him on weekends, and they were thrilled when John and his fiancé disappeared for a weekend in the guest room in their house in Lisbon.

----------

In May 1942, Gerald received an offer to go into business with the Andreas brothers, who purchased the food commodity firm, Archer Daniels Midland. In his response, he made a counter offer to Albert Andreas, to which the latter never responded. The company name was later abbreviated to ADP. Gerald was already considering various options for military service, but this was a tempting offer. However, when ADP became infamous after the war, he was glad that he had made this decision.

18 May 1942*
[Lisbon, Iowa]
Dear Albert:

I have delayed writing this letter until a late hour for I felt in fairness to all concerned it should be written after the most complete consideration had been given to your proposition to me last Thursday ... It would hardly seem proper for me to leave an assured income such as that without approximately the same in a new location, in view of the fact that the expense of moving and the higher cost of living in a large city must be recognized. ... I could

* Carbon copy of letter from GLH to Albert Andreas, in Cedar Rapids, Iowa, in GLH's letter file. Andreas's brother, Dwayne, would soon begin converting the Andreas family's food commodity firm into ADM. Several officers of ADM later went to prison for price-fixing, although Dwayne was never charged personally. The sordid affair became the subject of the film, *The Informant* (2009), starring Matt Damon.

not make such a change of locations at this time for less than $5,000. per year with any bonus arrangement to be held in abeyance. ... I sincerely hope you will feel free to write to me an answer at your earliest convenience.

Yours very truly,

[G. L. Hill]


In the summer of 1943, Gerald and Essie Mae began quietly to explore the issues involved if he went on full time active duty, in uniform, with the Red Cross. There were certainly financial and social risks involved, as well as potential danger of injury, or even death. It would be an adventure, though, and opportunities might be seized for advancement after the war. Essie Mae concurred, and in October 1943, Gerald traveled to St. Louis for an interview with the Red Cross. He said that he wanted to be trained to go overseas, into a combat area, preferably serving with the Air Force. The Red Cross interviewer heard this. But what he saw in front of him was a bald-headed, bespectacled businessman in his late 30s, wearing a dark suit, polished shoes, with a stiff white shirt and an unremarkable necktie. He saw a businessman, not someone who could work with front-line troops. The interviewer believed that Gerald would be a good fit for a temporary wartime position on the Red Cross staff, somewhere in the U.S., or possibly in an area far removed from the front lines. He probably didn't tell Gerald what he believed; or perhaps Gerald didn't hear what he said. Or Gerald thought that once he was accepted, he could persuade the Red Cross to let him do what he wanted. The misconception of goals – whether Gerald would have administrative duties, or whether he would be a Field Director with a combat unit – would be an issue for the next year.

After he was told that the Red Cross would accept him, Gerald and Essie Mae agreed to do what was necessary: they would sell their house in Lisbon; and he would ask for a leave of absence from the bank. And Essie Mae would accept an offer to teach cadets, and she and the boys would leave Lisbon and move to a rented house somewhere further west in Linn County. Her initial plan was to accept an offer to teach Army Air Force cadets at Coe College in Cedar Rapids, and that she would move to Mount Vernon or Cedar Rapids with the boys. However, over the next few months, it became likely that Cornell College would have a Navy Flight Preparatory training program, and she would be to teach in it. In the meantime, she would continue to teach at the Cedar Rapids CAP Squadron meetings. She and Gerald found that most of a house near the college was available for rent in Mount Vernon, in which one room would be reserved for the maiden sister of the owner, and another room would be occupied by a man who would offer some assistance with chores. The boys would complete the school year in Lisbon in the spring of 1943, and they would begin their new school year in Mount Vernon in September of that year.


----------


The profound influence of the Methodist Church on Gerald Hill and Essie Mae Thompson, and also of her Quaker ancestors, can be seen in the letters that follow, which they exchanged during World War II. They were guided by the Ten Commandments of the Old Testament and the Two Great Commandments of Jesus in the New Testament, even though they never explicitly referred to these Commandments. Gerald and Essie Mae were always faithful to these Commandments, and they never used "bad language," even as they wrote intimate letters to each other.[*]

---

[*] Deuteronomy 5:4–21, Mark 12:30-31.

13

# G. L. HILL TO BE RED CROSS ASS'T FIELD DIRECTOR

## Will Report Nov. 22 At Washington, DC

G. L. Hill received word by telephone from the Red Cross on Wednesday of his appointment as an assistant field director with the armed forces. He is to report in Washington, D. C. on Nov. 22, for a short period of training. He returned from St. Louis on Tuesday where he was requested to appear on Monday for personal interview.

Mr. Hill has been cashier of the Lisbon Bank & Trust Co. for seven years and will be granted a leave of absence while with the Red Cross. Active in Civil Air Patrol circles for more than a year, he has recently been named Flight Leader of the Lisbon Detached Flight of C.A.P. which has grown to a membership of almost 60.

Previous to coming to Lisbon he was assistant cashier of the Mt. Vernon Bank & Trust Co. for five years and employed in various capacities by the Iowa Electric Light & Power Co. division office in Mt. Vernon for three years.

He is a member of the Lisbon Town Council and has been secretary of the Mt. Vernon Lions club for 15 years. Mrs. Hill and their sons George and Tommy will remain in Lisbon for the present. They will move in early November from their house which was sold last week to Mr. and Mrs. George Young.

Mr. Hill will be in the Military and Navy Welfare Service branch of the Red Cross. This branch interprets the Red Cross service to the commanding officer and subordinates at what ever station the Red Cross is located. An assistant field director is the go-between between the enlisted personnel and the people at home.

*Mount Vernon [Iowa] Hawkeye-Record (28 October 1943)*

"The most important attributes of the field director were understanding people and knowing the ropes of the Army camp or naval base where he was stationed. Throughout such installations there were often posted large signs: KNOW YOUR RED CROSS FIELD DIRECTOR – YOUR PROBLEMS ARE HIS CONCERN. When the harassed serviceman came to the Red Cross office, he expected help no matter how far removed his problem might actually be from the field director's experience, and without regard to whether it really lay within his province . . . If he was sympathetic and experienced, he could do a good deal in advising an applicant how best to present his case to the Army authorities. . . . They were often called upon to inform men in camps of the serious illness or death of members of their families, and would then do everything they could to help them obtain passes and transportation for their return home."

– Foster Rhea Dulles, *The American Red Cross: A History*, 399

"Since Cornell College is inseparably a part of Mount Vernon, war measures at the college were reflected in the life of the town. Just as the young and active men were being drawn out of the town, so the college quickly lost its vigorous men students. Negotiations were begun to make the college a part of the base training program for the armed services. Plans begun by President J. B. Magee were completed after his death by President R. D. Cole with the able assistance in Washington of Col. William C. Rigby, an alumnus of the college and a former resident of Mount Vernon, and Leo Paulger of the Federal Reserve Bank, a trustee and alumnus of the college. The college was to receive a unit of 600 men to be called the Naval Flight Preparatory School at Cornell College. As its part of the contract the college loaned eight men from its instructional staff and the use of Merner, Rood, Altoona, Guild, Bowman, the conservatory practice house, classrooms in Main and Law buildings and partial use of the gymnasium. One of the comically common sights of those exciting days was the moving operations of the girls as they tried to compress their belongings into half or less the space they had used before.

"With the arrival of the first group of 200 men, the Navy took over. Names of the buildings were changed to names of ships and nautical terms – decks, bulkheads, shore leave – became accepted speech; squads of vigorous young men were routed out at early dawn to be marched to the rhythmical 'Hup, two, three, four' to chow, Bowman Hall, or 'The Wasp' [Merner] and to an incredible number of classes. All this activity crowded to capacity the facilities of the campus with an enrollment in college of about five hundred students."[*]

---

[*] *Centennial History of Mount Vernon*, 178.

# Chapter Three
# Letters in Time of War

**Essie Mae Is Alone – She Teaches Navy Cadets**
**November 1943 - October 1944**

**November 1943**
**Essie Mae and her children are in a rented house, and she begins teaching**
**She writes to Gerald, "It doesn't seem possible that you are so far away"**

The first plenary meeting of the Cairo Conference (which was given the code name "Sextant") was held at the president's villa on Tuesday, November 23. Its purpose was to outline formally to Chiang Kai-shek and the Chinese delegation the proposed operations in Southeast Asia. Thanksgiving Day, the fourth Thursday in November, is a feature in American life. Two enormous turkeys were brought in with all ceremony. The President, propped up high in his chair, carved for all with masterly indefatigable skill.
    – Winston Churchill, *The Second World War: Closing the Ring*, 333, 340-1

Mount Vernon, Iowa
November 19, 1943          Friday Night
Dear Gerald,

| MRS. GERALD L. HILL | 312 NORTH THIRD STREET WEST | MOUNT VERNON, IOWA |

    I can't seem to get used to the idea that the "weekend" doesn't start Friday night, like it does for most school teachers. We are spending the evening at home – or at least until George goes to the Junior class play. He got an activity ticket for a reduced price. Tommy is in the living room singing thru that patriotic song book that I brought back from Des Moines. He came home tonight so pleased, because he was the last one left on his side in a spelldown. There were three left on the other side, and then the teacher called it off. I guess the time spent in teaching him to spell was worthwhile. Last night at C.A.P. really worked out very well. The time went very rapidly for everyone, and we really spent two hours at C.A.R. Albert [Fischer] took notes along with the rest, and then after every "unit," he would get up, and give illustrations of the rules and cases which he knew of when they're being broken. I guess there was a lot of excitement around the C.R. airport yesterday when the inspectors were there. An instructor from Ottumwa, not knowing they were there, buzzed the field – with the result that he is probably looking for a new job. It made C.A.R. awfully interesting, and quite amusing at times. There was an instructor killed in Cedar Falls yesterday – cut his speed too low, when he was only 100 ft. off the ground. Pupil injured, but expected to recover.
    I took the kids with me to see the movie up at the chapel last night, and this time Lt. Dailey and several other officers were around. The kids wouldn't sit with me, and I had fear and trembling for fear they would get bawled out for being there. I had to leave early, and wasn't able to contact them when I left, so I was curious to know whether they got along O.K. This morning George said that sure enough, as he was going out, Lt. D. stopped him and asked who said he could come! George said, "My name is Hill, and Mrs. Hill is my mother," so Lt. D. let him pass. I got quite a kick out of it! Hanna [their dog] acted kind mopey all day Thursday, and I thought she didn't feel just right, and when I got home last night, I found that she had thrown up right in front of the front door. She seems to feel better today. Have kept her in, most of the time. Bertha Andre said if they had realized that you weren't to leave until Thursday morning, that they'd have had another party for you. She said they were coming up here some time (with the same "ammunition" they had that moving day) and help me settle. Eva West was at C.A.P. in spite of her saying that she was going to drop it. Ken West had three prospective cadets with him, and I was glad we had something to "shoot right out at them."

We got your first card today, and were glad to know you thought of us. I suppose by this time you are on your way eastward again. It's to bed early tonight. Heaps of love,

'S'Mae

Mount Vernon, Iowa*
November 12, 1943          Saturday night
Dear Gerald,

This is the night you are at Barkers'!! It doesn't seem possible that you are so far away, and doing something so different from our quiet evening here at home. George is up taking a bath, I have on my dressing-robe, and am typing at the kitchen table, while Tommy looks at *Life*. If you see a copy, look at the Munsing underwear Ad on page 75 – it shows a woman in very brief undies and high-heeled shoes, shoveling coal into a furnace. Tommy was much amused when he saw it. It is very possible that I will be teaching as usual on Thanksgiving – at least that is the office gossip now. This was quite a tiring day, with exams, altho my boys did much better than last week.

The kids spent quite a bit of time in the college library, and then met me at the building at 5:00 and helped me record grades. It was 5:30 when we got home, and I remarked to Tommy that we'd all pitch in and get supper. He said with a sigh, "My, wouldn't it be nice to have it all ready, so we could just sit down and eat!"

If I don't get the kitchen floor scrubbed tomorrow, I'm got to do something drastic!!!! Bath is over, and altho it's only 8:15, I'm on my way to bed – I suppose you're just about finished eating and are set for the evening. Me? I'm so tired, nothing looks good to me but bed.

Love – 'S'Mae

[s, in Tommy's hand]          Good night Daddy          Love Tommy

November 22, 1943          Mon. night
Dear Daddy,

I was the first one to get a hundren today in a Arithmetic (Mom spelled it for me) here is the way they came
Tommy Hill / Nancy Gasten (the rest dint get a hundren)

Have you seen the white house yet, if you have des it have any canones in front of it. If you turn this over you will see some brown stop on it. Well that is some coco I spelled. So mom wped so me off and put on the stove. Mom said tell dad abut it and when mom put it on the stove George said tell him to that I accidently droped it on the stove one it got stors only it dint

Mom is woresing your flannel shirt (with the tail stiking out) but we have to keep ours in (the boys) she says alos has her corduroy bands with the leg rolled up

I got to shov one hod full of coal / Me my self I
Lots of kisses / Tommy Hill

November 23, 1943          Tuesday
Dear Gerald,

I hope that mail is getting thru to you by this time. Your Sunday letter came today (Tues.) so the airmail service is really pretty good. I am so anxious to hear how you are situated down there. Are you to continue to make your headquarters at the hotel? How many of you are quartered there? How many new people are there who are just starting as you are?

A new officer-in-charge is coming, whom they say is a real Lt. Commander – not a Reserve officer. It will be interesting to see if some conditions don't change for the better.

---

* Richard "Dick" and Grace Barker were friends of the Hills in Mount Vernon when he coached at Cornell College.

Neil [Miner] wants me to teach Airplane ENGINES!!! Tie that if you can. There will be no Aerology taught during the next four weeks, and he is trying to distribute the work. I told him that it was out of the question, and then everyone started kidding me – for everyone has had to do it at some time or other – so I took the box of films home tonight and have been looking them over. If I lived thru that first four weeks in Aerology, I guess I can stand anything – but I never thought it would come to this. I am supposed to start studying Navigation – visiting classes, etc., with the thought that I will fill in in that dept. some time.

I seem to keep so darn busy all the time. We have been having extra conferences, etc., and I have been ironing etc., here at home – besides doing a little more straightening up all the time. When work is over, it is nice to get into old clothes, and just stay home here with the kids – who really have been so good and thoughtful.

Rachie [(Thompson) High] has invited us down there for Thanksgiving. I can go down after my last class in the morning is over, and come back by 3:05 for the first one in the P.M. if we DO have to work that day. So we'll have a Thanksgiving after all. For the kids' sake, I was feeling quite regretful, because on Saturdays when I am not at home, and they are, they do get lonesome. George went to Lisbon at 5:00 this P.M. with [Richard] Nelson to eat supper with Mother, and go to a B.B. game. Tommy and I are going over in a few minutes to bring him home. He said he would come about nine o'clock, no matter where they were in the game.

One of the cadets got sick Sunday night with spinal meningitis and is at death's door in Iowa City hospital. He ate dinner at Watson Davis's that day, so a lot of the faculty and students have been woozy today with sulfa shots. Must close for this time. And I do hope that these letters are finding you.

Much love,
'S'Mae

# December 1943
## Essie Mae is with her children at home. She is sick and lonely
## "I'm not sure that I am quite sane!!" but "I'll try to do the best I can at this end"

*Although the time I had spent teaching at Coe College seemed difficult, as it turned our however, it was like the preliminary bout before the main event, which was, of course, those war years in Mount Vernon. I personally shoveled thirteen and a half tons of coal that first winter.*

– Essie Mae Thompson Hill, *Prairie Daughter*, 92

Mount Vernon, Iowa
December 11, 1943          Saturday P.M.
Dear Gerald –

Your card mailed at N. Platte came this morning along with one from Ruby [Woodin] wondering "why I didn't answer her letter." She said too that Myron [Hill] wanted to know what you wanted for Xmas.*

I am feeling better, & expect to go uptown later this P.M. I kept Geo. at home from school yesterday (cough) and after 2 days shut up here in the house with the kids, I'm not sure that I am quite sane!! They have gone to the Xmas matinee (Little Theatre) where they will probably cough their head off, but in the meantime, "Peace." Norman & Bertha Andre stopped in Fri. A.M. on their way to C.R. – very nice of them – and Bertha Johnson brought us some soup & cookies last eve.†

Our Xmas cards turned out pretty well, I think, and I have about forty ready to go out. I stick the edges together with a Xmas T.B. seal. I am to go on studying navigation with very little teaching the next two wks. – so hope I won't have to work quite so hard. Few people realize how busy I am – and how I have to "manage" my time.

Must go and rest now – Love – Take care of yourself and don't worry about us.
Yours – Essie Mae

---

* Ruby (Hill) Woodin and Myron Hill are GLH's siblings.
† The Little Theatre in the Drama Department at Cornell College was directed by Al and Bertha Johnson.

December 12, 1943 [Sunday]

Dear Dad,

Here I am lying on bed in Sunday. Please excuse the bad writing because every once in a while I cough. Yesterday I went out to Mrs. Dean's to get my washing. She had 20 washings, and there were two dry cleanings. Rex and I took our loads up and delivered them. It was a madhouse up there. I got home at 1930 o'clock for supper and boy was I tired. I had Eddy Bostrom & tommy to help me. When I started counting the money mother nearly fainted – prepare yourself for a shock – I used to count my money in stacks of 5¢ each – Now I count in stacks of $5 each – I had $30!! and still had 8 left to deliver. $24 was the Deans' and the rest was mine

Beside my bed we put two chairs together and set Hona on them. She lay's there while I pet her.*

We moved the encyclopedias into my room, and put my insignia in the candy box. I stayed away from school Fri. I had milk toast for breakfast and hamburgher & onions for ~~dinner~~ lunch. There is a good movie this aft. *Iron Major.* I went to the ~~"Lexington"~~ Merner this day at 1315 o'clock, to deliver washing. Out of 8 I got 4 delivered. The rest weren't there. Going back at 1800 tonight. "Beastly" weather – cold – windy. Say – I found out what a "Salamander" was. I was reading in the encyclopedia about animals that never lived. (A salamander is an animal that lives under fire.)†

Yours, George


December 13, 1943          Monday, 5:00 P.M.

Dear Gerald,

Your card from Ogden came today. I suppose you are "on duty" now – How is the S.F. weather?

I am waiting for the potatoes to cook for supper – Geo. is still in bed but feeling better & Tommy has gone up town to do some shopping. I went to school today – have no teaching to do – am working navigation. Am feeling pretty well – but tire more quickly than usual. Lots of sickness everywhere. I got the Clarion Xmas packages off today and that leaves only Min and Alice May Large. It has been bitterly cold here today. Snowing now – very light. Am having a kind of rash that comes & goes on various parts of body that I think may be a reaction from the sulfa which I am still taking. I'll call Dr. V. L. if it continues.

8:00 – 20:00        George is acting as my secretary. I have been drinking lots of water in the last few hours. Mary Van Metre was here on Saturday and was surprised to learn that the slipcovers on the furniture were one & one-half years old, and she had never seen them. Tommy made 65¢ tonight in tips from the cadets, doing 3 errands, and Geo. is gloating over 2, $5 bills, all his own, including Granmaw's Xmas dollar. The latest word is we'll have 2 days off at Christmas time. I have 60 Xmas cards addressed. Tommy was happy to get back to school today, and he seems to be feeling very well except for some coughing. George had his homework brot home so that he can work on it. ‡

All of us send our love and a special Xmas kiss.

Essie Mae        Tommy        George                P.S. A letter enclosed from Grandma


December 14, 1943 [Tuesday] night

Dear Dad,

It finally snowed here last night and the paper says it will be 20° below zero tonight.

One of the cadets asked me to buy him a launder hit he have me a ten dollar bill. When I took him the change he gave me fifty cents (50¢). I took some pants to the cleaners and I suppose I will get some more for that.

---

* Their dog was named for Tommy's girlfriend in Lisbon. EMH usually spelled the dog's name as Hanna or Hannah.
† Mrs. Dean = Did laundry for the U.S. Naval Air Cadets at her house. George picked up, delivered, and collected money from the cadets, and shared in the profits. The cadets lived in two Cornell College dormitories, renamed for military purposes. He was helped by his friend Eddy Bostrom, who was the son of the Methodist minister in Mount Vernon.
‡ Min = Minne (Mohn) Kharas, her classmate in high school. Dr. V. L. = EMH's physician, Dr. Von Larkum. Mary Van Metre = wife of Douglas Van Metre, banker in M.V.

The sulfa poisoned mother so she has not been very well today.

At school we ar having long division like this

[He shows 52633 divided by 2 = 26316R1, confirmed by multiplying 26316 x 2 = 52632 + 1 = 52633]

George is back to school and is going to the movie while I stay here with mother.  I will go tomorrow night I thing

Hope you have a happy Xmas, and <u>Be Sure you tell us about it</u>

I am back my self and am having a nice time.  Did you know George has been sick well he has.

We have got presents from virginia [Thompson] and I got one from Nancy Gaston.  Thats all I can think of for now.  Keep 'em moving.  Kisses for a merry Xmas and Happy new year

   Tommy Hill

  Mother send her love to[*]


December 15, 1943   Wed. a.m.

Dearest Gerald –

I am writing this in bed, but I am feeling better.  That sulfa really did make a toxic condition in my blood, and I have spent an agonizing two days.  I called Dr. V. L. and he said there wasn't anything to do, but quit taking the pills & drink lots of water & <u>wait</u>.  My skin, especially <u>feet</u>, legs, arms, and face burned and itched so, I thought I'd lose my mind – but it is getting better, now.  It turned so cold there was lots of coal shoveling to do, but I am thankful to finally get the kids back in school.  It isn't so bad when just one of us is sick at a time.  I guess I'm a softy, but it was the first time I've ever been sick without you or Mother or Auntie Runkle around to baby me.[†]

I have spent the morning writing long delayed letters, so there is one good thing about this after all.  I don't know how I'll feel when I am physically fit again, but just now, I'm in a mood to tell Neil [Miner] that if I can't teach Aerology that he can just <u>count me out</u>.  The job of preparing "Navigation" and working out all those problems just looks now like a Mt. I can't climb.  But that may be just my "present" state of mind.  You wouldn't be too disgusted with me, would you?  I know you wouldn't tho' Honey.  I wonder what you'll be doing Xmas day – You know the fact that this is our <u>13th</u> anniversary should have warned us that it would be <u>different</u>.  I'm glad this flu didn't come over Christmas.  We miss you very much, but it'll be something to tell our grandchildren about I guess – I mean our part in the Great War.  I know you're going to do a wonderful job at your part – and I'll try to do the best I can at this end.  Everything will be fine when I get to feeling physically OK.

Must quit and get lunch now.  We'll have baked potatoes.

   Lots of love,

    'S'Mae


December 16, 1943   Thursday

Dear Gerald –

Your first letter from S.F. came yesterday (from Sun. nite till Wed.) which was very good time, I think.  It is 2 wks today since I got sick, and Thank Goodness, I really can see that I'm getting better this morning.  I slept pretty well last nite, and while my feet still itch & burn, my arms, hands & face are quite normal.  I am appalled at how much work of all kinds has accumulated & piled up in the last 2 wks, but I try not to worry about it.  I wish it would warm up, so there wouldn't be so much coal shoveling, but that goes with Iowa winters, I guess.

Yesterday, while I was in bed, I wrote about a dozen letters, including ones like Mary White that I've owed for six months or more.  I finally have all the Xmas packages and all but the local cards in the mail, too.[‡]

Boy! how the money goes.  With Christmas expenses over & the rest of the coal paid for, next month, there should be more of a surplus tho'.  I haven't been to Lisbon for two weeks, but I want to go within the next few days – and get our Xmas tree, and I hope Bish will "insist" upon my taking a wreath.[§]

---

[*] Nancy and Bobby Gaston were friends of the Hill boys.  Nancy was in Tommy's class, and Bob was in George's.
Virginia = Virginia (White) Thompson, wife of their cousin, John Paul Thompson.
[†] Auntie Runkle = Mattie (Rundall) Runkle, her mother's sister; son, Robert Lester Runkle, sent Xmas cards
[‡] Mary White = Wife of Wilbur "Pete" White, of Two Dot, MT.  He was a fraternity brother of GLH.
[§] Eldon "Bish" Stahl = Lived near the Hills in Lisbon; owed a grocery store, greenhouse, and vegetable garden.

I'm glad to hear your head cold cleared up. If you escape having the flu, by being home here with it for four days, it'll be a miracle. I hope you can see something of S.F. – pick out the nice places, so when the "duration is over," we can see them together. We might <u>fly</u> out, while we're at it. Might as well build a <u>good</u> air castle while we're doing it! Must go stir up the fire. Take good care of yourself and don't worry about us. I wonder if this will reach you by Christmas time. Wish I had been on the train when they were singing. It seems strange not to be training someone to sing Xmas music.

Bye, Honey, Lots of love,

'S'Mae

December 17, 1943          Friday

Dear Gerald –

I am wondering whether you have gotten any mail by this time – I guess I should have written sooner after you left – I am feeling much better this morning. Neil called & asked me to teach one class in Aerology next week (3:15 P.M.) and I am glad. Everything will work out all right – and the days seem much brighter when I feel well physically. The weather has moderated, too. I finished up my siege of letter writing last eve by writing to the Pitts.* That was a difficult job, but I'm glad I finally got around to doing it.

Geo. is all enthused about going to Mpls. – I hope the weather is good. School is not out until the 23d so he may not go till Sun. or Mon. after Xmas.

What has your work this week comprised? Have you had actual contact with soldiers? Is there really a "Knob Hill" in S.F.? Time to get lunch now – We're on the upgrade now – so don't worry about us –

Heaps of love,

Essie Mae

December 18, 1943          Saturday †          1945 hours

Dear Daddy,

I suppose you notice that I am writing in ink this time. I got myself a – oh, to begin with, this morning we decided to go to Cedar Rapids. We got all ready, but Tommy was sick. So after dinner we had to go without him, providing mother would buy him a Xmas present for him to give to me. He had Hona [their dog] to keep him company and he slept the afternoon. While we were in C. R., one of the first things we did was to look for some ice skates. We finally got some new ones – size 5 that looked 2 years old. They cost $2.85 out of my own money. Then mother got some things and then I bought my fountain pen for $1.50. It is a Do Write. Then mom bought some things [to] give to Tommy, and I bought a book to read along the way. This morning mom bought me some long Jockeys (to my disgust). At Penny's mom bought me some more clothes and ran out of (I am trying out George's pen) checks.

Tommy has a temperature of 103 and Mom is quite worried because Doc Ebersole is sick too. Mother is dictating now – I am so glad that you like the setup out there. We try and try to picture what it must be like. Was it grand to be out on the watch? I bought <u>George</u> a lot of new things today, including a nice corduroy sheepskin, shoes, bootsocks, corduroy pants, and JOCKEY LONGS. I got myself a large Double Frame for the two Lasswell pictures of the kids, and a personal file for your letters, and other "important" documents. We saw Arleta Smith in C.R. today.

I can't imagine what can be the matter with Tommy. I look forward to night without much sleep.

Much love,

Essie Mae (and George)

Merry Xmas to All and to all a good night.

---

* Pitts = Marc Pitts was the bombardier on the B-17 "Floozy," which made a forced landing in November 1942 near Lisbon, Iowa. He stayed with the Hills at that time, and became a role model for Tommy. He was killed on 13 June 1943 when his bomber was shot down over Germany. The story is told in the Prologue

† Letterhead of Write a Fighter Corps (WAFC) drawn by GJH.

St. Luke's Hospital
Cedar Rapids, Iowa
December 20, 1943          Monday 12:30 P.M.
Dear Gerald –

Tommy had an attack of appendicitis on Saturday – he is better now (Mon.) & will <u>not</u> have to have an operation. He woke up Sat. with a temp., feeling bad. Doc. Ebersole sick in bed. I did everything I could to reduce temp. but finally got hold of Doc. Gardner Sunday morning. When his tummy hurt & he was nauseated, Sunday P.M., he advised bringing him to hospital for blood count. Rachie & Jim came with me. He is quite a lot better thank goodness! Is sitting half way up in bed looking at pictures. You can imagine my state of mind, & I sure hated to leave him last night. He is so sweet, patient, & cooperative tho'. I'm feeling almost normal again for the 1st time in 2 wks & a half – altho' it seems like a million years. I am supposed to start teaching today – but of course I'm spending the day here. I ran over to Coe a minute – I am wondering if Cornell will dock my salary this month. Can't blame them, I guess.[*]

Isn't Dorothy Johnson's letter interesting! You might drop her a line. I will too, when I have time.[†]

I almost phoned you last night when I got home from the hosp. last night – it would have been wonderful to hear your voice – but I lived thru it and will "save the money" for the doctor bill. I am waiting for Doc. Gardner – who is somewhere here in the Hosp. to tell me when I can take T. home. He said he didn't mind staying if he could get home by Xmas. Johnsons have invited us to Christmas dinner in the eve (7 P.M.). Geo. is getting his own lunch at home today to save the lunch money I gave him. "Hannah" has been "off feed" again too – with messes to clean up – but I just haven't had time & strength to give her much attention.[‡]

Sorry I've had such discouraging news to write all the time – but that's just how things have been. Everyone is busy, so I can't really blame the "world" for not being much concerned about my well-being, but it has been lonesome. I'm over it now too – and have my "chin up." It is so nice to have your "newsy" letters. They will make a grand record of your experiences.

Have a nice Christmas Honey – and tell us all about it – Heaps of love,
            Essie Mae


Mount Vernon, Iowa
December 20, 1943          Monday
Dear Gerald,

This is a strange package of mail I'm sending, but I thought you'd like some of the interesting cards we been getting [enclosures not preserved]. You don't need to save them after you've read them. I've saved so many yrs. - & they're just harder to throw away, as "time goes by."[§]

I was so thrilled to get your grand long letter (Dec. 17) when I got home from the Hosp. tonight. Tommy was mighty homesick when I left him, but taking it "like a soldier." I hope he can come home in a few days! Geo is down now with a temp of 102.2°, but as long as I am feeling better myself, I can take care of everything. I surely hope he gets over it in time to make his trip to Mpls.

I hope you have your cold & bad feeling licked by this time! Stay in bed, and <u>drink lots of water</u>. I wanted to talk to someone, so I ran over to the Johnsons for a few minutes, & had a chinfest around the fireplace. I told them about your seeing *Kiss and Tell* – and they were pleased to hear about you & that you like S.F. It surely does seem long since you went away because – as you say – "so much has transpired." I'm glad you like the kids' letters so

---

[*] Rachie and Jim = Rachel Edith (Thompson) High was EMH's sister; her son was James High. They had a farm near Mechanicsville, Iowa. Dr. Ebersole was the Cornell College doctor, and he cared for the Hills in Mount Vernon; Dr. Gardner had been their family doctor in Lisbon. She was offered a teaching position at Coe College, but turned it down to stay at Cornell.
[†] Dorothy Johnson was a distant relative of EMH's who lived on a farm near Lisbon; as a teen-ager, she was a "mother's helper" for the Hills, and she then moved to California.
[‡] Al and Bertha Johnson invited them to Christmas dinner. The dog, "Hannah" had developed distemper and was euthanized on December 25.
[§] The song "As time goes by" was made famous by the movie, *Casablanca* (1942).

much. I think they do awfully well for their age. It will be an interesting record when they grow up. I am pleased at the way they do stay around home here. They never have had the habit of "being on the streets" and they show no inclination in that direction. Geo. went caroling last eve, & had a chili supper at the church afterward. He said "I got myself a girl." He ate supper with her.

I guess you're right "that we are better prepared for a 'separated' Christmas" than a lot of folks. We been mighty lucky all our years, in lots of way. We'll get along on the money end, too, and it's swell to think of the "reserve" we are building up. Tommy recognized the Runkles' card as the same one they sent in 1941 – but with the date changed. It is so good of them anyway. I think I have sent cards to everyone – including the Hisatomis in Cincinnati. I must have sent about 80 or more – so we don't need to feel apologetic as I did last year. Everyone thinks they are nice – and I'm glad, especially, that you like them. They never would have been possible if you hadn't arranged for the pictures. They made a much better "cut" than I imagined. *

I'm hoping these letters reach you by Christmas. The mail service has really been very good, hasn't it? The weather has been very mild & the snow has disappeared. My! I hope your cold is OK – you are in Calif. Can you see the sunset across the bay? Much love – "My Christmas Husband" – across the many miles. "May the Lord bless you and keep you while we're absent, one from another" †

Essie Mae

Mount Vernon, Iowa
December 21, 1943          Tuesday
Dear Gerald –

I am going to C.R. as soon as my class is over this P.M. Geo. is in bed with flu but his temp is going down & I think he'll be OK by tomorrow. He has semester tests coming tomorrow, which I hope he won't miss.

What did you mean by the "big blow" and ensuing damage? I am going to ask Harry Sizer for the loan of a suitcase for Geo. I didn't realize that our two remaining bags were absolutely "shot" in the moving. The Runkles are all set to give him a grand time. Bob Runkle is working downtown in the package department of a big store this vacation – and is to be one of the "guests of honor" at a Christmas dinner at Ft. Snelling as a result of being a member of a Red Cross committee which raised money in their school for a recreation room for soldiers. Nice, Huh?‡

I do hope the letters which I mail today reach you by Christmas. We will be thinking of you, needless to say, and I hope you can see the "silver lining" in the clouds, as I can now.

Much love – My arms – and a kiss –
Essie Mae

December 23, 1943          Thursday
Dearest Gerald,

I haven't mailed a letter to you for several days, altho I have started several. Now that the days are over, I can summarize it all by saying we have had two plenty sick kids, but they are getting better at last. I was able to bring Tommy home from the hosp. Tuesday eve, and luckily, for the flu came back, after he got over his appendicitis attack, and Geo. was sick too. It was like a hosp. ward around here, but Bertha and Al came over one eve and helped me, and I got along all right. Tommy is still in bed, very, very weak, but out of danger, and Geo. is on his feet too, at last. It has turned so terribly cold again. Geo. is SO disappointed about his trip to Mpls. and I am sorry too, but none of us could forsee all this sickness. I hope you haven't gotten the "germ" too – it would be awfully tough to be away from home and sick. I'll be anxiously waiting your next letter to find out. This was CAP night, and since Tommy was sleeping soundly at eight o'clock, and Geo. was willing to stay alone, I went over for just an hour, and took along

---

* Charles Hisatomi was a student of EMH's at Cornell College; he was relocated into a camp for residents of California with Japanese ancestry (internment camp) in WWII.
† "My Christmas Husband," was then a popular song. The second quotation is from *Genesis* 31:49.
‡ Harry Sizer succeeded GLH in his position at the Lisbon bank.

the CAP films. They did appreciate it, and while I hated to put the car away, I found everything all right when I got home. I got my chevrons.*

We have gotten lots of Xmas cards, some with notes. Aunt Emma wants to know where you are. I wrote Ruby a letter to read at their Xmas dinner. Got a card from Manly, saying only that he had rec'd our "unique" card, so I know he must have been getting our mail. Virginia sent an interesting copy of John's describing a visit to a native hut and a special dinner that was put on for four of them. The host turned out to be a native METHODIST preacher, who sang a hymn and said a prayer in dialect, but after the feast they all played a kind of Rummy. It was a most interesting description and he gave all the details of food and customs – and a note from Marie says Paul will be home for Xmas.†

I hear the Pre-flight at Iowa City is to be closed in March. I wonder what the future for Cornell is, at that rate. The I.Q. of each Batt. gets lower and lower! Tomorrow night is Xmas eve. We have our gifts under the tree, but I don't think I'll have the kids hang up their stocking. Tommy has missed you while he has been sick. He is so thin, but he's so terribly sweet, and takes his medicine like a hero, and Geo. has helped all he could. It's late now – So to bed. I set the alarm for 3:30 to put on more coal. I must order some more. Your bonus of $300 arrived from the bank.

Much love –
Essie Mae

December 23, 1943          Thursday
Dear Daddy,

I am in bed now listening to the radio in bed. Last night my temperature was down to normal and mother and I played checkers. I couldn't find my fountain pen, but when I wasn't feeling good I must have left it at school on Monday. A pen answering my description turned up in Mrs. Fisher's room at school. Mother is going over to get it today. Last night Mom was plenty worried about Tommy but this morning [sentence completed with 4 charts, showing gradual improvement in Tommy's temperature and overall status; and of his own cough and status].

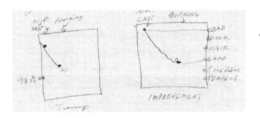 [Left Tommy]

[Right me]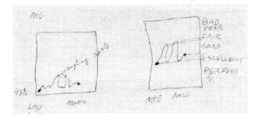

Mom went to Lisbon to get grandma just now and when she went yesterday she found that Virginia had sent her a letter from Johnny about his going to a native feast. Another interesting thing is that every pilot is supposed to pick out one native and call him the native word for friend and then he is to call nobody else his "friend." I don't have any idea when I will get to Minneapolis. We got a letter from the Runk's yesterday. They sent us a "Sunday before Xmas" bulletin. Doc Gardner is giving Tom all the pills and medicines he can think of.

Yours, George

Christmas Day, 5:30 P.M.   Saturday‡
Dearest Gerald,

Thirteen years ago, we were in Des Moines!

The weather has moderated, so it is grand outdoors, altho there is no snow. Your good letter, written Thursday (special delivery) came this morning – and it was just wonderful to get it. I got a long one last eve too when I got home from the office. Thank you, dear.

---

* She was a M/Sgt. See letters of 7 Jan 1944 and 18 Mar 44. GLH's chevrons in the Christmas card picture of 1943 are of a 1st Sgt., with a diamond in the center.
† Ruby, Manly, John, and Paul are relatives of GLH or EMH. See Glossary of Principal Names, and Names and Places. Emma Stockwell was GLH's mother's sister. Virginia was John Thompson's wife; Marie was Paul Hill's wife.
‡ They were married on Christmas Day, 13 years ago, and they honeymooned at a hotel in Des Moines

I do hope that you will be assigned to an airbase, but I just know that you will find it interesting wherever you are, when you are "on your own." You are used to sizing up situations and making quick, good decisions. I have always marveled at how you could do it.

Shall I tell you about the events of the past two days, since I wrote to you. Friday, the kids were definitely getting better, because they were so cranky we could hardly exist. Geo. was so disappointed over not going to Mpls. and he thought I was just being mean to him. Grandma has not been well enough to come up at all through all of this sickness, but she finally did come yesterday afternoon, and ate supper with us. Tommy just suddenly realized that it was Xmas eve, and wanted to hang up his stocking, so I had to dash out and get things for that. It just happened that I was able to get a chemistry set for Geo. and an electric football game for Tommy, so with some apples and nuts, and a couple of candy bars, that was taken care of. Geo. has been thrilled to death with his chem set, and Tommy has been able to be up today, and playing, so they have been happy.[2]

This has been a much better day than I anticipated yesterday (When I practically burst into tears anytime anyone wished me a "Merry Christmas.") We opened our tree presents after breakfast and then about eleven o'clock I started out. Then I went over to Johnson's and had a good visit with many friends who asked to be remembered to "Toot." Everyone wanted to know all about you, and you were much in our minds. I am to go back there tonight. This is absolutely the first social life I have had since you left the first time, and I do appreciate it, but I miss you.[*]

I am sorry to have to report a sad element, but it is just one of those things. I had to have Hannah [aka Hona] "put to sleep" this afternoon. Now that it is over, I can write about it, but I'm telling you now that on top of feeling so miserable myself, having the kids so sick – then to have a sick dog too, was almost more than the breaking point. I took her to the vet on Friday morning – (I just couldn't leave the kids long enough to go to Cedar Rapids, as you realize). He gave her some sulfa tablets, and said it might be distemper. She seemed somewhat better today, until about two o'clock. Then she began having spasms, we put her out on the back porch – saliva hung in strings from her mouth – and she thrashed around. I called the vet again and he came over – Was I ever glad Jim was here. I was afraid of rabies. He said not – that it was either worms or a brain condition that would take a long time to get over – if ever. So I told him to put her to sleep so she wouldn't suffer any more. One more thing on Christmas day!!!!! I have had a sample of everything that CAN happen, and altho I don't think I handled it all as well as you would, had you been here, I did the best I could, so I hope you'll feel that we're "carrying on."[†]

I do hope that you have had a pleasant Christmas, altho I know you have missed us, as we have missed you. I am going to "take you along" (your picture) tonight when I go to Johnson's. I must get supper for the kids now –

Much love – Essie Mae

Sunday night – the day after Xmas 1943        [December 26]
Dearest Gerald,

Your long telegram came this morning and I have been going around all day telling people I got a long letter from you Xmas eve, a special delivery on Xmas day, and a telegram the day after!! It was swell. I took the telegram over to Johnsons about noon, and they did know all the places you mentioned. I am so glad you had a nice day, Christmas. We did, too, in spite of the one sad episode. We got up late this morning, and were dressed by noon.

George has worked with his chemistry set, and seems reconciled to not going to Mpls. He feels pretty good, but is awfully thin, and still has some head cold. Tommy is still so weak and very irritable and no appetite. Hope I can get him over to the doctor's for a tonic, etc., if he doesn't "pick up soon."

I can imagine how you are looking forward to tomorrow when you will get your assignment. I do hope your luck holds out. When we stopped at Johnsons this morning, Gordon Meyers was there, and he also spoke about what wonderful work the R.C. does at the camps. The night that Johnsons were here helping me with Tommy, they told me in the greatest confidence their most important project. They are going to adopt a child. We discussed it at great length, of course. They want a child about four or five years old, but of course, will be glad to get anything. I don't know when anything has struck me as being so sweet as this plan of theirs, and I think it is simply wonderful to be included in the secret. I saw one of my California pupils down town this morning, and of course I told him about your being there.

---

[*] "Toot" was GLH's nickname before the war.
[†] EMH is paraphrasing the words of Winston Churchill on many posters: "Keep calm and carry on" (1939).

Oh – by the way, last night, when I went to the Johnsons, I wrapped up a bottle from the top shelf of the cupboard and took it along (I seem to have little or no use for it) and told them that it was TOOT's gift to the party. They thought "that it was swell of you" --- It is eleven o'clock now, and while that is not late, I start to work tomorrow, so I guess I better hie myself to bed. It is so hard to get up in the morning. It is only nine o'clock in S.F.!

Good night, my dear. Love, Essie Mae

December 28, 1943          Tuesday

Dear Gerald,

When you finally get this letter, you will perhaps find some of the news rather old, but I have hesitated to mail it, thinking every moment I would hear where your assignment is. In the meantime, the letter "grows and grows." The only real news I have now is that he [George] is in Mpls. at last. I put him on the [Milwaukee, St. Paul & Pacific RR.] *Rocket* last night at 1:00 A.M. and he was due in Mpls. at 7:30 A.M. Since I have not heard from them, I know everything was OK – but it was a tense and dramatic time for me. We had a long wait, but Geo. was very good – he got a seat (I was able to go on the train to see him settled) – and he had a special pillow with him. He was highly disgusted at my sewing a five-dollar bill into his shirt pocket – so he'd have some money in case he lost or had his billfold stolen. Tommy spent the P.M. with Grandma & took a nice nap. I have spent long hrs. at the office today – So he had to be pretty patient & good to be alone. He is looking better – but still so thin. Denny [DeNio] says there's a gift for us in C.R.. I surely think I'll hear from you tomorrow, and then I'll send this on its way. Hope you haven't been sick.                              Love – Essie Mae

December 29, 1943          Thursday

Dear Gerald –

The first letter to your "permanent" address. I wrote a long letter Christmas night – the day after – and then again last night – and when your night letter [telegram] came, saying you wouldn't get your assignment for several days, I sent the letter to S. F. (Headquarters) – so you'll get it eventually, and will know all about our Xmas – which was nice, altho we missed you terribly. The telegram telling of your assignment came Tues. night after I had gone to bed. You are on your way there now, and I know how glad you are to be really headed for work.

Mrs. Tull just called & invited me over for supper with the Van Ettens. I accepted for both Tommy & myself and it was OK with them. I bought 3 *Prophecies of Hope* (English club books) for Min, Alice May, & myself for Xmas – I think Toppy appreciated it. Must close now – lots to do. Best of luck & wishes for grand days in Camp.*

Lovingly – Essie Mae

December 29, 1943 – 8:45 P.M.          Thursday

Dearest Gerald –

Tommy and I took your long Sunday-after-Xmas letter over to the Johnsons, so we could enjoy it together – then went to the Tulls for dinner. It was really very nice altho' conversation was slow sometimes. I got this nice letter from Mrs. Pitts tonight in answer to the one I sent just before Xmas. I know you'll like to read it. She says she wept to read my letter – (I could tell her I wept when I wrote it, too). I told her that I have made it my own tradition to tell my classes about Marc on the last day I meet with each group, etc. Navigation has been going much easier, since I've started working on it again. Johnsons had a new letter from Ben Hoover – he's been made a Captain in the Marines – pretty good for working up from "an enlisted man." He has been right in the thick of it – buddies shot to pieces, etc. – and he says the war against Japan has just started. They also heard from Rowena Stuckslager.† Ward was with her for the holidays. She was raving about catching mice and cockroaches. I can't imagine her emptying mousetraps unaided, can you? My that Sunday letter of yours was grand.[3]

Good night, dear – Lovingly, 'S'Mae

---

* Clyde "Toppy" Tull was Professor of English at Cornell College; he and his wife, Jewell, lived on the street immediately to the south of the Hills' house. Winifred (Mayne) Van Etten (a prize-winning author) was at Cornell with the Hills. Min Mohn and Alice May Large were classmates of Essie Mae at Cornell College.

† Rowena "Rowdy" (Stuckslager) (McConologue) Friedrich (1896-1989) was a contemporary of Essie Mae's in Lisbon. She married and divorced Ward McConologue; they had a son, Ward McConologue, Jr.

December 31, 1943 – 11:00 A.M.      Friday
Dear Gerald –

Just got back from Lisbon, depositing my check (for $180.00). I was about thirty dollars overdrawn and Harry Sizer was anxious to get my check before Jan 1st. He said to tell you that he got notice this morning that he will be called to the Army March 1st. He is going to Des Moines for his physical exam right away, and if he does <u>not</u> pass it, then he won't have to worry any more about it. And if he <u>does</u>, then it will be settled.

Margaret Moffat called last night about 10:30 inviting me to go to the C.A.P. New Year's Eve dance in C.R. tonight. I appreciate their thinking of me, but I just can't take it. I suppose I'll make some people sore before I get through "living alone" – but my job & looking after the kids is just about all I can take care of. I didn't get to sleep tired Wed. night till 2 A.M. for coughing – so last night I went to bed at 7:00 in order to catch up. That's the way it goes. Karl Andrist said they were at a big party at Dr. Gazda's last night – <u>very</u> gay and <u>very</u> late hours – but Alice can sleep the next day!

I'm anxious to get your letters from Camp Roberts, and to know (1) your set-up, (2) how you like being on your own, (3) how you're feeling physically, (4) whether you've seen any more old acquaintances, and (5) whether you can live "on the base."

Nelson's invited Tommy and me to eat dinner with them at the church New Year's Day. I promised him I'd take him to a show tonight – and I <u>don't</u> expect to hear the Midnight bells ring.

I'll be glad to get on a regular mail schedule again and I'll bet you will too. I am appalled to think how little "settling" & sorting I've gotten done – and it's nearly two months since we moved.

Heaps & love & kisses – Essie Mae


# January 1944
## Essie Mae receives her sergeant's stripes in the Civil Air Patrol
## "This time is something to tell our grandchildren about"

*After I had finished my day's work with the Cadets in the Flight School on the Cornell Campus, I still had to keep the family fed, clothed, and entertained, as well as make weekly trips to Lisbon to continue my teaching in the Civil Air Patrol. All in all, it was just about all that I could manage.*

*– Essie Mae Thompson Hill, Prairie Daughter, 92*

Mount Vernon, Iowa
January 1, 1944    4:00 P.M.            Saturday
Dear Gerald –

Happy New Year! The ground is still free from snow, but we had a beautiful hoar-frost this morning – We have had only <u>one</u> very thin covering of snow which didn't last long.

Were you "on duty" all day today? It is no holiday in the armed forces – as my students reminded me several times in bitter tones. Last night (New Year's Eve) I took Tommy to see the movie *Victory Through Airpower* – which was boresome part of the time, but the *History of Aviation*, a la Walt Disney was interesting. We were home in bed by ten o'clock. Al Johnson called me about eleven P.M. (I was asleep) and wanted me to come over – but I asked them to excuse me – and they understood. I went over to their place this morning for coffee, etc., about eleven A.M. – many friends were there. They said that they were alone last eve at midnight, but they faced West and drank a toast to you – then SW – to Ben Hoover – and so on. That was sweet of them, I think. I hope you can get time to write to them soon.*

It's a durn shame you couldn't have been assigned to an air base, but undoubtedly Caif. winter will be milder than Utah – if that is any consolation. Have you met any more folks that you know? In connection with <u>Jan.</u>

---

* *Victory Through Airpower: History of Aviation* (1943), was an animated Walt Disney film, the first of its kind.

1st, Tommy says he's not making any <u>revolutions</u> this year. I think he's got something – don't you? Geo. seems to be having a grand time in Mpls. I wrote Lester [Runkle] asking about reservation for camp next summer. It seems like a long way away, right now – I wonder what we'll be doing by that time – life seems to bring so many changes. I hope it's going to be clear sailing from now on – – – It seems ages ago that you left Iowa.

Tomorrow is Sunday – No office work! Must close this rambling & throw in more coal.

Heaps of love – Essie Mae


January 2, 1944          Sunday
Dearest Gerald –

I am wondering how a R.C. man spends his Sundays. This has been both a lazy and busy day for me. It was wonderful to lie abed this morning till I felt good and ready to get up (when both kids are here, it seems like I have to get up & stir around fairly early). Since I have been up I have been busy, however – mostly putting away the Christmas things.

It is so mild outdoors (above freezing). Tommy has "given up" that there ever will be snow this winter. I had Doc Ebersole "look me over" yesterday because I hurt so around my rib-area. He said it was muscular soreness from coughing (and shoveling coal) and he put on a "corset" of adhesive tape. It does feel better today.

Rachie and Mother came while I've been writing. Mother is better now. They were <u>much</u> interested in your good letters. I promised Tommy I would tell you about the nice stool he made. I brought home a car full of crates for kindling and he has gotten a lot of fun out of building with the boards. We can't find our saw, but in spite of that, he made a dandy solid stool, as well as boats & airplanes. And that cellar is <u>so</u> dirty and messy!*

Hope there's a letter from Calif. for me tomorrow.

Heaps of love – Essie Mae


January 3, 1944    5:15 P.M.          Monday
Dear Gerald,

It was only 40° this afternoon and just like Spring outdoors. Tommy was happy to go back to school. Runkles gave him a bright orange sweatshirt for Xmas and he wore his bracelet. I was paying bills this morning including Stahl's [vegetables] $8.67; Bauman's [clothing] $10.00; our Eastern Star dues $4.00; Dilley's [grocery] $23.06. My balance at present is $57.10 (according to my figures) I want to pay Elsie [Meffert] for the magazines – and that is about all the "big bills" I know of. Gee, it costs a lot to live!

What're you going to do with all <u>your</u> money? How do you like Camp Roberts by this time? I tho't maybe I'd hear from you today – but I hope tomorrow. What sort of problems do the soldiers have? And what kind of living conditions do you have? Jim [High, her nephew] is going to bring me a load of corn cobs this week. Alice Andrist asked me over to dinner tonight – a hen party – guaranteed "No Bridge." People invite me out at their own risk, for the Lord only knows when I'll return the invitations. I can't imagine how women can justify spending time these days, just getting ready for parties!

Lots of wasted time & energy in the R.C. – the armed forces – and at home – that utilized could get this war over a lot faster – it seems to me! How about it? That's the impression I've gotten from your letters about R.C. Headquarters. Must get supper for Tommy now –

Heaps of love – 'S'Mae


January 4, 1944    9:30 P.M.  Tuesday
Dearest Gerald,

Your wonderful, long, letter, written New Year's eve, came today, Honey, and it was simply grand. I think it was undoubtedly the longest letter I EVER got – and you did give us an awfully good idea about what your work and working conditions are like. I hope my letters are coming thru to you directly by this time.

My boys from California said that today was typical winter California weather – so you know it was foggy drizzle. Not much like Iowa in January, but there is snow prophesized for tomorrow. It is certainly good that you can get your room and board at such reasonable rates – that business of restaurant eating is so unsatisfactory, isn't it?

---

* At this early age, Tommy shows his skill as an engineer; he later majored in aeronautical engineering in college.

You wouldn't have missed this experience for anything would you?  Life during these times for you and me both will be something to tell our grandchildren about – no one can say we didn't have a part in it, anyway.  I will read part of your letter telling about camp and your work to the CAP tomorrow night – your telling of the drill field reminded me of the famous "inspection and review."  Doesn't that seem a long time ago!!!

I spent long hours at the office working Navigation.  I was issued one of the Navy "suitcases" with all the equipment – plotting board, etc., today – so they really mean business.  It takes me about twice as long to do the stuff as it should, but it's coming – and the staff in the Navigation dept are very nice – and promise to help.  I have been amused at some of the tales Geo. has told about his experiences in Mpls.  He is like you in some respects.  He had a grand time with a bunch of college girls who knew Russell Coles' [wife] Betty.  He has gotten SO much pleasure, and a lot of knowledge from his Christmas chemistry set – but is much disgusted because he can't get a lot of chemicals that he would like to use.

Wish I could be in two places at the same time.  It would be wonderful to see the places that you are seeing, and be with you, and have a chance to talk.  These letters of yours are going to make a swell collection, however.  Besides, I'm "frozen on my job" – do you ever tell your acquaintants that you have a workin' wife?

I am sorry that Ruby and Adelia can't see "eye to eye" – especially since they are your only two sisters, and I know from my own case, how much satisfaction it is to have a congenial sister.  We all have to live our own lives, and I can understand how both of them like to be working.  It is too bad that Ruby couldn't have worked out Mildred's case differently – but that too is her problem, and we can't decide things for others, can we?  It was good for Tommy to be alone with me for a week.[*]

I guess this will be all for tonight – I miss you very much – but it doesn't seem nearly as far separated as if you were overseas.  Good night, Darling, and Thank you for your long letter!
>Essie Mae

Cedar Rapids, Iowa[†]
January 4, 1944    Tuesday
Mrs. G. L. Hill / Mt. Vernon, Iowa
Dear Mrs. Hill:

The society editor of the *Gazette* called me today and said that she would like to feature the women's angle of the Civil Air Patrol in this Sunday's *Gazette*.  She asked me to get in touch with various members of the C.A.P. in Cedar Rapids to pose for pictures.  One such picture she had in mind is someone apparently teaching two or three of the other girls some subject, shall we say C.A.R.?  I naturally thought immediately of you and suggested to her that she have one of you as a ground instructor.  The outcome is that she would like very much to have you and two of the other girls pose, in uniform, either tomorrow evening or Thursday.  I imagine you would much prefer Wednesday evening so if it is convenient will you be at the Y.M.C.A. at 7:15?  If not, will you please let me know sometime tomorrow morning.  My telephone number is 2-9831.
>Thanks loads,
>Margaret Ann Twogood

Mount Vernon, Iowa
January 5, 1944                    Wednesday            11:00 P.M.
Dearest Gerald –

Just a note while I get my feet warm before I go to bed.  (It snowed last night and I just got home from C.R. C.A.P.)  The back of this letter speaks for itself – isn't it exciting!  I went over to C.R. tonight and had the pictures taken – I was glad for my Sergeant's chevrons!  I'm like a kid now – waiting for Sunday!  C.A.P. was swell tonight.  Everyone was so cordial and sent their greetings.  I hope you have gotten the Xmas letters I sent to S.F.  They tell of Tommy's recovery.  The kids enjoyed sliding with sleds today.  Geo. looks the best this winter he has ever – I think.  His new clothes really look nice – Dark blue corduroy pants & blue corduroy sheep-lined [jacket] – and both of them

---

[*] Mildred Woodin was developmentally disabled, probably from brain damage from measles as a baby.  Ruby never admitted that Mildred had a problem, and her stubbornness about this caused tension with her siblings.
[†] Margaret Twogood to EMH, on letterhead of Hunter Flying Service/Army Flight Indoctrination School, Cedar Rapids, IA.

fit him – not so awfully big. I'm going to Lisbon C.A.P. tomorrow night – Goodnight, my Love – wish you were here to finish warming my feet – A Big Goodnight kiss, Essie Mae

January 5, 1944    Wednesday
Dear Dad
    I hop you are having a good time at Camp Roberts.
    Gorge just got back from Minnaplos 3 days ago.
    I am now out of the hosptol and at school having reading.
    I was the some on done with nubers these morning.
    School is about orut so lots of love from
    Gorge and myself and more from mother
            Tommy Hill
[EMH adds]: (Written in "spare" time at school – EMH)

January 6, 1944    Thursday
    Just a note, Dear, while lunch cooks.  Am sending your O.E.S. card – and Tommy's letter.  It was interesting to hear at CAP last night that the girl who went to Kans. City to study "Communications" is making a great success of it.  Is now on her way to N.Y. for some additional training – specializing in teletype-machine.
    I am gaining weight.  Been taking extra vitamins – huge appetite – and feel better now than in months.  So thankful.  Hastily – but with much love,
            Essie Mae

January 7, 1944    Friday
Dearest Gerald –
    Winter has certainly arrived – Boy, it's cold this A.M.  The kids are coasting on Pres. Hill all the time – and I'm so glad we live close – so they can warm up in a hurry.  I promised I'd get Tommy a fur lined helmet that would buckle down around his face to keep him warmer.  I guess he deserves it – Geo. has had so many new clothes.*
    Good turnout at C.A.P. in Lisbon.  A couple of strangers there whom I did not meet – I started Meteorology class with the film on clouds.  The D.M. *Register* reports this A.M. that the Cornell College N.F.P.S. is definitely to be closed June 30.  No more cadets after March – I'm in a mood now to say I'm lucky to get a shot at Navigation, 'ere it's too late – for no matter how punk I am, it won't last too long and it is valuable training.
    I wore my uniform to class today & everyone was quite agog over the "M. Sarg." emblem.  I haven't had much time for housekeeping this wk. – but it doesn't worry me – like it does when I'm not feeling well physically.  Hope you continue to like your set up and work there at C. Roberts.
    Must get lunch now –
            Much love – Essie Mae

January 9, 1944    Sunday  10:00 A.M.
Dearest Gerald –
    Just finished the painful process of getting the kids off to Sunday School – and before I "tackle" the mess around here – I'll relax with a visit with you.  The CAP picture turned out fine – didn't it?  Of course, they didn't include all the dope I gave them – but you "know newspapers" – sometimes they print what you don't want and sometimes they don't print what you do want!  I got a kick out of it anyway.
    It has been 10° below zero the last few days!  And it takes coal shoveling!  There's going to be some changes made if we live here another winter – such as more storm windows.  I forwarded a gov't letter to you, that I assume is the income tax blank.  If you have time, you might send a paragraph – to be given to the *Hawkeye* – about your situation, work, etc.  They have been asking me – and I hesitated to do it – for fear of "giving away Military secrets."

_____

* Pres. Hill = The Mount Vernon Presbyterian Church is at the corner of 1st St. W (then called Main St.) and 3rd Ave. N.  A steep slope descends to the north from 3rd Ave. for three blocks from the church.  It was closed to traffic after a snow storm.

I took the Navy Navigation test yesterday, which included Radio "fixes" – with Mercator corrections – and got them all right – so I feel quite encouraged! Did I tell you that Jim High bro't me a load of corn cobs this week? I was surely glad to get them! I still have tape around my "middle." The coal heaving keeps my muscles sore, and that does help. Karl Andrist and I have been getting along O.K. now. Alice had a narrow squeak. She squeezed a pimple on her cheek, and in 2 hours her whole face and neck were swollen & infected. She took sulfa and got it checked.* Much love – I am awfully proud of you – and I'm merely "carrying on" till we're together again.

Essie Mae

January 10, 1944   Monday 5:30 P.M.
Dearest Gerald –

The mailman was late today, but I waited as long as I could this noon and saw him & got my mail on the way to class. Your wonderful letter written Jan 4th (telling your schedule & some of your cases) came – and I was so thrilled. I think it was the "best ever." I am writing this in the car outside Merner, so I can't hope to answer it adequately – my fingers get too cold. (Geo. decided to collect laundry tonite & not finding anyone to help, Big hearted Mother gets out the car to help, altho' I warned him he's "on his own" from here on).†

Those cases you described were so interesting. In the sheltered life I've always lived – I really have no idea what many folks are up against.

To answer your questions –
1. The Lasswell pictures are wonderful – as my letters probably have told you. Your family rec'd theirs.
2. The Washington picture came – fairly good – I'll send one if you wish.
3. I told Harry [Sizer] to put bond in our box – O.K.?
4. I told C.A.P. your address & appreciation.
5. Doc Andre is in Lisbon (altho' I have not seen him) on his way to east coast and presumably overseas.
6. I rec'd notice of Insurance due for Tommy – 1/28/44 for $21.10 (Dividend $2.82) and for you Jan 22 $67.10.

We are really getting along O.K. now – but I surely do appreciate the swell "pat on the back" in your last letter. It was tough, but now that it is over, it doesn't seem too bad – and when I think what so many are going thru because of this awful war – I'm just glad to feel that we are part and parcel of it. I sent the C.A.P. picture to Marie, Mrs. Pitts and Mother. If Blacks or Frank Runkle doesn't send Lester's one, I have a copy for them.‡

Heaps of love Darling – And thanks so much for the sweet letter – Essie Mae

January 10, 1944   Monday [night]
Dearest Gerald,

The supper dishes are done now, the kids are working with the chemistry set in the lav., and I am set to finish the answer to your long letter, which I started in the car waiting outside Merner. I am so glad to hear that you are getting your mail again – and I know from experience how much it helps to buoy up a person's spirits to get letters. It would be swell if you got a chance to fly – I hope you do. It will be good practice for you, to help that girl with her "writtens" – every field that they cover is stuff that one has to constantly keep up on.

Since it is definitely settled that the Navy will close June 30th, several of the men whose deferments only last until spring, say that they are not going to make any further moves in that direction. Gossip has it that even teaching of this kind is not considered essential, as long as there are women available. I – perhaps egotistically – don't think there are a great many women available – at least not in communities like this. Frankly, I don't think most women could or would put forth the energy and effort that it involves. It is swell of you to say that I was brave to carry on when the kids were sick – but the truth is – I wasn't at all. The Sunday nite I left Tommy at the hosp. I had a real struggle to keep from phoning you, and the only thing that really carried me thru was the knowledge that if I had to, I could – which would not have been possible if you had been overseas.

---

* "squeezed a pimple" must have caused acute streptococcal sepsis.
† Merner Hall was a dormitory at Cornell College, used by Naval Flight Preparatory cadets.
‡ Marie = Marie Hill, wife of his nephew, Paul Hill. Mrs. Pitts = mother of Lt. Marc Pitts, USAAF bombardier, killed in Europe. Blacks = Lester Runkle's parents-in-law. Frank Runkle = his father.

We have all been taking vitamins and have more than gained back all our lost weight. Tommy has been sleeping in the north twin bed. He has your old picture on the cedar chest beside him, and I have your new picture hanging on the wall beside the double doors between the two bed rooms, so I can see it as I lie in bed. I keep a five watt bulb on all the time, because I want the curtains pulled down to the sills, and it is too dark to see whether the kids are covered, etc., I change your picture around frequently from one place to another.

Goodnight, Darling. Don't worry about us – we are "carrying on" and I know you are doing a wonderful job. Much love, and all that goes with it.

Essie Mae

January 11, 1944   Tuesday noon
Dearest Gerald –

Scuttlebut! – It looks now like I'd be back teaching Aerology & Engines. Relief! I'll try to keep learning "fictitious ships" etc., tho, for one never knows! Hope you had a good time in S.F. Very mild weather now – but my cold still hangs on. It will be much easier for me if I can keep on with Aerol. Plan to take CAA exam Thurs. –

Love, EMH

January 11, 1944   Tuesday [afternoon]
Dearest Gerald –

Tommy is down cellar, sawing something, and G. is in the Lav with his chemicals. He was able to get some at the drugstore in Lisbon which he couldn't get at the M.V. drugstore. I got him some test tubes at the Cornell Lab. Gosh, he's a pest – every two seconds he comes in and wants me to listen to some new experiment. But of course, he is learning a lot – and I am not unduly appreciative.

Would you be interested in how my days seem to go now. Set the alarm for 6:30 – get up and turn the draft on and start the kitchen fire, and then sneak back to bed for fifteen minutes while the kitchen gets warm. 7 to 8 – get breakfast, get the kids up and dressed warm enough for the day, eat breakfast, dress, make sure the fires are all right to leave – dash to school. 8 to 10 I am teaching in Navigation class, then until about eleven-fifteen I work on the stuff by myself, and get my things ready for my afternoon class [teaching] in Aerology. 11:15 to 11:30 I dash downtown for groceries, then home to get lunch & fix fires. We start eating by twelve or thereabouts, then wash and wipe the breakfast and lunch dishes, and have time to relax for about fifteen minutes and read my mail before dashing back to class. Then class from 1 to 2, and then more Nav. until I leave the office from 4 to 5:15. Home again to build up the fires, warm up Tommy's cold feet, spread up the beds (sometimes) get supper, empty ashes or go to Lisbon for an errand or two.

It takes me so long to get that Nav through my head and work enough problems so that the technique becomes habitual!! And you know how often I read 116 miles as 121 or do some other dumb stunt. I felt like weeping this morning, but after having lived thru those first weeks of Aerology, I know I'll survive! If they just had a few squares blocked out on the plotting board to make it look like a cross word puzzle, it would be easier!

I just sit here, and think up something else to write, instead of getting to work – But, Goodbye, Dear, – all is calm and peaceful around here, wish you were here too.

Much love, Essie Mae

January 12, 1944   Wednesday 10:30 A.M.
Dear Gerald –

I decided to come home early this morning (so I'll write a note to add to last night's letter before I put it out for the mailman). It was -2° this morning – and that's chill when one wears a "service cap." One reason I came home early, was that Geo. needed a compass & I knew we had 2 somewhere. I dragged out all the boxes from the closet again & then discovered them in the file. So now I must put the stuff away. I have been having them lay out their clothes & necessities the nite before to minimize confusion & hurry dressing when the house is cold. The days are getting longer tho' – and spring will come eventually!

The kids go to a social gathering of their age groups at the church tonight –

Much love, 'S'Mae

January 12, 1944          Wednesday
Dearest Gerald –

Two swell letters today written Jan 8 and 9 came from you today – This is C.A.P. nite - & so I can't take time to ans. in detail. I hope your bad feelings from the "shots" are getting better. I don't wonder your arms got tired from that long letter. Another ins. check for $21.25.
1. Please tell me about paying those insurance premiums.
2. If you don't use your ration books, send them back sometime.

I'm doing a miserable job of letter writing – have so much to do – I dread C.A.P. tonite – sore throat & already weary. That Navigation can surely get my goat! Dishes to wash – – – – – hate to leave the kids tonight. I miss you – – Love – Essie Mae


January 14, 1944          Friday morning
Dear Gerald –

'Fraid I haven't clicked very well on the letter writing for a couple of days – altho' this is the third "Start." Tommy will mail this on the way to school – so you'll know we're all O.K. – Got your two typewritten letters of the 8th & ninth yesterday & will ans. them soon in detail. Hope you are O.K. from the "shots." We'll live in hopes for the future, and enjoy our situation as it is – as long as it lasts –

Much love, Essie Mae


January 14, 1944          Friday [night]
Dearest Gerald,

This is Friday night, and it seems like it should be the end of the week – this week has seemed unusually long! George had some laundry to deliver so Tommy went with him and they were going over to Johnsons' pool to skate until eight o'clock. It has been mild today – above freezing. When I was up in Neil Miner's office today, he seemed to want to talk, and he told me to tell you that the Lion's are planning a Minstrel in March – also that Rex Dean gets pretty confused about some of the reports, which he is called on to make in connection with the sec. work.*

I can imagine how worried you were about the C.R. long distance call. Physically, the kids are fine now, and even when I think they are kinda contrary, I guess it is mostly my fault, for being short of patience. It just gets on my nerves, when I am awfully busy and kinda tired to keep eternally after them to "wash your hands – put on your rubbers, drink your milk, stop arguing, shut the doors," ete., etc., etc – . The kitchen stove is a blessing, but it surely is a dirty thing – ashes, coal dust, on a white linoleum and floor border. You would have a fit because this place is so disorderly – it takes me all day Sunday to put everything in apple pie order, and in between times, it just has to go.

Tommy just came in from Johnsons. George went on to the H.S. to play in the band for a B.B. game, and he brought a big wagon full of laundry home alone from the Grill. T. helped as far as that. They dragged it all the way over to J. from Merner, and got lost up around the President's house, but I guess they thought it was kinda fun.

It seems strange to think of you wearing GI heavy shoes, costing less than $4 – do they seem to feel all right? I am amazed and pleased at how careful Helen Dean is about keeping the laundry straight. When I stopped last time, Rex was running the ironer, while she was doing the hand work. Roy Nelson said Harlan's wife got 14 letters from him in one day. Can you imagine that! Sometimes I think I should number mine, so you'd know if any were missing in the sequence – since they seem to arrive erratically.

Wish I could write long, grand-reading letters like yours – but y' know I just don't live that kind of a life. I have dawdled away over this one all evening – – – I think I'll go to bed early.

Much love – "dreaming of a lovely weekend together."
                    'S'Mae

---

* GLH had been the secretary of the Mount Vernon Lion's Club for many years, and Rex Dean had taken on his role. In the Minstrel show, EMH sang *St. Louis Blues*, "vamping" in front of the curtain between acts.

January 15, 1944  Saturday
Dearest Gerald,

The kids are still skating at Johnsons, so I'll start this letter while I wait supper for them.  Your letter written the 11th, telling of your purchases at the commissary came today.  It is hard to realize that you have been there less than three weeks, for you seem like a seasoned "service man."  I have been on a "dead run" most all day – and in the course of twelve hours since I got up, have run the "full gamut of emotions" from despair (an upset with the kids which has now blown over) to a very nice trip to Lisbon, where I saw a lot of people who seemed glad to see me and anxious to hear about you and to be remembered to you.  After class today one of my boys asked me where my husband was, and how he was – and it developed that he was an old Delt and had come to our house to be paddled.  He has been one of the best students, in grades and attitude.  He finally just figured out that I was your wife, and we were both so surprised.  He was surprised to find I was Mrs. TOOT Hill.[*]

I think probably my morale went up because I bought myself a new hat – I felt kinda guilty, for there are so many places for money.  But it is very nice I think – and I haven't had a new one since my "funeral hat" two years ago.  This one is quite similar to Bertha Andre's with a band of black fur across the front to match my fur coat.  It really looks quite snouzy.  Cost $4.00.  Lots of people have spoken to me about seeing my picture.

I see in Tommy's letter that he has given you his honest opinion of his mother.  He's probably right – but you know, as well as I, that the bulk of my difficulties lie with the other youngster – This will work out tho.  Geo. has gone to the movie tonight because there "wasn't a thing to do around here, or anything to read," but that's OK with me.  Wish you were here and we could, too, together.

Much love,<br>
Essie Mae

Sat Mor          January 15, 1944
Dear dad

I don't know what is gotten in our mother's head because she atc's like she was crazy.  She said we cood go to C.R. This afternoon then she said we cant then she said we cood again so I dont know for now if we are or not.  I have been doing my best I think around home.  In geog. I drew a picture of or school room I was a good picure so I think Ill draw one for you [sketch of school room, with locations of "windos, radiators, black board, door, desk, 'my desk', girls bathroom, boys bathroom, bookcase"]  Don't you think that was a good map I sure do, of corse there are some thing rong but its all about right.  In school I have been getting good grades acsept penmanship [3 A's, 3 B's, 5 C's and D in penmanship]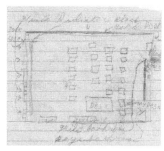

That all for now / Tommy Hill / I did go to c.r. This afternoon and got me a pair of shoe skates
Lots of love / Your son / Tommy

January 15, 1944  Saturday
Dear Gerald,

I am sorry to bother you with my problems, but By gosh I am so upset over what the kids' attitude at home is this morning that instead of waiting until I cool off, as I have before, in order that I only write "cheerful" things, I am going to just tell it to you.  If you think my place is at home, then I'll resign my job and stay at home – if that will do any good.  When I left at 7:50 this morning, I had everything laid out for the kids' breakfast, the kitchen nice and warm, and a list of things that G. was to do.

1. Take the laundry to Mrs. Dean and her money
2. Call Albert Fisher about a cadet's pants
3. Bring up a bucket of coal for the kitchen fire

The first two things as you see, were G's. own responsibility, and he knew already that they were to be done – I simply took the trouble to write it out so that he would not forget.  When I came home at 11:15 with the car, so that I

---

[*] GLH was a member of the fraternity Delta Phi Rho, the "Delts," at Cornell College.

33

can make a special trip to C.R. for their benefit – What do I find.  The front door and the hall door standing wide open.  Every light in the house still burning.  George not dressed completely – no shoes on.  Face and hands unwashed – two kids here with them – and DOING A CHEM experiment in the lav.  Not one bit of work done, not even the coal brought up, let alone the laundry delivered.  Boy oh Boy, I just saw RED.

If anyone can make an excuse for that, I'd like to hear it – I am simply boiling.  It is embarrassing, too, with the people upstairs to have these kinds of "set-toos" downstairs.  Now just what is my method of procedure.  I admit I told the kids they could stay in bed this morning as long as they wanted to, but I had NO idea that meant Eleven o'clock – since EVERY other morning – including Sunday, when I would like to stay in bed a little longer, I have to get up and get the house warm – simply because they insist on getting up.  George nearly had a hissy, when I said he could do no more Chem experiments for a week.  My gosh, you should have seen the awful looks he gave me, the sputtering and the generally hateful attitude.  I'm telling you an affair like this upsets me so – altho, by the time you get this I know it will have blown over – I suppose I should not write at all when I am so upset – but this is practically the first time – and darn it I just feel stymied.

I have a suggestion – When you have time to write one of your swell long letters, if you would take a scrap of paper and separately write just a short note to each one of them.  You seem very far away to them, and the letters you write to me apparently do not seem like they are to them, too.  I don't know if that would help, but you might try it.  The answer to this letter, of course, should come to me – but some suggestions to them would help, too.  I really mean it, if you think my place is here at home, then that's what it will be.  Some how, I guess I have failed, somewhere along the line.  It is very baffling.  Much love to you and confidence in your judgment.

These things, I wrote some time ago – but didn't mail, because I didn't want you to worry.


Wed Morn          January 19, 1944
Dear Dad
I for got to tell you I think tat I got a new gril firnd.  I might have told you that all ready.  we started out a good morning to today hope it's the same every morning.  I was the frist one to know what the time tables to 12

You can see my grades were good from the last letter
I got a book from the library that is about the Gremlins
Gorge is now getting in to more naschief
Honna dided Cristmas afternoon (we had to put her to sleep for good)
I havent much more to say but I got A in spelling in the 3 six week.
Keep the camp fires burning with a good time
                    Tommy Hill            Love from all            Tommy


Methodist Parsonage*
Lisbon, Iowa
January 20, 1944  Thursday
Dear Friend:
I am writing this letter to some of you whom I have known in other Churches . . . When any of you do come home on furlough, I hope you will come to Church, and to the parsonage, and we can meet face to face . . .

Some day, and we hope and pray it will be soon, the war will be over and you can be back home with your loved ones who are so proud of you . . . [s] Dear friend Hill: I visited with your wife for a few minutes this afternoon, Friday.  She still looks a little tired, but has recovered from the "flu."

George came in while I was there and is as peppy as ever.  I didn't see Tommy.  Your wife read that character estimate of yourself to me.  I wish I was as good at judging men as that Red Cross official.

Hope you are well.
            Regards –
            Charles Arnold

---

* Charles S. Arnold, Minister, Methodist Church, Lisbon, Ia., to "friends . . . in the Armed Services." Excerpt of Mimeographed typed letter, 1p., with handwritten addition to GLH.

Mount Vernon, Iowa
January 20, 1944   A.M.       Thursday
Dear Gerald,

I suppose you are back at came after a nice time in S.F.  I finally had an appointment with Doctor Gazda (Navy) this morn. and he gave me a new line of treatment for my cough & cold, which I hope will do the biz.  He seems to think so – honestly I have gotten so disgusted with Ebby [Dr. Ebersole].  The poison in my system has come out with a boil on my nose!  He thinks it will not come to a head tho'.

The kids have been pretty good lately.  As T. says, "I guess they are trying."  Geo. is back at the laundry business again.

Will be anxious to hear about your S.F. experiences & ans. to my questions in other letters –

Hang on, and I think the Lisbon Bank situation will work out OK.

Love, Essie Mae

January 23, 1944          Sunday P.M.
Dear Gerald –

Rec'd the package of pictures from S.F. and they are _very_ interesting.  It's hard to imagine what varied, and magnificent sights and settings you have seen while we here in M.V. just move around in our little "squirrel cage."  Enclosed is a clipping about you which was in the Red Cross column of the _Gazette_ today.  Sorry they didn't wait to get a picture before it was released.  The evaluation which you sent was very good.

I start teaching Navigation tomorrow, but will probably change back to Aerology & Engines the 1st of Feb., when the teacher goes back to the Navy.  I don't know how it will go to be on full-time schedule again after so many weeks – not easy, I know.  There just doesn't seem much to write –

January 24, 1944          Monday, 10:45 A.M.
Dear Gerald –

I feel better today – My boil is almost gone now.  Had good rest last nite.  This was my first morning of Navigation (which went OK).

When I left for school at 7:45 – they were eating breakfast – George's lunch was ready (he has been taking lunch to school lately) and all they had to do was wait ¾ hr. till time to go to school.  Sometimes Geo. is not inclined to follow the rules & this morning it was T.

I hinted to you before about this situation, but have not wanted to worry you – but it is something I must decide – whether to quit work & spend my time looking after the kids.

Love, Essie Mae

MOTHER*

Dear Mom,

I am sorry this morning had to turn out like it did.  I had hoped to get some studying done.
Tommy has been terrible.  He wouldn't let me listen to the radio.  He almost tore the plug.  He was in a tough mood when he does the opposite of what he is supposed to.  I just put him in the hall to cool off.
It didn't work.  He threatens to tear things.  He's plenty boiled.  I said he'd have to go to school if he wasn't good.  He won't do anything either.  I had to throw his address book in stove to keep him quiet.

George

January 25, 1944   Tuesday morning
Dear Gerald,

Rec'd your letter telling of your new watch yesterday.  I know you must be very thrilled with it – it has everything but an alarm clock device, doesn't it?  I guess there's one "pain in the neck" in every office – and evidently yours is no exception.  Hope you get a good evaluation from the F.D. – both for its own sake & for the salary increase.  Mild weather continues – it is only 50° on the porch this A.M. and seems like spring.  The new coal is in very large

---

* Handwritten note, written by GJH at 8:20 a.m.

chunks – very little ashes – so it holds the fire without roasting us. Life for us just stays in the same old groove – Everything O.K. – Hope you have time to comment on my letters –

> Lots of love –
> 'S'Mae

January 25, 1944          Tuesday 11:30 A.M.
Dearest Gerald –

Your long letter with the *Hawkeye* enclosure & messages to T. & G. came just now – and it was wonderful to get it. It gave me the "lift" I needed – and have needed for sev. wks. I am feeling definitely better now – but it surely has been a long drag (and the boil on my nose was the "capping climax"). I have been on the verge of "giving up" – resigning my job, etc., - quite a few times – but I'm glad now I hung on from day to day. You probably guessed as much from my letters, altho' I tried to not let it show too much –

"Navigation" this week has been an interesting experience, and the hours I've spent the last few weeks struggling with plotting have certainly meant this week's teaching has been shorter hours than I've spent studying in the previous ones. Next wk. I go back to Aerology & Engines (prob. 6 classes a day) – but I hope to feel even better physically by then. Have to quit now – but will write more later. Thank you, Honey, for your "visit" this morning –

We're over the hump now – and I'm sure your advice to the boys will help –

> Much love – Essie Mae

January 26, 1944   Wednesday
Dearest Gerald,

As I said in the brief note which I mailed on my way to class this noon, I was so thankful for your letter today, with the notes to the kids. As I look back on our difficulties here the last few weeks, I can see that it was largely my fault, because I was feeling so punk, but you can imagine what Dr. Gazda thought of my general welfare, when he ordered four big tablets of iodine and calcium, a day, besides NINE Unikaps (a vitamine preparation), the juice of three lemons and three oranges, every day. He also directed that I soak my nose and face in hot Epsom salts water as much as possible in order to stimulate the circulation so the poison of the boil would be absorbed rather than drain externally. It was a slow process, and of course I looked terrible, but this morning, I looked practically normal for the first time in ages (Or so it seems). But that is all water over the dam now. George is all industry, earning money for his camp experience this summer. He is scheduled to deliver 28 washings on Friday.*

I took that paragraph to the *Hawkeye*, but it probably won't be in until next week. It was very good, and I'm glad you took time to write it. I was surprised to hear that they are training no more RX classes in Wash. – it looks like things were closing down in many quarters. I am thinking especially, of course, of the closing of many schools like the one here at Cornell. When we "build" our new house we surely will have to have plenty of closet space – – – After living in this place. Glad that you finally had admittance to the Officers Club. It is hard to imagine you sitting on the sidelines at a dance, but, as you say, "It's a place to relax."

When I wore my uniform this week, several of my new students put down on their "experience sheet" that they had belonged to the CAP. I have one boy who has 800 hours in the air as a radio operator. One boy was an engineer on a PBY for a year, one was an instructor in "Instrument flying." All have been in the Navy for some time – from five months to several years. One of them told about seeing the CAP planes way down below them over the Gulf of Mexico many times. Harris [Thompson, her brother] was looking very well. He and G. had a session with the Chem set, of course. He has had several articles published in scientific magazines lately, and designed a clever computer that indicates the amt. of boiler scale, on the same principle exactly as our computers.†

I do appreciate your letters to the kids

> Lots of love – Essie Mae

---

* George went to YMCA "Camp Wapsie Y" on the Wapsipinicon River in northern Linn County in the summer of 1943. He expected to go there again in the summer of 1944.
† Harris Thompson was a vice president of the chemical manufacturing company, Nalgene.

January 27, 1944          Thursday
Dearest Gerald –

Just a note to add to the letter. It has been <u>pouring</u> rain all night and morning. Tommy said this A.M. – "I hope we move back to our big house in Lisbon when this war is over." In the course of the conversation, it came out that he had never gotten it thru his funny little head that we were thru living there <u>forever</u>.

                    Heaps of love – Essie Mae


January 28, 1944          Friday
Dearest Gerald –

Tommy is at home from school this A.M. – contentedly staying in bed, to get rid of a head cold. Seems like – "if it is not one of us, then it's another." I think we'll get this checked right away tho'. Your article to the *Hawkeye* was swell. It makes a swell contemp on the front page & I'm so glad you wrote it. Our warm rain of yesterday has given way to a raw cold wind & I think we're in for winter weather. I have an appointment to have Prall look the kids' teeth over tomorrow A.M. Don't know if I can get G. to go, tho'.

Hope your "office problems" have been going smoothly & that you'll soon have a desk of your own. The forms you fill out look very complicated to me.

                    Much love – Essie Mae


January 30, 1944          Sunday Eve
Dearest Gerald –

We have been listening to Jack Benny, and are wondering if you are listening to the Sunday programs, too. How is your cold? This has been quite a nice day, with a lot of hard work, but a pleasant trip to McVille, and the Lisbon airport. Yesterday, I should have mailed a letter to you, but I honestly didn't have a minute all day and the kids were so good – otherwise I never could have gotten thru. Tomorrow, I start on a six hour day – which means really from eight in the morning till five thirty at night.*

We have been daydreaming about a trip to Calif. this summer, if you are still there. I think you will find that the kids have been growing tall. I am so glad they don't have extensive dental work to be done, and they were just thrilled to death with Prall. Tommy says, "Why it even smells good in there." Even Geo. was satisfied.

I have to go back to teaching Engines, along with Aerology, and I went out to the Airport to get some help. There have been a lot of inspectors around lately, and that along with the fact that a new Skipper is coming is giving rise to the rumor that maybe the school won't close July 1st after all. I have my fingers crossed about lecturing SIX hours a day! I was really surprised after I got into the swing of teaching Nav. at how swell it really was. Of course, I had worked so darn hard at it for four weeks, that I really had it down pat, and I could sympathize and get a kick out of helping the slow ones, and the others were so darned good that their tests were practically perfect. The boys like it, and it seems so much more practical than the other courses. I suppose I would feel the same way about the other subjects if I had ever had any real instruction in them myself. I wore my red velvet jacket blouse yesterday after wearing my uniform, and one of the boys said, "Oh, you've changed to the NW Mounted Police now."

I'd like to begin building a little cash reserve out of my money, just in case I can come to Calif. or where ever you are – at least for a visit this summer. I get pretty lonesome for you, you know, Honey. All three of us just "get along" without you – we don't even pretend to be adjusted to not having you with us. We've lived in a house of our own too long to ever like apartment dwelling, where you listen to other people's radios more than you do your own, etc., etc. Geo. is begging for another dog, but I tell him we'll have to wait till we get a house of our own for that.

I hope you will "forgive and forget" my unhappy letters when I was feeling so punk. I swear I won't let myself get so low again. Thank you for all your grand letters.

                    A lot of "snuggling and love,"
                    Essie Mae

---

* Jack Benny (1894-1974) was a radio comedian, violinist, and actor in film and TV. He was previously in vaudeville.

31 of Jan [1944] [Monday]
Dear Dad,

I still have a bad cold But is going to school. Gorge also has a cold and is staying home with it, the same I had to go to school at 8:30 not long from here. Maybe you can send me lod you can send me a preaple snow shovel I can work it. that's oll for to nigh  good night

Wed. Feb 2

Daddy, Nancy [Gaston] my girl came over to play to night when she went home I went to help mom do som shoping I've been wining more marbels read tomorrow page now          [Tommy]


January 31, 1944   Monday
Dearest Gerald,

You certainly must lead a very busy office life to handle so many calls, appointments, etc., all in one day. How interesting it must be! Is your roommate finally located with his family?  Do any of the wives seem interesting – the kind that I would like, and be congenial with?

This was my first day of six classes, and it really was much less tiring than I imagined it would be.  George had a cold, and I let him stay at home – in bed until mid-afternoon.  I left at seven thirty, came home at ten.  Scrubbed the kitchen and waited on him, and got lunch.  Went back to the office at twelve forty-five, and didn't get home till quarter of six.  The kids had been very good in the meantime, however.  We have all spent the evening straightening up the house and doing the many odd jobs that there are to do.  Tommy is writing you a day-by-day letter to be mailed next Sunday.  I dreamed last night about MOVING.  It was just one place after another, each worse than the one before, until it finally ended up with a dirt floor in the kitchen.

Guess I better get the kids rounded up for bed soon and go in that direction myself, altho it is only quarter of nine.  Very much love, My dear.

Essie Mae


# February 1944
### Essie Mae teaches Navy cadets from before sunrise until after sunset
### "This week has been a killer . . . The kids have been so darned quarrelsome"

"I began to see those four years of the war as a kind of inadvertent revolution in America, a time when, while men were not really watching, women all over this country from every walk of life learned they could accomplish things they had never been allow or asked to try before."

– Emily Yellin, *Our Mother's War*, xiv


Mount Vernon, Iowa
February 2, 1944          Wednesday
Dearest Gerald –

Just a note to tell you that we are OK and loving you.  I just didn't have a minute all day yesterday to write you – Geo. is still at home with a cold – it's not very bad, but he is so good & contented reading the Encycl. that I think he's better off here.  Yesterday, during my brief respite from classes in the morning, I deposited my check in Lisbon, paid some bills, etc. etc.  Then I didn't get home in the P.M. till 5:45 and had to be back to the building to proctor make-ups at 6:45.  By the time I got home, & prepared my engines lesson, I was <u>very</u> weary.

Just sent you a telegram.  Must close now and start hustling again –

Much love,

Essie Mae

February 3, 1944          Thursday
Dearest Gerald –

        Your grand letter, containing the FD's evaluation of you, and the clipping from the paper, came yesterday. That was a particularly nice letter – and I am anxious to share it with Mother. The FD's opinion of you is wonderful! And of course, so TRUE – but I'm so glad he has come to realize it in such a short time.

        Harry Sizer called last eve. He said he really would have liked to have gotten into service. He said he would write you soon – but he has <u>lots</u> of work piled up. He is 4F now. That clears the atmosphere for any decisions you want to make about returning to Lisbon, and I know you'll be keeping your eyes & ears open.

        It is just like Spring outdoors again this morning. After one or two awfully cold spells, I never can remember such a mild winter. It's a good thing, too, for I am simply not going to buy any more fuel. I am thankful to be feeling "almost normal" – Still have a little soreness in my ribs – but after wearing a "bandage" for a whole month I finally took it off. When I first started, I could hardly lift the "demonstration plotter," which is quite heavy.

        Am wondering whether to get some more beef. We're nearly out.

        Must get lunch now. Very much love to you from all of us. Tommy is writing you every night – to be mailed at the end of the wk.!
                Essie Mae


February 4, 1944  Friday*
Dear Dad,

Mon. I still have a bac couf, but is going to school. Gerge nw has a cold and is staying home (remember this is a monday) with it (the same I had). I go to school at 8:30 not long from here
We had supper uptown. George is now wasing the dishes with mother wile I wirte a good letter.
Tue. 1day of Feb.
George had to stay home today to. I started playing marbels today wich was lots of fun. I learned some more in Arith in Division. I'll put one in tomorrows leter were learning lots more in scholl.
Wed. Feb 2
Nancy (my girl) came over to play tonight when she went home I went to help mom do some shoping
I've been wining more marble.
Fri: I had a cold and stade home Friday.
Sat: Today was the worse of all at first but not later    The woorsest was the dentist only went to find what was wrong we both had bad toothe and some bunched    I got a good hair cut in the afternoon
Sun: In Sunday school we had a quiz the girl won of course
Keep the camp fires burning plan to camp out there in the son  love from all
                Tommy Hill   your son


1944  FEB 2  AM 10:

FA 109  10=MOUNTVERNON IOWA  2 1110A†

GERALD L HILL / =CARE RED CROSS KZ= / =HARRY FAILED TO PASS PHYSICAL EXAMINATION RELIEVED MIND FAMILY WELL / =ESSIE MAE


February 4, 1944  Friday    Cornell College
Dearest Gerald –

        Your grand letter telling about your visit to L.A. came yesterday and was <u>SO</u> interesting! I think it is absolutely true that we can't really appreciate your work because we've had nothing like it in our own experience. The kids we so interested in our visit to the "cemetery" from having seen *Life*. Geo's first question was "Did he see Tom Mix's grave?" I didn't know enough of the geography of that region to realize that Glendale, El Monte, etc.

---

\* Excerpts of EMH's transcription of Tommy's letters.
† Western Union telegram.

were close enough together to be able to visit them at one time. I have heard of the window "The Last Supper" so many times, it was interesting to know it really is as beautiful as they claim. Can you imagine what it must be like in Europe where so many priceless things have been destroyed.*

The staff meeting yesterday was nothing startling. The new skipper is taking over, and there is to be a tightening up of discipline, etc. – which will be a good thing. It still throws most of the responsibility on the instructors and after having the Coe experience, I still resent that. Six months ago today I started teaching! You can imagine my surprise when I got word from Mother that she would stay with us for a while. I really feel that after this week, the worst is over, but we are all delighted! Tomorrow (Sat.) I will be gone from home from 7 in the morning – till six at night (practically) and the kids are delighted to have her at home with them. After supper last night I was able to relax – while she did dishes), and it was wonderful.†

Our spring weather still continues. The days are getting longer too – so it makes life so much more cheerful. The kids are playing marbles. Geo's cold seems better. Mother was <u>much</u> interested in your letters. Virginia says Johnny [Thompson] is flying 8 hours a day with only a couple of short rests. He likes combat.

I am writing this at the office. Must go home thru town, so will sign off.

> Much love,
> Essie Mae

February 6, 1944        Sunday
Dearest Gerald,

Two days have gone by, without getting around to write to you – but life is very complicated! I suppose I would have managed some how, altho I don't see how, if Mother had not been here – but it certainly has been lots easier since she WAS here. This week has been a killer, and yesterday, I left the house at 6:45 to give an exam at 7:00, and didn't get home from the office until 5:45 at night. I was home from 11 to 12:45 at noon, but had only about fifteen minutes rest. There were papers to grade, and record, besides the regular six hours of class or study hall. I thought that this coming week would be easier, but until this Battalion leaves, we have to hold our regular class periods as study periods, and to me that is just as tiring as class because of the fight with discipline. Then I have 2 sections of Aerology besides. As I told you, I have it arranged so I am not teaching Engines, but they are prophecying around the office that when the new schedule come out that I WILL be. But that is just where some one is going to get fooled. They'll have to find another Aerology teacher first – and sometimes I think they will anyway. Don't be surprised if I decide it isn't worth the struggle. The kids have been so darned quarrelsome today, that I don't feel rested and relaxed either.

I went to church here in M.V. this morning, for the first time since we moved. There is lots of to do about a Christian Peace, but with the actual details left so much to politicians, I am so cynical about the possibilities that I can't say I was much thrilled over that part of the service. I stopped at Nelsons for a few minutes this afternoon on my way home from the office where I was doing some work for tomorrow, and Richard asked me to ask you to send him a postcard or two for his collection. He is collecting picture postcards or anything of that nature from all the different places he can. Harlan had sent a picture of Mt. Etna taken from the plane – pretty high up.‡

I haven't told you before, because I was waiting to see if we caught it too, but Helen Dean was quarantined with scarlet fever a week ago yesterday. I guess we won't be getting it – from her at least, although there are quite a few cases in sickbay. I hope to get time to get my hair fixed pretty soon. Maybe I'll cut loose and go to a show tonight.§

> Much love, and wishing you were near,
> Essie Mae

---

* Tom Mix (1880-1940) was a film actor who played in many silent movies and in later in sound; he defined Western films.
† The new CO of the Naval Flight Preparatory School at Cornell College was LCDR Totten P. Heffelfinger, USNR. He was a scion of the Pillsbury family of Minneapolis, a wealthy man with Ivy league connections.
‡ Richard Nelson was a classmate of GJH at Mount Vernon; his brother Harlan was later killed in action.
§ Scarlet fever is a highly contagious and potentially fatal disease, caused by Group A Streptococcus. A yellow "quarantine" placard was affixed to Mrs. Dean's door. It responds to penicillin, which was not yet available for civilian use.

G. L. Hill has written a fine letter in answer to the letter that was recently sent out from this Church.  He has a position of serious responsibility in the Red Cross. We are proud to know that one of our members from Lisbon can be of such real service in the present crises.  Good luck "Toot," and write again soon.

February 7, 1944          Monday
Dearest Gerald,
        All is calm and peaceful here this eve.  The kids have gotten out the Erector set, and have been playing with it for the first time in many a long month.  Tommy has been working so hard on his music, and he came home all aglow with the hope that he might be chosen for a special singing group chosen from the fourth, fifth, and sixth grades.  He said if he wasn't, he was going to ask his music teacher to give him some singing lessons.  George found it very handy to get a report on Joyce Kilmer (author of *Trees*) from the encyclopedias.†
        Our staff meeting this noon was very interesting.  The new CO is a very commanding sort of person – about six feet three, tall, and well built.  He is all business, altho very gracious, and insistent upon meeting each one of the faculty personally.  He says there is going to be DISCIPLINE and from the way he said it, and his general manner, no one could doubt it.  He made the civilian instructors feel that that is what he expected of the cadets, and if the teachers didn't insist upon it, it would be too bad for them too.  He is going to visit classes, too.  Everyone thinks it is swell, and personally, I am delighted – you know that has always been my gripe.  He is going to have a staff meeting every Monday noon, too, so at last we really will be able to know what's going on and what is expected of us.  It seemed very peculiar to have been here for four months, and just see some of the officers for the first time, and to know them by name, today.  I wrote to Lester [Runkle] last night, that we had not yet decided about camp – it depends on whether you are still in California, and whether we save enough money – and (altho I did not tell him) whether the results will justify the expenditure.
        Good night, My Dear, Much love, Essie Mae


February 8, 1944          Tuesday
Dear Gerald,
        We have been looking for Manly [Thompson] today, because another letter came FOR him, forwarded from Camp, so apparently, he left that as a forwarding address.
        The last time George was sick, he simply railed at me for not doing anything to relieve his stopped up nose, after I have told him for days, to blow it, instead of sniffling it back up into his head.  He feels neglected, but if I could only make him realize his responsibility toward a happy household, and that I really DO know one or two things about how things should go, the battle would be practically won – but he feels constantly abused no matter what he gets, or what is done for him, and he knows much better!!  Darn it, I wish you were here for more reasons than one, so please tell us what is what.  Much love.  I sent you a Valentine today, which I hope you'll get by next Monday.
                Essie Mae

February 9, 1944          Wednesday morning
Dearest Gerald,
        Your letter telling of "celebrating treating the office" because your wife still loved you – just came.  Can't imagine what I wrote – but's very true I do.  If I haven't told you how much I miss you, it's simply because I didn't want you to be homesick – for I <u>do</u> miss you terribly!  Can't hardly stand it sometimes.
        This is a very hasty note – but wanted to tell you I mailed you a Valentine yesterday with my love.
        Mother's being here is <u>such</u> a help.  Geo. is mailing this on the way to school.
                Very much love, Essie Mae

---

* Excerpt from mimeographed program of Lisbon Methodist Church.
† Tommy eventually became a very skillful horn player and he was selected for membership in the school's glee club.

February 9, 1944          Wednesday 12:10 PM
Dearest Gerald,

This will reach you the same time as the letter I wrote last night – but I wanted to tell you that we were <u>SO</u> glad this morning to get your long typewritten letter written the night (Thurs) you got back to camp. I kept thinking all day that day – about your being back – but of course didn't dream that you had had such a hectic ride.

<u>My spirits are revived again</u>, over what they were last night. Classes went smoothly this A.M. The new CO has called a meeting of all the staff, both military and civilian, at 12:45, so I'll have to dash down town with this to get it into the mail. Grandma seems happy to be useful – Very hastily – but much love.

Essie Mae

February 10, 1944          Thursday 12:10 P.M.          Cornell College
Dearest Gerald,

I am writing this while I proctor a study period for the outgoing Batt. I had no idea that I would have four hours a day of this all week, so I am <u>SO</u> grateful that Mother is with me. It looks like winter has finally arrived. It is cold, snowy, and windy this morning.

Rumor has it that the new CO is a millionaire. He certainly has an air of great authority – and it wouldn't be surprising if the rumor was correct. Went to bed last night at 8 o'clock. It's a killing pace – but it <u>can't</u> last much longer! Feel OK this morning. The kids were both out to Church group meetings. Geo. says he's going to learn to dance. Tommy drew a picture of our Lisbon house at school t'other day & he said very few kids would believe that we once had such a fancy place.

Continued at home – Boy! We are having a real blizzard! Worst storm of the year, I think! You can be thankful you're not in blizzard country today, but we do miss our Daddy very much – and love him heaps and heaps.

Your Essie Mae

February 11, 1944          Friday A.M.
Dearest Gerald,

Just time for a hasty note. Will answer your grand letters soon – I hope. Got telegram this A.M. saying Manly [Thompson] arriving Sunday P.M.

Have to start tomorrow at 7:10 again. Awfully wintry today – Lots of snow and temp nearly zero. Doc Prall suggested consulting orthodontist about straightening Geo's teeth – said upper ones were protruding some. Tommy's are O.K. except for 1 small filling + cleaning. Geo. spent the evening last night practicing dancing. The space is so small around here, but he does very well. Has the waltz step down pretty well & I can follow him.

Sent a package of cookies to you yesterday – Watch for it. Hope this reaches you by Valentine's day – with my love. A big embrace and very special kisses for my Sweetheart –

'S'Mae

Mount Vernon, Iowa          Cornell College
February 12, 1944          Saturday          Lincoln's Birthday
Dearest Gerald,

Another so-called "study period" – at 7:10 in the morning. I bro't along a half dozen copies of *Life* for the class to read & told them that the rest of us could write our "daily letter." I was <u>SO</u> cold this morning, but the moon was shining bright as day. Mother got up and ate breakfast with me, but the kids were still asleep. I hesitate to think what it would be like at home, if she weren't there. I get so sleepy about 9:30 I can't hold my eyes open. Then I dream – too much to rest as completely as I might – usually about fitting our furniture into another strange place.

One of the cadets brought an "up-to-date" C.A.A. map to show me, showing the new width of the airways, 3 types of Airspace Restrictions (instead of the former "Reservations," etc.), which he had "acquired" when he was plane captain at a base down in Georgia. He seemed to get a kick out of pointing out the Florida swamps, etc., which he had flown over. Says a lot of crashes happen there – they spot them from the air, then send out a rescue party.

Tommy went to the show last night with Nancy Gaston & her Mother. Geo. wants a girlfriend now, but he can't think which one he likes best.  He is taking a lot of pains with his hands & hair.  Even puts hand lotion & fingernail polish on.  T. had quite a time when I told him I didn't think he should kiss Nancy [Gaston] any more.  He said she was mad at him when he told her he wasn't supposed to, but she got over it, & he said they "held hands" at the church party the other night.  He is so funny telling about it – without any inhibitions.*

        Later:  10:10 A.M. and just –5°.

            Much love – Essie Mae

February 14, 1944          Monday

To My Valentine –

        Your night letter telling of move to H. Liggett came yesterday P.M. (Sunday).  Much surprised & anxious to hear details.  Manly [Thompson] arrived yesterday, too, & was able to give us some idea of its location & nature.  He says they have "everything" there – from ocean to rugged country.  Manly doesn't know his future.  17 of 18 of M.P. companies have been disbanded & assigned to different work.

        It is snowing again today.  Mother made Valentine cookies for Tommy to take to school.  Am so anxious to hear details of your move.  Looks like I'd have an easier schedule for this week, at least.

            Much love – Essie Mae

February 16, 1944          Wednesday A.M.

Dearest Gerald –

        Manly left a few minutes ago – so I'll write you before I pitch in to get the house straightened up.  Your grand letter to Geo. came Monday – It was a wonderful letter and I'm SO glad you wrote it.  That kid is so talented but is always such a problem.  He needs the "pat on the back."  Manly says I show decided favoritism to Tommy, so I'm going to try to be more patient & sympathetic to G.  Actually, I <u>do</u> much more for G. than for Tommy, but of course T. is always more appreciative & responsive.  It is snowing again – a light, wet, flakey, snow.  Temp. not much below freezing.  I had one of the most unexpected & gratifying "breaks."  I went to work Monday at 7:15 – tonight two classes & came home.  Soon afterward, Neil Miner called & said the post has been quarantined for scarlet fever – no more classes till Thursday A.M.  Of course, we'll have to make up the time, but I have been entirely free to enjoy Manly's visit.  He bro't us all lots of things.  The kids' "military collection" now includes a 105 mm. shell besides many others, Johnny's dog-tag, a G.I. athletic suit, belt, insignia, G.I. eating utensils, etc.  He bro't me a couple of books, a grand stainless steel silverware case that they used in the officers' mess, etc.

        I heard Mother & Manly talking last night & it appears she is very homesick & disgusted at having to be here, so I'm going to get her home as soon as possible.  If I can't swing it alone, I'll have to quit.  I do feel as tho' I should start next month to save most of my salary, and live on what you can send us.  It will be good practice for the time which is eventually coming, and I think we can do it.

            Much love from all of us –

              Essie Mae

February 17, 1944          Thursday A.M.

Dearest Gerald –

        It is snowing heavily again this morning, but not cold.  I start classes this P.M.  I got the car out & took Mother to Lisbon & did the bank business.  Found that Mother's neighbors were very worried because she'd left a light burning since she was there last.  Geo. is home in bed today.  Had temp of 102 last night but only about 100.5 this morning.  Coughs most of time tho'.  This weather is tricky.  Tommy came home last night, wet to the waist, but I put him to bed right after supper & he seems O.K. this morning.  Seems like its "one durn thing after another."

        Johnsons are going to Davenport this morning to see their 4½ year old girl.  Promised to call me as soon as they get back.  Hoping to get mail from you soon.

            Much love –

              Essie Mae

---

* At this time, George was eleven years old and Tommy was eight.

February 18, 1944   Friday – 10:30 A.M.

Dearest Gerald –

  –10° this morning.  Geo. feeling better.  I think he can get up this P.M. – but won't go to school until Monday.  Awfully tired of sickness!!  I still plan to take Mother home Sunday.  Don't know how things will work out – I have five classes a day, starting at 7:40 A.M.  Your letter written from H.L. on Sunday 2/13/44 – came yesterday after I had mailed your letter enclosing N.W. Nat'l report – so I got it out of the P.O. & readdressed it per instructions to Camp Roberts.  I sent one or two letters to H. Liggett.  Hope you eventually get them.  Johnsons have their girl.  Nothing else new around here.  We miss you – Much love –

   Essie Mae

February 18, 1944   Friday

Dear Dad,

  JOHNSON'S HAVE A 4½ YR. OLD BABY GIRL.  The happy moment came at 6:00 P.M. yesterday night.  They arrived from Davenport Orphanage with a girl, ANNE.  Mom said she had taffy colored hair and blue eyes.  Later she said that she had light brown hair.  We don't know what she looks like.  I haven't been delivering washings lately because though Helen Dean is out of Scarlet Fever quarantine tomorrow, the washer woman that I took to while she was sick caught scarlet fever.  Mom isn't worried about me catching it though, because she has tested my temp. and everything every day.

   George

*George's drawings in his letter to his father, 18 Feb 1944*

February 20, 1944   Sunday

Dearest Gerald,

  Another Sunday night!  I am wondering what you are doing, and whether you got the leave that you asked for.  How long will the maneuvers last – or is that a "military secret," how long will it be before you have time off again?  It is hard to imagine you living in a tent, and undergoing some of the inconveniences which you undoubtedly are having to undergo.  Does your tent have a floor in it?  And what kind of help you do you have?  Have you had any contacts with chaplains before going out to H.L.?

  The kids were real sweet last night, and practically shanghaied me into going to the movie with them.  Geo. paid the tickets for all of us, and as they said, "Mother, you just never go anywhere – you just HAVE to come with us."  So I did, and they seemed to get an awful kick out of it, and I enjoyed it too.  One of my present platoons is simply deviling me to death to be invited to "my house" for an "extra Aerology lesson" and cake.  (I think they heard my story about Floozy.)  It just happens that we were expressly told not long ago that we civilians were NOT to entertain cadets any more than the officers are allowed to.  They are an awful bunch of kidders, this Platoon 13.

  It has been more than three months since you first went away – in some ways the time has gone fast, but in others, it has seemed endless.  I suppose if we knew more about others, we'd realize that all of us have our problems – and they all seem awfully important to each of us.  You realize that on a big scale, don't you?  When I think of how many families who are separated for a year or more, I suppose I shouldn't dream about a visit to Calif. this summer.

  Time will tell!  Much love to you from all of us.

   Essie Mae

February 23, 1944          Wednesday
Dearest Gerald –

Just a note to tell you that I "still have my head above water" – I just live one day "at a time" and am thankful to have gotten thru it. Have been so very busy but Geo. is back in school (after another day, out) and the kids have been quite good. How is it in the tent at H.L.?

Hastily – Much love –
'S'Mae


February 27, 1944          Sunday
Dearest Gerald,

It has been three days since we heard from you, enroute to Needles, to get your motorcycle, and we are wondering how you fared. You are certainly getting a variety of experiences, and seeing a lot of country. It must have been very beautiful, in places at least. The Red Cross drive is on now, and I am wondering how much you think we should contribute to the "good of the cause." At "quarters" this week, the C.O. sent word that he "expected the fullest co-operation" in regard to it (RX), and one of the teachers added dryly, "And you know what that means in the Navy, even tho' it was not given as an ORDER. The kids and I have spent the day (Sunday) "cleaning up on the enemy – dirt." The braided rug was Truk, and we surely went after the "dirty Japs" there, as well as elsewhere around here. I had thirty-six hours of dirty dishes to wash, and other things in proportion. So you see, I have been busy, too – during the week. We all went to C.R. yesterday – got my shoes fixed again, and did numerous other errands. The kids saw *This is the Army* while I was shopping.[*]

Altho I was so tired I didn't care to go, we went to the *Comedy of Errors* last night. The Johnsons had done the best they could without any men, but it was rather dull. I happened to sit next to Libby Jolas, and was bored by her conversation of how busy she was, teaching AFTERNOONS.

Must change into some "Sunday clothes" now and take this to the depot to be mailed.

Much love from all of us,
Essie Mae


February 28, 1944          Monday
Dearest Gerald –

Yesterday was a Red Letter Day, for each of us got a letter – Tommy and I each had one from you – and Geo., from Johnny [Thompson]. T. and mine were written while you were waiting for the truck to take you to Indio.

Geo's grades were a disappointment – Reading 90, Arith 91, English 80, Spell 90, Geo. 80, Science 90, Penmanship 83, Conduct 80 – Effort 85. He was absent 4¾ da. – which only partially accounts for it. He is to bring his books home & "bear down" now. He "talks too much" (so Mrs. Fisher told him) but he denies it, of course.

Lots of love – Essie Mae


Boulder, Colo. / CAA-WTS Armory[†]
28 February 1944 [postmark]
Postcard addressed to Mrs. G. L. Hill / Mt. Vernon, Iowa, with mountain scene with stream in foreground: "In the Canon, Boulder, Col."
Hiya Lady –          Now almost settled here in Boulder and I have to admit it's nice as you said it was. It has been nice & warm until today, and it snowed – but it still is nice. Had two hours of flight yesterday & really like it. They keep us moving faster out here than they did in Prep. Say hello to the boys for me.

Bye now – Bob                    c/o R. S. Mortonson

---

[*] Heavy U.S. airstrikes on Truk were carried out on 17-18 February 1944. *This is the Army* (1943) starred Irving Berlin and Ronald Reagan, among many others. Kate Smith sang "God Bless America."
[†] Postcard filed with GLH's letters of February 1944, sent to him by EMH. From Robert S. Mortonson, Service No. 550-53-66 V-5 Aviation Cadet, USNR, enlisted 1 October 1942 in Miami, Fla. (Fold3 record, 30 April 1944, Naval Air Primary Training Command, Kansas City, KS, p.277). He was EMH's student in the NFPS at Cornell College, which he calls "Prep."

## March 1944
### The long hard winter is finally over.  Essie Mae continues teaching Naval Air Cadets
### "It nearly gives me heart failure to hear you talk about going overseas"

"The War Department must fully utilize, immediately and effectively, the
largest and potentially the finest single source of labor available today – the
vast reserve of woman power."

– Henry L. Stimson, Secretary of War[*]

Mount Vernon, Iowa      Cornell College
March 6, 1944      Monday 7:00 a.m.
Dearest Gerald –

    This is the longest time I have gone without writing to you, but I didn't want your "unanswered correspondence" to pile up too high, before the RX gave you enough time to answer it.  I am writing this in a "study period," when I'm supposed to be keeping watch over one of my classes, which has taken the Aerology final.  I had a very busy week last week, finishing the course – with extra tutoring at night and five classes as day.  Next week should be easier tho'.  It has snowed terrifically the last three days, and now it is turning cold – with a high wind ("Beaufort 6").  The kids have been having a grand time building snow forts, etc., with thousands of wet mittens, pants, and shoes!  I had to order more coal this A.M.  Friday night it was raining when I went to put the car away (9:00 P.M.) and the garage was so full I couldn't get in.  Next morning it was covered with 6" of snow, so I called for help to come & get it out!  Johnsons are having a wonderful time with their child.  They asked us over yesterday – but the kids got too hilarious with snowballing & it ended in tears, so I wouldn't let them go – and went myself in the evening.  Went to Tulls on Sunday eve & had a dull time – he insisted on listening to "Fred Allen," which bores me.[†]
7:00 P.M.
At home.  I had a little extra time at home today and baked the first pie in six months, as well as made corn sticks, scalloped potatoes with ham and some tarts.  We had a real feast for a change, and I mean CHANGE.  I thought I would have plenty of time this winter to sort things that were packed in bulk when we moved, but I haven't had time, or else was too weary to touch it.  Did you get the box of cookies I sent recently?  I hope you get things in your work arranged to your satisfaction, and that the "powers that be" are aware of the extra time and trouble you take to make things right.  How do you like your motorcycle, now that you are back at camp?  That must have been SOME trip thru the rain.  George nearly jumped thru the ceiling when he read your letter about Gen. McNair being there.  He really gets a big kick out of things like that.  He went up to the Library tonight and brought home *Dr. Jekyll and Mr. Hyde*, *Beau Geste*, and *The Thin Man*.  He just got it thru his head that Hearst is *Citizen Kane* – so he really is getting a kick out of your location on the Hearst ranch.[‡]

    Much love from all of us.
        Essie Mae


Tuesday, March 7, 1944      2:30 P.M.         Cornell College
Dearest Gerald –

    This is another study period & this is the only paper available.  It has been storming terrifically for 24 hrs. (Thank goodness coal came this morning.)  Trains are all very late & the mail hadn't come when I left home this P.M. Do you have to make your own bed?  Would you like the horse blanket pins to help keep your covers together (If I can find them)?

    Geo. told this noon about helping several kids on a test this A.M.  Two cadets were recently washed out – one for getting help, the other for giving it.  I hope Geo. was duly impressed with the seriousness.

---

[*] Henry Stimson, quoted in Emily Yellin, *Our Mother's War*, 37.
[†] Fred Allen (1894-1956) was a very popular radio comedian of the 1940s and 1950s.
[‡] George's three borrowings from the library were books that had recently been made into movies: *Dr Jekyll* (1941), *Beau Geste* (1939), *Thin Man* (1934). Orson Welles' movie *Citizen Kane* (1943), was indeed based on the life of William Randolph Hearst.

March 8, 1944     Wednesday          2:30 P.M.   Cornell College
Dearest Gerald,

        Another study period – I sit in the doorway between two classrooms & look after another class as well as my own – these two early hours.  The roads are so bad that it has been a toss-up whether the other teacher would get there are all.  Apparently the "storm" is over now, and it has turned bitter cold.  Got up at 5:30 in order to get the house warm in time for breakfast.  Geo. and Bobby Gaston collected washings & then Bobby stayed for supper.  He & Geo. are simply devoted to each other & he is the nicest & most congenial friend Geo. ever had.  They are both trying to make the honor roll this six wks.

        I was called down to HQ in regard to one of the teacher's "attitude" (Reed) and in talking to the CO, I told him what I tho't of discipline & morale here, when I first came, & how much I appreciate the new regime.  How I tho't it was terrible to have been here four months before there was any opportunity to even know him [the previous CO] by sight.  He agreed, & apparently appreciates the change also.

Mar 8 – Later at home – 10:30 A.M.

        I am hot both physically & mentally!  I got to digging around in the furnace after I came home & finally ended up by taking out enough clinkers to fill one of the ash cans downstairs.

        I'll certainly be glad when winter is over.  You have no idea what a grind it has been!

        It's nearly time for the mail man.  So Bye –

                        Heaps of love –
                            G'Mae


March 12, 1944     Sunday A.M.
Dearest Gerald,

        Two letters (written Mar. 7 and 9) came yesterday, the 11th, one slower than usual, the other faster.  You have been "on your own" at HL now for ten days, and I am wondering if you like it.  I know you like to be busy, and I hope you're still happy in the arrangement.  Do you eat with the officers there?  And what kind of recreation is available?  I am looking forward to the coming week – I have only three hours of teaching to do, the whole week long.  I have every day planned full however, but it will be a welcome change.

        I want to do some sorting of the stuff here.  It is so crowded!  If I knew what we would be doing this summer, and next fall, I could do it more satisfactorily, but I'll just work away on it anyway.  If we just had another closet and a few more shelves here, it would help so much, and if this were a more or less permanent arrangement (for the duration) I'd do something about it.  Scarlet fever is very rampant in Lisbon now – Patty Sizer got it Friday – the rest of the family are at Doc Gardner's, of course.

        Margaret Bourke-White, the *Life* photographer, is to be at the college lecture course this week, and we are planning to go.  *Madame Curie* is at the movie theatre.  A new directive has come out at NFPS which means the end of Geo's "racket."  He is bitterly disappointed, for he thoroly enjoyed his contacts with the cadets, as well as the money.  I have one of the same groups in Aerology, which I started in Navigation – I enjoy it, and I think it is mutual.  Geo. said one of them "almost hugged him" when he found out that I was his mother – said "Oh, she is my favorite teacher," and then gave Geo. a hint that they had made me blush in class on Friday, to their great amusement!*

        Things are in such a mess around here – I plan to clean and reorganize one room a day next week, when I am at home.  I am cooking one of the two chickens we have left in the locker.  We have no meat at all left.  Jim [High] got a quarter of beef butchered and promised me some of it, but I suppose they have been snowed in for the last couple of weeks.  Wish you were here to help us eat the chicken this noon.

        I was amused at some of the cadets last week when I was up at the Wasp coaching them for their Aerology final.  An announcement came over the loud speaker that the Catholic priest was in the lobby, and would consult

_____

* Margaret Bourke-White (1904-1971) was the first American woman to be allowed to be a photojournalist in WWII..
*Madame Curie* (1943) with Greer Garson and Walter Pidgeon; story by Madame Curie' daughter, Eve.  It was a great success.

with anyone who wanted him. I heard one of them say, "He must need some money," and another, "I guess this (the quiz section) will do us more good than he will!"*

Lots of love to you from all of us, 'S'Mae

DEAR DAD: I AM WRIGHTING THIS LETTER WITH GEORGE'S PRESS.  MOM IS SENDING YOU A CLIPPING ABOUT A C.R. AIRPLANE CRASH.  READ ABOUT IT.          LOVE, TOMMY

March 14, 1944     Tuesday
Dearest Gerald,

My first whole day of vacation!  I had planned to go to C.R. this morning, but it has turned out to be one of the worst days (weather) we have had all winter.  It is raining and freezing – slippery, as only M.V. can be under conditions like that.  We feel very "luxurious" at being able to sleep longer in the mornings, and have been staying up till the "scandalous" hour of ten or ten-thirty.  Last night I read to the kids the story of a Navy doctor, awarded the Navy Cross, for bravery in evacuating his patients from Java.  It was written by James Hilton (*Good Bye, Mr. Chips*) and they like it a lot.  I kept thinking that some women would have been scrubbing and scouring out the dirt and clutter around here, but "keeping the kids happy and contented at home in spite of the wartime disruption" seems to me much more important.†

George got a big kick out of riding me home from Johnsons' Sunday afternoon on his bike.  He and I get along pretty well lately, by a "give and take psychology."  He really thought he was doing me a favor by helping me home, but you can imagine how petrified I was at tearing along at a furious rate over bumpy road and campus hills.
Much love, Essie Mae

March 15, 1944     Wednesday
Dearest Gerald –

I am hurrying to get to "quarters" at 12:50.  No mail from you today – hope for better luck tomorrow.
Love,     'S'Mae

March 18, 1944     Saturday
Dearest Gerald,

We heard Margaret Bourke-White, the *Life* photographer, talk on Thursday night, and she was awfully good.  Looked lovely – much like Elizabeth MacFarland, prematurely gray, but beautiful.  She really has had some thrilling experiences.  I saw in the paper the other day, that there was a call for civilian teachers for illiterate soldiers – to teach them to read and write.  I wrote to the address indicated (7th Service Command in Omaha) for details, telling them about my experience and qualifications, including Master Sergeant in the CAP.  Probably nothing will come of it, but I thought I would investigate.

Since I finally got over all the after effects of the flu, I have been feeling swell, altho I was so weary last night, I was in bed a full twelve hours (from 7 to 7), but I weigh about 120 now.  Altho I have no classes today, I must go up to the office now, and Tommy is going with me to get some wooden boxes and crates at the "Wasp."
Love from all of us, Essie Mae

Dear Dad

The first thing I want to ask is do they have <u>a good</u> Jack knife that I could have, around there.
Well how is thing going on down or up there.  I'm having my trubuls althou I get out of them as soon as I get in.  I'm going out to play.     Love and kisses.
Tommy          George   and Mom          Tommy

---

* "Wasp" was Bowman Hall when it was used by the Navy.  It was renamed in honor of the U.S.S. *Wasp* (CV-7), which was abandoned and scuttled after being torpedoed by a Japanese submarine in 1942; the wreck was found in 2019.
† James Hilton's book, *The Story of Dr. Wassell*, became a movie in 1944, starring Gary Cooper as the heroic Navy doctor, Corydon M. Wassell.  Hilton's novels *Lost Horizon* and *Goodbye, Mr. Chips* also were made into successful movies.

March 22, 1944    Wednesday
Dearest Gerald,

Tommy is watching the mails every day to see if you have been able to find a knife for him. In the meantime, you never would guess what both he and Geo. are doing in their spare time. EMBROIDERING!!! Yes, sir, I have going to have the fanciest set of tea-towels, you ever saw. I think it is fine, for they are learning to handle a needle, and do fine work with their hands, as well as to appreciate some of the fancy pillowcases and table cloths we have always used, but that they just took for granted before.

Another funny episode came up recently. Tommy said, "Mother, what if you get a job, but they won't take you because you have to look after Geo. and me?" Just kiddingly, I answered, "Well, I guess I'll have to clap you into the clink." Well, of course, Tommy wanted to know what that meant, so I told him, and then said, "Well, maybe I'll put you in the reform school, they'll keep you safely." Well Tommy said, "Oh, I couldn't be bad enough for that – maybe you could send us to an orphanage." "No, I answered, maybe someone would want to adopt you." Then Tommy said, "Well, I'd just tell them that I already had a Mother." Mother: "Yes, but what if she was much nicer and prettier." Tommy: "Well, I couldn't love anyone else, as much as I do you, so I wouldn't go."

I think the kids are getting spoiled by their Mother's attention, but that's merely compensation, for having to be without a Daddy for the time being, and it will adjust itself when we are together again.

Getting sleepy, Much Love, 'S'Mae

March 25, 1944    Saturday morning
Dearest Gerald,

Your letter telling of your airplane experience came yesterday, and we were all so happy to hear about it. I shall certainly report to the "Flying Eagles" all about it. It must have been a wonderful sight to see San Simeon from the air – hard to imagine all that belonging to one person. It was certainly very nice of the Lt. to arrange it, and a tribute to your "personality" that it worked out so happily. Not many, I imagine, have that happen to them.

The Lion's Club show last night was very good. It was a simplified version, but everyone seemed to enjoy it, and it was fun to see it, from the very center of the first row of the audience. Neil Miner had been sick in bed, both days, with a temp of 102, and Al Johnson had been understudying his part, but he came thru and was the chief clown – as usual – and no one would have dreamed he was so ill. I went to CAP Thursday night, after having missed five meetings. They were having class in Morse Code, so it was a little dull, but I was glad to see the gang. They were much interested in your motor-cycle experiences.

Tommy wants me to ask you if you are sending his knife. He is just pining for one. You really should tell him how pleased we are about his fingernails – you wouldn't believe how well he has conquered that habit, and how pleased he is, over the looks of his nails. I have been putting a little "wave-set" on George's hair every time he goes to school, in an effort to train his hair, and make him look nice, and I told the kids, if I got those two things done, I would really feel like I had accomplished something.

I was amused at my cadets last night. When I took off my fur coat at the theatre last night, one of them said, "Mrs. Hill, we've been wondering what dress you would wear to the show tonight." I said, "What do you mean?" He said, "Well, you know you have the fellows all agog, because you wear something different every day, and most of the teachers always look the same." I haven't worn my CAP uniform for a long time, but before this bunch leaves, I think I'll surprise them with it.

Have you made up your mind what you are going to tell the bank June 1st? I think the patriotic thing for them to do is to extend your Leave of Absence, altho' I suppose we'll never go back. I hear that Youngs use the southwest room as a guest room, and have papered it in bright yellow. I think that would be glary on a hot summer afternoon. I wonder what they did with your map room.*

Must get back to class now (it is now 0945).

Much love from all of us, 'S'Mae

---

* Referring to the Hills' former house in Lisbon, purchased by the Youngs, with 4 bedrooms on the 2d floor. The master bedroom was at the SE; the boys' bedroom was at SW; the guest bedroom was at NW; and GLH's study (map room) was at NE.

March 27, 1944    Monday
Dearest Gerald,

   I took out Hartzell Spence's second book from the Library over the weekend to read, and I came across some passages that I think will interest you.[4] Chapter II starts, "My birth was so old-fashioned that it occurred at home. There was no proper hospital in the little county seat of Clarion, Iowa. Had there been, my mother would not have stood for any such nonsense. … A snapshot in an old album purports to be me, seated prim and neat on the parsonage porch watching Eileen attempt, with an innocence belying her temper, to take an orange away from Ruth Shackleford." The name of the book is *Get Thee Behind Me*, and gives more of the details of his early boyhood and life thru college than his first book, *One Foot in Heaven* does.

   I noticed that Lela Hill is the Wright county spelling champion this year (*Des Moines Register*), and Mrs. Ruby Woodin her teacher. The Hill grandchildren have almost a monopoly on that honor, don't they?*

   Tommy has been having a pimple on his nose that was developing into a potential boil, but I finally persuaded him to take the hot Epsom salts water compress-treatment, and he says it is better this morning. The kids saw the movie *Lassie Come Home*, a dog story written by Eric Knight of SUI, yesterday, and Tommy confessed that he wept a little. He is SO proud of his fingernails. No fingernails no Shows, you know, has been our rule.†

   Much love, from all of us,
    'S'Mae


March 28, 1944    Tuesday evening
Dearest Gerald,

   I wonder if the RX changes its mind about the routine way of doing things, as often as the Navy does here. We just get into one groove, and out comes another directive, to do it some different way. It has gotten so the cadets can hardly take a drink (I mean water) without getting a dispensation for it.

   Tommy is lying on the davenport with a hot compress on his nose. It is really much better, but he knows now that it is what MAKES it feel better. George is still out playing baseball.

   We got a letter today saying that Lester [Runkle] will be here on Saturday. You know Sunday is Mother's birthday as well as Palm Sunday, so it will be a very nice time for us. Wish you could be here. We'll be thinking of you. Mother is hoping Harris [Thompson] will come too. If the roads are good, we want to go to Rachie [(Thompson) High]'s for dinner [at noon]. The church in Lisbon is having a union service, and I promised Rev. Arnold that I would lead the singing and sing a solo. I took my music over to Johnsons this PM after school, and Bertha played it for me on their piano. We are so pleased that you are investigating the living possibilities for a month or so in California this summer. George says he would much rather do that then to go to camp. After all, in a dream, you might as well make it as good as possible. I think I will go to CAP in CR tomorrow night, unless something interferes. I may take the kids, and go over before supper, then let them go to a show. *The Sullivans* is on at the Paramount, and Geo is anxious to see it. It nearly gives me heart failure to hear you talk about going overseas.‡

   Did I tell you that I read most of *Thirty Seconds over Tokyo* out loud to the kids?§

    Much love, 'S'Mae
Mar. 29  7:30 A.M.  Blizzard again this morning!


March 29, 1944 [Wednesday evening]
Dearest Gerald,

   Because of the snow today, and the fact that I had to have an extra class tonight at 7, Geo. is at youth fellowship, although he is "under a cloud" because he got home late from Gastons last night, and hadn't told me

---

\* Hartzell Spence (1908-2001) was an author of several best-selling books, including the two mentioned by EMH. GLH's birth three years earlier in Wright County on his parents' farm was similar, and GLH had no birth certificate. The same Ruth Shackleford appears in this book (misspelled in Spence's recollections), sometimes called Ruth Shack, or just "Shack."
† *Lassie Come Home* (1943) starred Roddy McDowell, Elizabeth Taylor and Dame May Whitty.
‡ The Sullivans were five Iowa brothers who died when their ship, the U.S.S. *Juneau* (CL-52), was sunk on 13 November during the battle for Guadalcanal. A destroyer, The Sullivans (DD-537), was named for them. It was launched on 4 April 1943.
§ Captain Ted Lawson's *Thirty Seconds over Tokyo* (1943) tells of his participation in the 18 April 1942 raid led by Lt.Col. Jimmy Doolittle. It was made into a movie in 1944, starring Van Johnson.

where he was. Tommy is putting a puzzle together that he got for Xmas. We laughed at Tommy again today. I made some dumb chocolate cookies this morning, and in order to make them more palatable I put a thin white icing on them. Tommy saw them and exclaimed, "Oh, they have plastic frosting."

Have you forgotten that you have not sent Geo. the money for a subscription to his newspaper, or did you ever receive your copy? Tommy is soaking his nose again tonight. He still remembers what an awful time we had with a boil on his bottom, and is delighted to hear that this one will not be opened and squeezed like that one was. That's all for tonight.

Much love, Essie Mae

"The college received notification that the input of Navy students would cease with March, 1944, and all utilization of college facilities by the Navy would cease on June 30. In May it was announced that a Navy Academic Refresher Unit of 250 men would replace the larger Flight Preparatory school. The Refresher unit was made up of Marines and non-commissioned officers who had seen active service in the Pacific. These men were allowed to participate in sports and were the backbone of the Cornell football team. The unit's Saturday morning inspections and parades and their formal presentations of service medals were a colorful and interesting part of the life of the town and college."[*]

# April 1944

### Essie Mae continues teaching Naval Flight Preparatory Cadets, but:
### "I get so discouraged trying to be Mother and Father and everything to the kids"

"Without due recognition or validation, and most often unwittingly, wartime women embarked on an odyssey that would, for better or worse, begin to explode their time-honored roles within their own families."
– Emily Yellin, *Our Mother's War*, 36

Mount Vernon, Iowa
April 3, 1944      Monday
Dearest Gerald,

Tommy was simply delighted with his knife. It is just what he wanted. The candy, Dreft, and Kleenex are SUCH luxuries – we haven't been able to get any for so long. My boys [cadets] look at me with puzzled expressions as I read *C/O Postmaster* during study periods, for I almost laugh out loud at times.[†]

We had a beautiful day for Palm Sunday, and Mother's birthday. She seemed very happy. All the grandchildren, except Bill and Johnny, were there and remembered her, and everyone was very generous. I put the leaves in the drop leaf table for the first time since we have been here, and it seemed like a party.

I sang a solo in the Lisbon church and directed the singing (at a union service Palm Sunday eve), and Lester got quite a kick out of being there. Lester got a big kick out of discovering who our new C.O. is, here at the Navy. It seems that he and all his relatives are Blake graduates. "Pudge" Heffelfinger's sons are there now. He says that undoubtedly, he (our C.O.) is many times a millionaire. Lester wants me to come to Mpls. and look around. He says that if we lived there, Geo. could undoubtedly get a scholarship at Blake. I am not worrying at all about the future – taking each day as it comes.[‡]

Tommy's boil finally broke, and is pretty well drained now. I was putting hot applications on it Saturday night (his whole nose was almost purple, and SO swollen), when it broke and started to drain. He has been so

---

[*] *Centennial History of Mount Vernon*, 179-80.
[†] Corporal Thomas R. St. George, *C/O Postmaster* (1943), was a Book-of-the-Month Club selection.
[‡] Runkle was Head of the Lower School at Blake School; another "Pudge" Heffelfinger was football coach at Yale in the 1950s.

patient thru it all. One of the girls accidently hit it during recess, and he said he cried all recess, it hurt so bad. But he wouldn't let the boys "beat up on her," because it was an accident.

Much love from all of us, Essie Mae


April 4, 1944          0835 Tuesday          Cornell College          Study period
Dearest Gerald,

I let the furnace fire go out last night and am feeding coal during the day, a teaspoon full at a time. As soon as my classes were over yesterday P.M., we drove to McVille and ate supper with the Highs, Lester & Mother, who were staying overnight. We were the first car over the road straight out from town & it was sort of a miracle that we got thru. "Fools rush in" you know. Spring must be here! One of the platoons sang "Good morning to you," when I opened the door this morning! Then the instructor in the study hall next to mine got mixed up, & failed to show up, so I'm keeping an eye on both rooms & answering questions in Aerology.

That's all for this time – Love, 'S'Mae


April 4, 1944, Tuesday
Dear Mom,

We had a bad morning because George called for a be-be. I gave it to him. He came in for another. I didn't let him have it. He called me selfish. I didn't mind but he finely called me a basturd and that got me mad.

Tommy


April 5, 1944          Wednesday
Dear Gerald,

I found this note yesterday [above] when I got home from school. Tommy <u>does</u> have is "trubels" as he wrote you. We settled the problem by agreeing Tommy could use the gun for the same am't of time Geo. used his knife. Your bank balance shows $49.90. I put $100 from the insurance acc't onto my acc't last month, so I have a balance of $125.16. I've made arrangements about my classes for Friday, so I'm set for the CAA exam.

George was "waylaid" by four hoodlums last night on the way home from the Gastons about 9 o'clock. They were all set to take the BB gun away from him. By convincing them it was over 30 yrs. old, they decided it wasn't worth taking. He was in tears when reaching home. I certainly would have gone to bat if they had taken it.

Love, 'S'Mae


April 6, 1944          Thursday
Dear Gerald,

You know that spring must really be here, when I feel the urge to rake lawn, as I did when I got home from school this morning. There is considerably less of it than in Lisbon, but the leaves were very thick, and I have a huge pile for the kids to carry out and put onto the garden.

Tommy got wonderful grades this six weeks. He brought his writing up from a D to a C, which was what he was working for, wasn't absent or tardy, got A in Reading, Arithmetic, language, and Geography, B in Science and Music, and C in Penmanship, Art, Citizenship, and Physical Training. Geo. hasn't gotten his report card yet, but he is hoping to make the honor roll – everything above ninety. I was talking to Mrs. Chas. Fisher about him (She is his Math teacher, and he does not like her). She said he was very smart, but talks too much, as of course we can imagine.

The future of the CR airport is uncertain after the Aviation Unit pulls out. Scuttlebutt – Col. Hunter wants to be rid of it. And that's all for this time,*

Lots of love, Essie Mae


April 10, 1944          Monday morning
Dearest Gerald,

When I got home from CR on Friday (my CAA exam) I found the lovely flowers which you sent us for Easter, and your letter written Palm Sunday. It was wonderful to get them, and we surely appreciate the flowers. It

---

* Hunter Field was the Cedar Rapids airport until the 1960s. Dan Hunter was a lieutenant in the U.S. Army Air Corps in WWI.

was such a surprise, and awfully nice of you to arrange for them. I made two lovely bouquets out of them, and they really make the apartment look and smell like Easter and spring. The CAA test was very tricky, and I make no prophesies on how I came out. I told the inspector what I thought of the idea of using such antiquated station models, that a person couldn't even find a copy ahead of time to study them. He agreed, but said that no tests were being made until after the war. There was a very small crowd there for the exams, because the weather was too bad for check flights. We sang some of the songs from *The Red Mill* yesterday at Johnsons. I told them that you had seen it recently. Tommy gave me a nice Easter present. He got up quietly and built the kitchen fire, all alone, and then heated up some left-over coffee, and brought it to me in bed. I explained to him the night before, why I felt punk periodically, and he was quite impressed. He had felt, the night before, that I was pretty irritable, I guess.[*]

I have a very light teaching schedule this week. Just one study period at 1535 tomorrow. I think I will plan to wash, if the weather clears. Lunch time,

Much love, and many thanks for thinking of us "with flowers."

'S'Mae

April 10, 1944        Monday evening

Dear Gerald,

I was in such a hurry this morning when I wrote to you that I forgot to mention how very interested and pleased we were with your pictures. It certainly gives us a better idea of your setup. I somehow got the idea that you slept in the tent as well as worked in it. Where DO you sleep? You certainly look very business-like. I am wondering if you have been assigned to a new place by this time. I hope you get a place where you have more help.

In this morning's mail was the application blank which came in response to my inquiry about teaching Army illiterates. It was a very ordinary form, so in order to make my application "different," and thereby hope to have a better chance of being elected to the job, I wrote an extra page, telling of my CAA ratings, my CAP experience, and my Army and Navy teaching. I marked myself in one of the *Gazette* CAP pictures and underlined in red what it said about me underneath. I stapled the pages together and sent it to headquarters at Fort Leavenworth, Kansas.

Would you like to hear a very nice compliment which I got today? "I think you were the loveliest lady in the Easter parade yesterday." I said, "What do you mean?" "You looked so beautiful in that new blue outfit at church." I fixed the hat a little differently than it had been, and got a new blue veil. I was sorry afterwards that I hadn't worn some of my flowers, for there were quite a few corsages in the audience. I did wear a couple of daffodils to class on Saturday, and everyone was impressed at how nice my husband was to remember me at Easter.

We have brought both slipcovered living room chairs out into the kitchen tonight, as well as the radio, in order to keep "cozy" by the kitchen fire. It is rainy, cold, and strong winded out of doors, and I am rationing the coal. I have only one study period tomorrow at 1535 – the rest of the day is my own. I always find plenty to do tho'. Geo. is reading *God Is My Co-Pilot*, which I brought home from the Library tonight. My boys have been asking me if I had read it. They seem to like it. He made the honor roll this six weeks. I also brought home *Assignment to Berlin* by the man who took Shirer's place.[5]

I have been trying for weeks to get Tommy some overalls, and tennis shoes, but so far haven't succeeded. He is rather resentful at having to wear the patched overalls that he has had to, all winter, but you have no idea how hard they are to get. That's all for this time.

Heaps of love, 'S'Mae

APR 16 [1944] AM 3 47 / FA18        NL=MOUNTVERNON IOWA 15

GERALD L HILL (AFD)= *APO 303*

AMERICAN RED CROSS MANEVER HEADQUARTERS 3 CORPS /APO 303 CAMPROBERTS CALIF=

ANXIOUS TO HEAR DETAILS OF SF TRIP• PASSED CAA INSTRUCTORS METEROLOGY EXAMINATION• CHILDREN BOTH

ON SCHOOL HONOR ROLL THIS TERM. SOLD TOMMY BICYCLE FOR SEVEN FIFTY LOVE= ESSIE MAE•

---

[*] *The Red Mill* was a Broadway musical by Victor Herbert, first played in 1906. It became a silent movie in 1927, and had a Broadway revival in 1945. It was popular during the 1940s at many off-Broadway locations. Tommy was only 9 years old.

April 22, 1944     Saturday          Cornell College
Dear Gerald (Study period) 0800 –

Long time, no letter from home, for one reason and another – None of them important – but all together conspiring to not make a letter writing mood. First, the weather! It has been raining, or drizzling for about ten days straight! Very depressing. My clothes (washing) including the winter blankets hung out all night, last night, in pouring rain. It has been so cold in the house (I'm not buying any more coal, you know) that we have literally been living in one room – the kitchen! It gets so monotonous to shovel out the mud all the time, or else just tramp over it – especially "fascinating" after being mixed with ashes, which have scattered out of the range.

Second – I missed your letters terribly during the time when you were in S.F. and when they started coming, I confess I was a little disappointed that you were too busy to give some answers to things I had written about.

Got an invitation to Peggy Frink's graduation from S.U.I.*

Love – 'S'Mae

April 25, 1944     Tuesday 0845
Dear Gerald –

This is Inauguration Day and all the faculty are duly excited. My classes are at the back of Law building so I'm not sure I'll be able to see the procession. Sunday was another trying day. It was so muddy – and to see the kids come in plastered with mud on their "second" best clothes is hard to take. I drove the kids to the C.R. airport in the afternoon & got there just in time to see a "squall line" come in. The wind shifted 45° in ten minutes & it was a spectacular sight to see the cloud roll in. The torrents fell, but here in M.V. the west end of town was wet, but the east end dry, by the time we reached home.   I am becoming very conscious of the fact that my Navy job will soon be over. I think it would be a good idea to start practicing on living on what you can send us out of your salary.

Please Answer.

Much love – 'S'Mae

April 27, 1944     Thursday 1115
Dear Gerald,

Your ten page letter, answering everything I have been wondering about, came yesterday, and we were so thrilled and pleased. You surely do a swell job "when you get to it," and we much appreciate it.

It would be simply wonderful to have you come back here to see us – and I am trying to decide whether I would rather move from this goldarned place before you come – afterward – or during the time you're here. I would be ashamed to have even you see the awful way we live. Honestly, it has been so cold in every place but the kitchen this month that we have spent the evenings at the Library or someplace where it was warmer. I haven't started cleaning up the winter's dirt, because the incentive depends on how long we will be here.

Much love,
'S'Mae

28 April 1944     Friday evening†
Waiting for the play to start –

Ration books & pictures with insignia arrived. Swell! Thanks so much. Geo. thinks this play the best he's ever seen. He went last night (tonight to the Senior High School play) and Tommy & I are here tonight. Invited to Johnsons afterward. Surely wish you were here to meet their house guest – the bus. manager of the publishing house which bought the play. I hate going alone. I did get a ticket to the Festival tho' – I decided the Madame [Mrs. Eloise (Stuckslager) Thomas] would think it too strange if I didn't.

The kids have been especially interested in your letters lately. They like direct references to themselves.

---

* The Frinks lived in the same block in Lisbon that the Hills lived on. They were all close friends. Peggy Frink's sister Helen Lucille "Hona," wrote the Foreword to *Prairie Daughter* (2d ed.) S.U.I. = State University of Iowa (now University of Iowa).
† EMH to GLH, in pencil, on margins of *Theatre Headlines: Play Bill and Bulletin* (Cornell College, April 1944), including cast of *Days Without Daddy: A play in three acts* by Albert Johnson, purchased and published by Row Peterson Publishing Co.

April 30, 1944 1915          Sunday
Dearest Gerald,

The thing that has been on my mind lately has been trying to figure out whether it would be better for you to come home for a visit, or for us to try to go out to Calif. I swing from one side to the other, but just now, it seems to me it would be better for you to plan to come home.

I get so discouraged with trying to be mother and father and everything to the kids – I think they need their Daddy. Things have been pretty much quarrel and argue and scrap lately, and I just can't seem to cope with it. It is so disheartening to leave the classroom, where the cadets are so nice, and where I have the satisfaction of doing a "good job," and then come home and not have my own kids think I know anything at all about what is good for them, or best to do. I have the final exam to my group yesterday, and for the second time in succession my classes where the only ones who had no flunks in the Aerology Final, so I KNOW I do a good job of THAT. But at home!!!!

From the middle of next week – May 3d or 4th – I will be feeling punk, and I always get despondent beforehand, so maybe that is the reason for my mood today.
                    Much love, Essie Mae


## May 1944
### Essie Mae addresses the Lisbon Alumni Association banquet:
### "When the Lights Go On Again, All Over the World"

"The mail became the lifeline for many relationships. Many women wrote to their husbands every day. … Sometimes, both on the home front and overseas, weeks or months would go by without a letter, and then in one day five letters would arrive."
                    – Emily Yellin, *Our Mother's War*, 9

Mount Vernon, Iowa
May 1, 1944          Monday
Dear Gerald,

I have better news to report about the kids than I did yesterday, so I won't let my discouraging letter of yesterday go without an addition. I had to direct the singing in Lisbon last eve, and before church started, the kids got into a kind of squabble, and commenced batting each other over the head. I took Geo. out and told him to stay in the car, and when we got home, I took each of them down cellar and laid on the strap, for the first time since we came to M.V. Both of them took it without resentment, and this morning, they got up and went at things in an entirely different attitude. Geo. made his bed, got dressed and came out to breakfast just as nicely as anyone could wish, and Tommy had a sore eye, but was nice about everything. It looks like things were going to be all right.

I happened to see Libby Jolas down town this morning, and she happened to start in telling me that Helene [Runkle] says our kids are very popular at school, rated as very bright, and "cute" as the kids say. It was certainly wonderful news at this particular time, and I told her I appreciated her telling me.

It is wonderful outdoors today, really like spring. Everything is coming into bud, and the daffodils are beautiful. I must start lunch now, but I did want to assure you that I think the immediate future looks peaceful and satisfactory. I am going to send the letter I wrote yesterday, tho', because I think you haven't had a complete picture of our ups and downs, by my not mailing the others of that type which I have written.
                    Much love, Essie Mae

May 2, 1944     Tuesday     Cornell College
Dear Gerald,

This is a study period again, but I am anxious for you to know what a nice day we had at home yesterday. Tommy had pinkeye, but he rode along with me to C.R. in the P.M. & stayed in the car. For his birthday I tried to find a bicycle, & being unable, I got a very fancy scooter, with a platform geared to the back wheel so you could put both feet on it & propel it. I paid $12.⁰⁰ for it, but he didn't like it & I was just sunk. Well, I took it back yesterday & lo & behold, the Hall Bicycle Co. were very nice & handed my money back in cash without a question. We have the $7.50 from his old bike set aside as a fund for a new one, & I think I'll give him $5.⁰⁰ for your present, & tell me that is for his bicycle fund. Is that O.K.?

Your letter giving Geo. his special message came yesterday, & for a while I think he resented my having reported to you unfavorably about him. However, I am awfully glad you wrote what you did. In the evening I gave my consent for him to get a rabbit & he is so happy. So many kids have them & this is a pretty little red one – 5 wks. old, which we named "Toasty." He built a box for it, & paid $1.50 out of his own money for it. I think much of his trouble is due to the fact that he doesn't have enough to do. To keep them out of the garden & dirt Sunday P.M., I went over to the school house & played baseball with them & they were very pleased.

I hear Peggy Frink made Phi Bete at the University. I sent her a book for a graduation gift. The kids are both in a musical program at school tonite. I think T. will be able to go, altho' he's at home this A.M.

            Much love,
                'S'Mae


May 3, 1944     Wednesday     Cornell College     Study Period
Dearest Gerald –

It is raining today so we'll have to postpone Tommy's birthday wiener roast. He is quite content however, & has ordered his favorite foods for the day. Lunch – spaghetti dinner & lemon pie – Supper, scalloped potatoes & ice cream & cake. I got him a nice archery set, with six arrows, arm & hand guards, which Geo. says is nicer than the one they had at camp & he is pleased with it. You would have been proud of the kids last night at the musical program. Geo. is the littlest one in the band, but he really can do some fancy rhythms & rolls on that bass drum.

The latest scuttlebutt – The Navy will stay here until Nov. if the college will "cooperate" to the extent of allowing them to have Armstrong Hall for Head Quarters. Russell Cole is in Kansas City now seeing about it. I am prophesying that Cornell doesn't care enough to make the concessions.

            Much love, 'S'Mae

May 3, 1944
Dear Dad,

I got up at six o'clock to see what was in my boxes Mother had under my bed (or rather yours). She had two one was a long box the other was a square not oblong. I the frist was a bow and arrow set which cost mom $5 in case and in the other was a board that had 14 game on it. I did a lot more that Mom might tell you about  O yes Anne [Johnson] gave me this good Stationery thank you for the dogtag and money for the bike.

            Tommy


May 4, 1944     Thursday     Cornell College Study Hall
Dearest Gerald,

Your telegram to Tommy last eve, was the final thing which "made this the best birthday I ever had" (said Tommy). We took the cake & ice cream over to Johnsons for our evening dessert, and they had three gifts for him (Navy stationery, a waterproof helmet & candy bar). He is in bed this A.M. tho' with ½° of temp. & a cough. School is out next wk. & maybe when the sun shines warm again, he'll get his vitality back. He has grown so tall this winter.

I'm 'fraid Al is going to be "put out" if they take over Armstrong. He doesn't like to have them use the Little Theatre for cadet movies. Funny, how every person looks at things from his own point of view!*

I am going to tell my advanced class about Floozy this A.M. Brought the scrap book along. One of them told me they tho't I was "used to having my own way" and "I'll bet your husband spoils you!" The Navy answered

_____

* The Little Theatre at Cornell was (and still is) in a building attached to Armstrong Hall.

"Yes" to my petition for the use of the code room & equipment for the C.A.P.  I was surprised but pleased, of course. The Lions (at Minstrel time) didn't refer to you in the show, but privately said how much they missed you.*

I gave Tommy $1.50 in War stamps (he now has $1.80 in one book) and told him when he had $10, I would get him a bond.  I got a call last night, asking me to give a speech at the Lisbon Alumni banquet on "When the lights come on again, all over the world."  I suppose I'll do it.

Much love, 'S'Mae


May 5, 1944        Friday    Cornell College    Study period†
Dearest Gerald,

When I came to class this morning, someone was cutting grass in a <u>Snow Storm</u>.  Great big flakes!  Tommy has pink eye in the <u>other</u> eye today, and a bad cough, so he's at home again.  He got a live rabbit last night, a twin of Geo's., so he's happy.  Geo. went with me to code (CAP) last night.  Will probably find out in a day or two whether Cornell keeps the Navy program.  Bets are against it.

We were asked this A.M. to send word to H.Q. "if we would be available" in case the Navy stayed on.  <u>Very definitely</u> yes!  Also told them that Geog. was my training & interest.  They may be teaching English & Geog. & Math & Physics (like Coe).  Don't know yet whether college has agreed tho'.

Much love – Essie Mae


May 6, 1944        Saturday        Study period
Dearest Gerald,

To go to May Festival in a <u>Snow Storm</u> establishes some kind of a new record, doesn't it?  It was a mixture of snow & rain, but the ground was white when I came home.  Johnsons had a gang in, afterwards.  It didn't seem right without you – and I surely missed you – as did everyone.  Many asked about you.  The concert was given by a soprano, but I have heard better singers!  Nelsons asked me to come to their place, but I had promised Johnsons. None of the "Stucks" [Stuckslager] crowd were there.

Tommy still has a bad cold, but he surely is sweet & patient.  He goes to bed before I leave in the evening & the last two nights has been all alone, when he drops off to sleep.  The darned old kitchen stove smoked terribly this morning.  If it would only warm up!  Still no news about the Navy continuing.   Later – It is warming up – Thank goodness.  Trying to get the house cleaned up a bit to get ready to go to the P.M. concert.

Heaps of love – 'S'Mae


May 9, 1944        Tuesday        Study period‡
Dearest Gerald,

I thought you might be interested in what I am going to do for my part of the Lisbon Alumni banquet program.  I decided to write an "open letter to servicemen" (Alumni) and after some preliminary explanation – read that instead of making a speech.[6]  I hope you approve of my remarks – wish I had a "critic" to make suggestions. This is "my best" tho'.  Rec'd the "draft" and will use it to the best possible advantage.  You would have been pleased at O.E.S. meeting in Lisbon last eve.  Special "party" meeting (about 50 present) honoring wives & mothers of service men.  I got a red, white & blue corsage "for My husband" and it was <u>Very</u> nice.

Much love – 'S'Mae

---

* After EMH died in 1994, the "Floozy" scrapbook went to Tommy, whose mentor was Lt. Marc Pitts, the plane's navigator. It is sad now to recall that the annual Lion's Club show was always a minstrel show, in blackface.
† EMH to GLH, written on back of mimeographed Navy form for "Aerology Review Questions Continued."   Paper was scarce in America in WWII, and people used every scrap they could find.
‡ EMH to GLH, on back of p.5 of a carbon copy of a 5pp. draft for her talk on 12 May 1944 entitled "When the Lights Go On Again, All Over the World," the title of a popular song in 1943.

May 10, 1944     Wednesday     1235     Cornell College
Dearest Gerald,

Your grand long letter written Saturday arrived & was simply swell. I have just a few minutes now before "quarters." Tommy is off on his final school picnic & Geo. has pink eye, but went to school wearing dark glasses, so he wouldn't spoil his record. I still have to finish my enormous washing when I get back from quarters.

I think the military frowned on my going out to the depot yesterday P.M. when my Platoon left, because they all crowded around the car & told me goodbye, but I'm not worrying about it. One of them said, "Would your husband be jealous if I wrote you all the things I'd like to?" He was the one whom I told reminded me of my own child, for he was so restless. He stood 1st in all grades in the Platoon, & then he was always wanting to wander around or be fidgety.

Geo. has decided not to go to camp, and we won't have to decide about going to Calif. or not right away. I am singing in Lisbon church Sunday for Mother's Day. Must dash off now –
                    Heaps of love, 'S'Mae


May 11, 1944     Thursday     Cornell College     Study Hall
Dearest Gerald,

It is really nice & warm today & for the first time, I didn't have to build a kitchen fire this morning. Geo. has pinkeye in both eyes & has a "compress" & bandage over them, pretending he is blind. The CAP getting permission to use the Navy equipment for Code is quite a long story of "red tape." I finally wrote a "memorandum" to the CO, telling the whole set up of the CAP (the "acting" leader & his job, the no. & type of membership, etc.).

Tommy has his annual sunburn, as a result of his school picnic yesterday. I dashed to C.R. after the washing was done. Ordered your pictures from Lasswell's (It'll take a wk. or 10 da) and was lucky to find a pair of overall pants for each of the kids. It looks like Tommy could have his birthday wiener roast this P.M. The kids both wear their dog tags all the time & are very proud of them.


May 12 – 1135

Been dashing around since 0600 – and finally got Geo. off to his Pal Day & Tommy & I are settled in for the day. The kids both did SO well in school – I'll send their grades when I have more time. (The mailman is due any minute). Yesterday I cleaned house – then took the kids to the C.C. for wiener roast and to CAP in eve.*

Marie [Hill] writes that she & Paul plan to be here next Wed. and I want it to look as "comfortable" as possible. I'm looking forward to Mother's Day. Evidently the kids have a surprise – there is much secrecy around here. Thinking of you – with much love – Essie Mae


Inserted here: The program for the "Fifty-seventh Annual Banquet of the Lisbon High School Alumni Association in honor of the Class of 1944" on the evening of May 12, 1944 in the School Gymnasium. Dinner Menu is shown, and the agenda included a Short Talk by Captain Alvin Ehresman, '18. The program concluded with "When the Lights Go on Again, All Over the World" by Essie Mae Hill, '20, followed by the High School Song and Dancing.†


May 13, 1944     Saturday     Study Hall –
Dearest Gerald,

Wish you could have been to the Alumni banquet last night to have boosted my morale after the last speech. There were about 165 there – surprising in "these times." I'm afraid a lot of people didn't get the point of my "letter" – if a remark which Frank Runkle made is at all indicative. Coming home I asked him how he liked my speech & he said, "Fine, but who did you say that letter was from?" Boy! I was burned! But it's water over the dam now.

---

* The Palisades Park on the Cedar River near Mt. Vernon was a place for picnics, such as those at the end of the school year.
† Program on 4x8in. cardstock paper, folded.

The kids had a wonderful picnic day yesterday. Geo. put his camp experience to good advantage & when the bunch found out he could row, he had all the boat riding he wanted & plenty of blisters today. Time is going to hang heavy on their hands now that vacation is here & this A.M. they were wanting to know "what to do today."*

Sunday Eve – (Mother's Day)

Your telegram came this P.M. and I was so pleased. I'm so glad you liked the speech. I believe it will be printed in the paper. This has been an awfully nice Mother's Day & the kids were really tickled to have your telegram. Tommy picked out a lovely big box of cosmetics and they could hardly wait for morning to come, to present it. I was very much thrilled by your thoughtfulness, Honey. Rachie asked us & Mother to come down there for dinner, and Tommy took along his suitcase planning to spend next week there. By the way, the kids were measuring height the other day, and Geo. is just exactly one foot shorter than you (5', even) and T. one ft. less than I (4'5"). They have grown this winter! Tommy has been taking vitamins & his appetite is much better. Geo. left home (AWOL) for Abbé Creek yesterday about 9:30 A.M. and didn't come home for lunch or even tell me where he was till after 5 P.M. He was very indignant over the "corporal" punishment which awaited him, but which I felt was necessary to make him understand that "outings" like that involve getting permission at home, and making adequate provision for lunch, etc. It is hard for me to take, but I feel it is absolutely necessary for his own good & future welfare, – I will not let him run wild without supervision.

Your story of the Mother & 3 children coming to camp had been on my mind so many times. Fact is, it made me teary just to read about it. I really meant every word I said about "When the lights come on again," and I'm so glad you liked it. I really kept thinking I was writing to you – as you may have guessed. I'm so glad you have had this chance to get actively into the war's work, and I just feel that the whole rest of our lives is going to be so very much richer for having had the experiences you are having. I'm terribly proud of you, Honey. I just know you're so well fitted by personality, for it. No matter how it all turns out in the end, the "satisfactions" will be something never lost. Thank you again for making this a lovely "Mother's" Day.

Much love, 'S'Mae

May 15, 1944     Monday

Dearest Gerald –

You should get two "double postage" letters today. When Frank came with the mail this A.M. he bro't your pictures, so I'm sending them on immediately. I hope you like them. I really caught up on a lot of letter writing last nite. Wrote to Helene [Runkle], telling them to "count Geo. out at camp [Lincoln] this summer. We have been going "round & round" about his swimming in Abbé Creek, where they've been building a dam, but I guess we have it settled now. He is going to help me put on screens this P.M.

I'll have Geo. go uptown & mail this.

Much love – Essie Mae

These grade reports were written by EMH on the back of the program for the Methodist Church service in Lisbon on May 14, 1944, when Mrs. G. L. Hill gave the Solo, "A Flower for you, Mother Dear."

| George's Grades Semester Averages | | Tommy's Grades Semester Averages | |
|---|---|---|---|
| Reading | 94 | Reading | A |
| Arith | 94 | Arith | A |
| English | 90 | Language | A |
| Spelling | 92 | Spelling | A |
| Geog. | 90 | Geog. | A |
| Gen. Sci. | 92 | Science | B |
| Penmanship | 90 | Penmanship | C |
| Music | B | Music | B |

---

* George had gone to Camp Lincoln on Lake Hubert, Minn., in the summer of 1943, on an arrangement made by Lester Runkle, who was camp director.

| P.T. | B | Citizenship | C |
|---|---|---|---|
| Days absence | 5 ¾ | Art | C |
| Tardy | 3 | P.T. | C |
| Conduct | 78 (last 6 wks) | Tardiness | 0 |
| Effort | 85 (" " ") | | |

May 16, 1944     Tuesday 1845     Cornell College
Dearest Gerald –

My chance to write a letter today comes while I supervise make-up exams tonight in the old Geol. Lab. It is so hot and "humid"! I have been cleaning up the apt. for Paul & Marie [Hill]'s visit tomorrow & have caught a cold (disgusting!) Did a big washing today including curtains. Geo. has been very nice today – helping me wash & helping with the dishes. He found that old Linn Co. atlas & got a wonderful time this P.M. reading the descriptions of Lisbon & M.V. – and "fine business centers, etc." Yesterday P.M. he and I went out to the lumber yard & I got a piece of wall board 4 x 6 for him to put his maps on. The Navy is having a Code class for officers, Instructors & enlisted men, which started today & which I plan to attend. Our training by "saying the dahs and dits" was all wrong, for I constantly have to fight "breaking up" the sound, instead of listening to it as a whole. So, I am extraordinarily slow – but stubborn as always. I am planning to iron your khaki pants which are here & send them, probably day after tomorrow. I imagine you are needing them in the Calf. heat.

May 18, 1944     Thursday 1010
Dearest Gerald –

I am in the library now, with half an hr. before Code Class. I have been on the jump ever since I started the first part of this letter – getting things in shape for Paul & Marie [Hill]. Got up at 5 yesterday to iron, but had the apt. nice & clean, with fresh curtains & all "clutter" at least out of sight. As well, supper ready – chicken salad, fresh asparagus with mushrooms, potato chips, pickles, toasted rolls, chocolate cake & ice cream with honey on it. They had the kids with them, but Geo. was unusually helpful & Paul took movies (colored) of the three of them playing with the rabbits, as well as a few pictures of Geo. & me. It will be fun to see them sometime when we go to D.M.

After Bobby Gaston's mother clamped down on him for "getting home late," Geo. doesn't feel so unjustly treated by his "corporal punishment" over AWOL last Saturday & he really has been very considerate.

The cadets would get a bang out of the difficulties that the officers are having with code. They heave a sigh of relief over 2.5 words per minute, which is barely passing. I am awfully slow – but I'm not giving up.

(Continued) Lunch is over & I want to add just a little more to this "continuous" letter. Your letter telling of the last S.F. trip was in the mail this A.M. I appreciate your investigation of jobs for me – and I certainly don't interpret it as an effort to "keep me on the job." I know you just "know me" – and that I like nothing better than a "job." It all depends on how the kids get along. They are pathetically pleased at my being home more, lately, and I have spent every spare minute at home – I mean like turning down PBK banquet, Entre Nous, etc. I think I ought to improve my typing, don't you? That would be a help in being useful in Meteor. at an airport. In fact, any new skill is useful & that's why I'm sticking to Code.

My cold is better, but it is cold & chilly outdoors today. Must iron your pants now –
Much love, 'S'Mae

May 19, 1944     Friday 1230
Dearest Gerald –

I am mailing you a box today with three kinds of cookies in it, which Geo. & I made the last 24 hrs. Much love goes with it, of course, & feel free to dispose of them any way you want to, for there's probably more there than you can eat alone before they get too stale.

Imagine my surprise last night to be asked to present my "letter to service men" (Alumni banquet) at the annual Rotary-Rotary Ann dinner on Monday night. It seems that "someone told some one, and they told someone else, etc., etc." – till it got around that it was "worthwhile" – so there I am. I really feel quite honored, but highly amused. You probably saw the small portion which was in the *Hawkeye*. I am supposed to give the program at Thursday Club next week and I think I'll just tell them about what I've been doing the past year & give them a little idea of what the cadets are expected to learn & know in schools of this type. The idea being, of course, to make the folks at home realize what these kids are up against, & so help to be home folks to appreciate them more.

Do you think that would be all right?

Much love, 'S'Mae

[later] May 19      2200
Dearest Gerald,

Geo. and I just got home from the movie, *A Guy Name Joe.** I wonder if you have seen it. I like it very much – and so did Geo. It is thundering and lightning very badly again. Altho we didn't hear it last night, I guess the storm was really terrible, with 4 1/3 inches of rain, and the railroad yards in the south of Marshalltown under three feet of water – tornadoes in the western part of the state.

I have to be at the building at 7 in the morning to give an exam for one of the teachers who is spending the weekend in Chicago. So I guess I better hie myself to bed. I give the 3d week Aerol. tomorrow, and I don't expect the kids to do as well as previously. These are cock-young V-12ers, and they think they know so much they don't have to study like the fleetmen, and as a result they'll have to learn the hard way.

Much love, 'S'Mae

Sat. A.M. [20 May 1944]

No additional news this A.M. It stormed again last night very badly, but warm and clear this morning. I'm not sure how I'll spend the rest of the day. Wish George could find some work to do.

Much love, 'S'Mae

Monday, May 22, 1944      1015
Dearest Gerald –

Just time to write a few words before Code class. We have been having such awful storms that R.R. & highways have been blocked, so I imagine I'll be getting some "delayed" letters one of these days. This has been a good time (appropriate) to teach "Thunderstorms & Tornadoes."

Rachie [High] called yesterday P.M. and said Jim was going to town & if I would drive down, I could pick up Tommy – which I did. He wasn't ready to come home – had had <u>such</u> a good time – but was running out of un-muddied overalls. He would like to spend some time on one of the farms at Clarion. What do you think would be the reaction, if I should write – to Julia [(Woodin) Hill] for instance? He really is pretty good help at running errands, so Jim says, & I know he would be welcome to spend more time at Highs.

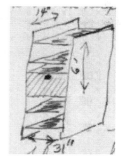

*Essie Mae's sketch of Tommy's redwood desk and book case*

Geo. earned 40¢ for a little work at Dilley's Sat. P.M. helping clean out the basement & Harry promised to call him again. He and I did a job Sat. P.M. that I have been wanting to do for years. We made a book case. It fits into one corner of the back bedroom. It is made of redwood (which I want to wax) six ft. high, with six shelves, variously spaced. Between 2 of the shelves we are putting an up-right board on the front – which will let down to form a little desk for Tommy. I was lucky to find the necessary hardware in Lisbon. I borrowed a plane from Roy Nelson to smooth the edges of the boards (quite a job, too, on the six ft. ones) and then Tommy sandpapered them.

May 23, 1944 [Tuesday]
Office   1012
Dearest Gerald –

When people asked me about "the latest news" from Toot, I tell them that the latest is probably held up by the floods. We have really been very lucky right here – in spite of what seems to be constant rains. The Rotary

---

* *A Guy Named Joe* (1943) starred Spencer Tracy; it is a fantasy movie about a bomber pilot and his guardian angel.

dinner was last night & my letter was much more enthusiastically rec'd than at the Alumni banquet. I really enjoyed the party very much – and <u>many</u> people spoke to me about my "contribution."

Home again. Lunch is cooking now – The kids have put a "high jump" in the grassy alley & are busy "developing muscles. Hope the mailman brings me some mail this morning.

2100    The kids are both so engrossed in their books, they hate to go to bed. Your letter telling of moving to E.G. [East Garrison] in the BOQ came today. How do you like your new quarters and new work layout? It's too bad you have to spend such long hours. Tommy and I finished his bookcase & desk this PM. & he is just delighted. Of course, if we had it to do over again, we could improve it a little, but the desk really works, patent "catch" and all, & we are most awfully proud of it. We put the books & things in it, & will wait for another day to wax the wood. It is still in its "raw" state. Tommy really likes things neat, and he is just so happy over his desk, all his own.

The floods are still the big news. Much love, 'S'Mae

May 24, 1944    Wednesday afternoon    Cornell College

Dearest Gerald –

Still raining – so I won't plan to go home this hour and then come back for Code. Scuttlebutt this morning is that the Navy will be staying (using Merner, Armstrong & Bowman dining room) and that only 8 teachers will be needed. Characteristically indefinite tho' – that Washington must O.K. the deal.

May 26 – A couple of days have gone by since I started this – busy ones as usual. Yesterday, I washed before school – did my Thursday Club program – dashed back to hear Russell Cole tell the faculty about the Navy staying at Cornell – then CAP, etc. Your wonderful long letter came yesterday & was simply swell. I want to get this letter in the mail right away so won't take time to answer yours now. The "camp folder" & dog tags came too.

It looks like they wouldn't need me in the new Navy program – but more of that later – Must hurry now.

Much love, 'S'Mae

May 27, 1944    Saturday    Office 1010

Dearest Gerald –

Another final over – probably my last one. And again – the only one who didn't have any flunks! ("Pardon my puffed out chest"). It is a lovely sunshiny cool day & I can take six words a minute without <u>any</u> mistakes & am steaming up on eight. When I pass <u>that</u> test, I'm going to quit & concentrate on house cleaning. The kids and I are much interested & entirely "willing" to live on some far away shore or land, if the Pan American wants you. I would be swell. The more new experiences the better. Later: Am singing in a quartette in Lisbon for Memorial Sunday Service in Meth. Church. Elizabeth Smith Ford (*No Hour of History*) died in N.Y. this week. Lt. Com. Heffelfinger takes Code, & I introduced Geo. to him yesterday – he shook hands & was very gracious.[*]

(Note from Geo.)

You'll be glad to hear that I got a *C.R. Gazette* Route this morning. It's all taken care of. I get the route June 11. A man named Parker gave it to me. He said he would remember you to all your friends. The old carrier gave my name as Toot Hill. He asked what my first name was and I told him Geo. Then he thought my name was George Toothill.

May 29, 1944    Monday

Dearest Gerald –

Back to a week of "hard" work – one study period a day to proctor! But it's hot & there's someone over at the Chapel practicing a trumpet – very much off key – so it's hard to settle the kids. Tommy's latest project (since he saw *Mark Twain*) is building a raft. After fussing about it for a couple of wks, unsuccessfully, Grandma finally gave him an old door. We took it out to Abbé Creek Sat. eve – to prove to him that it wouldn't hold him up. It sank into the mud immediately, of course, but was he discouraged? Not at all. He is busy now, fixing "floats" on the bottom. The floats consist of gallon fly spray cans which he salvages from "dumps." So sometime today, I'll have to take it out to the Creek for another trial "launching."[†]

---

[*] Elizabeth Smith Ford, Cornell College '15, attended graduate school at Columbia University. She was a journalist in New York City, and wrote two books about Mount Vernon. The house she inherited in Mt. V. is now owned by Cornell and used as a B&B.
[†] *The Adventures of Mark Twain* (1944) starred Frederick March. It was a box office success.

Yesterday was "Memorial" Day – Union Service in our church. There was a large crowd & the total effect, I think, was very satisfactory. We took some flowers over to the Norwich cemetery. The kids hadn't been there for a couple of years & they were quite interested. The pine tree Mother set out a few years ago is simply beautiful.[*]

I am so anxious for a vacation – to catch up on housecleaning etc. at home – that I'm making no immediate moves for a job away from here. In figuring your vacation – consider this (May 29) as X-day.

Much love,  'S'Mae

May 30, 1944  Tuesday    Decoration Day
Dearest Gerald –

I cleaned the closet yesterday & "de-mothed" everything in the hot sunshine & then used the spray and crystals. I took the kids out to Abbé Creek for another unsuccessful attempt to launch the "raft." Tommy is still confident that he can eventually fix it up. In the evening, we all three lay on the double bed and I read O. Henry stories to them. One of them is about a couple of bankers and an examiner. It is very clever. I bo't a cheap edition of all of O. Henry's stories in one volume, & I've enjoyed it a lot.[†]

May 31, 1944  Wednesday
Dearest Gerald –

I simply slaved yesterday washing & ironing & cleaning up the house – because Johnsons were going to stop here to see the bookcase on their way to the Lion's picnic. Geo. marched to the cemetery and was the biggest child in the parade, much to his disgust. The kids had a grand time at the Palisades Park with all the ice cream they could hold. The kids seem to need me here this summer, at least until they get routinized & altho' I'd like both the work & money better, I think that is my first obligation for the present at least. We can size up the whole situation when you come home, of course – and then "other openings have come so unexpectedly that anything can happen, I've come to believe." Helene & Dorothy [Runkle] are coming the first of next week. She is in Marion [Iowa] now.

Must get back to ironing –
Much love – 'S'Mae

## June 1944

### D-Day: The invasion of France is launched and the college bells ring
### The Navy Flight Preparatory School at Cornell College winds down

> "As American men were marching into combat to change the balance of power throughout Europe and the East, the wives, mothers, and sisters of America found themselves thrust into a quieter revolution of their own."
> — Emily Yellin, *Our Mother's War*, 36

Mount Vernon, Iowa  Cornell College
June 1, 1944  Thursday
Dearest Gerald,

Several interesting coincidences.
(1) One of the books I read out loud to the kids last winter was *Doctor Wassell*, so we surely will want to see it in the movies. It was an awfully good story.

---

[*] Several generations of EMH's mother's ancestors (Rundall family) are buried in the Norwich cemetery near Martelle, Iowa.
[†] Two of the novels by O. Henry mention bankers and bank examiners: "Friends in San Rosario" and "A Call Loan."

(2) Geo. and I have been reading a continued story in the *Post* – "The Devil on His Trail" – and in it was a reference to the difficulties of eating artichokes. Geo. had never heard of them before, and only yesterday he asked me how to eat them, and I tried to explain, altho I have never eaten them myself.

George earned forty cents at Dilley's again this morning, and since he has the *Gazette* job, his summer is pretty well blocked out. I have just about got Tommy talked into talking a course in "Art" at the college for the first five weeks this summer and then go to camp later, and since you speak of coming home early in July, I am sure that is what we will do. You made your calculations OK – and it will be just perfect if you make your trip home around the 4th of July – or shortly after.

I PASSED THE NAVY TEST ON EIGHT WORDS A MINUTE IN MORSE CODE this morning. I don't think I could do it again without more practice, but at least it "is on the books." Geo. is still working on the numbers now, and they are tricky – they still bother me, even with lots of practice.

The faculty are invited to a tea in honor of Adm. Leahy Sunday afternoon, and I have promised that Geo. can be my "man." He is thrilled to death. If he could get his autograph, he would be the happiest mortal alive. I am on my way to Lisbon now to cash the check and draft, get my hair curled, etc. Another teacher has taken my one study period for the last two days, and I will take hers tomorrow and the next day, and then I am thru. I am really just reveling in the extra time, altho I have been busy all the time. I have a bushel basket full of mending to do next.

Much love, S'Mae

Later, at home. 1300

Something new happens every day, sometimes it's bad, sometimes very good. We are very thrilled and happy over George's prospects for a job with the *Gazette*. This came very suddenly. Mr. Parker had heard of you, and said to tell your friends that Toot II was now on the *Gazette* staff. The route has 58 customers, the largest in town. He is really too young, by rule, but he said Mr. Parker asked about Geo. and got very favorable comments. I'd like to know whom he asked. It will be a headache (to me, at times) I know, but I'll try to be as kind and patient as I can, and I am very much pleased that he has the job lined up. He is supposed to spend this week learning the route. I advanced the initial $8, down payment on his bond. He plans to make out a budget, including 10% in war stamps, and a certain amount for clothes, etc.

The kids and I are invited to the annual spring Lion's picnic at the Pal next Tue. So happy that you liked my Alumni letter. You really must be prepared to "tell about your work" when you come home. Will look for the Kodak (I think it is with the stuff over the bank). Tommy will take this down, so it will go out this afternoon. We are looking forward to having you home in a few weeks. Hope it will work out that way.

Much love, 'S'Mae

June 1, 1944        Thursday
Dear Dad
I just got done Breakfast and now I'm writing on are homemade Bookcase (or desk, you might call it).
On the top shelf ther is a number of thing the second is the game shelf, the next two are Georges, the bottem two are mine where my Desk is. I was at the farm and fell in the [corn] crib will I was ther. I've got alfull bad mosasbeto bites. And have to bathe them. Mom gave me another hair cut yesterday.
With love   Tommy

June 2, 1944        Friday    Cornell College
Dearest Gerald,
Back at study hall this morning! When we went out the car yesterday P.M. to go to Lisbon, we found we had a <u>very</u> flat tire (nail). It was nearly 4 P.M. when we got started. We got the red camera & the hose. I'll send the camera to you today & the kids used the hose to wash the car when we got home. I looked at my watch this morning and then <u>jumped</u> thinking I had just ten minutes to get to class. After I was all dressed, I discovered the time was 5:35 instead of 7:25 – so I had a lot of "time on my hands after all" & got all the beds made, dishes washed, etc.*

---

* "Time on My Hands" (1930) was recorded by many, including Glenn Miller, who died when his airplane was lost in WWII.

1330 - No typing given this summer!  The Morse Code teacher gave Geo. a nice colored picture of a plane, for passing his 4 word-per-minute test _perfectly_ this A.M.  He's thrilled.  The kids are going to _polish_ the car this P.M.

                Much love, 'S'Mae

June 3, 1944        Saturday

Dearest Gerald,

      Nothing new since yesterday, but I want to send "Love" and "Hello" at any rate.  Geo. will soon be out collecting on his paper route, Tommy and I are going to Lisbon (I have an appointment at the beauty parlor) then dash back and see if I can't pass my test on ten words a minute, so Geo. and I will both be at a "stopping point."  There is no more Code until after Commencement, and if we don't get any more it won't matter.

      The kids and I waxed the car yesterday, and BOY! it surely looks nice.  I bought a five gal. can to put the anti-freeze in.  It's pretty rusty, but it will be very scarce next fall.  We are counting on your coming home the forepart of July.  With much love, 'S'Mae

June 4, 1944        Sunday

Dear Dad,

      I have just gotten back from a tea given for Admiral Leahy.  I was the only boy there.  He doesn't look like his picture.  He looks older and friendlier.  He was wearing his "Undress" uniform.  Everybody shook hands with the Coles, Admiral Leahy, Col. Rigby, and the Heffelfingers.  He asked me how I was.  Then Mom and I talked a while and I got her pen and a newly boughten autograph book.  I walked up to him, and he asked me where I wanted him to write his name.  He saw his picture and said, "Oh, you've got a funny picture of the old guy haven't you.[7]

         I ate one Cookie for refreshments,

           Yours truly, George

Mount Vernon, Iowa

Monday A.M.     June 5, 1944

Dearest Gerald –

      As you may judge by Geo.'s letter – he is a _very_ happy boy!  Everything "clicked" in a very lucky way – haven't time now to tell details – for Helene and Dottie [Runkle] are coming this A.M. & we are getting ready for Commencement.  One of the profs nearly split at Geo. getting the autograph – said "he was surely a chip off the old block" – More later – Much love, 'S'Mae

"Admiral William D. Leahy, Chief of Staff for Presidents Roosevelt and Truman, gave the address for the ninety-first Commencement June 5, 1944, at which time he was given the degree Doctor of Laws.  Had original plans been carried out, this would have been the date for the Normandy invasion.  The following morning when the news of the successful landing of troops in France came on the radio, Admiral Leahy relaxed and told President and Mrs. Cole a great many details of the plans for winning the war in Europe."[*]

June 5, 1944        Monday

Dearest Gerald,

      What did you think of the application pictures?

      This has been quite an eventful two days, as you can guess from Geo.'s letter.  I finally got up nerve to take him with me to the tea yesterday afternoon.  We were very pleased at how cordial Adm. Leahy was in the line – and Cmdr. Heffelfinger explained to his wife that Geo. had been taking Code with him.

      It will surely be wonderful to have your home again, altho I'm beginning to "cross the bad bridge" of thinking it will be harder than ever to see you go again.  I surely wish we could be together again.  There's hardly a day goes by, but what I wish that you were here to help solve some problem that comes up – I guess I am just getting

---

[*] _Centennial History of Mount Vernon_, 174.

lazy. It has turned very cool again – about like my birthday last year, when Forbes[*] was here and we lit the fireplace for a steak fry. I guess I'll have to wash again tomorrow. I just noticed today that your name is up on the Cornell service roll. Must get supper started now – Boy the cost of groceries is surely going up!

Much love, 'S'Mae


June 6, 1944      Tuesday
Dearest Gerald,
D-Day in Mt. Vernon, for the Record!

Our radio is continuously "turned-in" this morning – as it is everywhere. We were lazy this morning & were still in bed when the chapel bell started ringing at 7:45. I suspected what it might mean & told Geo. to turn on the radio. He jumped! and sure enough it was true. He dressed and went up to the chapel for the special service which had previously been planned. Geo. had the thrill of telling the Gastons the news when he got home – they had not yet heard it. I am wondering how you heard the news and what were the reactions in camp.

It has been cold & drizzly this A.M., but the sun is coming out now. They had to make some changes in the program at the chapel since the students have gone for the summer. – – The radio just now is describing the streets of San Francisco right now – at 8:15 A.M. – it is two hrs. later here of course. – – Now the radio changes to Los Angeles. I wonder what more will happen to US, personally, before it is all over. "The Lord only knows, I guess."

Much love – Essie Mae


"June 6 – Washington learned officially of the invasion of Europe at 3:32 A.M. today when the War Department issued the text of the communiqué issued by the Supreme Headquarters, Allied Expeditionary Forces. This was D-Day and it has gone well. ... At daybreak Anglo-American forces dropped from the skies in Normandy, swarmed up on the beaches from thousands of landing craft and renewed the battle for France and for Europe."[†]


Mount Vernon, Iowa
June 9, 1944      Tuesday
Dearest Gerald,

Your long letter, with the pictures and letters to the kids came day before yesterday. We all enjoyed them VERY much, and the kids were pleased to hear directly from you. They have just gone to swimming now – the Lions are sponsoring free lessons, and we surely appreciate it. It is rainy and cold again, but they don't seem to mind the cold pool water. I started teaching Navigation at CAP last night, with about ten there. The Flying Eagles reported that their plane has been grounded for some time, waiting for an oil cooler. Lack of leadership is certainly killing the CAP in Lisbon, but I haven't had enough active concern with flying to go ahead and stir things up.

Doubtlessly you have rec'd my letters telling of Tommy's camp plans for later in the summer. Whenever you get your reservations will be fine, and we will be all set for you. So far Geo. seems to be getting along fine with his papers. Mrs. [James] McCutcheon overheard the conversation, and before we got thru, she told me to tell Geo. she would like to have him order and deliver her paper too. So that is the way "good service" helps. He has gotten two new customers. I have personally introduced him to several of his customers who knew him when he was little, and I thought they would have an added interest if they knew who he was, now that he was their paperboy.

Tommy spent the morning gluing together a dozen or more match boxes into a "unit" for his desk, to keep odds and ends in. He is going to put a label on each "drawer," and I'll sew a button on each one, so it will pull easily. We are very lazy in the mornings, but it seems grand not to HAVE to get up and dash around.

Must hurry uptown with this so you will get it when you get back from S.F.

Much love, 'S'Mae

---

[*] Captain Robert Forbes was pilot of the B-17 "Floozy"; he was later killed in the war.
[†] *The New York Times: Complete World War II*, 436.

June 13, 1944        Tuesday

Dearest Gerald,

I am wondering what you found out on your trip to S.F. – I'll probably hear soon. I must be getting rested up, for I woke up a little after five this morning, and got up about six. I baked a hot coffee cake for the kids' breakfast, which they thought was fine. We have rain, rain, and more rain. The cellar is so damp, and smelly. However, I washed and ironed yesterday, and am catching up on mending again today.

The kids are enjoying the free swim and lessons very much. So many Lisbon kids turned up yesterday that there "was standing room only," so those in charge had to tell the Lisbon kids that they would not be allowed. G. and T. are glad they are eligible.

Rachie, Jim and Mother were here Sunday P.M. Farm work is way behind, everywhere, and continues to be, as the rains keep up. Geo. started a savings account yesterday at the M.V. bank, with a deposit of $3.87. He plans to buy a dollar's worth of war stamps today. It was interesting to get the S.F. paper telling of Admiral Leahy. The local papers claim that he knew about invasion day. He went from here to Hampton [Iowa], his birthplace.

*Tommy Hill*
*June 1944*

The pictures which we sent with your Father's Day card were taken last week when T. and I were in C.R. G. preferred to stay home and play "Monopoly," and so didn't get in on it. We just did it on the spur of the moment, but you see how Tommy has changed, and how much we look alike.

Much love, 'S'Mae

June 15, 1944        Thursday

Dearest Gerald,

You really broke all the records, with the letter which came this morning. It was a wonderful letter, and I really do appreciate your going into detail on your S.F. trip, the way you did. The staff pictures are very nice, but of course we wish that you had shown more conspicuously. They are a good looking crowd tho'.

Naturally I was very MUCH surprised to hear about your pushing the overseas angle. I'd much prefer to take an ostrich attitude, and not even comment on it, but I know that wouldn't be fair. It will certainly be very hard to get along without you, as I know now after nearly eight months. I appreciate your confidence that I can "manage," but I am far from being so sure. If I were working, so I had "adult" contact, and the mind-diverting stimulation of doing something creative, I wouldn't dread it so. But with no social life, and so few people that I care to see, time goes very slowly. Life has been very uneventful around here for the last few days. I have been at the sewing machine or mending basket, and have it nearly empty. Every time I mend a pair of socks, I think I "have earned a dime." Geo. is scheduled to work at Dilley's tomorrow.

This is a very inadequate answer to your grand long letter, but please know that it was wonderful to hear in all the detail, all about what you've been doing. We will be thinking especially of you on Father's Day – Sunday. Virginia said John [Thompson] had been in New Zealand, but was now back in combat.[8]

Love – 'S'Mae

June 17, 1944        Saturday

Dearest Gerald,

I went to the play at the Little Theatre last night, and happened to get there at the same time that Mrs. Thomas, Rowena [Stuckslager], and Elizabeth [Eke] arrived, so I sat with them – next to Eke [MacFarland]. She says that Packy [MacFarland] was in Cairo the last she heard, but he was probably back in Turkey now. They asked about the nature of your work, how you liked it, etc. Lisbon is quite agog over a meeting which Dr. Gardner had with a Red Cross man on the way to Chicago recently. They asked a strange RX man to share their dining table, since the train was very crowded. To make conversation, Doc asked where he had been stationed, and he said on the west coast. Doc then asked if he happened to have run across a man named Gerald Hill, and he SAID HE HAD BEEN WORKING WITH HIM FOR THREE MONTHS. He told Doc that you were working on an overseas assignment, so

67

it is a good thing you broke the news to me first. The Stuckslager group mentioned the incident, so evidently it has "gone the rounds in Lisbon," as one of those remarkable coincidences. And it is quite unusual, don't you think? Doc got a big kick out of it. I promised the Presbyterian church here that I would sing a solo, Sunday morning. I think it was nice of them to ask me – it is the first time I've been asked to sing in MV, and I did get a kick out of it.

Much love, from all of us, 'S'Mae

June 19, 1944      Monday
Dearest Gerald,

Your letter telling of the Reservation for July 11 came today, along with the things you sent the kids. I think that will work out just fine, and we'll plan on it. In regard to the story I am writing, I am trying to think of something that I can do here at home, and am experimenting with writing. It seems to me if I get the knack of it – that I don't lack for anecdotes that might be enlarged into stories. The Presbyterians seemed to appreciate my singing yesterday – I sang a prayer hymn for sailors from the hymnal. The minister asked me if I would sing it again at the union service with the M.E. Church.[9]

Much love, 'S'Mae        Tommy goes to camp June 25, to stay till July 9th.

June 20, 1944      Tuesday
Dearest Gerald,

It was so nice to get your letter of the 17th today. From the description of the am't of work you have been turning out, I think you are surely justified in the "snifters" which you anticipated getting. I am sure they tasted very good. It is the limit the way a person has to keep hammering all the time to get any recognition in their work, and not to have the work speak for itself – but I guess that is the way life goes. I went to the Johnsons yesterday for the first time in about three weeks. I read my story about "Daddy" to them, for suggestions, and Al's suggestions were very good and constructive, but it involved rewriting the whole thing, from an entirely different angle – and I woke up this morning feeling very Blue. It is just like pulling teeth to get set for a job like that, with all the traffic in children which there is. BUT – I am all up in the air again! Not too much – I won't let myself get too steamed up!

I happened to see Mr. Reed downtown in the bakery this A.M. and he told me he was writing a High School text on Aviation, and he would like to have me write the chapter on Civil Air Regulations. I am going up to the office this A.M. to see about it.[*]  Hastily – with much love, 'S'Mae

June 22, 1944      Thursday
Dearest Gerald,

We are so thrilled to think you are all set for your coming home. I selfishly hope we don't have to gad around a whole lot for to me, it will be much nicer to spend the time as a family together.

It surely seems crazy to think that a year ago, I knew less than nothing about CAR, and now I "am writing a book about it." It is fun, and I may do the chapter on Meteorology also. Reed asked another man to do it, last spring, and hasn't heard from him – so it looks like I would have the chance at it, if I care to. This chapter on CAR is much more to my style and ability than fiction, I am sure, and it is an interesting experience. I may try my hand at drawing the necessary diagrams for it myself. It is nearly noon now, and I must get lunch. Much love, 'S'Mae

June 23, 1944      Friday
Dearest Gerald,

Imagine my consternation when X-day came yesterday, the 21st. That is several days ahead – and if you want to do a little figuring and change your home-coming dates, you will know the set-up. Whatever you decide to do, will be okay with me. I leave it entirely up to you. Tommy passed the physical to go to camp, but he was pretty disgusted last eve because he couldn't go swimming at the Pal – that is human nature to never be satisfied.

Nearly time for the mailman and to get lunch. Much love, 'S'Mae

---

[*] EMH completed this chapter for Mr. Reed, whose first name is unknown, and she then wrote several more chapters for his proposed high school textbook. It was never published, and the work that she did for this book has been lost.

June 26, 1944     Monday
Dearest Gerald,
          We are already for Tommy's camping experience tomorrow.  Am working on the chapter on "Communications" now, and will know in a day or two, whether I will do "Meteorology."
                    Much love, 'S'Mae

June 27, 1944     Tuesday
Dearest Gerald,
          Your lovely birthday card came yesterday, and I really appreciate it.  The kids got a kick out of Red Skelton being at Camp Roberts.  We saw *Marine Raiders* last Sunday, with Pat O'Brien, and thought about the time he was there.  It was a very good show. * Sally [Thompson], Dottie [Runkle] and George are playing Black Jack in the bedroom.  Martha [Thompson] has just arrived and they'll all be here all night.  Cousins are as thick around here as they are in Clarion.  I have the chapter on CAR all done, including the diagrams, and am working on the unit on Meteorology, which will include about six chapters.  Nothing may ever come of it, but I am willing to take a chance on "getting into print" – and it is good practice for me in organizing and expression.
          The show we saw Sunday – *Marine Raiders* – gave me a number of views of the Army camp at San Diego, and gave us a better idea of the kind of what you see all the time.  The picture also gave a good idea of what the fighting on Guadalcanal was like, too.  It is just impossible for us, isolated and inexperienced in the "ways of war" to imagine what these things and places and fighting is like.  Aren't I right – "ain't it so"?†
          "It won't be long now" – – – Much love, 'S'Mae

June 30, 1944     Friday
Dearest Gerald,
          Your telegram came about noon yesterday, the 29th.  If you have decided over-seas duty is what you want, I am surely glad you will be able to get home for a little visit before you go.  I am still trying to adjust my mind to the thought of your being overseas.  You will certainly have some interesting and no doubt thrilling experiences.  We certainly will have lots to talk about and plan when you get home.
                    Much love, 'S'Mae


# July 1944
### Jerry comes home on leave for the first time in eight months
### "War really came to Mt. Vernon today" as Harlan Nelson is Killed in Action

> "There were very few guidelines on negotiating the practical issues that women had to deal with during the war.  Many young wives turned to their own mothers for aid, some in closer quarters than they ever expected."
>                    – Emily Yellin, *Our Mother's War*, 14

Mount Vernon, Iowa
July 3, 1944     Monday
Dearest Gerald,
          I am wondering very much – and often – what decisions you are making these days.  As I told you in the telegram Sat., I am sure you know the picture best, and whatever you decide will be just all right and fine.  Now I have the picture, I think, and will understand any future messages that may come.  Geo's temp. is down nearly to normal today, but I was quite worried about him for 3 da.  His ear was very painful and the pain extended out

---

* *Marine Raiders* (1944), starred Patrick O'Brien; it was about U.S. Marines on Guadalcanal.
† Her question is a play on words from George Gershwin's "It ain't necessarily so," which has been recorded by many artists.

around & behind his ear, which is the mastoid bone. It is better now – thanks to sulfa & the ice bag, but he has lost 10 lbs. this summer and looks very badly. I have been delivering his papers. Tommy was fine when I visited him at camp yesterday. He had made a lanyard & a belt and was brown & freckled. He was quite tearful when he saw me & tho't he wanted to come home. The Wapsipinicon river is high & swimming is not good, but he is getting along fine. His talking soberly about the "latrine" amused me.

I am going to sing "Angels of Mercy" – Irving Berlin's Red Cross song – and lead the Community singing at the USO Wednesday night. I am glad to do it, altho' wish I had more time to work on it. It will be fun to sing for the cadets anyway. Florence & Roy [Nelson] spent the eve here last night (Sun.). They are anxious to know when you are coming. It is kinda hard to visit with them, for when Florence talks "social events" Roy is bored, & when I talk Navigation, etc., with Roy, Flo. is bored. But I appreciate their visit & I know we'll see them when you're home.[*]

It almost seems too good to be true that you will be home next wk. I am waiting anxiously for any word that may come from you about job-decisions you may be making. When they come, they come fast – like it was last fall when we sold our house – moved, etc.

Most impatiently waiting to deliver my love in "person" –
Yours – Essie Mae


July 4, 1944          Tuesday
Dear Gerald,

The war really came to Mt. Vernon today, for the news came that HARLAN NELSON WAS KILLED IN ACTION OVER JUGOSLAVIA ON JUNE 21. It is just too terrible to imagine – probably the finest kid that Mt. Vernon ever had – at least he seemed like that to those of us who were so fond of him.[10]

As I told you in my last letter, Nelsons were here Sunday night, and we talked a lot about Harlan. Monday night the message from the War Department came, and it was delivered to Roy, altho of course it was addressed to Catherine. He went over and told her. I did not know a thing about it until I finished delivering the *Gazettes* today, nearly 24 hours later, altho it was on the front page. I went right over, and there was a mob of people there, all sitting around very stiffly. I surely felt sorry for Catherine having to face that mob. I stayed in the background until they left, and then visited with Catherine about things in general – trying to help her get her mind off of it. Florence has been so worried all along – too much for her health, and so has Catherine, but she is always the poised and gracious hostess. Roy as you can imagine is just himself – quiet, and looking after things. Catherine's folks are at Nelsons. Of course, one can rationalize, by knowing that these things happen all the time.

George is still in bed, and his temp., altho normal during the day, comes up every late afternoon. He is very weak, and is willing to lie quietly on his back – so you know he has a long way to go before he is "himself." He is still taking sulfa pills, and he ate a little better today. Every day brings you a little closer home – a week from now you will be well along your way – if all goes well. Every time the phone rings, I wonder whether it is you calling. It will surely be wonderful to have you here, and be able to talk "in person." These eight months have never seemed as long as the last few weeks, when we could count the days till you'd be here. The kids and I would be glad to live in California, I'm sure. In fact, I have no set mind about any place, just as long as we are together.
Much love, 'S'Mae


July 6, 1944          Thursday morning
Dearest Gerald,

It is now nearly nine o'clock in the A.M., and Geo. is still sound asleep. His temp. is down now – to stay, I hope, and I am glad he is catching up on his rest. A letter from Tommy yesterday ended, "I wish I was home," so I think he must be getting a little homesick. The camp this summer had a large proportion of kids his age however, and Mr. Salisbury said he never had such good kids. The "weed-pulling" which Geo.'s cabin had to do last year for group discipline was unknown among these younger children.

---

[*] "Angels of Mercy" (1941), by Irving Berlin, was dedicated to the Red Cross; recorded by Glenn Miller and Bing Crosby.

It certainly is aggravating to work and get no recognition or commensurate pay for it, or to see the way other people slide along, and get just as much money, as you – who do your work so much more conscientiously. But we can discuss more of that when you get home – if you don't go overseas.

It was a lot of fun, singing with the USO last night. Of course, I knew most of the cadets, who were much surprised at my new "role." Before I announced my songs – "Angels of Mercy," and "Comin' in on a Wing and a Prayer" – I told them, "I suppose the only appropriate song for an Aerologist to sing would be "Stormy Weather," or "There's a silver lining, through the dark clouds shining." That got a laugh, and they were a very responsive audience. I led group singing afterword. Snooty M.V. has very "definite" ideas about music, but I feel I <u>can</u> and <u>know how</u> to make people like to sing. I think singing should be <u>fun</u> even if fancy technique is sacrificed.*

A week from today, we'll be eating breakfast together, I hope. This will probably be my last letter, as long as you plan to go to S.F. early in the week.

Bye, Darling – Till I see you –

Much love, 'S'Mae

There is now a three-week gap in Essie Mae's correspondence with Gerald. He left Camp Roberts for San Francisco on July 9 and took the train from there to Iowa on July 11. He arrived in Mount Vernon on July 13 and was on leave with his family until he left there on July 26, arriving again in California on July 28. Her correspondence resumed on July 28, and he wrote to her on the same date.

On July 20, *Since You Went Away*, David O. Selznick's movie about the Homefront was released. It depicted the life of a family with a father in service overseas while the mother and their two children were coping at home. The movie was set in a suburb near Chicago. It featured a woman who was the same age as EMH, and who worried, as she did, that her husband would never return safely after the war was over. [11]

Also, on July 20, Franklin D. Roosevelt accepted the nomination for a fourth term as President. He said, "It seems wholly likely that within the next four years our armed forces, and those of our Allies, will have gained a complete victory over Germany and Japan, sooner or later, and that the world once more will be at peace, under a system, we hope, that will prevent a new world war."†

Mount Vernon, Iowa
July 28, 1944        Friday
Dearest Gerald,

I suppose you are out in the heat of the "great American desert" about now, while we are shivering with cold this morning. It was interesting to watch the COLD FRONT come in last night, and know what was happening. Great dark cumulo-nimbus clouds tumbling over each other, and then showers lasting only about twenty minutes, with a beautiful double rainbow afterward. I took Geo. to McVille as soon as we had the papers delivered after you left, and we stayed for supper. That helped to "ease" over a lonesome time, but it still seems very lonesome here.

The CAP last night decided to have one more meeting on Map reading. They did very well on the exam in Navigation. I feel that they have learned quite a lot, and I know that I am much more secure in my own knowledge about it. Mr. Reed wrote that he had rec'd another very encouraging letter from the publishers, and that they had given him until Aug. 15th get the manuscript in, so I probably will have a chance to finish the chapter on "Communications," and revise the Meteorology. I am keeping my fingers crossed, but will be pleased if it does amount to anything. I hope you find that your new work is just as thrilling as you anticipate.

Much love, Essie Mae.

---

* "Comin' in on a Wing and a Prayer," recorded by Kay Keyser, was the only song with a patriotic theme to be in the top twenty on Billboard pop chart in 1943. "Stormy Weather" was first recorded by Ethyl Waters in 1933, but in 1943, it became immensely popular, when Lena Horne's version appeared in the movie by the same name. "There's a Silver Lining," was a World War I song which included the wistful words, "Till the boys come home again." It was often sung in WWII.
† *New York Times Complete World War Two*, 447 – July 21, 1944.

July 29, 1944     Saturday
Dearest Gerald,

I have been thinking about you this morning as I baked a pie and cake, and made some jam out of juice I had in the basement. It is nearly time for you to be rolling into San Francisco – and How I would love to be seeing it with you. It was mighty hard to see you go away, and realize how many interesting sights and people you would be seeing before you came back again. Day and night, I try to think of something I could do (and still look after the children) to keep from growing so stale and dull – as I'm afraid I will seem when you come back again.

But enough of that! Geo. got back from McVille this morning on the bus in time to do his collecting. He had a very nice time, and told of cleaning out the tool house, including sorting all the nails and tools for Jim [High]. He rode the combine, and helped with the chores. Tommy has been very happy and contented to make a small loom, and weave some more hot-pads. He is really very handy with his hands, and he loves to make things like that.

Hope you had a nice trip – We'll be anxious to hear what you find when you reach Obispo.

Much love, 'S'Mae

## August 1944
### Essie Mae continues her work at home, while planning for the post-war world
### She writes, "If Fate decrees, I'll meet those problems"

"During World War II, more than six million women joined the workforce. ... In addition, three million women served as Red Cross volunteers."
– Penny Colman, *Rosie the Riveter*, 16, 19

Mount Vernon, Iowa
August 2, 1944     Wednesday
Dearest Gerald,

Your letter with the shoulder patch, written from S.F. – much enjoyed. The pictures you sent the kids are really beautiful. We'll have to think up some way to display them in our "house" when we build it. I sometimes wish we had taken the "bull by the horns" and come out to Calif. this summer in spite of everything. Everyone thinks you looked so very well, when you were home. A uniform is very becoming to you – and you stand nice and straight. The kids still row & quarrel a great deal, and I took T. down to Lisbon Sunday night to clear the atmosphere. I'll probably bring him home today. I surely feel like "throwing in the towel" when I come home and find them screaming and fighting. We have made out a budget, and are all cooperating to "abide" by it. Please don't forget you said you'd send me a RX insignia to wear – I like to "show the world how proud I am of my RX husband."

Much love from all of us –
Essie Mae

August 3, 1944     Thursday
Dearest Gerald,

I am glad to hear that you are planning to do some climbing and flying. One's muscles certainly get soft, and I know you are right that I should get more exercise. I have been taking some "setting up" exercises and AM I stiff. You will be glad to have a chance to swim. I went down and watched Tommy the other day – to his great pride – and was amazed to see him dive off backwards and forwards into the deep end. He would come up – look around to get his bearings and then strike out towards the shore. He has no fear of the water at all. Wish I didn't.

This week's *Saturday Evening Post* has a cute story in it – "A Room for a Soldier" – about an ex-soldier, who got a job driving a taxi in SF. It said "four drunks wanted to be driven to San Luis Obispo," but decided that the Mission was far enough. It is funny how much more interesting stories are and magazine articles, since these places "mean something." Tommy got a letter from Bill [Thompson] yesterday, from Milwaukee – he has been detached from the *Ludlow*, and doesn't know where he will be next.* George is looking forward to Johnny [Thompson] coming in Sept. I got a letter from Aunt Grace [Stockwell] – she said Paul [Hill] was on sea duty, on a ship commanded by F.D.R. Jr. She is going to Clarion this weekend, and was sorry to have missed you.[†]

Got a swell letter from Lester [Runkle] today, urging us to come to Camp Lincoln and spend two weeks in a cabin – rent free. They want us to be there August 13. He is very anxious to have me come up three and investigate work opportunities. He wrote, "There are so many opportunities in a city and life is so much more interesting. Sure, I know it takes some guts. I survived, didn't I? You are smarter and have a lot more talent and ability than I have, and you know that. Shake the dust off of that stinking little Cornell College free from your feet. Plan on coming to the hub of the universe." It seems very glamorous, doesn't it? If I decide to go, what do you suggest I take along as "ammunition" for getting a job? Do you have any suggestions, based on your own experiences in S.F.?

Much love, Essie Mae

Mount Vernon, Iowa
August 4, 1944     Friday
Dearest Gerald,

A note this morning before I get busy with the ironing. We are making some plans towards going up to camp as Lester suggested. George has arranged for a substitute paper carrier, and I am investigating bus schedules. We don't have enough gas for the trip, and anyway I think we might be criticized here, if we did drive – Although a car would be very convenient and I could probably help the Runkles bring back some of their stuff from camp – as camp will be closing at the end of the time we plan to be there. The kids have been very nice, since Tommy came back from Lisbon, and both of them are definitely trying to keep peace. They have been very busy with the tools on the back porch, and have made several little wooden cut-outs that are nicely sanded, and cleverly designed.

We go to Rev. Arnolds' tonight for supper. I know they will be wishing you were here too, to go.

Much love, from all of us, Essie Mae

August 5, 1944     Saturday
Dear Gerald,

We are making plans to go to Mpls. on the *Rocket* a week from tonight. The kids want me to tell you that a B-29 went over just before lunch. We were all much thrilled to see it.[‡]

We had a very pleasant evening at the Arnolds' last night. It had been so long since the kids had been invited out to dinner that I wondered how they would act, but they were very nice, and I was quite proud of them. Mrs. Arnold had a nice dinner, and he seemed quite steamed up with stories, etc. They have the parsonage completely redecorated and it looks very nice. That's all for this time,

Much love, 'S'Mae

August 8, 1944     Tuesday
Dearest Gerald,

People are always asking me about you, and incidents like your telling about James Roosevelt being there at SLO are nice to report – to show the interesting things that are happening there.

The Flying Eagles picnic was nice and the kids went swimming. It was fun to watch the kids swim, and I was delighted to see how well they did. They were out in the deeper part all the time – and two years ago they wouldn't even get out of the wading pool. Tommy looked so cute, diving, and then his head would come and he'd swim out like a veteran. He says he just "flutter kicks" automatically now – in fact, has to look around and see it, to realize he is doing it – so you know he can take care of himself in the water pretty well.

---

* The destroyer, U.S.S. *Ludlow* (DD-438), saw heavy battle action in North Africa, Italy, and France. Its crew suffered many casualties, downed enemy planes, and finally returned to the U.S. for repairs. Bill never told us about this.
[†] Paul Hill was on the destroyer escort, *U.S.S. Ulvert M. Moore* (DE-442), commanded by LCDR Franklin D. Roosevelt, Jr., which shot down two Japanese aircraft and sank a Japanese submarine. It was in Tokyo Bay at the surrender of Japan on 2 September 1945. Paul never spoke about his experiences on the ship.
[‡] They planned to take the *Zephyr Rocket* of the "Rock Island" railroad (Chicago, Rock Island and Pacific R.R.).

Yesterday – Monday – was Johnsons' first day out of quarantine, and they invited us to go out to the Pal with them for supper. It was a lovely night, and we all had a speed boat ride afterwards. We went to the Upper Palisades to get way from the crowds, and found that the Rotarians were having a family picnic – so we came back to the Lower – in great haste.*

My greatest problem in going to Mpls. is to get luggage – but it will work out all right, eventually – with borrowing, and perhaps buying a canvas bag of some kind. A man from McVille came back from the RX in the south seas, for just the same reason that you were ready to quit domestic service. Inefficiency – lack of supplies – no way to get the work done that needed to be done. I surely hope you don't run into a situation like that.

Much love, 'S'Mae

August 9, 1944    Wednesday
Dearest Gerald,

Your letter yesterday was "extra fine" – it was interesting to hear about your living arrangements, and the prospects for a hutment of your own. I went to C.R. yesterday and got a couple of canvas overnight bags for the kids to put their stuff in, to take to camp, and a small sized duffle bag for our heavy clothing. I hope we can get bedding up there, but I think Lester [Runkle] will take care of that. I bought a bathing suit, and when Tommy saw it on me, he giggled, and said, "Well, I think the skirt COULD be just a little longer." George and Bobby [Gaston]'s newest craze is to learn Spanish. I am quite pleased. He is up at the Library now trying to find a Spanish grammar with a vocabulary in it. I am once more disgusted to think that another one of the things we have kept so many years, and finally discarded when we moved, is now "wanted." The Gastons know quite a little Spanish from having lived in

*Jerry Hill's RX pin for his garrison cap*

Panama. Thank you for the RX pin – I get a big kick out of wearing it. Florence and Catherine Nelson called the other afternoon. Catherine looks very badly, but Roy told her right at the beginning that if he had to go back to work, and "carry on," she should too. I think it is the best thing for her, for it keeps her mind occupied part of the time.†

The over-seas preparations you mentioned sound very exciting – but I've made up my mind not to worry or get unduly bothered. I think you can take care of yourself, and if Fate decrees otherwise, I'll meet those problems when they come. I hope that you get to see a lot of the world, and have all manner of unusual experiences. And if when you get over there, you see some nice shady palm tree that you'd like to sit under the rest of your life, don't waste money asking us how we'd like to live there too – just cable "Come one, I've found it."

Much love, 'S'Mae

August 10, 1944    Thursday
Dearest Gerald,

Your letter of the eighth, written in red ink, just arrived. I am so glad you like your new set-up. I really had not realized until just near the end, how distasteful the situation was at Roberts. I surely do hope you pass your final physical exam, for I know it will be an awful let-down, if you don't.

Tommy has been having an ear-ache the last couple of days, but he is better now. We have postponed our trip for a day, however, starting early Monday morning, instead of Sunday. We arr. in Mpls. about seven thirty in the morning, and the bus for camp leaves about two-thirty. That will give me several hours in which to contact the U.S. Employment Service. Everything is problematical, but we are looking forward to a nice vacation, if nothing of a business nature does materialize. I have the kids' clothes in ship-shape condition – for school or anything. It has been so terrifically hot, and sultry lately. It is hard to imagine that it will probably be "frosty" at camp.

I was interested to hear that you were taking more First Aid, and "medical." Sounds like they were really getting you ready for anything – you might not be so far away from the firing, as you might think. This week's *Hawkeye* tells that Catherine Nelson had heard a little more about Harlan's death. The plane and contents all burned, but the bodies were all recovered, so one of the men in the squadron wrote.

_____

* In those days, quarantine was imposed only for scarlet fever. Anne had it, but all occupants in the house were quarantined.
† "Keep calm and carry on" was a popular phrase by 1944; it first appeared on a British propaganda poster in 1939.

Geo. got a letter from Paul [Hill] today.  Quote – "my mail was somewhat delayed, but it is catching up with me out here in the Atlantic Ocean aboard ship.  I rec'd orders July 15 and was to report to the east coast on the 19th, so I had no time to see or write anyone before I left. ...  This ship is a new one, one of the Navy's best.  I hope that everything goes well, so we can be in warmer climates this coming winter ... This letter is written while we are underway, and it's rough, so please excuse the mistakes.*

I am so glad that we had a chance to see Paul and the family – they were here for supper in June, you know.  He asked about your plans, and had heard from Aunt Grace that you had requested over-seas assignment.  Wouldn't it be exciting to be in the same "theatre" – perhaps.

Must make a trip to Lisbon, and lots of other things to do, so –
Much love, 'S'Mae

"In August 1944 the article 'Women at Work' appeared in *National Geographic* magazine.  According to the article, 'The balance of power rests in women's hands.  Literally'."

– Penny Colman, *Rosie the Riveter*, 7

August 11, 1944   Friday
Dearest Gerald,
Ten o'clock, 2200, and I have just finished filling out two of the USES application blanks, to take with me to Mpls.  Geo. thinks that anyone would "want to hire me after reading them."

It would be just too bad, if we should happen to get unexpected company for a meal, for I am certainly "cleaning out the cupboard and refrig. these last few days."  We had some of the sauerkraut that I canned last summer for dinner today.  I bought myself a "trench coat" at Bauman's today – with Geo's approval.  The kids were weary tonight and admitted it, and have been in bed quite a while.  Tommy's ear is better.  Must get to bed myself.
Much love, 'S'Mae

Lake Hubert, Minnesota
August 15, 1944   Tuesday          4:15 P.M.
Dearest Gerald,
We are cozy in a cabin with a woodfire burning and wearing "heavies" and flannel shirts.  The sky is overcast, but there are several sailboats out, and the kids just got in from swimming.  In other words – we are <u>here</u> – we are calm and peaceful and very happy and cozy up here among the pines, far away from the hustle and bustle and heat of the city – which was <u>very</u> evident yesterday in Mpls.  <u>Travel</u> is all that you have said it is.  The *Rocket* was very crowded.  We finally got one seat for the 3 of us – till Waterloo, and then we each got one, but the rest rooms were jammed with people who didn't get one at all.  We got to Mpls. right at 7:20 A.M. & had breakfast at the station.  Geo was willing to sit there & take notes on all the servicemen he saw and T. & I went out to find the USES.  Luckily, it was only <u>3 blocks</u> away, and we got there about 8:15, and no one else was there yet, so we got wonderful service.  They said however that they had nothing in their files about military teaching or airport work & so sent me to the Civil Service man.  He was a Ph.D., who was pleased to find someone with my background for him to help.

I visited various offices with no results & then the girl (to my surprise) said, "Are you Mrs. Hill?  (Yes).  Well, Dr. Phelan (USES) just called & asked you to call him about a job in <u>Panama</u>."  I nearly keeled over, but back we went to the USES.  Dr. Phelan introduced me to a Civil Service Procurement man from Panama.  We had a long interview which will come to nothing, but it made me very happy, because both he & Dr. Phelan seemed <u>so</u> impressed with my record & <u>so</u> anxious to help.  I was <u>much</u> flattered (especially as I didn't look any too well after being on the train all night and "X-Day" too).  The Panama job is "Assistant Meteorologist."  Not forecasting, but taking records & readings & doing some traveling around among the various stations.  The job calls for a man.  He said my qualifications seemed so <u>perfect</u> to him that that might be overlooked.  It was very gratifying to my ego, to have such pleasant interviews from complete strangers, who seemed so anxious to help.  It was nice, tho', and will give me a nice "glow" next winter, back in M.V when I get to feeling low.  They were really just grand.

---

* USS *Ulvert M. Moore* (DE-442), commanded by LCDR Franklin D. Roosevelt, Jr., won 5 battle stars in the Pacific theatre.

The bus station was simply a mad house. We stood beside the gate to our bus for an hr. to be sure to get a seat & we did. The kids were very helpful all the time, and I never saw them so good. It took about 5 hrs. to get here. Everything is simply swell. We slept till ten o'clock this A.M. It is delightfully cool & so lovely & peaceful. Helene will join us Wed. night. The kids have been swimming twice & we went on an unsuccessful fishing trip with Lester. I am to have complete charge (music & all) of Sunday morning "service" at camp. (The Minister couldn't come) – & I'll tell Marc Pitts' story to the boys. Met a woman about my age up here from Ft. Dodge – whose father (a banker) was a RX man – overseas – in the last war. Her husband manages the Gypsum plant – knows Mrs. Thomas & admires her. She is also a CAP, chairman of "motor corps" RX in Ft. Dodge, & hates bridge. I must quit now & get supper. It takes a long time to cook vegetables on an oil stove. I tho't about our trip up thru Anoka, Little Falls, etc., as we came up on the bus –

> Much love – 'S'Mae

August 17, 1944   Thursday
Dearest Gerald,

Time passes very fast, but we are entirely relaxed. I went in the Lake this A.M. for the first time & the water was swell. There is a boat for our exclusive use & the kids have been in it about 8 hrs. a day. Geo. tried to take the chimney off a lighted lamp & found they're hot – Result – 1 broken chimney! Lester has kept us supplied with fish. Helene was here last eve & we talked till 2 A.M. The rest of the world doesn't even seem real, up here – it is unbelievable that such remoteness from the war exists. It is nice for a vacation, but I wouldn't be satisfied to not be "contributing something to the times" – after a brief rest. We have been working with some lovely pieces of birchbark. Will write more soon – Much love & wishing you were with us. Essie Mae*

August 18, 1944   Friday
Dearest Gerald,

We are going to Nisswa (3mi) with Helene this P.M. The lake is rather rough today, but the sailboats were out & it was quite a thrill to have Bob, who was the "skipper" of one of them, come in so close to our dock, it seemed as if he would have to land. Then just at the right time he maneuvered it into a quick circle & was headed "seaward" again. The beach where we had our hamburger fry & the one along the boat house was all eroded away by the ice last winter. A lot of birches along the water were uprooted also, in the big "push." Albert Andreas's little girl (6 yrs.) was in Helene's prep camp this summer. She got whooping cough & her mother had to take her home. Helene didn't realize who she was at the time – but she was quite the talk of camp for the front "exposure" of the dress she wore. The little girl was very sweet, Helen said. Lester has 2 "Pillsbury" boys in camp. I am to talk at girls' camp a week from Sunday. We wrote a lot of "letters" on birchbark yesterday & Tommy has been making some little things out of it – canoe, wigwam, etc.†

We are thoro'ly enjoying this trip up here as a "vacation" & I pretty well satisfied myself as to jobs, as I wrote you. I'll try to concentrate on writing or something like that, that I can do at home.

> Much love, 'S'Mae

Lake Hubert, Minnesota
August 21, 1944   Monday
Dearest Gerald,

Life moves at a very leisurely pace, with launch rides, fish fries over the fireplace, etc. as "high lights." Geo. and I made biscuit "twists" (Boy Scout) and cooked them over the fireplace for supper Sat. night. I had a lot of fun conducting "church" at camp yesterday. I had the whole service, including prayer, solo, & "sermon." One of the "high up" Pillsburys was in the audience, but it didn't bother me. I was gratified at the response to my "Marc Pitts" story & lots of the visiting parents as well as the boys came up to talk to me afterwards.

---

* Helene Runkle eventually, and perhaps already in 1944, became the Director of Camp Lake Hubert for Girls on the north side of the lake. She said she used "Nature's alarm clock" to wake up in the night: "Drink a lot of water before you go to bed."
† For the Hills' relationship to the Andreas family, see GLH's letter to Albert Andreas, 18 May 1942. The "Pillsbury Boys" included the Heffelfingers. The family scion was Lieutenant Commander Totten P. Heffelfinger, CO, NFPS, Cornell College.

I like it in the daytime up here – but not particularly at night.  A kerosene lamp in the big house, doesn't show much light (The living room is about 30′ long) – so we go to bed early, unless the Runkles are here.  I'll surely look for "shower soap" when I get home.  I liked hearing about your "landing net" practice!

Heaps of love – 'S'Mae

Lake Hubert, Minnesota
August 23, 1944   Monday
Dearest Gerald,

Your letter, written the 18th & mailed the 19th came yesterday – pretty good service for the "wilds" isn't it?  You probably have mail from Hubert by this time and know we are really enjoying our vacation.  It must have been very interesting to hear & see the Kay Kyser broadcast.  We saw him in a movie not long ago, called *Swing Fever*.  Wish we could have heard the broadcast, knowing you were there.[*]

You certainly have the most interesting experiences in meeting people, whom you know – or know of!  I can imagine how pleased the boy from Battle Creek was to talk to you.  We were interested in hearing of your "grenade" experience.  We saw a cartoon lately, about pulling the "safety pin."  I was beginning to get worried about the bus travel from here to Mpls. over Labor Day weekend (when we plan to go home), for even on regular "runs" people are often not able even to get on – standing or otherwise.

We had a lovely ride in the sail boat – bigger than the one we rode in 5 yrs. ago.  Bob R. was the "skipper" & I really (to my surprise) was not at all nervous.  We "high-sided" & had to change sides several times, riding up on the "deck."  Wish I liked to swim!  The kids go in 2 or three times a day – but I just sun myself – You can see a white spot on my wrist where my watch is – so I'm getting tanned.  Your plans for "debarkation" surely sound like the real thing.  I'm really awfully glad you had a chance to have these experiences.  Much love – 'S'Mae

*Essie Mae & the boys*
*23 August 1944*

August 24, 1944   Thursday
Dearest Gerald,

Wish you could have been here last night.  Helene & Lester & another Camp couple were here "after hours" and it was so nice in front of the fireplace, eating & chatting – with beer if you wanted it.  Two of Helene's little girls had birthdays today, so we have quite an addition to our "larder" in the way of leftover chocolate birthday cake, etc., etc., etc.  Tommy has made me a nice lanyard today & he now knows the required 62 parts of a sailboat, besides being able to tell a yawl from a "ketch" from a schooner.  Every day brings your preparations that much more nearly complete.  I am better "set" psychologically now for your going overseas than I was last year, for I was so busy then, and had so many things on my mind.  This vacation up here, so relaxed, has really done me a world of good, I think.  Take care of yourself and get all the new experiences you can.  Much love, 'S'Mae

August 26, 1944   Saturday morning
Dearest Gerald,

Your letter of the 23d, with the evaluation came this morning – pretty good service!  The evaluation was simply wonderful.  I can't see how anyone could get a better one, and it was nice that the SAFD wrote all that he did.  I wish they would "act on" his suggestion that you would make a good FD.  It makes me very proud to read such nice things about "my husband."  I was interested to hear your comments on *Dragon Seed*.  I read the book a couple of years ago and thought it was wonderful.[†]

We had a very pleasant experience last night.  Bob took us out on the camp's newest sail boat & gave us a sailing manual.  About 8:15 last night Lester dashed in and said Bob was going to take us all sailing again.  He had a little gaff-rigged cat-boat this time – and was alone in "charge."  He was so pleased at the progress the boys had

---

[*] *Swing Fever* (1943) starred Kay Kyser; the cast included Lena Horne.
[†] The movie, *Dragon Seed* (1944) starred Katherine Hepburn. It was based on the book by Pearl Buck (1942).

made in sailing that we stayed out about 1 ½ hrs. & he taught them all the time & tested them. He is going to sign a certificate that they are "Able Seamen," the first "step" in being at "Boatswain" at camp. Tommy helped him "put the boat to bed" – tying the sailcovers on, pulling up the bilge boards, etc. Tommy has a natural aptitude, it seems.

Love, 'S'Mae

Lake Hubert, Minnesota
August 27, 1944   Monday
Dearest Gerald,

We are beginning to get ready to go home – so I don't suppose you better mail any more letters up here – after you get this. The Runkles are quite determined that I look for jobs in Mpls. before I go home. Camp is out on Wednesday, then they will move into the cabin with us. We plan to go to Mpls. pm Thurs. A.M. if we can get on the bus. They plan (if the weather is good) to take a two or three day canoe trip and come to Mpls. on Sat. or Sunday. If I can get the kids on the train, I think I'll send them

*George's "camper's stove"*

to C.R. (have Rachie meet them) on Thurs. eve, and then I can be free to scout around and see the job and living places alone. It is just about impossible with the kids along.

Geo. cooked our super for us in the clearing behind the cabin. He made a camper's stove out of a gallon can. We had our bread all buttered & ready for the bacon and eggs & it really was quite an interesting experience. The rowboat got away from them this morning, and Geo. pulled on his pants, and waded into the lake, up to his chin, and rescued the boat. He had a sweatshirt on, but it didn't make a very good "swim suit."

G'Night, Honey – Take care of yourself. Lovingly –
'S'Mae

Minneapolis, Minn. / Milwaukee & Rock Island RR. Depot
August 31, 1944   Thursday
Dearest Gerald,

I have just put the kids on the train for home – so now, I'll "bring the news from here up-to-date." The time has dragged for the kids the last few days, because we had just about "done everything," as you can imagine from my letters. Runkles took us to Brainerd about 6:45 A.M. today & got a bus which is made up at "Aiken," [Aitkin] only one station west – by doing that we got seats. When the buses from north (Bemidji, etc.) are so loaded by the time they reach Nisswa that they haven't even been stopping there – passengers are left standing on the road. We got here about 12:30, and by the time we ate & got to this depot it was about 2 – with 3 hrs. to wait. The kids were really good, and I went with them to the train, & saw that they had seats, tickets, lunches, extra money, and I phoned Rachie, & she said she would meet them & take them to Grandma's.

We were very lucky about weather at camp – Yesterday was the first "damp" day we've had & a big fireplace fire made even the bigness of the living room warm. I spent one of the last PM.'s at camp making some birch bark baskets & things. I bound them around the edges with grass & decorated them with acorn clusters, & the Runkles were intrigued. They never have time or inclination for that sort of thing, & that's more in my "line."

It looks like tonite would be a "test" of my endurance, for there's not much doubt that my "hotel room" will be a chair in the women's lounge here in the depot. I've investigated all the hotel "possibilities" within walking distance, with no luck – and I won't mind too much. Just chalk it up to experience!

*Essie Mae's birchbark basket*

Was so glad to get your telegram. Have been wondering about you "needless to say" – I'll go "stretch my legs" now and think about you & the kids –

Much love – 'S'Mae

Sept 2. – Tell you all about it later –
EMH – Got along O.K.

## September 1944
### The new school year begins for Essie Mae and the boys
### "What will people say if I start working for Al Johnson?"

"Shortages and rationing altered the lifestyle of all American civilians during World War II, but the impact on the lives of the women in charge of running a home reached into most aspects of their daily routines. … One wife wrote, 'Last week we didn't have a scratch of butter in the house from Monday until Friday'."

– Emily Yellin, *Our Mother's War*, 20, 22

Mount Vernon, Iowa
September 3, 1944        Sunday
Dearest Gerald,

I sent a night letter today telling about getting home all right, for the last I wrote, my plans were not very bright. To make a long story (or night) short, I did sleep in the depot all night, last Thursday, because the people who rented Runkles' house were so hostile about my coming out there. It was QUITE a night as you can imagine, especially since they lock the place up at two o'clock. The attendant asked me at that time what my plans were, and when I explained, he "assured" me that I would be safe. – but it was pretty lonesome. I went out to Runkles' about nine o'clock the next morning, and went to bed for a couple of hours.

I had a seat all the way home on the train, and I appreciated it, for the aisles were crowded all the way. Lester called a couple of friends of his who know the school situation in Mpls., and they said they were filling all vacancies this fall with their regular substitutes, so they would not have too many teachers when the war is over. The housing situation is so bad, that I was not at all tempted to stay. It was a pretty disillusioning experience to realize how a city "bothers" me.

The kids were fine when I got home. They had stayed here two out of the three nights. They were both happy to get back with their friends at school. Bertha Johnson stopped in this morning after she had taken Anne to school, and was rather emotional at the "first grown-up step for their child." They certainly love that youngster. There is to be a professional Hollywood production of their play – *Days without Daddy* – and Zasu Pitts almost bought the film rights to it. They are very hopeful that the stage production will eventually mean the movies.[*]

When I was taking my nap this PM, I dreamed that the telegram you sent was a last minute hasty message, just before you "pushed on." I was so real that when I woke up, I looked up the dates on the letter and telegram to make sure. Do you have any time to give a message to the *Hawkeye*? I'll be busy the next few days, getting the immense washing done, cleaning up the house, and really getting things organized for the kids' school.

Must close now – with Much Love, 'S'Mae

September 5, 1944        Tuesday
Dearest Gerald,

Tommy was happy to start out on a study of the Indians, and he took a big piece of our birchbark, and some of the little things we made from it. It was nice to have the benefits of our vacation show up so very promptly. George is taking his "honor roll goal" quite seriously and has been studying all evening. He and Bobby Gaston have their locker together. Bobby was elected president of the 8th grade class.

Johnsons called me over last night to visit and they were very gracious about the report of our trip. One other thing of interest happened before I left. Al asked me if I would be his sec'y next year. He had been thinking about it for some time, but had waited until after I had my try in Mpls before he said anything about it. He wants to devote more and more of his time to writing, and the job would involve more research than actual typing and letter writing. It would be my job to find and edit material which he would want to use in his writing. It would be interesting to learn another new "field," and it would serve as a good apprenticeship for me, but I am very hesitant

---

[*] Zasu Pitts (1894-1963) was a well-known film actress and producer who transitioned from silent films to sound films.

79

about accepting it. I think that it is best not to mix business and social life, and I would certainly hate to have anything happen to the very wonderful friendship which now exists.

Wed. Morning – Rev. Arnold is clerking at Sears in CR four days a week. Mother is "disillusioned." The Rust College singers are to be in Lisbon next Sunday morning. Do you remember when we kept them? I guess no one has volunteered yet to keep them, and Mrs. A. thinks she'll have to do it alone.

Must close now – Much love,
'S'Mae

[GLH added a note to this letter in his handwriting, with a line pointing to ⸜, writing: "SF comment on Race"]*

Mount Vernon, Iowa
September 7, 1944          Thursday night
Dearest Gerald,

Congratulations on all the good exams you've been writing. I think it is wonderful, the way you're taking all the "tough practice," like crawling thru barbed wire and the rest.

I got the bright idea, that it might solve the problem of "what will people say" if I start working for Al Johnson – if I enrolled in an individualized course in the Dramatics department. There is such a course called "Theatre Production," in which each student works on an individual problem. I still want to take Math, and then the time I spend at the Theatre or looking up material in the Library would just be "in connection with my study." I talked to the Johnsons again tonight, and Al plans to do a good deal of his writing at home – in the mornings. Nothing definite, tho' – would like your reaction. X-day again – they seem to come around awfully fast. I'm going to have to watch my weight – I have been so lazy that I weigh over 126 now – the most in many a long year.

It is a very good idea to "keep yourself in the public eye back here, I think," and as you know, a little publicity never comes amiss. I think your ability to adapt yourself to new situations is quite remarkable – I am "withdrawing" more and more, and you are branching out! I wish I had more of your nerve for tackling new places.

Much love, 'S'Mae

September 11, 1944          Monday night
Dearest Gerald,

Your letter, telling of your 14-mile hike, and your buying "heavies" came yesterday. The kids were much impressed with your hiking experience, and are hoping you will take some hikes with them when you come home. Their expression was – "I think Daddy will like to do things outdoors with us more than he ever did before – he'll be more FUN." I think it is wonderful that you have these experiences, and glad that it doesn't leave you too pooed.

Tommy and I went to Lisbon to church Sunday and heard the girls' quartette from Rust College. They really didn't sing very well – not nearly as pleasing to hear as the boys, but it was a good experience for the church. I guess they had quite a bit of trouble providing for them – One woman was very outspoken against them – but Harry [Sizer] said they entertained them for breakfast, and they had an all-church basket dinner Sunday noon. Rev. Arnold said he never had had such a lack of loyalty and interest. "You're telling ME, says I."[12]

I have forty-five quarts of tomatoes canned, and am ready to start on a bushel and a half of peaches. They are very expensive, but not as much as they are if canned. The new A gas coupons came this morning.

Much love, 'S'Mae

September 14, 1944          Thursday night
Dearest Gerald,

Your wonderful long letter written last Sunday after you got back from SF, came this morning. It took "postage due," but it was worth a million, in the happiness it brought to me. I think it was one of the nicest, and most thoughtful and appreciative you ever wrote, and I appreciate every word of it. I was interested that you saw the show "Wilson." I have been listening to a broadcast about him tonight, and I am very anxious to see the show and have the kids see it too. Public opinion of him has changed so very much, in these later years, that the kids won't ever be able to imagine how folks like my Dad (rabid Republican) felt about him.

---

* The Hills hosted the African American Rust College singers in 1943 and they all believed it was a wonderful experience.

Is there ever any suggestion that the war in the Pacific may be over before you get a chance to get across? I can't help but be glad that you won't be shoving off right away, but if that meant that you would lose out on your foreign experience, I wouldn't have you miss it for anything. I'll just miss your letter so much, Honey, during that long interval while you're "enroute." (Mustn't be selfish, 'S'Mae!!)

I hope you have a very happy birthday, and know that all of us back home wish we could be with you to deliver our love "in person."

Always, 'S'Mae

Mount Vernon, Iowa
September 20, 1944          Wednesday afternoon
Dearest Gerald,

I have just finished my shorthand class for the day, and while I am here at the office, I will take advantage of this nice new typewriter. I have been very negligent about my writing lately – and like all college "beginners" – I have only the excuse of being "very busy." I am glad you told me all you did, about your plans for the future, and the directions for getting in touch with you if necessary. I hope you will like the new camp as well as you have Obispo, but at any rate it will be one more new experience and place that you have seen.

Getting started in college again has really been something. If I didn't want the work so badly, I certainly never would do it just for the thrill – for it's a grind, and it seems strange to be in class instead of teaching. I checked in on the typing at 38 words a minute, much to my surprise.

Much love, 'S'Mae

September 21, 1944          Thursday afternoon          Cornell College
Dearest Gerald,

You will recognize that I am up in the typing room again. Your two letters describing your birthday came today, along with the money order. It was wonderful to hear that you did have a nice birthday and got a lot of mail. I am glad it all got there in time. The kids were happy that you liked what they sent you, and Tommy was especially proud. He is remarkably handy with his hands, but this fall, all he thinks of is football. He plays on the fifth grade team – which call themselves the "Blue Boys" – and they wear a white BB on the front of blue sweaters (if they can persuade their mothers to sew it on for them). Up to date, Tommy is the only one who has his decoration in place.

In one of the reading exercises in Shorthand, there was the sentence, "Ray made merry in the dale." Of course, merry and Mary are spelled alike in shorthand, and when one of the girls read it slowly, she said in a puzzled voice, "Why that just doesn't make sense." At which the class simply howled.

I am sending an original draft of a theme George wrote for school. I did not see the finished production, but I thought he did very well with it this far. He never pitched in to school with the enthusiasm that he has this fall, and he reports excellent grades, and seems to be learning a great deal. The H.S. has a dance Friday night and the Junior High is allowed to go, so he is planning on it.

I am to go over to Johnsons' in a few minutes to see what Al has for me to do. I am supposed to work a couple of hours a day for him, at 50 cents per hr. Charley Brackett, who has been a script writer and producer for Paramount for a long time, has been here with Rowena [Stuckslager], and he has been reading Al's newest script. They were to have dinner together at Rowena's last night, and I will be interested to hear what happened.*

Much love, Essie Mae

September 24, 1944          Sunday evening
Dearest Gerald,

This week has been quite a hectic one – getting started in school – getting my program ready for Entré Nous tomorrow nite, and trying to work for Al, and do some typing and writing for Mr. Reed. I don't feel I've done much for either of them, and I don't care about Mr. Reed's problems, but I hope I can soon get the hang of what Al wants.

_____

* Charles Brackett (1892-1962) wrote many prize-winning films, including *Titanic*. He received an honorary Oscar in 1958.

He and Karl Weber are collaborating on a farce, which is so fantastic I can't catch to spirit of the thing yet. Mr. Brackett, who writes and produces for Paramount, has been here for Elizabeth Ford business, and he and Rowena [Stuckslager] have been entertaining the Johnsons. They hope he will be interested in some of his writing, and he has arranged to have good Paramount coverage at the Hollywood production of *Days Without Daddy*.

Al says he thinks you are kind of a "lodestone" for Iowa people.[*]

Bye, and G'night, Honey. I'll not be so long about writing next time.

Much love, 'S'Mae

Mount Vernon, Iowa
September 25, 1944     Monday morning
Dearest Gerald,

Your description of the simulated landing was very graphic – I wish I could share it – but I don't know how much of it was "military information." My program on the weather at Entré Nous "went over" better than I was afraid it might. They want me to give another program on it – for they had to leave early to hear Dewey's speech.[†]

I always get involved in more things than I have time to do well, and just now I am not sure whether to start on last night's dishes, to wash, to study, to type for Reed, or to do some research for Al. I solve it all, by writing to you, but I MUST get lunch started.

Bye – with heaps of love, Essie Mae

September 29, 1944     Friday morning
Dearest Gerald,

I have just learned that one should make two spaces between sentences – new to me. I only got a B plus on the first quiz in shorthand, and I was surely disgusted with myself. The last of the cadets left yesterday, and it made me sort of sad. The code room is all dismantled, and no one would ever dream that the elaborate code equipment was once there. Most of the temporary partitions are down in the Law Building. I am glad I had a chance to see the whole program, when it was at full height, for it is all ancient history now. I told Mr. Reed that I could not help him anymore, so I am not quite so rushed – but still busy.

With much love, 'S'Mae

## October 1944
### Essie Mae accepts an invitation to speak at Cornell College Chapel on "Weather" And she is taking classes in shorthand and typing

"One of the most dramatic changes during World War II was the extraordinary job opportunities for women. As the armed forces filled its ranks with *manpower*, industry filled its jobs with *womanpower*."

– Penny Colman, *Rosie the Riveter*, 15

October 1, 1944     7:30 P.M.     Sunday
Dearest Gerald,

The kids and I just came back from McVille, where we left Grandma for a few days. 12 years ago, on the Sunday before George was born, we were there, too. I happen to remember, for I felt sick from "then on."

Your Geology has stayed by you unbelievably well, I think, to take you up on the mountain seeking a "dike" – I'll be interested to see the pictures which you took of it – Stone wall and all! Bertha says "sunburn" in a fog is the very worst kind ever – for one doesn't realize how penetrating the sun's rays are.

---

[*] Karl Weber (1916-1990) Cornell College '37; was at Winding Way Productions, N.Y.; many acting credits on radio and film.
[†] Thomas E. Dewey was the Republican party's candidate for president, running against FDR.

I am becoming more amazed at the reception my talk on the "Weather" got. Quite a few "non-members" in town have heard about it, and have mentioned it to me. I went to an AAUW dinner meeting Friday eve, and was asked if I'd consider giving it in Chapel! (Much comment then on my "Palisades" talk, etc.). Jim High is very much interested in my shorthand project – He has always wanted to learn it – and wants me to get a book for him, and teach him as fast as I learn it. We started working on it today, and it will be excellent practice for me.[*]

So G'Night, Darling – We're thinking of you – We think we have a mighty swell "Daddy" – and we wish we could see him. We're going to be mighty glad to all be together again.

Much love from all of us – 'S'Mae

Mount Vernon, Iowa
October 6, 1944    Friday morning
Dearest Gerald,

I have been doing some reading on "business practices," etc, and I can appreciate the pride you take in your filing system. This business of "taking care of business" is so new to me – but it is good for me, and I think it will make me a better wife for you even if I never use my new skills. I've been getting A in shorthand tho'. Typing is so aggravating because of habits I have to unlearn.

I get sort of paninc-y when I think of your being out on ship-board for ten or twelve days. I hope you have good weather, and enjoy the whole trip.

Do you realize that a year ago this week I started teaching at Cornell, and that we had the CAP review and entertained the C.R. gang on George's birthday? In some ways the time has gone very fast – but in other ways, it seems much longer than a year, because out activities are so different now. I know I couldn't "take" what I did last winter. X-day was this week, and for about three days before and three afterward, I just felt rotten.

Well, I've officially been asked to talk in Chapel – and officially accepted! I got up early this A.M. and am writing this before breakfast. This is the first A.M. this week that it has not been raining – By the way – I shortened that old trench coat (raincoat) of yours for George, and he just loves it. Wish there was a Boy Scout group George could affiliate with now that he is twelve.

Much love, Essie Mae

October 8, 1944    Sunday 4:15 P.M.
Dearest Gerald,

Ed Franks' funeral has taken a "lot out of me," but I was very glad I was asked to sing. I certainly missed you, and kept thinking all the time, how strange it was, for I know you would have been sad at losing a very good friend – as I was. I have never seen a larger crowd at a funeral in Lisbon, and I have not sung at one, I'm sure.

And now to a happier subject! The suitcase you sent came yesterday and we were all simply delighted. I would have been disappointed if it hadn't gotten here for George's birthday. You were certainly a thoughtful and loving Daddy, to remember us with our favorite things. Thank you – and kisses – for everything. I have a Hershey here beside me – and it is so delicious! George had a very happy birthday – I gave him $5 from "us" – and had his bike fixed. George insisted on treating me to a hot fudge sundae – which I thought was very sweet of him. We went to *Mark Twain* in the eve, and I was very proud of how nicely they looked and acted.

I am wondering how your new location impresses you. Your last letter, telling of the "accidents" on the overnight experience last Monday was appalling – I read it and shuddered. I think your part in it must have been a wonderful experience – I can imagine you "pitching" into the bad details of a tragedy like that, with outward calmness, but it must have been mighty hard. Your first trip "out at sea" will be interesting and exciting, I'm sure. It gives me a kind of "panicky" feeling, but I'll have to get used to it. I have increased my typing speed to 45 words per minute – largely in eliminating errors – rather than faster typing, and I have been getting A in shorthand. As in typing – nothing less than perfection counts with me, for just one error throws the whole thing off.

'Bye, My dear. Take care of yourself and come back soon.

Much love, Essie Mae

---

[*] EMH became proficient Morse Code, and then in typing and shorthand, and later in Braille.

Mount Vernon, Iowa
October 10, 1944   Tuesday     4:30 P.M.
Dearest Gerald,

Your letter of Oct. 8 mailed at 1:30 P.M. came this morning! I am glad you told us about that tragic incident – I won't worry – and it makes me realize much better, just what you are doing. Please don't "censor" or soft pedal anything, and we all will just take what comes – you as well as we, here at home.

In the test-minute today, I wrote 60 words without a single error! That was more luck than management, but it made me feel awfully good. I got a bang out of the teacher asking me to allow her to put my name down on a list of possible speakers at a Woman's Club conclave in Manchester in Nov. I guess I better get busy and get a speech organized – even if I don't do that particular one.

Tommy has been very thrilled to think that he and you met Wilkie. I think he did a little bragging at school, but no one believed him, probably.*

Will close now – with heaps of love, Essie Mae

October 11, 1944               Wednesday
Dearest Gerald,

Just a note to tell you that a letter from Helen Thompson came today, saying Harris is in the hospital and will have an operation this weekend. He is satisfied that nothing else will relieve the pain, and we are all hoping, of course, that he'll come thru all right. I feel that I must be ready for most anything, tho'.

My new glasses came this A.M. and the kids think I look better with them on than without them! They do seem very comfortable. Hope you are finding your new location very satisfactory. Hope, too, that you have gotten rested from your troubles. Have so much to do – but my shorthand and typing are a great satisfaction.

Hastily – but with Much Love, Essie Mae

October 15, 1944               Sunday 9:45 A.M.
Dearest Gerald,

What a surprise to have Tom Meredith hand me your telegram last eve when the kids and I stopped at the drug store on our way to the show, for our weekly "night out" together. George went to a dance Friday eve, and learned by sad experience that "two cannot live as cheaply as one." He decided to ask a girl to go with him because a "couple" could get in for 25¢, while single admissions were 15¢. He figured that he could get the girl to pay half. I bet him 5¢ he couldn't! Of course, he had to pay the 15¢ plus the 5¢ to me, and then she (Mary Thompson) had so many other dances, he didn't get to dance with her once the whole eve. I think it showed up her poor training in social obligations, but it showed him that a fellow has to be on "his toes," when he gets involved with "women."

Must dash off now – If I don't get any more written now – I'll write as soon as I get your letters.

Thinking of you – Much love – Essie Mae

October 18, 1944               Wednesday
Dearest Gerald,

I wonder if you are really "out on the water this morning"? I am thinking of you, and wondering how you like it. Sorry about the mix-up in addresses on your mail. I had that one letter addressed to Callan, and then a letter from you came saying it should be "Cooke." The candy in George's package has been simply luscious – My! we have enjoyed it! We haven't seen anything like it for ages! Tommy can "ration" his share, but George and I have a hard time to limit ourselves.

Tommy and I went to bed last night at eight o'clock. I have learned from last year, that when I begin to "ache around my neck & shoulders" that means quit – and I intend to do it, even tho' I have to stop in the middle of something. I just "can't take it" like I used to, and I realize more than I did last year, how close I was to doing some permanent damage to my health. My chapel talk has been postponed till sometime after election & my mind is much

---

* Wendell Wilkie was the Republican candidate for president in 1940. The Hills saw him at the Cheyenne Rodeo, and then followed his train to meet him at a whistle stop east of Cheyenne, Wyoming. Tommy and George shook his hand.

relieved. I have my "good and bad days" with my "school" work – but I don't have the "pressure" about it that I did last year. Must get breakfast now. It's a beautiful day here, and I wonder what you are doing "on shipboard" –

Much love, 'S'Mae

"October 20. American invasion of the Philippines was officially proclaimed today by Gen. Douglas MacArthur. He announced that his Navy and air-covered ground forces had landed in the archipelago."[*]

Mount Vernon, Iowa
October 20, 1944          Friday morning
Dearest Gerald,

I suppose you are back "on shore" again – did you get sea-sick? I'll be anxious to hear all about your trip to sea. This is Homecoming weekend here in MV, and imagine my surprise at being asked to "pour" at the tea after the game at Armstrong Hall. I can't imagine what has come over the college! Altho you may not believe it by looking at this letter, I made 65 words per minute yesterday in class, without any mistakes. I use the machine very little for private use, however, but I thought I could save a little time on this letter.

It is nearly time for the kids to get up and have breakfast. Harris is getting along all right from his operation. It will take a long period of convalescence, tho'. I have been writing him a note every day. Monday night there is an Entré Nous dinner at Nelsons', and the lecture by a geologist. It should be a very interesting evening.[†]

I did my typing for the day so Tommy and I are going to C.R. this afternoon. I am anxious to hear from you.

Much love, - 'S'Mae

October 21, 1944          Saturday
Dearest Gerald,

So many people asked about you today, and asked to be remembered to you that I feel "moved" to write to you right away. As I told you, I was asked to pour (the kids want to know, "Pour WHAT") at the tea, and it gave me a good chance to see people. George has a regular hospital of modeled little people, complete with wheel chairs, and crutches, and all. Tommy has been following the pattern we do in class – making a little bowl. I just thought today, if you land in Japan, you might refer to the picture Aunt Emma [(Stockwell) Lum] gave us, showing the cherry trees in Wash., D.C. I'll hope to get a letter soon telling about YOU.
Sunday P.M.

Just to bring the record up to date. Imagine my amazement last night to hear Lester Runkle's voice on the telephone. He was calling from Marion. Mrs. Black had a bad heart attack on Friday night and is in the hospital with an oxygen tent. The whole family came down, but all of them but Helene went back home today. Lester was here for a short time this morning, and then we went to Lisbon and Mechanicsville.

That made a very busy morning, because we got back to Lisbon just a few minutes late for church, and I stayed for choir practice afterwards. Mother had a grand letter from Manly [Thompson]. He says Bill has finished his work at Princeton, and is heading for Harvard for more training, which I think is pretty nice. He says Johnny is back in California, and will be at San Diego for several weeks making sure he hasn't any tropical bugs.

Am thinking about you, and wondering what new adventures you have been in since we heard from you.

Much love, 'S'Mae

October 23, 1944          Monday
Dearest Gerald,

George came home this noon declaring he would not go back to school, until something was done to make the kids let him alone. He has had his protractor, compass, several pencils, etc., swiped this year, and the older boys in his grade take their fun in hiding his book and equipment. Today they took his bike and left it in an alley. I have wanted to go over and talk to the Supt. but George didn't want me to. But now he said he didn't care – HE JUST WASN'T GOING BACK, AS LONG AS HE HAD TO PUT UP WITH THAT. However, I notice that George brought

---

[*] *New York Times Complete World War II*, 476.
[†] He had surgery for peptic ulcer disease, probably a partial gastrectomy. He was always thin, but he lived to the age of 77.

his books home tonight to study, so I judge that he is going back. I have not asked him any of the details – I thought he might like to keep that to himself.

Much love – Essie Mae

Mount Vernon, Iowa
October 26, 1944  Thursday A.M.
Dearest Gerald,

Your note written last Sunday came yesterday and we were pleased to know you were thinking of us. I think your letter to Mary Franks was a better and finer tribute than anything at the funeral. It may be "old-fashioned" to eulogize the deceased, but it still appeals to me!  So glad you went to Mexico. George seemed especially pleased to think you have been in both neighboring countries.  It seems a long time "no hear" from you, but I am getting my mind adjusted to it.

George led the Youth Fellowship meeting today & is giving a Chem. demonstration in one of his classes today.  I gave the kids breakfast in bed this A.M. so I could go to 7:45 class, knowing they had had a good "nourishing" breakfast.  They are getting very lazy in the mornings.  Tommy had tears last night hoping Daddy would do things with him & George when you come home.

Much love,
Essie Mae

October 26, 1944
Dear Dad,

I haven't written to you for a longtime but when the box came I thought that I would write and thank you for the planes and purse.  Mother and I were trying to figure out what the planes were in order of but know matter what they sure are good.  I've been playing football lately the 5th grade have a team of their own and we played and beat the 6th grade.  I am the center on our team.

When you sent the candy on George's birthday I made mine last longest.

Love
Tommy Hill

10-26-44
Dear Dad,

I sure was very surprised and happy when I got both your birthday package and the planes.  Those candy bars sure tasted          good.  A while ago you sent us some 7th Division and some other insignia. The other was shaped:          You said that it was a division ins.  It isn't in the *Geographic* so it must be a regimental insignia of          some division.[*]

In school I was kept off the honor roll because I got a 89.  If I would have gotten a 90 I would have made it. Right now I'm doing pretty good.  In English today we were supposed to tell how to make or do something.  I picked ammonia gas.  I actually made it.  I took $NH_4Cl$ (Ammonium Chloride) and $Na_2CO_3$ (Sodium Carbonate) and boiled them in a test tube I borrowed from Miss West, my science teacher.  I did the experiment fine but then I broke the tube washing it when I turned the faucet the wrong way and it was blasted out of my hand.

I've been monkeying with my Chem set and have typed 64 labels for my chemicals.  I also double filed them in alphabetical order by having first the chem name and after it the name we          call it and then vice-versa.  It was really a job.  I went up to a little pile behind the chem bldg.          at the College and after ½ hr.'s digging I found a chipped test tube and a partially broken one.          Also a glass funnel and a lot of tubes.  Mom taught me a little Spanish a little while ago.  When I          was on my paper route on foot I met some college kids who were practicing their Spanish.  One of them said "hasta la vista" and the other looked puzzled.  I said "How are you," and as they walked by they were wondering how I knew that.  Then the boy yelled back "Thanks Boy."[†] George  Toot

---

[*] It is probably the badge of the U.S. 29th Infantry Regiment, the motto of which is "We Lead the Way."
[†] George, who called himself "Toot II," got a Gilbert Chemistry set on October 7, for his 12th birthday.  The only mis-spelling is "Spanish" (sic), and his punctuation is shown as it was in the letter.  He drew three pictures and inserted them in his letter.

Mount Vernon, Iowa
October 27, 1944 (before breakfast)                    Friday
Dearest Gerald –

We were all so surprised and pleased yesterday when the big packages came.  It was <u>such</u> a nice thing – and it made us all very happy.  I checked in at 67 w.p.m. yesterday, but the day before I was <u>terrible</u>.

Coffee is ready now – So 'Bye – Much love, 'S'Mae


October 29, 1944                    Sunday afternoon
Dearest Gerald –

I am "unsettled" now, however, because Miss Leigh just passed away.  It came quite suddenly, and she was conscious up to very near the end.   I am wondering whether this will mean any change in our living arrangements.  Fortunately, several new storm windows are already installed.  Johnsons asked us to go out on a picnic with them last eve, and we went to a place near the river.  This has been a beautiful fall, and the picnic was a great success – moonlight and all.  The kids are very sweet with Anne and she just worships them.

That's all for this time – Much love, Essie Mae


October 30, '44
Dear Dad,

We had our homecoming dance and boy was the floor decorated.  The whole thing was covered by a blue cloth covering.  The sides were covered by twisted, alternating blue and red crepe paper streamers.  At 2 of the sides were elaborately decorated doors.  They didn't have a band but they have a <u>beautiful</u> phonograph.

On Saturday when I collected I was supposed to make $4.20 not counting deductions for bond, but I made $4.25 and felt happy about.  On Saturday when I was getting a bank draft for $8.70 which was my bill I asked Mr. Van Meter to let me have 3 silver dollars for 3 dollar bills.  He told me they were low on Silver Dollars so he didn't give me any.  That disappointed me because our Am. Hist. teacher said any bank is supposed to be able to give you silver dollars for paper ones.

Your son,
George          <u>Toot</u>


8YF8  NL  PD=MILWAUKEE  WIS  OCT  31  1944  0920* / GERALD HILL = AFD  AMERICAN RED CROSS CAMP CALLAN

SDGP= JOHN AND VIRGINIA GRANT HOTEL SAN DIEGO BELIEVE THEY WILL SOON LEAVE CALIFORNIA ALL FINE HERE

SOFT LIFE FOR ME BILL LEAVE TONIGHT 4 MONTHS AT HARVARD.  PROPER WAY TO FIGHT WAR SAYS ME.  TAKE CARE

YOURSELF = MANLY

---

* Transcription of Western Union telegram from Manly Thompson to his brother-in-law, GLH.  He mentions his sons Bill and John, and John's wife, Virginia.

# She Waits and Worries on The Home Front
## November 1944 – February 1945

### November 1944
### Another Thanksgiving passes for the Hills, with Father away in service
### Essie Mae rents a room in her house: "One of my dreams was to live with another 'war widow'"

*It just seemed too good to be true to hear your voice last night. ... Where were you when you telephoned? And what had you been doing to pass the time while you waited? And how had you spent the day? Do you still have to keep up the pressure of hurrying and long hours? ... Much love to our wonderful Daddy*

Essie Mae to Gerald, 27 November 1944

Mount Vernon, Iowa
November 1, 1944          Wednesday morning
Dear Dad,

I'm writing this at 10:55 in the morning during a spare study hall. I did most of my work for today, yesterday, so I only had to do a little bit this morning.

We had our Rotary Halloween party last night. It was a lot of fun for a while. We had boxing matches that were 3 min. long and 4 couples boxed. There were corn stalks and pumpkins in the hall. Some kids got the idea to throw corn and so there was regular fight. It was really terrible. I came home with little nicks and scratches all over my face and hand. We allso had a rather dumb but funny movie. Then there were folk dances that weren't much fun and I bobbed for and got 2 apples. They gave out free pop and cookies. I had 2 bottles of that and 2 cookies. Then I was so tired I didn't want to dance so Bob Gaston & I just went home about 11:00. This morning we saw people picking up corn around the halls to throw in class.

We had a brain-buster test this morning in Am. Hist. I tied for the highest score which was 14 out of 16. Bob only got 7. We're going to have a test that will cover about 50 pages on Thursday or Friday. We have a test today in Science.

(It's now 6:45)     I did no good. The highest score was 2 out of 9. I got 2 along with about 7 others. I'm going to a lecture by a former Russian Gen. at the college tonite so I'll have to be studying.

Your Son, George*

November 2, 1944   6:15 A.M.          Thursday
Dearest Gerald,

This is in the morning I go to 7:45 class, so I always give the kids their breakfast in bed. I am looking for the letter you said you were going to write Monday – so I am answering it "ahead of time." When you go overseas, I'll make carbons of my letters so you can refer to them by date & I'll know what I wrote.

This has been a <u>wild</u> week, – but everything has gone smoothly. Tommy was <u>so</u> touched & pleased when the Leighs gave him an incense burner that belonged to Elda, to remember her by. Feel sorry for Clint Keubler – he seems so lost and lonesome. He'll stay on, and I've asked him to look after my ashes, etc. He is so nice with the kids – brot George's bike up on the porch Hallowe'en & takes the *Gazette*.

---

* George's 12th birthday was October 7, 1944.

George went to the Lecture course at the college last night all alone.  He wanted to get the autograph of the Russian general.  He has been <u>such</u> a good boy – so companionable and so conscientious.  I know you enjoy his letters – which are all his own "wanting to write to you."  I almost never "jump on him" – just let him work things out himself, and he really tries very hard to do the right thing (when it's something <u>important</u>) and I just don't nag him about little things which used to irritate me.  Rev. Rowley says he gave a wonderful talk on "temptation" at Youth Fellowship.  He practiced it at home & I read him the background from *The Story of the Bible*.

Love, 'S'Mae

Mount Vernon, Iowa
November 6, 1944   Monday 7:30 A.M.
Dearest Gerald,

Anne Johnson was a very sweet little overnight guest, and we thoroly enjoyed her.  We all got up early Sunday A.M. and helped George with his papers, and she tho't that was lots of fun.

I may go into the "real estate" business.  Earl Leigh has taken over this place & wants to rent me the whole house for $25.  If I can rent the upstairs for $30, I may take him up.  He has been very nice, and it all came about from an inquiry from a man who will be employed at the college heating plant if he and & wife can find a furnished apt.  The man would want it from Dec 1 to May 1.

Much love – Hastily, Essie Mae.

November 7, 1944   Election Day      Tuesday
Dearest Gerald,

Kids are both fighting off colds.  This is a legal holiday for the bank, but the Red Cross "carries on" I suppose.  Did I tell you George is very proud of the autograph of the Russian general?  He went to the lecture all alone (at his own expense) and was the only child there.  The general wrote his name both in English & <u>Japanese</u>.  Hoping for mail from you today[*]

Love, 'S'Mae

"On November 7 FDR carried out his election day ritual at Hyde Park … If he genuinely feared Dewey, no sign appeared in Roosevelt's cool and unconcerned demeanor.  By 1:30 A.M. … it was clear that he had won … FDR not only took the popular vote handily but also the electoral college vote by 432 to 99."[†]

Armistice Day      November 11, 1944  Saturday
Dearest Gerald,

We were certainly happy to get your long letter (and a short one) this week.  The long one telling of your sea-trip was so interesting an account, that I couldn't resist reading part of it to Johnsons.  They think as I do that you certainly <u>can</u> write & that you should plan to "publish" sometime.

Tommy is <u>so</u> thrilled to be in the Thanksgiving play at the College – *Family Portrait*.[‡]  He appreciates the honor, and is simply "walking on air."  He is doing it <u>very</u> well, & it's a wonderful privilege for him.  Tommy's Character Education Class has been giving the 5th grade some personality tests & I was so interested that I have conferred with Miss M. about Tommy's reactions –

For instance:
What 3 people would you like to have with you on a desert island? – Mother, Father, brother.
What kind of boy would your Mother like best? – The one who gets the best grades.
What kind of a boy would your Dad like best? – The one who minds & keeps his Mother.
(Among the choices were – Most athletic, strongest, best looking, smartest, etc.)
What do you want to when you grow up? 1. Inventor.  2. Aviator.  3. Capt. of a PT boat.
What age do people have the best time? 9-12 yrs. [Tommy was 9 on May 3, 1944]

---

[*] "Keep calm and carry on" from the British war motto.
[†] Joseph E. Persico, *Roosevelt's Secret War*, 351-2, 368-9.
[‡] *Family Portrait*, a three-act play by Lenore Coffee and William Joyce Cowen (1939), was about Jesus' family.

What do your parents want you to be?  A normal, happy man.

Who are your best friends?  Mother, Daddy, Brother.

What do you want most?  More money (for a football suit).

Of course, the test was made up very cleverly, but these are typical results.

I was asked to be vice-president of the P.T.A. (stepping stone to president) but turned it down.  I am giving the program at Lion's next week (or the next) on "Weather."

That was a grand letter of yours in the *Hawkeye*.  Johnsons & Jay McGregor have especially asked me to compliment you.  I'm so glad you wrote it.  I just can't tell you how much we enjoyed your graphic acc't of your recent experiences.  They make it seem <u>very</u> real.

Must hurry now – Much Love, 'S'Mae

Mount Vernon, Iowa

November 13, 1944          Monday 0800

Dearest Gerald –

I completed arrangements for renting the upstairs – to a young couple connected with the Navy.  He is in the refresher course, so will be here 6 mo.  They are <u>so</u> nice.  Both from Oakland, married 3 yrs. – but together now after 2 yrs. (he was at sea).  She is a <u>flier</u> and was set to go into ferry-service before they cut out women.  Both seem <u>very</u> intelligent & interesting, and she is apparently quite a natural "home-maker" too.  This California couple thinks Iowa weather is <u>very</u> strange.  Never had <u>heard</u> of a storm window till a couple of weeks ago.  That sounds plausible to you.  They have spent a lot of time at La Jolla & think it is <u>beautiful</u>.

Much love to our Daddy –

Essie Mae & the boys.

November 16, 1944          Thursday

Dearest Gerald,

Your grand letter, with the RX assignment came today, and it was so very interesting, and I know it took a long time to write, that made me feel guilty, for I haven't had time to do a very good job of writing lately.

I am glad you told me about your possibility for hospitalization.  I hope and pray it won't happen for I know – as well as you – that it will be a real ordeal, but I know too, how much you want to say with your group.

The Lion's Club evening was quite interesting, and I never had a more attentive audience. They were really grand.  There was quite a write-up about it in the *Hawkeye* which you will get in due time, but I hope no one who knows anything about Weather will think I actually said some of those things.  I think it is just grand that you are allowed to wear the Division patch now – and your contact with General Halsey sound very impressive.  I think it is wonderful – the way you do take hold of things and put them across.  I know too, that there wouldn't be any unfavorable reports about the RX if all the men were like you.

Must get to bed now – so many things to get ready for.  Heaps of Love, Essie Mae

November 21, 1944          Tuesday morning

Dearest Gerald,

This is Founder's Day, and we got out of class a little earlier than usual – so I dashed back up to the typing room, to write to you and practice a little.  You see, I will have to cut class again this afternoon, to go to Lisbon and sing at TWO funerals.  Sunday night will be a fine time for you to call, and we'll stay close to the phone.  Have you had any more trouble with the hernia problem?  You have a job before you to keep in good physical condition, but I know you realize that even better than I do.[*]

Al Johnson has it doped out that you will be going to the Philippines, and if you do, all you need to say to give us the information is "Al was right," or something like that – that is, if you want to.

Much love, Essie Mae

---

[*] EMH uses the word "hernia" here for the first time, in referring to GLH's problem that will need surgery.

Mount Vernon, Iowa
November 24, 1944          Friday morning
Dearest Gerald,

I have much to tell you this morning, and such a short time in which to do it, for we have school today, as usual. In addition to that, I have a washing to do, and singing at another funeral this afternoon.

It was so sweet of you to send Tommy a telegram – it came about the middle of the morning yesterday. He will have quite a few things to save and remember this by, when he grows up. The big event on Wednesday was Tommy's Minstrel show. His teachers had worked it out very cleverly to make it a unified project. In Music they studied Stephen Foster, in Art they designed their stage, to represent the deck of a show-boat, complete with railing, life preserver, pilot wheel, cabin windows, etc. In Language they composed and wrote their invitations, after they had learned to spell the words. Tommy played a "solo" on his "hum-a-tune," and his costume was really SOMETHING. He wore a pair of YOUR shoes, white canvas pants, rolled up to show one red boot sock, and one blue one, a suit coat, a white shirt with the collar starched high in points, with a bow tie. He wore a negro wig he got for Hallowe'en and your red plaid corduroy sales cap. He burned cork to black his face, and carried the old Yellowstone suitcase, with a piece of long underwear trailing out of it. He did really well, of course, and afterwards his little face was covered with perspiration, just like yours when you get thru with a Minstrel show. There were about 125 people there including the grade school kids, and Bertha Johnson took time out to go and take Anne. The combination of working in this school show, and the late rehearsals for the college play have made Tommy so very tired, but he has kept going, and he simply covered himself with glory last night in *Family Portrait*.

The Runkles were here a short while in the afternoon, but they are starting back to Mpls. this morning. Helene has been away for five weeks and the family are needing her. Mrs. Black is SOME person, I say, with the persnickety way she insists on everything being done, and the family has nothing very happy to look forward to, even when they get the house built for the Blacks. Mr. Black is so helpless, and was sick himself for more than a week while Helene was here. Mrs. B. will not hear of having twin beds – she has always slept with "papa" and she is not going to quit now – even if both of them are sick.*

It is hard to realize that you will soon be far away!! I wonder how you have been feeling physically – do take care of yourself! Must close now and get ready to dash to class. George is awake, but I hope Tommy will still be asleep by the time I get home.

Much love, my dear! 'S'Mae

November 27, 1944          Monday morning
Dearest Gerald,

It just seemed too good to be true to hear your voice last night. The Johnsons came over about half past six, and we had a highball – from that bottle you brought last summer, and we all drank a toast to "Toot" – the kids had grape juice, but they joined in, too. Then we had supper, which we ate in the living room, and which included hot ginger bread and ice-cold applesauce for dessert. Bertha took Anne home about seven-thirty, and then we just sat and talked until the call came.

Tommy was trying to tell you about his boat. He has a strange combination of talents. Friday night, while he was waiting to go to get his make-up on, he read the new *Life* magazine. There was a long, and well-illustrated article in it, explaining the theory of jet-propulsion and giving a picture of a little raft, with a flask on it filled with water. Under the flask was a little flame which kept the water boiling, and as the steam came out of the tube at the top of the flask, the boat moved. What does he do, but get up Saturday morning, and make one, all by himself. Fortunately, he got it balanced just right, and just happened to get a board that was not too large to be propelled by the amount of steam he could generate, and lo, and behold, the thing actually ran.

It was the most surprising thing. After that the kitchen was real workshop, with sawing, test tubes, rubber hose, and what-not, but the kids had a wonderful time, and it was about the most ingenious little device I ever saw. He certainly had "vision" and faith to start out on the project, for I didn't at all suppose that it would work.

---

* Mr. Black had juvenile diabetes. He had an infection in one leg as a child, which resulted in an amputation.

Mother, Rachie and the Runkles all told me to remember them to you. They are all thinking of you, and wishing you the best of everything. John Woodin's girl [Betti Gray] told me this morning that he called her yesterday. He is getting along fine and likes it very much.

It still doesn't seem real that we actually heard your voice last night. I do so little long distance telephoning that it all seems like a miracle to me – that we could hear you so plainly and yet it would take days to actually be there in California. I am so glad you called us, Honey, it just makes all these intervening months just melt away. I know you will take care of yourself, but I can't resist cautioning you to "take care of yourself," and know that whatever you have before you, you can take, and we'll be pulling for you.

Much love to our wonderful Daddy, Essie Mae

Mount Vernon, Iowa
November 28, 1944        Tuesday 0700 At the breakfast table: (George working Science Problems) -
Dearest Gerald,

It's a good thing to be busy! I'll bet you felt that yesterday – as I did – it keeps one from thinking too much – when thinking might bring on the blues! Yesterday, it seemed to me that everywhere I went, I overheard snatches of conversation telling about some loved one who was about to go overseas, or who had just gone. Of course, they didn't know that I had just talked to my Honey the night before, but it surely "got" me. I kept busy! I really believe you'll have a nice Christmas, too – everyone will do all they can for each other. We'll be very conscious of you, and you'll be very much with us in our hearts.

I must get down to business on our Xmas cards. Nothing has clicked in my mind yet, but something has to be done soon. Our school runs until Dec. 19 and that doesn't give a great deal of "vacation."

Must rouse Tommy now & get ready to dash to 7:45 class – G'Bye, My dear – Lovingly, 'S'Mae

## December 1944
### Essie Mae plans to put his letters in a book, *The Life of a Red Cross Man in World War II*
### "Last year, I was so scared at being alone, I used to keep a 'night light' burning all the time"

"For the many women who stayed on the home front, volunteering through such organizations as the Red Cross, the USO, and the Office of Civilian Defense was their avenue to war involvement. These women were also less threatening to the status quo than their military counterparts, though they discovered a similar kind of satisfaction in using their skills and talents in public life."
– Emily Yellin, *Our Mother's War*, 167

Mount Vernon, Iowa
December 1, 1944  6:15 A.M.        Thursday
Dearest Gerald,

Up at 5:30 this morning to dig the clinkers out of the kitchen stove and get things organized for the day. The ground is covered with snow now – and we really know "winter is here"! You would be very happy over the kids' grades. George is way out ahead of all his class, with A's in everything except penmanship (raised from C to B) and Conduct, C–. Eloise Littell got F in Conduct, so George is still a pretty good boy. Tommy raised his grades by +'s and got A in several, including Music, which he got C in, last year. He and I have been making "spatter pictures." I think he has a real artistic "sense," and he loves to do it. I feel we are much better set for the winter than we were at this time last year. I was so scared at being alone, I used to keep a "night light" burning all the time! Am glad to know that your physical condition is par. I am hoping with all my might that you "get by" your last physical exam. I suppose your never take extra vitamins. I have been feeding the family on vitamins, as a precaution, and we are fine.

Much love – Essie Mae.

Mount Vernon, Iowa
December 2, 1944          Friday morning
Dearest Gerald,

What a life! It is now ten o'clock and we have just finished getting dressed. I warned everybody last night that this was one morning that I was going to stay in bed. I have been getting up at five-thirty for so long. There was a telephone call at 0700 for the girl upstairs, so I got up and built the fires and then went back to bed. How I hate winter – I have shoveled about three tons of coal so far, and it is the kind that makes so much soot and ashes.

Tommy's teacher called me in to her office yesterday, and showed me the most interesting thing! It seems that her class in character education made a study of the social tendencies among the grade school children. Each child was asked to name his three best friends and then they were charted to see how the bonds of friendship ran. In the fourth grade, the girls were all in a little clique and the boys in another, which is not so good for children of that age, and there were four little boys, who all named each other, thus giving a "double" bond.

Would you believe it! The chart which she showed me looked like this, with Tommy in the center, and practically everyone in the room – both boys and girls – naming him as their best friend. To cap it all, Tommy had named as his three best friends, Mother, Daddy, and George – which I though was particularly significant. She said such lovely things about Tommy – what a sweet and talented child he is, and I thought the tribute of his classmates was very touching. He said, "I don't have ONE best friend like George has Bobby Gaston, but a lot of kids come to help me when I get into a fight!"          Much love, from all of us. 'S'Mae

December 6, 1944          Tuesday morning
Dearest Gerald,

Your letter came Monday explaining why we didn't hear from you after Monday of the week before, and I confess I had begun to think that you had shipped out. I don't see how you stand those long trips – aren't you just about dead for days afterwards? – – – – After class: 1000 – This bodes to be ONE OF THOSE DAYS! George finally got up on the wrong side of the bed, and we had a round or two before he finally left for school, altho I had said that he could not go unless he ate his breakfast. He stalked out of the door, with a "Oh, is that so," so I have some unpleasant times ahead of me, I am afraid, until I get him in line again. Please "advise." Must close now, and get to work. Will write again soon.          Much love, 'S'Mae

December 9, 1944          Friday morning
Dearest Gerald,

George and I are on good terms again & all is peace & quiet. He sprained his hand sliding, but is getting better – altho' still swollen. I plan to take the kids to C.R. tomorrow for their one Xmas trip & will get the bicycle repaired. Tonight we are addressing Xmas cards. Am renting the upstairs as two apartments for a total of $40. Now I won't worry so much about the amount of coal I have to shovel. Am wondering how things are going with you.
          Much love, Essie Mae

Editor's Note: Sometime after EMH wrote this letter to GLH, he was suddenly given leave to spend two weeks at home in Iowa. There is a gap of 14 days in his letters. While he was away from Camp Cooke, a surprise German counterattack on December 16 occurred in France. This is now known as the Battle of the Bulge. It lasted until January 25, and it set back the Allied plan for the war in Europe. The 97th Division was then retrained and received new equipment for combat in Europe, instead of the Pacific.

KW1 NL PD=CAMP COOKE CALIF DEC 13 1944[*]
GERALD HILL= AFD AMN RED CROSS MTVERNON IOWA = SUGGEST LEAVE MT VERNON 18TH OR 19TH UNABLE WIRE EXPLANATION SITUATION HERE REGARDS TO FAMILY
          FLD DIR ARC 97TH DIV CAMP COOKE. 18TH 19TH          97TH.

---

[*] Western Union telegram.

Mount Vernon, Iowa
December 15, 1944          Friday
Dearest Gerald,

By the time you get this letter, you will undoubtedly know that a telegram came for you about 1:30 on Thursday saying that you could have stayed at home longer. I am enclosing the message, and am very curious – anxious – to know what brought about the changes "which could not be discussed in the telegram." It is a shame that it did not arrive twenty-four hours sooner, but by the time it did get here, I thought it would be useless, if not impossible, to try to contact you. I am thinking of all the things we could have done in that extra time, but am very grateful for having the unexpected luck in having you here, for the time that you were here.

What kind of luck did you have in getting a plane from Omaha? I surely hope you did get one, for it would have been a long and tiresome trip if you didn't. It was six below zero in CR on Wednesday night, but it is very mild this morning. I got kinda spoiled for coal-shoveling while you were here!

Did you meet any interesting people on your trip back to California? I hope you find everything working out all right when you get back there, but you know I'll be very anxious to hear all about it.

Much love, 'S'Mae


December 17, 1944          Sunday night
Dearest Gerald,

I am thinking about you, and wondering what you found when you got back to camp. Tommy has been in bed a long time, but George went out with a church group to sing carols, and have a chili supper at the church afterwards, and isn't home yet. They have been skating a couple of times this weekend, but it has been so cold that their enthusiasm has cooled too. They took along materials for a fire today, but some big kid threw snow on it – doesn't it beat all, how mean some kids can be, and think it is fun? The pictures from Lasswell's are all very good. It has been hard to decide which one is the best, but Bertha Johnson and I have agreed on one, so that will be the choice. I have seen them only very briefly since you left. The kids and I went to the movie last night and saw the *Great Moment* – the story of the man who discovered the use of ether. It was very good.*

Saw the Nelsons at the *Messiah* today, and they were very regretful at not having had a chance to visit with you. I feel mighty sorry for them this Christmas – Harlan's wife is going to Kansas, and she said they had no plans at all – I mean none of their relatives were planning on being here.

Much love, 'S'Mae


December 20, 1944          Wednesday
Dearest Gerald,

I have the Christmas preparations pretty well completed, and I bought one last thing for each of the kids, that so delighted them, that it brought the tears. George has been embarrassed several times lately because he had no really good clothes – nothing but corduroy pants, and no coat – so I got him a tan coat, brown pants, and tan shirt. They look lovely, and I have never seen him so pleased with anything in his life. I showed them to him, so that I could judge how they fit. He looks so nice, and has wanted them so badly, that I think he will take care of them. I got a size 16 coat, so he should be able to wear it several seasons.

For Tommy, I got a reversible coat, tan gabardine on one side, and bright red wool on the other, with a detachable hood. He just danced when he saw it. I have been worried about his outdoor clothes, for his sheep-lined coat was "done for," and that little leather jacket just isn't warm enough for below zero weather like we have been having. These things made quite a hole in the budget, but I just thought it would be worth it to "starve along" – and after all, the kids have to be clothed. Just as an "extra" (not for Christmas) Lester [Runkle] sent George a Bunsen burner, and a high school chem work book, and he is surely happy about that, too.

My school is out, and since this is X-week, I am glad to be sort of lazy today. I got three tons of larger sized coal this week, which holds the fire longer, and doesn't mean so many trips to the basement for shoveling. I must wash again, tho', and I have the rabbit in the basement now – it just got too awfully cold outdoors.

---

* *The Great Moment* (1944), starred Joel McRae; it tells the story of the first use of ether anesthesia in surgery.

I hope you find a place among your friends' Christmas festivities so you will not be lonesome. We will be thinking about you, as you must well know. Several people have mentioned that it didn't seem possible that it was "fourteen years ago." Take care of yourself, and a Christmas kiss.

Much love, 'S'Mae

Mount Vernon, Iowa
December 23, 1944            Saturday
Dearest Gerald,

Rachie went to C.R. this P.M. and got our pictures – Aren't they nice! This will be our Christmas "visit" together. I am so happy that they are finished in time for Christmas, and I hope you like them. The house is shining clean, and piled high with gifts. I surely wish you could be here to enjoy it with us. George's customers have been very generous & he is so surprised and happy. The Gazette Co. gave him a "wrist light." We'll be thinking of you, Honey, and remembering all our other Christmases –

Lots of love, Essie Mae

December 27, 1944            Wednesday
Dearest Gerald,

The telegram telling of your promotion just came and I am so VERY proud of you. I think it is simply wonderful. I feel like just going up and down the street and telling everyone about it. As it was, I stopped at the *Hawkeye*, and had the address on your paper changed, and I assume they will mention it in this week's issue. It has been rather difficult to think up answers to people's questions about you, for the most important news has been about your trip to the hospital, and of course I couldn't tell them about that.

That has been very much on my mind yesterday and today, and I have been hoping I would hear from you. I suppose that by this time the operation is over, and I surely hope and trust that you are getting good and sympathetic care. It is hard to imagine you down without me being there to look after you. I know you will be a very good patient, and be "patient," and then will be well and fine "forever more."

I am sending the Xmas cards, which I thought you might like to read as you "recuperate." If it is not too much trouble, I wish it might be possible for at least the ones with the lovely notes on them to be saved and sent back to me sometime when you are sending things. I would like to keep them to read, when I get to feeling kinda low. It has made me very happy to realize that people apparently appreciate my work so much. I admit it has been a burden to keep on with the music in Lisbon, but you can see now, that I feel that it has been worthwhile.

Lester [Runkle] sent me the most beautiful chimes for the door, designed and hand made. I was so pleased with the string of Mexican bells that George gave me, and he had several other surprises (as well as Tommy) which he picked out and bought for me. To cap my bell Christmas, Bostroms sent me a great big scrap book, about a third filled with pictures, articles, stories, and poems, about bells. Johnsons had their usual open house in the morning, and then I came home to dinner with the family, and we had one of Bish [Stahl]'s capons, with all the trimmings, ending up with "plum pudding," with a sprig of holly on the top, and I poured brandy around it and set fire to it, and I brought it in, with the blue flame actually burning around it. It really didn't taste very good, but I have always wanted to try it, and it was quite spectacular.

The kids were both so tired that by bedtime they were glad when I suggested that I read them a story out of *Daddy's Christmas Book*. George lay on a comforter on the floor and Tommy and I on the bed. When Tommy finally was ready for sleep, he put his hands under his head, and lay on his side, and I patted him and said, "You know you're a much loved child, don't you?" A big tear rolled out of the one eye that was "up," and right over the bridge of his nose.

It is just wonderful to think that your ability to do a bigger job that you have had in the RX is at last recognized, and I am certainly very happy and proud for you. I hope too that your operation is all over, and successfully done, and that you have only the best of health from now on.

Heaps of Love, Essie Mae

PS: Your telegram on Christmas day was so lovely, and it was very sweet and thoughtful of you to send it. I just wish you could have been here to help us enjoy our "simple," but very sincere pleasurers. Love, again, EMH

Mount Vernon, Iowa
December 28, 1944          Thursday morning
Dearest Gerald,

Just received your telegram telling of the failure of the general to OK your promotion. I know how disappointed you are, and I am just terribly so. I sent your wool clothes to SLO yesterday, so you will have to send out a tracer for them, but you won't be needing them right away, if you go to the hospital – you are probably there right now. I am thinking of you, and hoping that you are feeling better soon. The *Hawkeye* was all set to carry a story about your transfer – for from the first message, it seemed a sure thing, but I phoned them right away, and I hope they can "kill" it. Please don't be mad at me, if they can't – I was just so darned thrilled! And I wanted to give them your new address for this week's issue of the *Hawkeye*.

We are still reading "folktales" for a good-night story-time. The kids are very much interested in it, and I keep thinking how glad I am that they are learning all these new stories. George works chem alone now, for he has read in the books which he has received lately, just what is really dangerous and what is safe for children, and he really sort of "looks down" on the other kids, who "don't have sense enough to let good enough alone." These books give lots of simple, yet interesting experiments, with "home" things, like potatoes, and soap which can be done without danger, and yet show real chemical results. I am very happy to know that he finally realizes that we haven't been just "mean" to him – in discouraging his more dangerous experiments.

I am so glad you're getting physically in shape, and I know that you will have other opportunities to "be of service," and have your ability "pay out." Good luck, my dear, in everything.

Much love, from all of us, Essie Mae


December 28, 1944          Thursday evening
Dearest Gerald,

I hope this reaches you as you are feeling on the "up" after your operation. After I wrote to you this morning, I received your long Christmas eve letter, with all the enclosures, and your Xmas day letter, too. I was certainly glad to hear the details of your conferences with all the RX men and the military in explanation of the telegrams that have been coming. I am perfectly satisfied to leave the decisions to you, for I feel that you know the situations best, but I just hope that eventually you will be given a position that I feel is comparable with your ability. I am just so thankful that it has been possible for you to have that operation as long as it was pending, and necessary. And I hope and trust that it will be and is a complete success. Please really take it easy during your recuperation, so you have a real opportunity to get strong and well again.

The kids are really thrilled over the shoulder patches, and I am confident that they appreciate, and will take care of everything that you can send along that line. I think ahead twenty and more years, and know how proud and happy you will be of that collection in the years to come. The *Hawkeye* killed the story, and I am so thankful. I just must stop in and thank them for it – for the presses were running by the time I called them, about your change in plans. It is time to put the kids to bed, so I will quit my letter writing for the night. I hope you can get that package of clothes and the Christmas cards which I sent to SLO. I think you will be glad to look at them, while you lie in bed. Don't worry about not writing long letters while you are convalescing – I'll understand – just so I know that you are getting along all right. Much love, my dear, and "Happy Dreams."          Essie Mae


December 31, 1944          Sunday Morning
Dearest Gerald,

This will be another way of spending New Year's Eve for you, won't it? I am hoping you are feeling pert by this time, but, of course, I don't know much about the nature of the operation, so all I can do is hope.

On Friday we all went to Mechanicsville, and took Anne with us for her first visit to a farm. She was so excited about the prospect that she got up at three o'clock in the night and got dressed all by herself, and then went in and told her folks she was ready to go. The weather was perfect, and I am glad it worked out so that she could go, for she behaved beautifully, and she really had the time of her life, with the corn-sheller, the calves, etc., not to mention the kittens. It was that same evening that George got sick, so if we hadn't gone then, we wouldn't have made it. Tommy is just now complaining about his tummy, so I suppose this bug will go the rounds. I am very thankful that we got thru Christmas all right, and that it will be over before school begins. Mother came home with us from McVille for a few days.

Are you getting good care in the hospital? Perhaps you can tell us all about it some time, but don't worry because you can't send us the long letters as is your custom – we understand. It is very mild outdoors today – thank goodness. There was just enough snow on the sidewalks to make the sled pull easily, and yet it was hardly below freezing. Hope that the package of Christmas cards reaches you soon, for it will help to pass the time away to look at them. I started my scrap book – "for my grandchildren" – of all the programs that I have had a part in, and newspaper clippings, and "fan mail," etc., and I would like to have some of those "appreciation" cards to put in. It is really quite a scrap book, and I'd like to make similar ones for you and each of the kids. I got a different type of scrap book than any of our others, for they are bound like a regular book, and only library shelves would eventually look like a "set" of books – just larger in size than the encyclopedias. In fact, I think a scrap book of all your letters would be interesting, and would make a "real" book – *The Life of a Red Cross Man in World War II.*

We are having scalloped potatoes and ham, and squash, for dinner today, and roast beef loin for New Year's dinner. I'll probably wash "to start the New Year out right."

January 1, 1945.

Last night, Tommy and I stayed up to see the New Year in, and when twelve o'clock came we rang our bells, drank toasts to all our loved ones, and each of us made three wishes on our candles. Of course, we kissed each other and sang "Auld Lang Syne," too. Tommy's wishes were (1) that he would be the best boy in the fifth grade, (2) that this New Year would be the happiest one yet, and (3) that Daddy would soon be home. I wished that the war would be over in 1945, that we would all stay well, and that we would celebrate 1946 together. He is still in bed this morning (9:30) but he is awake, and feeling fine. George was feeling quite disgusted to think he couldn't get out and celebrate, but he is up and around this morning and I hope will be able to deliver his papers today.

It is cold and windy this morning, and the house is cold, for I didn't get up in the middle of the night and fix the fire as I have been doing lately. Tommy is calling for help in getting up, so I guess I better bring this to a close, and Wish you happy days, and Happy New Year.

Much love from all of us, Essie Mae

Gerald's hernia operation was performed on Tuesday, January 2, 1945

# January 1945
### "The war now looks like a long drawn out affair"
### "We are still having sub-zero weather … the kids have good warm clothes"

"Genevieve Eppens, whose husband, Glen, was in the Coast Guard, recalled: 'I read and reread his letters … Neither of us had much news to write, but we poured out our hearts to each other, longing for the day when we could be together again'."
– Emily Yellin, *Our Mother's War*, 8

Mount Vernon, Iowa
January 2, 1945    Tuesday evening
Dearest Gerald,

Since I mailed your letter to you yesterday, we have had three letters from you, one to each of the kids, and to me, and the package has come, too. The package was simply wonderful. I think my Mexican basket is SO nice – and I certainly can put it to good use for "special" occasions. I haven't anything like it at all. The boys are tickled pink over their shoulder patches, and we are dreaming up a suitable way to mount them.

School starts for all of us tomorrow, and we are ready for it. We all look forward to vacation, and then we are glad to get back to routine again. I have been glad to have Mother here for a few days, and we have gotten the washing, ironing, and mending all done. George was short eight papers tonight, by some mistake of the company, for the correct number was listed on the package, and it took SOME maneuvering on my part to help him, to get a paper for each house – altho' there are a number of places where there are apartments, where the people had to use just one paper instead of two. I washed Tommy's and my hair tonight in the kitchen sink – the shaking of ashes, and shoveling coal certainly makes my hair dirtier than it has ever gotten before. We are still having sub-zero weather!

We had a nice evening tonight, just doing spelling words. I pronounced the words in my shorthand book, and the kids wrote them. I sat on the oven door, and grandma and the kids crowded up as close as they could to the stove. Altho' it is only nine-thirty, I think I better get to bed, for this has been a strenuous day, and tomorrow will be a busy one. I must remember to set the clock for 3:30 to refire the furnace.

Love, 'S'Mae

Mount Vernon, Iowa
January 3, 1945    Wednesday morning
Dearest Gerald,

I am enclosing a letter from Mrs. Forbes which came today, and which was quite a shock. It is always the "best of the lot" that are taken, or so it seems. I wrote to her at Christmas time, and this is her reply. It was very nice of her to send all these clippings, and I will put them in the scrap book, as soon as you send them back.*

Your letter of December 29 was in the mail also, telling of the delay in getting to the hospital. Since I have been assuming for a week or so that you have already been there, maybe my letters will be timed better than if I had known the real facts. At any rate, you know that we are wishing and trusting that you are getting along as well as can be "expected." The kids were happy to get back to school and came in this noon all bubbling with news. Tommy is so disgusted with me for not accepting the vice-presidency of the Parent-Teacher's, for as he says, "I would be so proud to tell the kids that MY MOTHER was the vice-president." I told him that that would mean that less time with him in the evenings, but he lavishly said, "I wouldn't CARE." Am just about ready to go up to typing class.

Hope you are getting good care, and that you will soon feel like yourself again,
Much love, 'S'Mae

January 5, 1945    Friday
Dearest Gerald,

Two letters from you yesterday – written Dec. 29 after you went to the hospital – and including the very welcome check. It is hard to imagine that you are having such balmy weather, for it is SO cold here. I certainly am pleased with my Mexican basket. We ration the Hershey's very carefully, and I am saving the precious Whitman's for some very special occasion.

Thank goodness, the kids are right in the groove about their wraps, and they dress warmly when they go out. The session that I was going thru with George when you were here is certainly bearing results, and he has been simply wonderful lately. Last night, the *Gazette* shorted him eleven papers, and I phoned them, and they sent the missing ones down about eight o'clock. You never can tell what kind of notion he is going to take – His latest is "to be the BEST boy in his class" and apparently, he is making some kind of new record. I am certainly pleased and all too happy to help him with his spelling, etc., so he can get out of the semester tests. He has spent a good deal of time in the evenings drawing pictures, and he has become quite skillful at pictures of "military." He knows a lot of the history connected with the various divisions, and how they worked out the designs for their patches, and I think he could work up a very interesting "speech" about it, if he would. He could even use some of his drawings in connection with it. I have to work on him about it "very subtly," for he doesn't care for speechmaking and he would just have to "lose himself" in his subject – but I think he could do it.

Hope your mail get to the hospital promptly, and that you are over the worst of your session.
Lots of love, 'S'Mae

---

* Captain Forbes was the pilot of the B-17 "Floozy" which ran out of gas and made an emergency landing near Lisbon in 1942.

Mount Vernon, Iowa
January 8, 1945    Monday
Dearest Gerald,

I have just written to Mr. Luecke, telling him how much I appreciate his having taken the time and trouble to write to me telling me that your operation was a success, and reassuring me that you are getting very good care.

I realize that I slipped in not getting a letter off to you on Saturday, but I was so darn busy. My main job for the day – as I had planned it ahead of time – was to take the shirts back and try to exchange them. It took me all morning to get the house cleaning done, and then when I called Johnsons to ask them if I could do errands for them in CR, it turned out that they had a whole list of things for me to do – which of course I was most happy to do – including buying snow pants for Anne. Since both the kids were busy, I took Anne with me, and we spent the whole PM in CR shopping for everything from snow pants to record-changers. The Johnsons were very grateful, and invited the kids and me over for supper last night – and I was delighted – and Bertha had that delicious chicken and rice, which she served to all of us just before you went away last year. The kids loved it, and took great pains with their clothes. George read out loud to Anne, and we had a nice time discussing everything under the sun together.

It is much warmer this morning, and the trees are covered with hoar frost. Tommy took me "for a ride" down Presbyterian Hill Saturday, and of course we "wrecked" about half way down, and I slid about half a block on the northwest corner of my anatomy. I was stiff yesterday, but it is practically gone now, and it was really fun. Tommy was very serious and quite nervous with the responsibility of taking me down.

Much love, 'S'Mae

January 9, 1945    Tuesday morning
Dearest Gerald,

Your first letter written after the operation, and one from a hospital worker, came yesterday, and made us very happy. We are so glad to hear that you are getting along so well, and that you are a "good patient." Tommy and I were particularly interested in the idea that you may be doing some craft work. I hope you do – it is very interesting, and of course, is right along the line that interests us so much.

You might be interested in a sample of some amusing table conversation last eve. Supper was late, for I didn't leave the Art lab until nearly five, and then I had to go down town for groceries. But the kids took the delay very well, and we talked very gaily. Tommy was telling about someone who didn't wash for ten years, so I started to tell him about the filthiness of the monks in the Middle Ages – and then asked, "You know what the Middle Ages are, don't you?" Oh, yes, that's what YOU'RE IN! So then we had to tell him the difference between middle age, and Middle Ages, with capital letters. Then we used the word, vocabulary, and I asked Tommy if he knew what that word meant. Oh sure – it means the words you DON'T KNOW. (Laughter, by Mother and George). Well, says Tommy, the teacher writes the word vocabulary on the board, and underneath it she puts down all the words in the reading lesson that we DON'T KNOW. That just goes to show how kids get some of the ideas they do. I hope we set him straight on that one tho'.

[ ] We learned how to make brackets in typing yesterday and I just demonstrated this for George. Tommy is busy after school these days skating on the tennis courts. That really is a very nice winter project for the Lion's to do. He has been playing BB with his pals from the fifth grade. They play in the cage at the gym, and he is "very hopeful of making the team, as a forward!"

I hope that you keep right on improving, and that you have a contented time while you are in the hospital – it was very nice of you to arrange for the "extra" messages.

Much love, 'S'Mae

January 10, 1945   Wednesday morning
Dearest Gerald,

Another day well started. I was so lazy this morning that I took a shortcut to warming up the kitchen, and just lit the gas stove. The kids both were slow getting underway this morning – they are both just on the edge of colds, and we had gargles to mix up, etc., etc. I can't ever remember a time when George has been on such good behavior, and after arranging a "point system" whereby he is given "paper" credit for helpfulness, he just stands around begging for jobs to do! It can't last, but I am certainly enjoying it. Between Clint [Keubler]'s being gone, and also the garbage man, life gets kind of complicated, tho", and I was very weary yesterday after carrying out eight buckets of ashes and clinkers. I just took them outside, and the kids have promised to carry them to the end of the lot, and dump them. George's semester exams start today and he is looking forward to some good grades – we have been studying together evenings – he pronounces my shorthand words, and I give him his spelling, etc. It works very well, and I, at least, have been doing better, and I trust he will be practically perfect. He has to learn to define meanings of words like "perambulations," and "ambiguous," so he is really "on the ball."

Jacques Jolas told me this morning that my name had been mentioned last night in connection with the Lion's show – I would much rather not perform, but if I am called, I won't refuse, because I really appreciate the skating rink and swimming pool which the kids have enjoyed. Our final requirement in Art is to write a paper on "something" – and I am going to write about the "Art in Bells." Not from the music angle, but from design, craftsmanship, materials, history, and the effect of different countries on the types of bells which are put out. I have been thinking that someday I will be doing a club paper about my bells, and this would be a good time to get the material organized. The teacher is quite in sympathy with the idea, and since I made my bell in pottery class, she has become quite interested. She says that no one has ever made a bell in her department before.

Hope you continue to feel better all the time. Much love, 'S'Mae

10 January 1945          Wednesday evening
Dear Dad,

I sure am glad you sent all the insignia you have sent a lot of them we didn't know what were.

Over at the tennis court the Lions Culb made a skateing place where I have been skateing every day except to day because I had a head cold. I think you remember the 5th grade football team well now we have a 5th grade basket ball team in which I am a forward. In the cage up at the college is where we practice.

I sure would like you to tell me what your craft work is.

### Hope you Get
### Well Soon

Sincerely,
          Tommy
          Hill  Hb

Mount Vernon, Iowa
January 11, 1945   Thursday morning
Dearest Gerald,

This was my early morning up here at the office, but we all went to bed about 8:30 last night, so it wasn't so hard to get up this morning. I was supposed to write a paper in Art criticism about modern paintings hanging in the exhibition hall, and since I didn't get it done, I decided to cut that class and stay and practice typing. Tommy's cold is better this morning. He wrote the enclosed letter last night, and it makes me realize that he needs some help with some of his school work. Nothing seems to worry him, and it doesn't matter whether he gets a few words misspelled, or not. George was the only one in his class to get 100 in his semester Spelling test. What really made George happy yesterday was the fact that that old watch of mine, which I took to C.R. before Christmas to be fixed, came yesterday. I was told that it would be the first of March before it would be fixed, so it was a grand surprise, and George is simply delighted. He said this morning, "Boy, I don't envy anybody in the world, now that I have my new suit, my new shirt, and my watch."

I gave Elaine Rowe, our renter, a can of my home canned peaches for Christmas, and last weekend she asked me if she could trade a can of apricots for a jar of peaches. We thought it over, and finally decided I wouldn't be a sucker, because she would have gotten the best of the deal, so I told her I didn't have enough peaches, and the kids don't like apricots anyway. Must be on my way home, now, and go around by town for groceries.

Much love from all of us. 'S'Mae

Mount Vernon, Iowa
January 11, 1945   Thursday evening
Dearest Gerald,

Your two letters, enclosing the Air Force patch, and telling of your operation and the big batch of mail you got one day, came today.  The kids were so thrilled over the insignia – that is a good way to send them, for it keeps up their interest, and makes them appreciate each one all the more.  Tommy was feeling pretty good, from his cold this noon.  George got 99 in his literature test, and said that History was very easy.  We were both saddened by the fact that the rabbit had got out and disappeared.  We have been doing a kind of awful thing, I guess – but we have been letting him run loose in the basement.  He has gotten very tame, but he found the door open and got out.  He will probably turn up again, however.  It is not very cold this morning, thank goodness.  I had made a reservation to go to an AAUW dinner meeting last night, and so I hurried up and got supper for three boys at home, and went to my dinner anyway.  It is really quite funny, how something always happens on AAUW night, and I have had to cancel my reservation time after time – I just didn't do it this time, and the boys got along fine.  Tommy was asleep when I got home, and George was out taking a walk with your nephew, Edward Hemenway, who arrived today.

Much love, EMH

January 13, 1945   Saturday morning
Dearest Gerald,

This looks like it would be a very busy day, but I do want to give you a summary of the last 24 hours.  Edward Hemenway contacted the college yesterday afternoon (I introduced him to Dean McGregor), and as a result of the interview I think he feels that Drake will suit him better.  He was at Columbia [Missouri] nearly two terms, but he flunked two subjects the first term and was still flunking in the second term, when he was "washed out," so he didn't get any credits for the second term at all.  Cornell will only give him 8 credits for his work, and he says Drake will give him 12½ - and in addition, he will have work in Des Moines for room and board.  I pointed out that Cornell has a higher academic standard than Drake and that they put great emphasis on good grades in HS in the selection of their students.  He is at the college talking to Dean McGregor again.

Bertha [Johnson] invited George and me to come over to their place last eve to hear the reading of Al's newest play, which is to be the next production.  There is a part in it for George – which thrilled and pleases us very much.  We didn't get home until very late, and I made myself as comfortable as possible on the davenport, when Tommy called about 2:30 and said he was sick.  Of course, I couldn't get the pan to him fast enough, and he had one awful mess in his bed.  He was nauseated every hour and a half or so until about six, and then settled down to sleep soundly until about eight thirty.  I was so pooed by that time, that I didn't get up until late, so we have just finished doing the dishes now at ten 'clock.  I have washing water heating, for I have a lot of bedclothes to clean up, in addition to the regular two-weeks' washing.  Will Durant has a new book, *Caesar and Christ* – of the "masterpiece" variety – not a novel, which is scholarly and interesting in the parallels that he draws between the Roman Empire of Jesus' day, and the United States of the present.  It is not a happy picture – but it makes one think.*

[Later] Before I could get back to this letter, Rev. Arnold came.  I cleared off a chair so he could sit down – the davenport was still made up as a bed.  He suggested that we all go down to the farm to see Mother some time – which I thought was very kind of him.  It is now eleven o'clock, and not much accomplished, but at least you know what we are doing, and that we are not wanting you to get lonesome for news about what goes on at home.  Tommy is getting dressed now.

Much love, Essie Mae

January 15, 1945   Monday 7:30 A.M.
Dearest Gerald,

Just a note, written on a corner of the kitchen table while the kids get "waked" up.  We were all "done in" this weekend, and spent most of the time being lazy – went to bed at 7:30 last night, so we should be rested.  X-day for me, and with an enormous washing Saturday, Tommy sick, Edward here, etc., I was really weary yesterday.  Feel all right now tho'.  Tommy is fine too.

---

* *Caesar and Christ* was v.3 of Will and Aerial Durant's eleven volumes of history; their 10th volume won a Pulitzer Prize.

101

It was very mild & foggy this weekend for a change. I delivered half of George's papers yesterday on the sled. He was tired and cranky, and I shouldn't have kept him up so late at Johnsons' Friday night. He is all steamed up about being in the play, and I'm sure he'll do a good job. Edward went home Sat. P.M. to talk things over with his folks in Clarion. Don't know what he'll decide to do, but whatever it is will be O.K. I can't think he'll ever finish college anyway – he thinks maybe he'd like to stay in the Army after the war – and I don't know but what that would be a good a solution as any. He is an awfully good hearted kid. It is too bad he has such a lack of "social polish" as a result of his background. But everything will work out all right, I'm sure.

I suppose you are able to walk around some now. Do take it easy!

Love from all of us, 'S'Mae.


Mount Vernon, Iowa
January 16, 1945  Tuesday
Dear Dad,

I am writing this just before I do to the movie "American Romance." I'll leave at about 7:05. I am also going to study American History. I was so pleased in my semester test grades. In English I missed 6 out of 237 points and got A. In History I had – 1 out of 88 and got A+. In Literature I had -1 and to A. In Science I had A. In spelling I had 100% and got A. I have not received my Arithmetic grades yet.

In American History we are studying about the 1850's in our History. Today we talked about the lives of R. E. Lee, Jefferson Davis, U. S. Grant and Abe Lincoln. We also talked about the "Compromise of 1850."

In English we are study how to write social letters. It is very dull and I'm not apply much of what I learned in this letter. In English we're talking and reading lyrics, "poems that sing." Today we had one of Carl Sandburg's and Robert Frost's poems. In Science we ware learning about heat, radiation, concuction, convection, etc. It is very interesting. In Arithmetic we are still talking about equasions.

Our insignia collection is doing fine but we now have FIVE of the insignia [diagram inserted] which is the Ack-Ack Artillery Command Western Defense Command. You just sent another one.

I'm glad your felling better and we all hope you'll ship out with your division.

Love,
George

Dearest Gerald –

Will just add a note to G's. letter for my "daily." OES last eve was very nice, but not nearly as "fancy" as Lisbon does. An amazing number of people I didn't know. Geo. goes to play practice tonight & I will tutor. Mrs. Rowe is going to sit in on the session. Must hurry lunch now – Much love – 'S'Mae


January 16, 1945  Tuesday
Dearest Gerald,

Your long letter written in pencil with George's letter enclosed was most interesting. I am so glad to hear that you are getting along so well – and of course, kind of disconcerted to hear about the changes in plans for your Division. I am just philosophical about it, hoping that if it is in "the cards" you will be allowed to go, and if for some reason, it falls to you lot to stay, it is all probably for the best. I am only SO thankful that your operation is over, and that you are getting along so well. I am sure that you have shown the military what good work you can do, and if they say "Nix" on shipping you out, it is just Fate, altho' I know how mightily disappointed you will be. You will have other chances, tho'. It is certainly a great joy to know how nice all the officers and your associates have been thru all of this, and I hope you have had enough mail to remind you of those far away, who love you and are concerned about you.

George and Bobby [Gaston] had a "falling out," but he seems contented and not lonesome. Bobby has been doing "dangerous" chem experiments, and I really am not sorry to have G. out of it, altho it was a nice friendship. Bobby has been slumping in his grades since the breakup, but G. has certainly been in the groove. Tommy has gotten interested in learning to type correctly, and he spent the whole eve last night, working on the "home row." I certainly would be glad if he learned the keyboard, even if his interests slip before he really gets very far.

Much love, 'S'Mae

Mount Vernon, Iowa
January 18, 1945   Thursday
Dearest Gerald,

If and when the day comes when you get overseas, and we don't hear from you for perhaps a month at a time, I guess it will behoove us to remember the days when you were in the hospital, and we got a grand big letter every day. Yesterday's letter told of the good news that you were up and dressed and going to mess. That is really wonderful – you really must have been in good shape physically to have gotten along so well. I suppose by this time, you are again getting things organized to go with your Division when they move. I hope all your dreams come true.

Tommy is all excited about making a model airplane, of the kind that is cut out of balsa wood, and then it is pinned onto a pattern as it is made. George had one at one time, but never finished it. He got the idea, and is working at it all alone, and is terribly happy about it. Geo. did the nicest thing for me last eve – the kitchen was simply a mess, but while I prepared for my tutoring session, he pitched in and washed up all the dishes and put them away, and even swept the floor – all alone. It certainly was a great joy to me, and helped me tremendously. He has been taking his "reward" in the form of "credit points," and he has accumulated over 200, one point being equal to the "work" of drying one plate. Geo. went to play practice last eve, and didn't get home till 10:30. I am afraid he is going to get tired before it is all over, but I am sure he will do a good job of it. After I finish my last classes of the semester tomorrow, one of my first jobs is to type his script. The man from the Cincinnati play company promises to come out for the production, as he did for *Days without Daddy*, when he was pleased enough to buy it.[13]

The kids both got their grade cards yesterday, and did exceedingly well – practically the same as they have done before. G. got a B in conduct, and all other A's except B in Science. He did get a D in music, however, which we are hoping won't keep him off the honor roll for the semester. If it does, he will just have to take it, for the reason is that he dropped Band. Tommy got B in spelling for the 3d six weeks, but his semester average was C. We are going to concentrate on Spelling, and try to keep it up to a B. He is like I am, I am afraid, however – he just isn't a good natural speller, like you and G.

Must go up town now for groceries, so will say "Bye." Much love, from all of us,
            'S'Mae


January 17, 1945   Friday P.M.
Dearest Gerald,

The mail was late today, so I'll just dash off a note & rush for the P.O. Hope everything goes O.K. & you keep well! Enclosed is your O.E.S. card. You should get the *Hawkeye* this week, for I checked the address & it was S.L.O.            Hastily – Love – Essie Mae


January 22, 1945   Monday A.M.
Dearest Gerald,

If plans are really going as you anticipate, I know you must be very excited and happy. This was a nice quiet weekend. I was rather poo-ed on Saturday, but played "lazy" and felt fine yesterday. The kids & I went to church yesterday (M.V.) and had an early dinner. The kids went the movie *Arsenic and Old Lace* while I went to Johnsons and typed for a couple of hours & then took Anne for a short visit to the Highs. The Rev. Arnolds and we are going down there for supper Wed. eve.*

George's English class had to write "something about the RX" and G. wrote a very nice story about a F.D. He expressed himself so nicely, that I hope he gets it back so I can send it to you. "His hero" was a successful lawyer instead of banker, but he went to St. Louis – Washington – SLO, etc. They are both working on model airplanes again & never have been so cooperative & appreciative of each other's work. Geo. just came home from school not feeling well – so I must tend to him. Don't think it's serious.

Much love,  'S'Mae

---

* *Arsenic and Old Lace* (1944) starred Cary Grant, with Raymond Massey; directed by Frank Capra; it was very popular.

Mount Vernon, Iowa
January 23, 1945   Tuesday
Dearest Gerald,

As you would say, we hit the jack pot yesterday with three letters from you, including the check.  The kids certainly get a kick out of their insignia in each letter.  I know you are happy today, in being released from the hospital.  I have been wondering how large an incision it took, and how many stitches you had.  From now on, if things go as you anticipate, you will be very busy, and soon on the move.  It doesn't seem possible.  I surely hope that nothing comes up to interfere.

It seems strange not to have to get out early in the mornings, and dash to school.  I have tried to work out a "budget" of time, so I wouldn't get too lazy, but it will have to be a very elastic one, to take care of emergencies, like waiting on G. yesterday, and helping him deliver papers, etc.  Tommy was proud to have gotten 100 last week in spelling, as a result of our "home work."  I forgot to tell you that Bunny came back, but I don't mind it, and everything goes smoothly on that score.

Heaps of love, 'S'Mae


January 24, 1945   Wednesday morning
Dearest Gerald,

I had hoped to get this letter written before the kids went to school this morning, but one thing after another has come up, and now it is 10:15.

Bertha Johnson came about nine o'clock, and brought some more script for me to copy.  She told me about **a** very hot session which took place at Lion's Club last night.  It seems that Russell Cole had said not to grant the Lion's any production date unless they guaranteed that the minstrel show would be absolutely "clean."  He suggested that a script be submitted for approval.  That didn't help Al's feeling about the matter, and so last night it all came out at the Club.  Luckily, Russell was there, and they all went round and round.  Rex Dean assured them that "he got around a lot" and had heard no criticism of last year's show – and when the committee tried to pin Russell down to name anything that was objectionable, he just couldn't do it.  The upshot of it was that the show was left "to the judgment of the committee" with the assurance that the Club would all stand back of them, even if criticism did arise – "and you can't please everyone."  Al Johnson is going to be one of the end men, and Bertha is going to direct the show.  It is too bad that all this unpleasantness had to come up, but it leaves a bad taste in their mouths.  It certainly reflects Russell's attitude toward the theatre, too, which makes the Johnsons quite unhappy.  The redeeming feature, however, is that Al was made a full prof., so he must be getting some credit for his work.[*]

George wrote a nice "fan letter" to a soldier whose picture he saw in the paper last night.  The man had service stripes indicating 27 years of service in the Army.  It was a very nicely composed letter and I think it was nice of him to write it, even though he never gets an answer.

Hope everything goes as you plan – I know you won't be able to write much of the details after you really get going, but try to remember it all.

Good luck, and heaps of love, 'S'Mae


January 25, 1945   Thursday
Dearest Gerald,

The days are slipping by so fast!  I hope that you haven't had any serious pains, as you described in the letter we got yesterday.  Mrs. Rowe tells of getting a card from of friend of theirs in England who has been required to take 6 months for recup. from hernia operation.  He isn't allowed to come home, nor is he allowed to do anything, so he just "chaffs at the bit" – I'm glad yours is over!

The pictures were swell!  That camera certainly takes remarkable pictures.  There are no films in town at the present.  It was nice to see how your friends really look, and to see the pictures of "where you are."  I was glad to show them to Mother & she liked them.

---

[*] A minstrel show opened with a "walk around" by two "end men" in blackface with an interlocutor.  President Cole was ahead of his time; most white Americans didn't realize how offensive minstrel shows were to people of color.  For history of minstrel shows, quoting Library of Congress: https://memory.loc.gov/ammem/vshtml/vsforms.html).

Russell Cole called Al Johnson yesterday & read a letter from Al's publishing Co. suggesting that Russell contact *Look* magazine for a feature on the premier of this new play. He is pleased, of course, and negotiations are under way. There is only a bare chance that it will actually go thru, but it was nice to have Russell realize that the "Little Theatre" was what was advertising Cornell in <u>some</u> parts of the country. The timing of the affair was perfect – just following Russell's seeming insistence on "censoring" what is put on in the Theatre.

George is going to have his church membership transferred to M.V. next Sunday – at his own insistence. We are scheduled to have the Junior Youth Fellowship here in a couple of weeks. I'll be glad to have them – although some will have to "sit on the floor" – about 20 kids usually show up for meetings. Geo. says he got very good comments on "extemporaneous" speech-ing in English class yesterday. He was pleased with the 27th Div. insignia, too. [EMH's sketch inserted]

***27th Infantry Division***

Glad to hear the bank is leaving your "status" as "is" – that is always nice to fall back on. The war looks like a long drawn out affair to me, tho'. However things work out will be all right with me, tho' – I feel the experience I have had in school this fall – is "something I'll always have" and I'm glad to have had the opportunity. The typing skill will never come amiss – even for private affairs – and I am constantly surprised at the demand for "public" typing. Must go uptown now. Heaps of love, 'S'Mae


Mount Vernon, Iowa
January 26, 1945   Friday
Dearest Gerald,

I thought you would be interested in the "story" George wrote as an English assignment [see Photo Album]. They had to write "something" about the RX, and this was George's contribution. It lacks much of course, from an adult point of view, but I thought it was real cute, and he got an A on it. It shows he has followed your experiences pretty closely. I was sorry to see in yesterday's *Hawkeye,* that his music grade kept him off the semester honor roll, but he is right out in front, and has been such a good boy that I don't mind too much. I didn't sleep very well last night and I am sort of weary today. The kids both seem interested in learning to type with the touch system, and if I can put it across to them, I will be satisfied that the project was worthwhile. They will use it more than I ever will.

It begins to feel like spring outdoors, altho' the ground is still covered with snow. It warms up and melts during the day, but of course, freezes again at night. It is nice and sunshiny, tho'.

It was disheartening to read about a troop ship being sunk, in last night's paper. Most of them get thru all right tho'. Dilleys have not heard from their son-in-law since Dec. 6th, and they surely worry about it. The CR paper is full of casualties every night.

Much love, 'S'Mae


January 27, 1945   Saturday morning
Dearest Gerald,

Another Saturday morning! Grandma was the first one up, and got the kitchen fire going. I was next, and got breakfast, just in time for George to get to rehearsal at 8:30. Tommy was lazy and refused to be budged until nearly 10:00. By that time, I was up to my ears in washing, - more than two weeks of dirty clothes. I heard yesterday that Stimson's grandson is among the trainees at Cornell now!*

All my exams are over now, and I wrote the fastest, in a timed five-minute writing that I have ever done – 58 words a minute, counting five strokes for a word, and subtracting ten for each of the two mistakes that I made.

We are so involved with our own little rounds of activity that it just doesn't seem possible that you are deep in the job of getting ready to go overseas. The last letter we got from you told about the pains you had after getting out and around for the first time, and I am hoping that you have had no recurrence of them. Am hoping for a letter this morning. We are having waffles for dinner. You would just be amazed at the prices of food, and things continue to get more scarce. I bought a bushel of potatoes yesterday, and Harry Dilley told me that his jobber says they are going to "run out," too. Much love, 'S'Mae

---

* Rumor untrue: Henry L. Stimson, Secretary of War in WWII, had no descendants. He was infertile due to mumps as an adult.

I had a bad moment the other night when Harold Ennis called me and "said he had gotten a telegram from the RX." He immediately went on to say, that Private Ward McConologue had requested the RX to send Mrs. Rowena Stucklager's address. I don't know the reason, of course, but I referred him to Johnsons. 'S'Mae

#1
Mount Vernon, Iowa
January 29, 1945 [Monday morning]
Dearest Gerald,

This is letter No. 1, and I am making a carbon of it. Each of your letters sounds more and more final – and they must be if plans go as scheduled. I hope when you get on the train, that you have good accommodations, for one can get most awfully tired, traveling. I trust you "got your innards" all straightened out and are feeling well – as can "be expected." You certainly have been very lucky, and I hope it keeps up. Winter has come back with a bang! My coal pile is getting low again, and the house was awfully hard to heat yesterday. Temp. below zero.

Tommy stayed at home from school this morning – his cold hangs on, but he plans to go this afternoon. I felt rotten yesterday, achey, etc., but used the heat pad on my shoulders most of the afternoon, and went to bed at 9:00, so feel pretty well this morning. I have been thinking, that it is just about a year ago, that I finally went to the Navy doctor, to get something done about my general "condition." I certainly feel a lot better than I did then!!

Bertha and Al [Johnson]'s thirteenth wedding anniversary is tomorrow – the 30th. He is getting her an unabridged dictionary - $22 – and I may go to CR tomorrow and pick it up. George joined the MV [Methodist] Church yesterday. Everything is fine here, and we'll be looking for letters, "as long as we can."

Much love,<br>'S'Mae

#2
January 30, 1945  Tuesday
Dearest Gerald,

Your #2 letter came yesterday, written the 25th, and surely sounded like the time was getting very short. I have been reorganizing things around here this morning to make room for the lockers when they come, and I found a sleeveless sweater which you left when you were here. WOULD YOU LIKE TO HAVE ME SHIP IT TO YOU? IS IT ALL RIGHT FOR ME TO USE THE RX STATIONERY WHICH YOU LEFT? I am sure we will be very thrilled over what you have sent in the locker – it will seem like Christmas again. And speaking of Christmas, it just occurs to me that it is possible that it will be more than "Christmas time" again before you are back home! I'm telling you IT JUST DOESN'T SEEM POSSIBLE!

It would be fine if you did write back some of your experiences, like the CR girl, whose writing I am including. I wish I could think of some way of using the material you have already written in letters, I am sure that few, if any, RX men have done such a thorough job of it. And, as I have said before, I think it should be "shared."

It will be a break for you if you can get a place on the train where you can rest and relax all that is necessary. It will be a long trip and you'll need all the rest you can get. It will be a break for you, too, to be able to see NY while you are in service. "From coast to coast," isn't it? I am so glad that you had lots of mail when you were in the hospital. I know the time must have passed pretty slowly, even at best – and I'm glad to know that you realized we were all thinking about you here at home. I certainly hope you have gotten the *Hawkeyes* by this time. I just checked with them on the address, and they have it correct now. By the way, would you like to have me clip the *GI Gazette* which comes in every Sunday paper, and the summary of Iowa news from the Sunday *Register*? We have been getting the *Register* on Sundays lately, and we decided that we would stop ordering a *Gazette* for ourselves, and put that money in the *Register*, by the week, so now we will have two papers for the same price, for we usually get a chance to read the *Gazette* anyway.

The kids saw *Arsenic and Old Lace* and enjoyed it. I haven't read *Leave Her to Heaven* but will try to get hold of it. Jim and Rachie have gotten quite interested in purebred Herefords. They are in CR today attending a cattle sale. Mother expects to home with them tonight. My cold still hangs on, so I had them do some shopping for me.

It is still below zero this morning, but Mother got up and had the kitchen fire going before I got up, so that was nice. Hope you are feeling fine, and that you get 100% of everything out of your new experiences.

We are realizing that we probably won't be hearing from you so often, but it has been wonderful to have had you in this country long enough to have gotten things routinized here at home, and to feel that I am "used" to looking after things, so I feel prepared. I just don't see how I would have done it a year ago, or even six months ago – so I am thankful. Love, from every one of us, and a "good by kiss" if this is the time for it.

'S'Mae

#3
Mount Vernon, Iowa
January 31, 1945  Wednesday[14]
Dearest Gerald,

I am writing this on the back of a "script" I wrote in honor of Bertha and Al [Johnson]'s wedding anniversary [see Photo Album]. It is a "take-off" on his latest play, which is called *Love Your Neighbor*. Three of the main characters are Tessy, Johnny, and Wingy, and you can see how I used the idea with my characters. Some of the expressions, such as "attractive matron in her early forties" are taken from his play. The catch to it, however, is that we weren't able to get the pencil sharpener after all, but they got a kick out of the "play" and appreciated the idea. Rachie got an unabridged dictionary in Cedar Rapids for Bertha – Al's gift – and Al was thrilled over it. It really is a grand book – to the tune of $22. This morning, I put your civilian shirts, etc., which were in the dresser in the lavatory into one of the lockers which you have here, and repacked linens, etc., tablecloths, napkins, etc., so that there will be room for the new lockers when they come. We certainly are crowded in this place, but I still have hopes of shifting things around so what we use is easily available.

I have a job of typing for Tommy this morning – He has been involved in writing a "radio" script to use at school, and nothing would do but that he must have 8 copies – one for each of his cast. I think the teacher set them quite a job – to write a 20-minute script, but they padded it with news, weather, etc., until they can do it, I guess. He made a microphone out of a broom handle, and has taken the whole thing very seriously.

My cold, and Tommy's, hangs on in a disgusting fashion, but we are drinking lemonade, etc., and it will eventually wear itself out I suppose. I got the fire going in good fashion this morning, so that is a satisfaction.

I hope you're able to get some "sight-seeing" done in NY. That will be most interesting!

I saw the book of "testimonials" which Judge Littell's students wrote for him yesterday, and it really is impressive. It is on display at the library, and Judge happened to be there when I was looking at it. He said he had heard from you recently, but that he wished you had written something for the book. Most of the letters were about a page in length, telling how much his teaching had meant to the individual, and how they appreciated his friendship, etc., etc. I certainly hope you have some *Hawkeyes* by this time. We didn't get a letter from you yesterday, and I know the time is getting very short! This letter will eventually catch up with you, and you will know that we are thinking of you, and wondering how you are getting along. Must get at Tommy's typing now.

Much love from all of us. 'S'Mae

## February 1945
## The 97th Division moves from California to New Jersey, and sails to Europe
## More Letters to Jerry Hill from the "Home Front" in Iowa

> "At noon on February 27 I asked the House of Commons to approve the results of the Crimea Conference. I said, 'Let Germany ever recognize that it is futile to hope for division among the Allies and that nothing can avert her utter defeat'."
> — Winston Churchill, *Triumph and Tragedy*, 399

#4

Mount Vernon, Iowa
February 1, 1945   Thursday
Dearest Gerald,

I am getting an earlier start on this than I usually do, for the kids are still in bed, and it is only 8:15. It is fairly warm, but I surely will be glad when spring comes, and fire building is a thing of the past. My head is still stuffy, and I am very grateful for the box of Kleenex that Bertha Johnson gave me yesterday. George was certainly thrilled yesterday to receive an answer to the letter he wrote to the soldier whose picture he saw in the paper. He wrote from Camp Blanding, and must have answered immediately. It was a very fine letter, I quote –

Dear George: Received your letter and am alway glad to hear from anyone expectaly children.

I am sending you 2 insignia, the one with the blue, yellow and red stands for Infantry Replacement center, and the other is Mobile forces in Panama. The service ribbons that I wear are the purple heart, Mexican Border, Victory, pre-Pearl Harbor, American Theatre of Operation, South Pacific with two stars, and the presidential citation, and the combat infantry combat badge.

Well, George, if I was you I would keep going to school til I was an old man, a person never gets enough schooling
Yours truly,

An old soldier          S/Sgt. E. T. Welch
P.S. I will try to get you some more insignia later.
Pappy.

I think it is a very nice letter, and needless to say, George was simply thrilled to death.

I copied Tommy's radio script for him yesterday morning – 8 copies in fact, but it wasn't long enough – this "dumb" teacher said it had to be 20 minutes long – so he is going to "pad" it by reading some jokes out of *Saga of American Folk Lore*. Al gave me my first assignment yesterday – some forty letters to write to producers and publishers. There are only two forms to use, however. I ought to have them memorized by the time I'm done!

I am glad that I will be able to get the "official" report on your operation. Hope you continue getting stronger, without any backsets. I agree that illness of yours four years ago Lion's show time was really an awful siege, but it was kinda fun waiting on you, reading out-loud, and receiving your guests. You certainly had lots of callers. That's all for today, I guess. I have to make a trip uptown in the cold, which I'm not looking forward to.

Much love, from all of us, 'S'Mae

#5

February 1, 1945   Thursday evening
Dearest Gerald,

THE FIRST LOCKER CAME TODAY++!! It has been a time of very mixed emotions, for your letter of the 29th also came with the beautiful goodbye messages to us. It was a wonderful thing for you to do, and I was deeply touched. I have forced myself to keep busy all afternoon typing, or I know I couldn't have been very "brave." As it was, the "letters ran together" part of the time, and I make no bones about it. I am really glad you wrote it out, instead of making a recording, for we could only get your message on a "borrowed machine" and this way we have it all the time. You are all set for some wonderful new experiences, and we'll be proud of you all the time. I'll be glad when the time comes that I can tell "the world" that you are "in the thick of it" or on the way at last.

I didn't tell the kids about the locker until they were well started at lunch, and then I had to be broad minded about "what a clean plate consisted of," for they could hardly wait to open it. It was really thrilling, and George has spent the evening arranging it on the wall hanging. It certainly looks impressive. We hung it above the book case, and put the other things on top of the book case. G. is especially anxious to have it in good order when the Fellowship group comes here next week. The *National Geographic* this month tells about a new supplement which is now ready for distribution, which is the most complete listing of insignia available. We are sending for it immediately. Just now, the kids have on their pajamas and are trying out the sleeping bag. There is much giggling and consultation, and planning of how they are going to use it "sometime in the future."

Tommy just said, "Have you told Daddy how glad we are about everything he sent us?" I haven't told you adequately, for I just haven't the words, and besides I get all teary thinking about it.

I got my new coal today, and here is Gaylord's address.

> Lt. Col. G. R. Andre, 0-345332 / Hq. 90th Infantry Division
> Surgeon's Office / APO 390 c/o Postmaster
> New York City / New York

The reading material you sent, I have not had time to do more than glance at. It looks very interesting tho' – Wish someone would ask me to do a speech or write a paper on the RX so I would have occasion to really learn all about it. Will investigate V-mail but it seems awfully small for "our kind of letter," and maybe airmail will go just about as fast. That was Harlan Nelson's experience anyway. I am making carbons of all my letters now, so all you have to do is refer to the number or date, and I'll know what I wrote.

T. just assures me that "Boy! This sleeping bag is sure warm." He wants me to let him sleep there all night! My cold is better tonight I guess – been taking lots of lemon juices all day. It has been awfully cold again today, but I did not have to do much outside today. Wondering "where you are, and how you are, and if you are" all right. I trust the Lord will take care of you, my dear, and bring you back safely. Goodnight, darling, 'S'Mae

#6
Mount Vernon, Iowa
February 3, 1945          Saturday morning
Dearest Gerald,

Your "change of address" card came yesterday. I steamed this open & corrected the date after I had sealed it. What a nice surprise it was to get a letter from you yesterday, (#5) for the note on #4 the day before, I had given up hope of hearing from you "for some time." This is Saturday, and George is out collecting from the customers on his paper route. He plans to put $9 into the bank today, for something he won't tell what. He has been saving very religiously since Xmas, but I don't know for what.

You may be interested to know how the sleeping bag experiment turned out last night. Tommy and I went to rehearsal with G. and when we got home the kids both got into the bag. I fixed their beds so they could go to bed there if it got too crowded, but I didn't hear a thing out of them until 4:30 when I woke up and found the bag empty! George says he remembers thinking "that if I don't get to sleep in about five minutes, I was going to get into my own bed." Then he looked at his watch and saw that it was 1:15, and realized that he had been asleep for some time. The covers were all mixed up by that time, and so they got up. Tommy claims he is going to try it again tonight, but G. is willing to use a bed! I gave them pancakes and sausage this morning for breakfast – camp style.

We have been wondering how long it will take to get all the men started on their way. Whether they go out very rapidly or whether they are sort of staggered. How long it will be from the time you leave until Luecke goes, for instance? – something to remember to tell us. This Youth Fellowship bunch met at Dean's this week, and George said the kids laughed and had a lot of fun looking at early pictures of Judd and the rest of the family. G. is really looking forward to having them here, and showing them his various trophies.*

---

* Judd Dean and EMH were members of the Class of 1926 at Cornell. He was hired by Cornell as a coach in the Athletic Department, and his wresting teams won many championships. He was a Lt. Col. in the US Army Air Force in World War II.

Tommy reports that his radio program at school went off very well and the "play" part of it which he wrote is going to be included in a composite program which the fifth grade will present to the sixth grade, as an audience. I will send you a copy. He said the moron stories from *Folklore* got a big laugh.

[later]   1100 now, and I must be thinking about lunch. It has snowed the last couple of days, and it is very treacherous outdoors, but I have lost my footing only once – there is ice under the snow. How you're going to miss that nice California warmness – I used your atomizer last night, and hoped that your sinus troubles wouldn't come back if you got into a damp climate.

Much love, from all of us, 'S'Mae

No. 7
Mount Vernon, Iowa
February 4, 1945   Sunday
Dearest Gerald,

I have been thinking that it certainly is a good idea to be numbering my letters, for you may be getting these that I mail to New York, sooner than some that went to California last week. I checked with the *Hawkeye* and they have your new address. This has been a lazy day – if you can call any day "lazy" that starts with an early paper delivery! Tommy claims to have spent a very good night in the sleeping bag, and has been unusually giggly all day. We didn't go to church – it sleeted and snowed and is now melting. I think I'll take a nap pretty soon, for Elaine Rowe came down last night, and suggested I use some of her sugar to make some candy, and she stayed too long, for folks who have to get up early in the morning. As to your question about Doug's part in the Lion's discussion about the minstrel, Al reported that Doug really "spoke right out" and asked Russell and Rowley why they had sat there week after week, and listened to the discussions and plans and never said anything – said he "just didn't like this beating around the bush."* He was the one who definitely tried to pin them down as to WHAT the criticisms has been – but which they could not answer very satisfactorily. Al is to be one of the endmen, and Bertha is directing the show.*

I am about to send for some vegetable seeds – aren't you surprised? Mother is the motivating force, of course, but I realize that the food situation is really pretty serious, and with the kids' help I guess we ought to plan on having some kind of garden. I will be completely "cleaned out" of vegetables from former years before this winter is over. Getting sleepy –

Love – 'S'mae

No. 8
February 6, 1945   Tuesday
Dearest Gerald,

It has been about eight days since the last letter we received from you was written, and I just keep wondering and wondering where your travels have taken you, and how you got along. I have been rereading *c/o Postmaster* out loud to the kids, and it takes on a new interest for all of us.

As you can see by the enclosed letters, George has developed a great interest in writing to you. He wouldn't let me read the one he wrote yesterday noon, so I don't know what "secrets" he divulged. He is quite intrigued with the idea of making carbons, and numbering the letters, and altho' he thinks he makes lots of mistakes, I think he does very well on the machine, using the touch system entirely. As soon as the play is over, and he has more free time, I am going to help him with various drills. He does say however, much to my gratification, that his typing lessons when he was in fifth grade have a decided "tie-over." It was such a battle at the time, that it is nice to know that he realizes now, that it was a good thing. He types a lot of the papers he hands in at school, too.

I guess we are lucky to have a coal supply, when we read in the papers about the shortages everywhere. I think the last batch I got is the most satisfactory I have ever had. It is just good sized chunks that aren't too heavy to lift, but which hold the fire well. Tomorrow will be a busy day, for I get a permanent in the morning, and then have

---

* The minstrel show was done in "blackface" at the Cornell Theatre, and would now be considered offensive for that reason. EMH sang *Saint Louis Blues* (W. C. Handy, 1914) in costume, between the acts: "My Mammy done tole me…"

this Fellowship group here in the eve. It will be the first time since we moved that I have had occasion to get out all the plates and silverware.

I wish I had thought to ask you to write out a descriptive article about yourself to give to the *Gazette*, when we get word that you have "safely arrived." I will do it soon, but you could have done a much better job of it.

Dreamed about you the other night – you were home, and it was VERY nice.

Much love, to MY VALENTINE!


No. 9
Mount Vernon, Iowa
February 8, 1945  Thursday
Dearest Gerald,

Our party of Young Folks last night seemed to be very successful. There were twenty-four here, including ourselves, and the kids had a great time ringing all the bells, looking at pictures, and examining the insignia. They sat around on the floor and on all the chairs, and really seemed to have a very good time. There wasn't a crumb left of the pumpkin pie and whipped cream, so apparently George's choice of refreshments was satisfactory too. George wrote in his last letter that I wasn't feeling very well. It wasn't anything serious – just a headache – and after lying down for a couple of hours I was all right. I really have been feeling just fine, but I have to watch myself, or I guess I don't get enough exercise. Tommy is so happy that he was elected by the class to be the announcer and general manager of the "radio program" which the fifth grade are putting on for the sixth grade. It was quite a close race between him and Nancy Gaston,* and Tommy confessed that he "voted for himself" – but I'm sure he will do a good job of it. He has everything planned so that each one on the program will be doing the thing that he wants to do. Tommy is in a boxing tournament on Saturday, altho' he doesn't particularly care for boxing.

Helene is coming to Marion today, and her folks, the Blacks, are having a sale on Saturday. They move to Mpls. next week. I hope everything on that deal works out all right, but it is going to be a big responsibility for the Runkles. I wrote to Ruby this week – got a letter from her saying that they had gotten your NY Postmaster address. She said everyone was fine, but she was very lonely. I am planning to write to Marie Hill today and send her your address. Florence Nelson warns me that when you ship out, it may be a month or so before we hear from you – I hope it won't be that long – but I'll assume that "No news is good news."

We're thinking of you, and hoping that all is well.

Much love, 'S'mae


No. 9 [sic]
February 9, 1945  Friday
Dearest Gerald,

After I wrote the letter yesterday, your locker came and we opened it at noon, with many exclamations of delight! The "special" things for me exceeded my wildest dreams, and I am SO thrilled. George signed up for Boy Scouts, recently organized, and is looking forward to camping trips. I am late getting started this morning for I read the *Yank* after I got home from the PTA meeting last night, and it was unusually late when I got to bed. I spent more than an hour last eve at the library looking up some material for special reports for Geo., while he was at play practice. Among the info. that I got was "it cost $5 a half ounce to send mail by the pony express." Compared with airmail service today, that seems mighty expensive, doesn't it? I am surprised at how interested G. is in Am. History. His teacher is a pupil of Judge's and she really makes it "live." He can just glance at the book and it seems to stick in his mind. A week ago today we got our last letter from you – we remarked about it this morning.†

Am washing this AM in spite of X-day, and have a full day of miscellaneous. Thank you for being so sweet to us – we love "our daddy" very much.

'S'mae

---

\* The Gaston family lived near the Hills. The father was a civil engineer, who had worked on the Panama Canal. George and their son, Robert "Bobby" Gaston were classmates, and Tommy and Sarah were classmates.
† "Miss Ralston" was George's teacher in American History; Mrs. Betty L. (Ralston) Anderson, Cornell College '45.

No. 10
Mount Vernon, Iowa
February 10, 1945 Saturday
Dearest Gerald,

Saturday morning, and we are unbelievably lazy! It is nearly ten o'clock, and Tommy is still in bed reading, and George and I have just finished breakfast. I think he dreads getting out to do his collecting, but he isn't saying anything about it. He has rehearsal this afternoon, so T. and I will deliver the papers – and earn some "Points" for ourselves. I just realized this morning that you must have decided to take the big pictures of the kids and me along with you. If you did manage to squeeze them in, I get a kick out of thinking that "we are traveling along with you."

Tommy went to a BB game last night, and I went with G. to practice. I got quite a kick out of going with him downtown afterwards to get a sundae – we haven't splurged like that for a long time, and he didn't seem to mind the fact that he was with his "Mom" while the other kids in there were with each other. It may not be exactly a normal situation, but he isn't an "average" child either – as his taking the part in the play testifies. He is in every act, so he has had six rehearsals this week, and will be continuing at that pace for three more weeks. He hasn't let his school work suffer either.

Did I tell you that the bowl Tommy made in pottery is in the display cabinet now at the college, and it looks very nice? I sent one of my vases to Harriett [Thompson] as a wedding present. Our rabbit episode is finally over. He got out night before last – the cellar door was opened a crack, and a neighbor called me yesterday morning to say that their dog had "brought it home" – dead, of course. The kids took it very well – altho' we were all sorry, for he had gotten so tame, and was really very cute, in the way he'd dash around in the basement to show his pleasure at anyone coming down there.

Am looking forward to seeing Helene tomorrow. I ordered a chicken, and will have pumpkin pie, and our own frozen peas to go with it.

To work now – With much love, and hopes that you are all right.

'S'mae


February 11, 1945          Sunday 9:30 PM
Dearest Gerald,

The kids and I splurged again tonight and went to the movies to see *Our Hearts Were Young and Gay,* which as you know is the story of a trip to Europe which Cornelia Otis Skinner took with a girlfriend back in 1923. Do you remember when COS was here at Cornell? I was trying to tell the kids about it afterwards. It was really very amusing and I thoroughly enjoyed it – the costumes and dancing of the time, etc. The movie was packed. *Kismet* is coming soon – which you saw, didn't you?[*]

We had a nice visit with Helene today – she got here about 10:30 and the Johnsons had already called asking me to bring her over so they could meet her, so we went over right away. Bob [Runkle] is on a committee to choose a senior class play, and Helene got some advice, and a catalog. I was surprised to learn that *Days Without Daddy* has already been produced by high schools in nearly every state. The colored cover picture on the publisher's new catalog is a scene from that play. When a play is published, they always put pictures of the original cast in it – so G. will probably have his picture "Immortalized."[†]

I hope you have plenty of warm clothes – the news reels in the movie tonight showed SUCH snow and coldness – the suffering in those countries must be terrible! I chatter on in these letters about what we are doing here at home, but I hope you can read between the lines, and know that all the time I am wondering what you are doing and where you are since we got that last letter from California. I know that eventually we'll know, and in the meantime, we are "carrying on" thinking of you, and loving you very much.

Goodnight, my dear,
'S'mae

---

[*] Cornelia Otis Skinner, *Our Hearts Were Young and Gay* (book, 1942; movie premiered in NYC, 12 October 1944).
[†] Albert Johnson, *Days without Daddy* (Row Peterson & Co., 1944) was the Junior Class play in Worthington, Ohio, 22 Nov 1944. See http://www.worthingtonmemory.org/sites/default/files/documents/document-118404.pdf (accessed 12/21/2018).

Editor's note: GLH sent a Valentine telegram to EMH on 11 February from Camp Kilmer, N.J. The telegram is transcribed in his letter file. The identical wording, with a different formatting, is in EMH's letter file, although the site of transmission is eliminated; it is stated as "Military."

No. 12
Mount Vernon, Iowa
February 13, 1945                    Tuesday 9:30 PM
Dearest Gerald,

We know what our expression "hit the jackpot of mail" means now, for we got four letters and a telegram from you yesterday. You could have heard George for half a block, when the mailman came – he knocked at the door, so we'd be sure to come right away. It was certainly grand to hear from you – and the telegram was simply swell. And so "at long last" you've seen New York City! So glad you stood the trip across the country so well – and we are glad to know that our letters are coming thru to you without delay.

This looks like another day filled with "odd jobs" including typing for Tommy's radio program at school, waiting on George, who is catching up on rest at home this morning from school, and getting out a lot of letters for Al. It is just like a spring day out doors, tho', and the fire tending is practically nothing. You must have seen a lot of snow where you are, from the accounts in the papers. George is resting in bed this morning, and both of us are satisfied that he not go to school – he can't bear to go unprepared, and it will take cooperation from all of us to get him thru the play, for they do have SO MANY rehearsals. Tommy went to the show with Mrs. Rowe, and after G. came home from practice, we had ice cream and birthday cake, and she appreciated it greatly. My angel food turned out very well. The Dramatics Dept. – including Mr. Johnson, and his SECRETARY are having a terrible time getting New York addresses. So far, we have mailed batches of letters to two of his friends in NY to be addressed and mailed by them, there in NY. If you saw a NY classified directory (phone) wandering around without any home, or needing a "new" one, we could give it a treasured reception. In other words, if you could finagle one, and send it to us, it would be much appreciated – but we realize that it would have to be "swiped" and so don't break the law (and get caught). Use your own judgment.

The war picture certainly is moving fast – I wonder if you ever worry for fear something will happen to change the orders again and that you may have to make your plans all over. It was a big thrill to get your letters – and know how you are and that you were thinking of us.
                    Much love from All, Essie Mae


February 13, 1945                    Monday 1750
Dear Dad,

Today I was so tired I didn't go to school. Mom went around by town on her way home from the College and brought home the papers. She also brought home some doughnuts and we ate so many of them we don't want supper right now. I didn't have any trouble getting the papers around as I was just tired, not sick.

If I would have gone to school today I would have had 4 tests and maybe a fifth. In Science it was a Problem test, in Arith. and Am. Hist. they were Chapter Tests and in Literature it was a test over all the poetry we have had this year.
                    Time Elapses.                    1810

I just got the assignments that I missed today. In Science we are studying about the weather and Mother likes that very much. Every morning on my way to school I go out and get the temperature, precipitation, wind direction, wind speed and the condition of the sky. When I get to school the teacher gives us the relative Humidity, and the barometric reading. The same thig happens at 2:00. It's a lot of fun. I joined the Boy Scouts and the first meeting is Friday but neither Bertha or Mother will let me go to it. The scoutmaster is Joe Cooper who runs the filling station just W. of the school.

We all went, on Sunday night, to see "Our Hearts Were Young and Gay" from the book by C. O. Skinner. It was really good. The theater was really packed.
                    Yours Truly, George

No. 13
Mount Vernon, Iowa
0900 Happy Valentine's Day        February 14, 1945        Tuesday
Dearest Gerald,

        I am really "on the spot" this morning, for it is up to me to bake Tommy's valentine cookies. You know he has always insisted on having cookies for his school valentines, and this is the first year that Grandma hasn't been around to bake them for him. He has been worrying about the fact that I have never learned how to bake "grandma's kind," so this is "survive or perish." Several enclosures with this letter – including a letter from George, which he wrote yesterday. He is feeling fine this morning after resting all day yesterday, and eleven hours of sleep last night. Tommy was the last one in bed last night, for he went to a HS basketball game and I went to bed about nine o'clock. T. came in shortly after. Tommy reports that the radio program which he MC'd yesterday was "the best thing he ever did." Also, that he had never worked as hard over anything as he did that.

        Your RX personal card is very nice – do you have occasion to use them much? It was interesting to get "censored" letters – but nothing was cut out except the return address on the large RX envelope. The weather here was warm enough yesterday, so I let the furnace fire go out – it was just like spring. Tommy fell into a big puddle of water and got wet to the skin, up to his waist, but I put him to bed with the hot pad while I got supper and he seems none the worse this morn. Will keep the khaki sweater – G. says lots of them being worn at school if the kids happen to have "service people" in the family. It is too large for him now, however.

        Your suggestion about taking the lockers (extra) to the bank, noted. It seems that we are always needing something from them, however, and I'll probably just make room for them here. For instance, I packed a lot of your civvies in one, and put it on the bottom of the stack, only to have to dig into it last night, to get your "tux" shirt to loan to the Theatre for the play. My cold is all gone now, and I am feeling fine again. We turned out a lot of work at the office yesterday, but it only balances the very light days I have had lately. I have a typist for an hour a day, to "supervise" and I am "much better at bossing the typing" than I am at doing it myself.

        I noted down the general "form" of the newspaper account of Byron Anderson which I sent to you yesterday, and when the time comes, I'll write something about like it for you – mentioning your position in the bank, and CAP. Our newspaper arrangement is working out very well, and it seems nice to have a morning paper again. Must get at those cookies now. It was certainly nice to get that telegram, and we'll be looking forward to hearing about your experiences in the "big city."

        Much love, from all of us, 'S'Mae


No. 14
February 15, 1945        Thursday
Dearest Gerald,

        Your letters 10 and 11 came yesterday, telling of the subway ride and "brownout." It was quite amusing to think of you fellows finding your way around – the "blind leading the blind" – I would have been terrified, but now you are "qualified" to act as the family guide, if and when. Hope you had a chance to see and visit with Rowena [Stuckslager]. She is a very poor letter writer, and even the Johnsons seldom hear from her.

        It was interesting too, to know that you have had the experience of meeting a "deadline" on leave!

        Yesterday was a nice Valentine's day for us. I spent the whole morning getting Tommy's cookie valentines ready, and he declared that "I must send a sample to Grandma, because they were the BEST cookies I ever ate." I burned one batch to a crisp, talking to Bertha on the phone, but the rest did turn out very well. Tommy hunted up his pocketbook before he went to school, and came in the evening with much secrecy – of course, it turned out to be a valentine for me, which both of the boys signed.

        I was happily surprised to get my grades from the college office, and learn that I am credited with A in Art, B in typing, and C in SHORTHAND! I am glad you liked George's letters – I think, too, that he does remarkably well. He is absorbed in getting "extra credit in History" for doing some drawing, and he is making a pictorial map of the "expansion of the west" and "discoveries of mineral deposits." He seems to be rested up now.

My "homework" today is to sort and reorganize your things. There have been so many fires reported in the papers lately that I have been having that on my mind, nights, and, while we haven't anything very valuable here, there are a lot of things, like letters – that couldn't be replaced, and I realize that they ought to be somewhere where I could get them all in a hurry. This place would certainly be a firetrap, if the fire should start in the basement.

      Much love, from all of us.

          'S'mae

No. 15
Mount Vernon, Iowa
February 16, 1945        Friday
Dearest Gerald,

      This seems to be my routine these days – Get up about 7:15, get the fire started, get breakfast, including putting the toothpaste beside G.'s plate, so he won't forget to brush his teeth, getting the kids off to school, and then writing to you, before I start on the morning housework. I forgot to include the clipping about Byron Anderson,[*] when I spoke about it the other day. George had his picture taken last eve, with his "father" – Junior Brace – for the *Hawkeye* next week. I think that will be nice. I plan to ask the Sizers to go as our guests – you know I asked Arnolds to see *Family Portrait*. The show is going very well – and G. is fine, but needs to work on the problem of deepening his voice, and slowing down. I guess I am getting the hang of my "secretarial" job a little better, learning addresses, style of letters, and "working a few of my own." Al is hoping I can rework some of his plays and stories as a "collaborator." He seems to have much more confidence in me, than I have in myself. And now to work – I didn't get your things sorted yesterday as I planned, and there is an ironing to do, if I get to it.

      Thinking of you – and wondering what the next few days, and months have in store.

      Much love from all of us, 'S'mae

No. 16
February 17, 1945        Saturday
Dearest Gerald,

      Saturday morning! And we are certainly slow about getting started. Even the typewriter keys and my fingers are stiff and cold. G. has been arguing with himself for an hour and a half, trying to crank himself up to going out collecting. I think we always notice the cold more, after having a nice warm spell like we have been having. Bertha just called and asked me to come over and eat dinner with them, and the kids plan to see *Kismet*. George really doesn't know which way to jump these days, or what to concentrate on – and as a result, it takes all my tact to keep him going right. You see, they are just now organizing a Boy Scout troop, and he wants to get right into the thick of it. His interests are very much divided, for rehearsals are going in dead earnest now.

      No mail from you for several days now – and of course, I am wondering if that means – you know! We certainly watch for the mailman – that's the high point of the day! George is gloating over the "equipment" which he will have for hikes, such as the canteen – I am really glad they are organizing the Scouts. My tummy seems to be "acting up" this morning somewhat, and I'm wondering whether it is my turn to get that kind of flu. Hope not, but there's lots of it going around. I'll sign off now, and get at the morning work. We are all fine, and thinking of you.

      Much love, S'mae

No. 17
Mount Vernon, Iowa
February 19, 1945        Monday
Dearest Gerald,

      Your long No. 12 letter came in the mail yesterday, after I had sent my No. 16, and it was certainly a grand letter. The bell came also, and it is simply wonderful. I am glad you sent the receipt, for it DOES give me an added respect for it, but I am simply delighted with the bell.

---

[*] A brief undated story titled "In France," from the *Cedar Rapids [Iowa] Gazette* was attached to this letter: "Byron K. Anderson, of Cedar Rapids, a Red Cross worker, has arrived in France and has been assigned to the 89th division."

It was most interesting to hear about your visit to NYC. I feel like scolding you for carrying two typewriters – that sounds like taking a big risk (for a "sick man"), but if you suffered no ill effects, it must have been all right. I surely hope you don't have too much of that for six months or more – but you can judge your own strength, probably. The way you can find your way around in strange cities, absolutely dumbfounds me, but I am certainly glad you have a preview of it, for NY is one place I certainly want to visit some time. How are you standing the cold? I certainly hope you don't suffer any ill effects of the change in climate.

The big pictures which you sent in the locker were in a pile of magazines that I had not examined closely – so they are found now. I hadn't discovered the pictures of the RX staff until I found our pictures, and it was nice to see what the men look like. I like the one of you very much, so I assume the others must be good, too. From their pictures, I can imagine the characteristics of each one, as you have described them, very well. Your new typewriter must be very nice. How do you like a Corona compared with the Royal? The new machines are certainly wonderful, and that's one of my "ambitions" for after the war. Geo. says to tell daddy he'll have to excuse him from writing until after the play is over, he's too busy, and that he doesn't expect you to answer his personally.

I loafed around all day yesterday – very lazy – nothing physical I guess – just kind of a mental let-down. I go along about so long, and then realize how much I miss adult "give and take" in the household. The kids and I have been getting along just fine, but it takes a lot of tact to keep them doing what I think they ought to do, and so I just relaxed yesterday and today. The kids were very nice, and washed and wiped the dishes today.

I went to Johnsons last eve – they were celebrating Anne's* arrival a year ago on February 17. Bertha had T-bone steaks from the locker, which she broiled in the fireplace – as well as frozen peas and strawberries, all of which tasted simply wonderful. Jacques Jolas is giving a lecture recital in the exhibition hall at Armstrong this PM, so I guess that will be my afternoon "exercise." I have promised the kids we'll open the cedar chest, and sort the things in it, and they think that will be a treat. Word received that David Blinks has been killed in Europe. Also, Paul Runkle [Lester's cousin] has been severely wounded in Luxemburg. Al's brother is in Luxemburg now.

And that's all for now. Extra and special love for my valentine bell.

From all of us, 'S'mae

No. 18
February 20, 1945          Tuesday
Dearest Gerald,

Snow on the ground this morning, but not so cold. I have been using that little nose spray of yours, and it seems to help keep my head clear. Yesterday passed very uneventfully, but I spent a long afternoon at the office, traveling "vicariously" to New York, Los Angeles, Northampton, Mass., Alabama, etc. Al has gotten replies to the letters I have been sending out, so they are intelligible, at least. Tommy and I went up to rehearsal last night, and it was late when we got home. It is certainly much more complicated to put on a new play, for Al is still making changes in it, as things seem to work out better on the stage, from what he had originally written. It means lots of extra rehearsing. G. was there more than three hours last night, and I insisted that he come home before they were all through. I wrote to Faye Sizer yesterday asking the whole family to be our guests at the play and she phoned last night. The sectional basketball tournament is the same nights, and she and Harry have some kind of jobs there, but she was pleased with the invitation, and said they would try to make arrangements to come to the play.

Sunday PM, after the Jolas recital in Armstrong, I overheard Ruth Pinkerton telling someone, "And little Tommy Hill made that bowl." She was showing the pottery exhibit, and I was quite proud. I came across an old "engagement" calendar in the cedar chest the other day, and saw it was five years ago March 2nd, that we were invited to the broiled steak dinner at the Johnsons. Remember? It was very nice. And now to work. Just as soon as the kids leave for school, I have been writing these letters, to get my mind cleared for the morning.

Am wondering how things are shaping up for you – and if you are "on your way again." Happy landings!
Much love, from all of us.
'S'mae

---

* Al and Bertha Johnson had no children of their own; they adopted Anne in February 1944.

No. 19
Mount Vernon, Iowa
February 21, 1945          Wednesday
Dearest Gerald,

Yesterday afternoon, after we finished work at "Summit End" we had tea out on the terrace, and it really seemed like spring. BUT! This morning the sidewalks are covered with sleet, and it is so dark and gloomy – but the kids got off to school in good spirits, and all is fine. I bought some V-mail stationery yesterday, and if I don't hear from you in a day or two, I'll write a letter that way. Thought I'd warn you ahead of time. I indulged myself in a "luxury item" yesterday, by subscribing to the Literary Guild. That is a "book of the month" – four books a year are the minimum to be bought, and a free book with each four you buy. The original free gift book is *Leave Her to Heaven* – so I'll be reading that before long, and if you don't get a chance to finish it before you come home, it will be here "waiting for you." I am looking forward to reading it! because it is certainly "much talked about."

This is a short letter this morning – no special news – but I do want you to know that I'm thinking of you, and of course wondering whether you are on the move again – I watch for the mailman most eagerly.

Love, from all of us. 'S'mae

No. 20
February 21, 1945          Wednesday
Dearest Gerald,

Your No. 13 letter arrived yesterday – written Feb. 17, and reached here Feb. 20. Came straight through, without any evidence of censorship. I'll be most interested in knowing how long this letter is enroute. I can imagine what a kick you got out of seeing the hockey game at Madison Square Garden. I am reminded of the famous telephone call made from our house to the gang at the hockey game in Chicago – Packy [McFarland]! Remember!

Johnsons are much pleased with George in the play. He has "come out" wonderfully, and is really doing a grand job. I certainly wish you could see him. I'm just terribly proud of him. Tommy says, "Why, they all seem so natural you wouldn't think they were just waiting in the wings for their cues to come on." His experience in the Thanksgiving play just whetted his appetite for more.

George has been following the battle on Iwo with great interest, because he has the insignia of the divisions listed as taking part there.

Bye, my dear, for this time. Thinking of you, and hoping you are warm, comfortable, and content.

Much love, from all of us. 'S'mae

No. 21
February 24, 1945          Saturday
Dearest Gerald,

My last letter was sent V-mail, but was delayed one day, because I forgot that there would be no mail pick-up on Feb. 22, Washington's birthday. I'll be interested in knowing how long it takes for it to reach you. Your vali-pack came yesterday, and the enclosures were simply WONDERFUL! It was very thoughtful of you to send them, and I surely appreciate them, and am putting them to very good use, in a rationed way.

Our lives still revolve about the play, and there's only one more week to go. George has an especially busy day today, and that means ALL of us do, for it takes the whole family to see him thru. Tommy is out helping collect this morning, we go up to the theatre at 12:30, then he goes to Scouts, paper delivering, and then more rehearsal this eve. I have an enormous washing all done, and will be involved in one thing or another until late tonight, I imagine. Everywhere we go we hear "how Tommy is growing" – some of the kids who played with him in *Family Portrait* three months ago hardly knew him – Helene remarked about it too.

We are eagerly waiting for your next letter, and thinking of you, and being proud of you – Love from us all.
'S'mae

No. 22
Mount Vernon, Iowa
February 25, 1945          Sunday
Dearest Gerald,

George and I tried to outdo each other this morning, in "helping" and he won. I had the alarm set to wake me up early, so I could deliver his papers for him, while he slept. However, he woke up first, turned off the alarm, and when I finally woke, his bed was empty, and he was gone to deliver them alone. I felt very chagrined, and tried to make up for it by having a "pancake" breakfast for him when he got home.

John Woodin's girl tells me that he was to get his Ensign's commission this weekend, and that he will be coming home in two weeks. Isn't that fine. He apparently has "hit his stride" for she says he has gotten very good grades. Bob Runkle has been breaking into print lately, according to clippings from Lester. His picture, with a "party" group at a formal, in the society section, and then on the "front page" as an article about his being a member of his school debating team which spoke before the House elections committee speaking in behalf of lowering the voting age. Bob's special part was to declare that youth are interested and informed on public affairs. I daresay they are – more so than lots of grownups, judging from George's knowledge about world affairs.

The papers are so full of European news, and every story makes me think about you, and wonder what you are doing. Much love, from all of us,
          Essie Mae


No. 23
February 26, 1945          Monday
Dearest Gerald,

The daily "broadcast" from the home front! Starting with the "weather report" – your (own) forecaster prophesies that Europe is in for more cold weather, for a REAL cold moved into Iowa last night. The sun shines brightly though, and spring can't be far away.

Am getting a special kick out of Max Gordon* and other Broadway Producers asking to see the script of *Love Your Neighbor*, because of "my own" letters about it which went to them – George and Bertha both under the weather with colds, but definitely improving – got our little radio fixed, after two months without one – now we're all set to hear all the "foreign" news – had my hair recurled this morning and bought a very gay red plaid flannel shirt – very definite morale builders – rejoiced to get George a pair of overalls and corduroys at Syndicate (by mail) when Bauman's didn't have, and couldn't get any – he weighs ten pounds more than last year, but still awfully thin – delivered the papers tonight for George – wearing his rubbers, and carrying a red hankie – "pride" (false) is one thing I'm not worried about. Am eagerly waiting for your letters – Tell us all you can about what you are doing, and any suggestions about what we can do for you – Take care of yourself. Hope all is well with you. Much love and a big kiss from all of us. †          Essie Mae


No. 24
February 27, 1945          Tuesday
Dearest Gerald,

I wrote you a V-mail letter last night, but I wanted to send these enclosures from Sunday's papers, and tell you that SUI won the final basketball game with Minnesota last eve, 55 to 48, for the Big Ten championship.

Life goes on in its quiet uneventful way. We see the cadets down town, especially at Meredith's [drugstore and soda fountain] about 4:30 every afternoon with the college girls goggle-eyed at the hope of being able to talk to a MAN, but that is only about the only "military atmosphere" we have. The papers and radio are so full of the terrific fighting on Iwo, and in Germany – I try to imagine what it would be like if the guns were pointed toward Cedar Rapids, for instance. Or as George said the other night at supper – "Just think, even a little town like Mt. Vernon, might be a target if we were in Europe."

---

* Max Gordon (1892-1978) was a successful Broadway producer, immortalized in Cole Porter's song, "Anything Goes": "… let Max Gordon produce his shows." In 1944, he produced *The Late George Apley*, but Al Johnson's play didn't make the cut.
† Bauman's was *the* clothing store in Mount Vernon.

There was an article in the new *Reader's Digest* on "how to treat the men when they come home." You know there has been so much said to civilian home folks, to the effect that we must handle our men "with kid gloves – not asking them any questions about their experiences for they wouldn't like to talk about them. This article, by a service man, said that we "should just be NATURAL," ask questions, etc., and if the men wanted to talk about it, they would. That seems like good advice to me, for I certainly want and hope to hear all about it.

George went to school this AM, but Dr. Ebersole is going to give him a doctor's excuse for PT this week – and with that I think he'll get thru the week all right, and be ready for the play production this weekend. The PT they have, I think it's good for him, but it is so awfully strenuous – pushups, and that kind of stuff, until he is absolutely pooed, even when he doesn't have a stuffed up nose and throat to contend with. I think he has a tendency to sinus, for he simply can't blow his nose to do any good. Tommy, on the other hand, is always "hocking" and whiffing. The ground is still frozen this morning, so their feet will be dry, and it was wet feet that caused all the trouble over the weekend, I think.

And this, my dear, is all for this morning – let me know, if I can send you anything, or if my letters are "all right." Much love from all of us.

'S'Mae

# She Receives Good News: It's V-E Day, and Gerald Is Safe
## March 1945 – May 1945


**March 1945**
**Essie Mae "can hardly wait until I get news" from Gerald**
**A telegram from Red Cross Headquarters says he has arrived in Paris, and he is promoted**

> "These men and women came of age in the Great Depression … They
> answered the call to save the world from the two most powerful and ruthless
> military machines ever assembled … They faced great odds and a late start,
> but did not protest."          – Tom Brokaw, *The Greatest Generation*, xix


No. 25
Mount Vernon, Iowa          Cornell College
March 1, 1945          Thursday morning
Dearest Gerald,

This would be a busy day, if you were in the bank, wouldn't it; I'm wondering what it's like, where you are. March comes in like a "lamb," here, with a beautiful sunshine, and it will probably be melting before long. The windows in the office overlook "lover's lane" and the trees are full of birds acting very excited!

Things about the play are concerning us night and day, and tomorrow night is the first production. Last night, was a dress rehearsal, with an audience of about 75, and it went very well. You would just be amazed and thrilled with George. He is really awfully good, and has developed so much, during the course of rehearsals. I'm afraid the stage crew have had a taste of his "temperament" however, for he "blows up" if anyone touches any of his props back stage. The big worry now is that Bertha is sick with a cold – she drags around, but shouldn't. Last night she couldn't talk out loud. I got up early this morning and baked an apple pie for them, and one for ourselves, so "we housewives" would be able to carry on, and still have food for our families.

The kids got their grade cards yesterday, and they are fully up to standard. George got A in everything except conduct (he just deliberately devils Mrs. Watson Davis), but he promises to be better, and actually that grade was C plus. Tommy got mostly B's with an A in art and C plus in history, which is a new subject this semester. It was a week ago today that I got your last letter – it seems much longer than that, but at any rate, I'm just glad that much of the waiting is over.

That's all for this time – "be with you tomorrow" – BYE, my dear – Much love –

Essie Mae


No. 26*
March 3, 1945          Saturday morning
Dearest Gerald,

Two days have gone by since I wrote to you; I am sorry to have "neglected" you. They have been filled with "play" as you probably guess. Bertha's terrible cold, which kept her just on the dizzy edge of being "incapacitated" for all of her responsibilities of the weekend – Tommy had a touch of intestinal flu, and was home in bed for a day (better now), and George fighting sore throat and stuffy head, – well, the combination kept me on the jump.

However, everything worked out wonderfully well, and the premiere of the play last night was an OVERWHELMING SUCCESS! The audience (a full house) was just in stitches, and I am so proud of George. He did wonderfully! I surely missed you all day yesterday, for I was very jittery with tension over him – wondering how

---

* Attached to this letter: *Theatre Headlines: Play Bill and Bulletin* (Cornell College, Mt. Vernon, Iowa, March 1945):
"Celebrities Hail Premiere." "Lee Owen Snook of Row Peterson Company Publishers … has option on publishing and amateur performance rights." The play opens with GJH (playing "Wingy Vaski") on stage.

he'd get along, and I surely wished for your "calming" influence. I think I hid it fairly well, from George, at least, and I delivered his papers for him, got him supper in bed so he could rest, etc., etc.

It was a terrible night, rain, and all that. Rachie and Jim came part way by truck, and partly by car, and then decided to stay all night, rather than try to navigate the road home thru the mud and rain last night. They got away by seven this morning, and will have a rough ride, for the ground is frozen hard this morning. I surely appreciate the effort they made to get here, tho', and it was fun having them here over night. Tommy slept in the sleeping bag, and Rachie and I on the studio couch. Al got a telegram from a Broadway producer, asking that the script be sent to him immediately. Having Mr. and Mrs. Snook here, is very interesting too, and I am going to a tea for them this PM, and party after the play tonight. I will miss you then, too, very much – I just don't like social affairs "without a man" – but I will get along, some way or other. SUI plays its final game tonight to decide whether they are the "sole" Big 10 champion – Jim heard over the radio that they could have sold 6000 more tickets. Ames won the championship of its conference, the paper announced this morning. I am baking an angel food cake for Bertha Johnson to serve tonight for dessert. Her birthday is March 14, and I thought she might find her birthday cake more useful now, than later – which she agrees to. George is just now getting up – 9:40. Tommy is still in bed. Much get breakfast for G.

Much love, from all of us.
Essie Mae

No. 27
Mount Vernon, Iowa
March 4, 1945        Sunday evening
Dearest Gerald,

If you had been at home this morning, I can imagine the eagerness with which you would have the sports sections of the papers, for they certainly gave very interesting accounts of SUI's winning the undisputed title to the Big Ten conference BB, defeating Illinois 43-37. It must have been a very exciting and memorable night. According to the papers, Lisbon won the sectional tournament Class B, and MV the Class A, which was held in Lisbon.

So much for the sports news. Family affairs now. Tommy joined the preparatory church membership class this morning, and had to go up front in church. He says he was more scared than he was in the play. I stayed at home with George, who spent the morning in bed, and we had a good visit – going over everything about the play.

It is a relief to have the play over, but it was certainly a grand experience. Mr. Snook, the publisher, was genuinely "taken" with George and his fine performance – Johnsons said he talked of it several times. He gave him a very cordial goodbye, and said, "I'd like to see you when you are about a junior in college" – implying that by that time, he would really be a very good actor. He will be good at whatever he sets out to – there's no doubt about that in my mind. Mrs. Snook spoke about what fine boys they both were – and confessed that she was very partial to boys. The Snooks have no children.

The audience reaction to the second performance was much "slower" and the cast did not really do as well as they did the first night. After it was all over, we found out that Stevie (Mary Stevenson, the principal actor) had just learned that her boyfriend had been killed over Germany. She hid her emotion, and didn't tell a soul, and went thru the performances like the superb "trouper" that she is. Al was just sick about it – he said he knew all the time that she wasn't doing her best work, but he just couldn't figure out why.

So many people have spoken to me about George's work in the play, and everyone was dumbfounded. Al made recordings of it, so you will be able to hear it when you come home, if you care to. I guess you know the secret for which George has been saving his money. It came out yesterday, when he presented me with $22.50 and said that was to buy my unabridged dictionary. I don't think I was ever so touched in my life. Really, that was the nicest thing, I think a boy ever did for his "mom." I never dreamed that that was what he had in his mind. I really shouldn't spend it for that, but he'll be disappointed if I don't.

This letter must sound strange – giving a "play by play" description of the events of the past few days, but that's just the way the days have slipped away – they'll certainly be a "continued story." We are going to "celebrate" tonight by going to the movie getting <u>ice cream</u> afterwards. Tommy is on a committee in his room to line up a "talent" program, the best of which will be selected from all the grades to be presented as a composite program to the public. We've decided that he will learn "The American's Creed" as the thing which he could do, which would have the best chance of "surviving" for the final production. That is what George presented in the HS in Lisbon, when you were in Iowa City having your nose operation, and he forgot, and felt so badly about it. Everyone thought he was so gritty and swell about it tho' and I felt badly, for I felt I hadn't taken enough time to drill him on it. It is very tricky to learn – but I am sure Tommy can do it. It will be good for him, even tho' he doesn't go on to the final show with it.

Tommy is also interested and keen about the printing press. He has been sorting the type, and wants to put out a newspaper, like G. has done at various times. I delivered the papers alone this morning so G. could sleep, so now I feel even, for his doing it alone last Sunday. It really is a back-breaking job, tho' – but I didn't mind it, knowing he was resting. We have been very lazy around here, and I must get after the dishes, and other house work. The only thing worthwhile that I've done, is bake a cake – especially for Tommy, for he felt so envious of the one I made for Bertha yesterday as a birthday cake. Wish you were here to have a piece.

By for this time. Hope you don't have to wait much longer for the mail to reach you – and <u>us</u>.

Heaps of love, 'S'Mae

No. 28
Mount Vernon, Iowa
March 7, 1945      Wednesday morning
Dearest Gerald,

The kids have just gotten away to school, so I'll visit with you for a little while. I had a backache yesterday (combination of various things) so I didn't do any typing – just laid around on the heat pad, and it's better today.

Neil Miner called and asked if I would be interested in teaching Geology at Coe next year – said he'd been asked to recommend someone. Don't think my health could take it, and the kids have been too happy with me at home this year to approve – but I think it was nice of him to think of me. The paper this morning tells about the 1st Army in Cologne. Questions: Were you seasick? Is there lots of work for the RX? Lots of other things too, I'd like to know, but I trust you'll use your typewriter to good advantage when you can. George has apparently gotten rested from the play, and is deep in Scouting now and keeping up his school work. They are very lazy in the mornings, and don't get up until about 8:20. Had to order another ton of coal yesterday, but it is really good – cold weather continues, but I guess that is only natural for the first part of March. Bobby Gaston and G. seem to have made up their difficulties, and are in the same Scout Patrol. He stopped here last eve – I'm glad.

Goodbye, my dear, for this time. Impatiently watching the mails. Certainly am enjoying your "last gifts."

Much love, Essie Mae

No. 29
March 8, 1945      Thursday morning
Dearest Gerald,

A beautiful spring day in Iowa! Snow is all melted, sun shines, and the birds are singing!

The *Saturday Evening Post* this week carries an article interested me particularly – on travel in the subways of NY. Lots of pictures of the crowds, etc. – I tried to imagine you among them. A follow-up on the Coe job. I went to a Geology Club meeting last week, at Neil's invitation, and a Dr. Wilson from Coe was the speaker of the evening. As soon as he finished his lecture, he came over to me, and commenced telling me about the job for next year – he continued with the build-up with many complimentary remarks about my teaching, etc., which were very nice to listen to. Apparently, it is up to him to find someone to take his place for the year, and he told Neil he "wasn't going to look any further." He'll <u>have</u> to, tho', for I am not going to take it, altho' it was nice to be offered the position. I would have two student assistants – the salary $2000 for the nine months. There were a couple of people from the Geologic Survey from Iowa City at the meeting, and I had interesting conversations with them – one of them a woman, who most cordially invited me to "come over." The chief of the Survey is off on some war work, I was interested to learn. Altogether, it was a very stimulating evening. The kids continue happy and healthy, and I spoil them outrageously – they spoil me too, I hasten to add. Thinking of you, and wondering what new sights and experiences you are having. How's your health? Are you under an awful strain, or can you rest?

Hoping all is well – much love, Essie Mae

No. 30
Mount Vernon, Iowa
March 10, 1945     Saturday morning
Dearest Gerald,

9:00 AM and George has gone to collect, and Tommy is out to "fly his kite." (Literally) The road out in front of the house is still so muddy that only the rugged 303rd could get thru, but it is nice overhead. The news from the European front is wonderful this morning – telling about the break across the Rhine.

A couple of interesting things that happened in the last few days. Yesterday John Howard [Woodin] and his girl, Betti Gray, came before I was dressed and the kids got away to school. He got his commission (ensign) and flew from NY to Chicago. He considered himself very lucky, for immediately following is final exams, he came down with chickenpox, and was in quarantine for six days. Received his commission in "isolation" – but was released a day later to come home. He looks wonderful in his new uniform – he is really a very good-looking boy. He and his girl left for Clarion (via Ames) on the PM train – Ruby was going to meet them there. He phoned his mother, and she said Adelia was sick, had to give up her job, and would be at their house in Clarion for a few days. Too bad!

Last night was the PTA benefit at the schoolhouse – a basketball game between the North and South sides of town. Huge crowd. I came home immediately afterwards, and George, Bobby, and I had ice cream and cookies here at home. Tommy, however, stayed for the dance – and guess what! When he finally got home (10:30) he said HE HAD DANCED SEVERAL DANCES. A sixth grade girl asked him first, and showed him the ropes, and after that he was no "wall flower." He simply smirked when he told about it! I am glad he had his first experience, before he was too old to be self-conscious about it. He said his feet "were surely sore, where other people had walked on them!"

I have been under pressure this week to get the script of *Love Your Neighbor* to the publisher. There are so many "bugs" to get out of it, and it has to be "letter perfect" and ready to go to the printer.
Love, Essie Mae

No. 31
March 11, 1945     Sunday afternoon
Dearest Gerald,

Sending you the news of the week. And I can hardly wait until I get news from you. I confess I go around feeling like I'd swallowed a handful of lead, but everyone assures me that this waiting is only "the natural course of human events." I hope you don't have to wait for "too long" for mail. Tommy and I went to Lion's show rehearsal this afternoon. They are going to give an extra show on Wednesday eve, to take care of the demand for tickets. It certainly hurries the men, but it will be fine. Very "pure" but the men sing wonderfully well. The kids both went to Sunday School this morning. RX has a major place on the radios and in the newspapers these days, with the financial drive on – and everyone praises it. I feel quite proud! Do you hear any radio programs from home? Must get some supper now – we had cinnamon toast and cocoa about five o'clock, so that took the edge off their appetites – I think we'll just have the good old crackers and milk. Wish you could join us.
Much love, from all of us, 'S'Mae

No. 32
March 13, 1945     Tuesday evening
Dearest Gerald,

Yesterday was REALLY a red-letter day, for we got your No. 15 letter (the regular airmail came thru before the No. 14 V-mail, which we have not yet received) and then in the PM came the telegram from RX headquarters saying that you had arrived in Paris. At noon, we had finished lunch and were all sitting at the front window hopefully watching for the mailman. When we spied him, George ran to the corner to meet him, and then when he saw your letter he began to yell, so I think the whole neighborhood knew about it. We were simply delighted! I had just reached the low point in waiting, and it was wonderful to hear from you. I hope my letters are coming thru to you, and that you had a batch of mail on arrival.

When George stopped to deliver Meredith's paper in the PM, Tom gave him the telegram. He ran all the way home with it, dashed into the front door so fast, he tore the lock from the storm door, shouting for me. I was at the office, so he really burned up the wires contacting me. Jacques Jolas happened to be the first person I saw, so I told him about it, and he was so very interested. He, of all people, can best imagine "Paris in the spring" and he went into raptures, as only he could. He said over and over, "But you should be there too, Essie Mae – don't you wish you were there" – etc., till I was ready to slug him – after all, what does he think I am! But I am so thrilled to think you are there – that is the place I have always hankered to see, and I am trying to imagine seeing it with you.

      I am writing an article for the *Gazette*, and for the *Hawkeye*, and sending your picture to the *Gazette* – will write to Ruby this AM. I am glad you had a "satisfactory crossing" and found conditions on shipboard agreeable. We simply drooled when we read about "pineapple" and the other good food. That is swell! Jacques says he will give me the names and addresses of his family, just on the vague possibility that you might run across them. I guess they are scatted all over Germany and France. There are lots of Cornellians in those parts, too. Tommy and I went to the lecture course last night (John Jacob Niles doing folk lore stories and songs) and walked home with Toppy and Jewel. They spoke about what a remarkable job George did in the play. Said he did about the best job of "child acting" they had ever seen in these parts. That was "music in my ears" naturally.*

      We are wondering what kind of accommodations you find in Paris – where your headquarters are. Anything you are able to tell us will be of great interest.

      Much love from all of us – waiting for your letters very eagerly.

      'S'Mae

No. 33
Mount Vernon, Iowa
March 15, 1945    Thursday evening
Dearest Gerald,

      Yesterday was another red-letter day, for your two V-mail letters written on shipboard arrived. They had not been microfilmed – were just as you wrote them. The fact that they did not come thru as fast as the regular airmail is just one of those unexplainable mysteries. It was wonderful to hear from you, and to know that you were thinking of us – of course, we knew it anyway – but it is wonderful to read it in words. As I figure back, with the reference to "pie" on shipboard, I realize that that is the time I felt sure you were taking off. I am certainly glad that you had no serious set-backs as a result of getting aboard with all your gear.

      I sat up till nearly midnight reading *Leave Her to Heaven* – it is a fascinating book, and I liked the descriptions of the north woods and the desert ranch. Ellen, the wife, doesn't seem real to me, and if she were real, I don't see how her husband tolerated her for so long. Deliver me from her type!†

      George is working at his Scout work, as hard as he did over the play – altho' he says he still has nightmares in which he misses his entrance, and is "disgraced." There is to be a paper drive on Saturday, and he thinks he's going to collect 1000 pounds all himself. Won't he be a wreck on Sunday! He was so pleased to get a letter from you – it was an awfully nice one too. I hope to move George and all his belongings into one of the rooms upstairs on Sunday. I simply <u>have</u> to have more room, and I think as a twelve-year-old he deserves a separate room for his things. The plastering in the kitchen is not done yet, and we are all so sick of this place we can hardly stand it – it is just in disgraceful condition. I plan to write a hot letter to Mr. Leigh this morning.

      It certainly must have been nice to get the coffee and doughnuts as you went on board ship – the RX is SWELL! No doubt about it! Am going to write to Rachie, Mother, and Runkles this morning, using carbons, and quoting from your letters. Hope all is well with you, and that you are really getting 100% out of your experiences.

      Much love from all of us, Essie Mae

No. 34
March 16, 1945    Friday
Darling,

      This is going to be a short letter, just simply to tell you how thrilled we all were to get your letter of March 3 yesterday, and how proud we are of you. I read the letter out loud to Johnsons and they are so happy (along with

---

* John Jacob Niles (1892-1980) was known as the "Dean of American Balladeers."
† Ben Ames Williams, *Leave Her to Heaven* (1944) was made into a film noir in 1945. Gene Tierney was the unstable "Ellen."

me) that you have the ability and take the trouble to give us such good accounts of what you are doing. So many people have spoken to me about how wonderful it is that you are in France – you know there are lots of people in MV who have been there so they have some idea of what you see. I am so proud.

The enclosed clippings will give you the important items of "news" from MV. The Lion's show is grand – beautifully staged, and CLEAN! But the review tells all about it. I hope you are satisfied with the job your "press agent" did. I was happy in writing about you – feeling that that was the one and only thing that I could do for you just now, even tho' you didn't know I was doing it – not just yet anyway. I made four copies of your letter written from the chateau, and sent one to Ruby [Woodin], and will send the others out to various members of the family, so they will know what you are doing. It gave a wonderful picture of the situation as you have seen it.

Hope you found some of your friends when you got to Paris, and that your stay there was simply super. Surely hope you found some mail waiting for you, for I've written a lot of letters.

Much love from all of us, and constant thoughts, 'S'Mae

No. 35

March 17, 1945    Saturday morning         0100

Dearest Gerald,

I am writing this at the scandalous hour of 1:00 in the morning, but I know I feel more like writing now, than I will at a "civilized" time when I wake up. I just came home from Johnsons and guess who was there! PACKY! How I know you would have enjoyed being there. To tell the story in sequence: We knew that Eke [MacFarland] was coming for the last night of the Lion's show, but when the gang came in tonight there was Packy with them. He arrived in NY on Monday, spent a few days in Wash. D.C., arrived in Chicago this morning, met Eke, and they drove out to here. We all got a shock on seeing Packy for he looks so OLD. Lines around his face, and hair much grayer, but when you talk to him, you soon forget it.

I was in the booth, and just shook hands with him in the lobby, but as the finale started, I went out to the house, and there sitting on the steps leading to the "house" was Packy, all alone. The house was sold out, and the rest of them were sitting on the steps on the other side. I sat down beside him, and we talked (I was glad to have a few moments' friendly visit and he was most cordial), then Mary [Van Metre] came and dragged him away, so that he could meet Doug behind stage as soon as it was over. Doug, of course, did not know he was there.

Johnsons asked me to come over afterwards, and while we were discussing things, the phone rang, saying they were all coming over. After a while Packy came over, and took me by the hand and said, "Come on over and talk to me" – leading me over to the davenport by the fire downstairs. He was most gracious, and I simply asked a few questions and he did the talking. After a while, I saw Al wandering around, and knowing that he was dying to talk to Packy, I called him over, and he was delighted to hear and join the conversation. Packy is getting out of the Army – he's a major now – but he has certainly had thrilling experiences, as the only American behind enemy lines in the southeast [sic: neareast], organizing guerillas. He says his work is finished, and he is delighted to be getting out of the Army. Really, it was most like old times I have had for years – we finally ended up in a mild singing session! How I wished you could have been in on it. But I was awfully proud you were a part of the whole show, and doing your share of the work in Europe. Packy wears a double row of ribbons & the "Near East" shoulder patch, which he promised to send to George. Seems strange to think that he has undoubtedly been the motivating force behind much of the *Times* news from that section, & knows all the big shots personally.[*]

Your V-mail of March 10 came this morning – six days – not microfilmed. I know you're a real "soldier" and it makes us all proud that you can "take it," sleeping bag, cold, and all. I hope things have eased up for you tho' and that you are warm and well fed. Hope that GI does a good job on your socks.

Good night, darling – I expect you are just about ready to get up – But I must go to bed.

Much love, Essie Mae

---

[*] Lt. Col. Lanning (Packy) MacFarland was the head of OSS operations in Istanbul, undercover, posing as an American banker. He ran "Operation Dogwood," which gathered intelligence on Nazi operations in the Balkans; he received the Legion of Merit.

No. 36
Mount Vernon, Iowa
March 18, 1945     Sunday morning
Dearest Gerald,

Sunday morning, and the kids have just gone to Sunday School – George gets credit in Boy Scouts for attendance, and Tommy gets his instruction for church joining on Easter. Your letter written on shipboard telling of the church service, came yesterday. They come at strange intervals, but I like it that way – spaced, rather than all at once – of course, I'm glad to get them, whenever they come!

I know you will get a kick out of the enclosed *GI Gazette*. You will know from the carbon of my letter to Tait Cummings, that he didn't print all the info I gave him, and got it garbled, but I think it's all right, and I get a great satisfaction from it. I am quite sure you'll be writing him yourself one of these times – or you can enclose a message with a letter to me, which would be still better. Went to PBK formal dinner last eve.

George and his pals collected about 1/3 of a train carload of papers yesterday, and had a good time doing it. It was a "trial" tho' for he certainly didn't give his paper route much attention. He is the only one in the troop that has a steady job, and he feels quite abused. I may have to enlist some "Scoutmaster" aid in building morale on that score. They are going for a hike down to the river this PM – it is in flood stage now. Am wondering what you are doing this Sunday morning. [Cornell Dean] Albion King spent 9 months in Europe at one time, and was telling me about their trip down the Rhine past Coblenz to Mainz. He says they nearly froze in Paris in the spring, so he can imagine what you are going thru. Was interested in your first contact with French femininity. Have you had much actual contact with the French people? Do you ever hear a radio? Glad to hear that you are feeling fine as far as your operation is concerned. Bye for this time. If I were a Catholic, I'd say an extra Hail Mary for you this morning, but I'll do it in my own way, and have faith that it comes thru to you.

Much love, 'S'Mae


Attachment: *Cedar Rapids Gazette "GI" Gazette* clipping: "Cornell Friends – of Gerald "Toot" Hill, former publicity man at Cornell, wouldn't recognize him in the above get-up which shows Toot on his motor cycle as a Red Cross man in Paris, France"


No. 37
March 20, 1945     Tuesday   7:30 PM
Dearest Gerald,

The first day of Spring, cold and very windy, but a WONDERFUL day! Your cablegram and V-mail letter written March 8 were responsible for my feeling that everything was and is beautiful. It is strange, but every one of your V-mail letters has been longer enroute than the straight air mail – I'm wondering if that is true of the ones that I have written to you. I got a big kick out of the cablegram, and it was very sweet and thoughtful of you to send it. We rejoice in the fact that you are an FD now, and I'm sure the three of you in your RX team will get along fine together. I appreciate the difficulties under which you work and write, so don't feel that you aren't "doing us justice" for you certainly do a grand job at writing. I know you will be pleased at Tait's brief note. I didn't tell him where or when that picture of you on the motorcycle was taken, and he just assumed it was Paris – Please don't disillusion him – I thought it was a good picture for the *GI Gazette*, and he apparently got a big kick out of it.

George went with his Scout Patrol on a hike to the river last Sunday PM and when they weren't back at eight o'clock, several of the fathers went out to hunt for them – everyone was plenty worried. They were all right though, and had had a grand time, frying raw potatoes – and I mean RAW – and burned meat. The boys have a list of regulations as long as your arm now, governing their next hike, for which I am very thankful. Anything could have happened, but luckily it didn't. George feels like a "man" in his room upstairs. He has one of the twin beds, his desk, one of the footlockers, a dresser, a couple of chairs and a closet, and a pin-up light over his bed. It is just a nice size for him, and gives us more room downstairs.

Love, S'Mae

No. 38
Mount Vernon, Iowa
March 22, 1945    Thursday    0700
Dearest Gerald,

Sitting here at a table in the bedroom, in my pajamas writing before the kids are awake. As I look out, the robins are "cavorting," the sun is shining, and the house is nice and warm. Makes me feel downright "guilty" to be so comfortable, knowing that you probably slept with cold feet last night, and perhaps writing to me by the light of a gas light. (The latter is wishful thinking, of course.) Your No. 26 letter came yesterday, and it was grand. So glad my letters are coming thru to you. Your telling of French money was interesting. I hear that the prices that are charged for things the Yanks want to send home (luxury items) are really scandalously high – nice that your wife would rather have a letter than a bottle of French perfume, isn't it! The Rowes are moving out on April 1, and I think I have another couple lined up to move right in.

The Johnsons gave me a bonus this week – celebrating the selling of their play, so now I have "made up" what I spent for tuition last semester, and have a "couple of months of experience." May I brag a little, when I think I can write a credible business letter, in form, and yet humanize it. At least, I know my own correspondence has improved with practice to you and usually Al says "answer so-and-so's letter" and then I do it in my own way.

Clint is spading garden, and making big plans – the only catch is that I'm afraid he'll do all the work, and not let the kids do it. We'll probably have a lot more vegetables, but I'd just as soon have the kids have the responsibility. He wanted to put lima bean vines on the front porch, but we finally compromised with morning glories. Tommy's teacher spoke about our very "talented children" last eve. I appreciate the fact that they have been able to do so many things the last two years here in MV – it is unbelievable the difference in these two towns.

I get a lot of satisfaction and pride in your being an FD now. It was nice to hear that the officers appreciate your work. It certainly spurs one on, and makes a person feel like "giving" when you know that it is appreciated. I know you do a grand job, and never spare yourself. After our experiences at camp last summer, I know how you feel when you say, "it takes so much time just to <u>live</u>" – the business of getting fuel, food, washing, etc., seems endless, but of course, we had the advantage, of just having nothing else to do, and it was warm.

The kids are stirring around now, and I must get breakfast. It seems strange to think of you drinking coffee three times a day. Have you learned to drink it black? I'm washing this morning, and I wish I could put your socks in – Much love from all of us.
                    'S'Mae

No. 39
March 23, 1945    Friday morning
Dearest Gerald,

Writing before the kids get up again this morning. Only two things of special import in the last 24 hours. Tommy reports that he has been chosen one of the few out of his class to be on the big composite grade-school program next week Wed. I think I told you he was on the committee to line up the talent. He felt pretty discouraged, because his "Citizen's Creed" wasn't flashy. When he spoke it, he said, "the kids just sat quiet and didn't say a word." That of course was high tribute. The other thing I have on my mind is Packy [MacFarland]'s visit. You know it just seems like a dream, for there was absolutely nothing about them in the paper, and I heard of saw nothing more of them, nor has any one mentioned them. Eke said a strange thing as she left. I said, "I know just how thrilled you are to have your husband home." She said, "Well, I don't know. I just get used to running my own life, and plop back he comes. I just don't know." She never was anywhere near him at J's – Packy was at one end of the room, by the fireplace, and she on a davenport over by the stairway. I don't understand it, but it seems screwy. Bertha commented afterwards about it – said she didn't think Eke was treating him very well. Packy obviously wanted to talk, and that she should have been the listener, if it took till 4 in the morning.

I have a hunch that I won't get any mail for a time now that you have moved up to the front. I hope that you are all right, and get the very most out of your experiences. Interesting to know the RX girls, as well as the men, are on the job. Goodbye, and good luck, my dear.
                    Essie Mae

127

No. 40
Mount Vernon, Iowa
March 23, 1945     Friday evening
Dearest Gerald,

Just a few lines this eve, to let you know I'm thinking of you. This has been another gorgeous spring day, and I hope your cold weather is over, too. I read with great interest an article in *Life* today, telling (with pictures) how the "ACS try to keep warm in Paris – wrapped up in blankets, or sleeping under a collection of coats." (THERE MAY BE SOME OTHE WAYS, NOT PICTURED?) The kids are going to CR tomorrow with Rev. Grant's to see *Thunderhead, Son of Flicka*, a highly recommended Technicolor movie. The Grants were good friends of the Hartongs before he became DS, and Mr. Grant was the father who brought the kids back from the Boy Scout hike last Sunday. I feel very much in a mood to go somewhere tonight for pure relaxation, but the movie isn't anything I want to see alone, so I'll try to persuade Tommy to go to the movie with me. George goes to Scout meeting.*

The chapel clock is just striking seven PM – I wonder if you are in bed asleep? G'Night, my Dear.

Love, 'S'Mae

P.S. I've been reading *A Tree Grows in Brooklyn* – a lovely story, which I hear is popular even with the GIs, if and when they have time to read. Plenty of realism to be interesting, but without the Bad taste in your mouth when you finish, that a lot of modern novels have. Love, EMH[†]

No. 41
March 24, 1945     Saturday morning
Dearest Gerald,

The kids are on their way to CR, Tommy haven gotten his hair cut for the occasion this morning, and George got his collecting done. G. was rather disgusted at having to take his small brother along, but he'll come thru in good shape, I know. Mr. Snook returned the playbill with an autograph for George, saying "To George Hill, a swell actor, and my kind of by, Lee Owen Snook." In a note he said he was "highly honored to be asked." Very nice of him, I think. No letter since the one you wrote the 12th of March. I am surely wondering what you have been doing the last twelve days. I am assured that you haven't "been standing still" at any rate.

Must dash to rehearsal of my solo tomorrow – will be thinking of you.

Much love, from all, 'S'Mae

No. 42
March 25, 1945     Sunday evening
Dearest Gerald,

Palm Sunday, with a warm spring rain all day. I sang "Open the Gates of the Temple" at the Pres. church, and got them "ajar" at least while the kids went over to the Methodist. They said they had a grand service over there – ours wasn't much, for it was McKibben's last Sunday. Thought about you, and wondered whether you were in chapel. I think it must be a wonderful experience to go to a service "at the front" or in the field.

A call from the McVille operator this morning about 0900 relayed from Mother, asking me to come down, for Jim hadn't come home last night at all. While I was debating what to do, for I knew the roads would be terrible from the all-night rain, and I had to sing in church, she called again, and said she had overheard [on the "party line"] Mrs. Davidson telling someone that Jim had stayed all night there, because the road from their place to home was so bad. She is so hard of hearing she won't answer the phone down there, and so it was impossible for Jim to contact her, even if he had tried. Glad it worked out all right, for I know how upset Mom gets.

The kids and I went to see Gary Cooper in *Casanova Brown* this PM for pure relaxation. An interesting short showing surgery at the front, not all of which I could stand to look at. Evidently they do wonderful things tho' – I tried to imagine Gaylord [Andre] in charge.[‡]

---

* *Thunderhead, Son of Flicka* (1945), starring Roddy McDowell, continues the story of his beloved horse, Flicka.
[†] Betty Smith, *A Tree Grows in Brooklyn* (1945) is considered a classic American novel. It became an award-winning movie starring Dorothy Maguire, Joan Blondell, Lloyd Nolan, and Peggy Ann Garner, directed by Elia Kazan.
[‡] *Casanova Brown* (1944), a romantic comedy, had its world premiere in France shortly after D-Day.

I guess I have my new renters lined up – Mr. and Mrs. Eisel. She is Roy Nelson's secretary, and he is a Marine, in the ship's company. They have been here quite a while, and have been quite popular around town. I have learned a little in my brief experience as "landlord," but I am not so optimistic as to think it will be all velvet – but it'll be worth it, I think. So many people have spoken to me about your pictures in the *Gazette*, and I'll be anxious to get your reaction – I surely hope you approve. It doesn't seem possible that Easter is nearly here, altho' the trees and everything are greener than they are usually a month from now. Everyone is raking lawns, burning leaves, putting in garden, scrubbing porches, and otherwise acting like spring is really here. I had a little fire today, for it seemed kind of damp, but lots of day, I let the fire go out entirely.

George would love to have the shoulder patches from the 7th and 9th armies, and Canadian and British, if you ever get a chance to get them. He is that strange mixture of little boy and man now, so that he surprises on both ways. Tommy's teacher told me she was so amused to see him riding his bicycle and dragging a little boat along after him on a string. Tommy made the boats and earlier in the season the kids of all ages sailed and dragged them in every creek and gutter. On the other hand, G. looks so nice when he gets dressed up – he can tie a four-in-hand now, and he is pretty good about washing himself and brushing his teeth. He does have nice looking fingernails, quite like yours, but isn't especially careful with them – altho' they're respectable.

Tommy tries to keep up with the bigger boys, and in some things can better them, then feels so hurt when he gets a slam. He can work people, including his mother, in his own way, too – and it comes out once in a while that he really expects to find his way smoothed out for him after the tears squirt. That's all right with me tho' – for he really doesn't abuse the love folks have for him. But enough of this chatter, for I must get the kids bedward – they are both up in G.'s room now – he likes company quite often.

Much love, from all of us, and I hope you are safe and happy and comfortable.

'S'Mae

No. 43
Mount Vernon, Iowa
March 26, 1945    Monday morning
Dearest Gerald,

The plasterers came this morning! This is the third time I've gone thru this business of having the kitchen torn up, but I seem to forget what it's like until it's started again. Nevertheless, I am simply delighted to have it going, and if we have to eat plaster dust with our cold sandwiches for a week or two, I guess I can take it. I remember climbing down a ladder to cook on the gas plate in the basement when we lived in the apartment just after we were married – now I wish I had a gas plate in the basement.

Your No. 21 letter came today, and we were so glad for it and the enclosures. Your telling of Dieppe and Rouen was swell. I know how the men must have appreciated your coming to see them at the hospital. Tell me if I'm right, but I'll bet that you are in Germany tonight. My, there has been so much activity over there lately, and there must have been some tremendous advance. Your letters are wonderful – you don't need to spend your precious letter writing moments commenting on unimportant things in my letters (altho' I'm glad you spoke of the play) – just keep telling us what you are doing. I have to do my "war work thru you," and I like to know all about it.

I never saw things grow like they are this spring. Iris is up ten inches, and lots of flowers and bushes are in bloom, and it's still March! Entré Nous had a picnic supper tonight but I elected to stay and eat with the kids. I must go to the meeting now. You're mighty sweet, darling, and I love you very much.        Essie Mae

No. 44
March 27, 1945    Tuesday afternoon
Dearest Gerald,

This letter won't be more than a "hello" and "goodnight" but it'll let you know I'm thinking of you. I have been scrubbing and scouring since the plasterers left at noon, but am making slow progress. Rachie wil be home in a few days, and I'm going to try to persuade Mother to come up and help me. Everything in the house will have to be washed, for the dust scattered and seeped into everything.

News from Europe is wonderful, and I am wondering how far from Berlin you are. Hope you can get into several countries before you come home – now that you are really in Europe. Had another offer of a job today – working in the Navy office. It means an eight hour day, tho' and I 'm not interested in that – besides I don't think it would be fair to Al, since I have only recently become efficient enough to be worthwhile as sec'y to him. It was nice to be asked, however, and it makes me feel that my struggle last semester was worth the effort.

I am a little irritated with the Boy Scouts tonight, altho' I was one of the boosters when it was organized. I think Joe Cooper doesn't get the whole picture (he's rather young himself in some ways) and I think he should make allowance for boys who have regular jobs (like George's paper route) – for G. hasn't had time to do one single thing around home since the Troop was organized – hardly has time to study, and NOW (what really set me off) was that the boys HAVE to take turns mowing Rev. ROWLEY'S lawn!! I don't' get it!! I am simply blowing off to you, so don't let it worry you. It makes me feel better to do a little spouting to you.

And now I DO feel better, and will go to bed. Goodnight, my dear. Sweet dreams.

Love, 'S'Mae

No. 45
Mount Vernon, Iowa
March 27, 1945     Tuesday evening
Dearest Gerald,

Another short letter before I go to bed. I have been reading a biography of Woodrow Wilson written by the sister of his first wife, and it was so fascinating that I couldn't lay it down – written from the human side rather than the political. I still hope to see the movie sometime. This has been an interesting day, beginning with house cleaning and ending with a steak fry in the back yard. This was the day of the grade school program and of course I was very proud of Tommy. He did very well with the big words in "A Citizen's Creed." I decided this would be a good night for George to try a little outdoor cookery practice, so we got steak and tomatoes, onions, apples, buns and potatoes (to fry) and had our supper over a fire – out near the alley. And that, my dear, is the picture on the "home front." Not at all exciting, but I thought as we were eating, that at least we were eating out doors <u>too</u> and even the mess kit was used. Hope you won't be too sick of picnics like that when you get home.

Much love, and a good night kiss. 'S'Mae

Al got a letter from MGM today asking to see script of *Love Your Neighbor*. He told me to "contact Hollywood" and this is the result!

No. 46
March 30, 1945     Good Friday morning
Dearest Gerald,

Breakfast all over – Bobby Gaston stayed all nite with George last night – and we are all set for a "different" day. The kids have no school, so Tommy and I are going to CR for the first time since the forepart of Jan. The boys are going on a Scout hike and will cook their own dinner. That's why I gave them a hearty breakfast!

Your V-mail letter No. 22 came yesterday, microfilmed for the first time. It certainly was small, but legible. It was very interesting, as all of your letters are. Bertha reads French very readily, so we won't have to wait long to know what they say. Are you learning any Fr. words or phrases? Glad you took some pictures … we'll be anxious to see them too. "We" have peas in the garden! Can you beat that? Potatoes planted, etc., etc. Some people have even mowed their lawns – never saw a spring like this. Tommy and I have a lot of errands in CR. I am going to get him a "pin-up" lamp for over his bed, and George a waste basket, for Easter presents. They don't need clothes, for the first time since I can't remember. Also plan to get the dictionary which George gave me the money for, get his watch fixed again, etc. We plan to stay for lunch. George and Bobby have a job painting Johnsons' fence. They are transforming their pool into a sunken garden, with a lot of flowers and shrubs. More chances to do more work – but I'm still content with the "status quo." Of course, you realize that I make quite a point of mentioning these offers, just so you will be convinced that you have a "private secretary of your own when you get home."

Belated Easter greetings, and lots of love.

Essie Mae

No. 47
Mount Vernon, Iowa
March 31, 1945    Saturday
Dearest Gerald,

        I've been up long enough to get a letter written to you, but if it wasn't one thing it was six, all day.  One set of renters moving out, and then a quick shift of what furniture I wanted to grab, before the next set moved in. Cleaning up the mess down stairs, etc., etc. Tommy and I had a wonderful day yesterday in CR.  It was almost like Christmas, for we had a lot of shopping to do. We had such good luck, getting things that the Johnsons had commissioned us to get.  I finally found a pin-up lamp for Tommy, and he has stayed in bed all afternoon, reading and drawing pictures so he can enjoy it.  A Scout axe for George, and he was delighted.  George and his pals had a grand time on their hike, and came home to enjoy a "home-cooked" meal.  Bobby Gaston was all set to cook his meat, and saw the dog just gulping down the last of it.  G. baked his potatoes in a hole in the ground, but forgot to prick them, and they "exploded" when they got full of steam – but a grand time was "had by all."

        The water is hot for a bath, and I'm just too weary for more letter writing now.  Excuse the shortness of this one – I'll write again soon.                 'S'Mae

## April 1945
### The Home Front listens anxiously, as the war comes to a climax in Europe
### Then Suddenly, the President Is Dead

"By the middle of April it had been clear that Hitler's Germany would soon be utterly destroyed.  The invading armies drove onward in their might and the space between them narrowed daily.  Hitler had pondered where to make his last stand. As late as April 20 he still thought of leaving Berlin for the 'Southern Redoubt' in the Bavarian Alps … Two days later, Hitler made his final and supreme decision to stay in Berlin to the end."
                                – Churchill, *Triumph and Tragedy*, 532-3

No. 48
April 1, 1945        EASTER SUNDAY
Dearest Gerald,

        The headlines this morning say that Eisenhauer [sic] demands Nazi surrender – tells of the new Fifteenth Army, etc.  We're wondering where you are, and whether, if peace comes soon, whether you will be coming home. Too soon to tell, I suppose, but one can't help wondering.  George started the day with an April fool that made me jump from the bed, in sound sleep, to the middle of the living room, wide awake, in nothing flat, when he came down about 6:30 yelling that the house was on fire.  It was just "April fool."  The next stunt was when I blissfully made an eggnog for Tommy for breakfast, only to discover that G. had filled the sugar bowl with salt.  He pulled several other good ones, but it was all good fun.  We had a lovely service at church – a class of 23 joined the church, including Tommy.  I was quite teary but "thoroly" enjoyed it.  Church was packed – a beautiful day.

        Then Rachie had such a nice dinner and we took our birthday presents to Mother.  Jim has a lot of little pigs, and everyone but me went out to look at them.  Mother came home with us, as scheduled, and we're just about ready to go to Johnsons' for supper.  Mother looks very nice in a black dress that Rachie fixed for her, with a fancy white frill at the neck that I gave her for her birthday.  I plan to take her to Lisbon tomorrow to make some calls.  She has had the best winter in years, I think.  Jim thinks that last V-mail letter of yours was something.  He said he didn't realize how it was straining his eyes, but he felt it for a couple of days. I had to have my glasses to read it, but it didn't do <u>that</u> to them. George with the Scouts are going to communion, tonight. He would like to know how far you got in Scouting when you were a boy. He is interested in getting any airborne Army patches, and the new Fifteenth Army patch. Tommy dyed Easer eggs on Saturday, and had a wonderful time, and did a grand job. He is young enough to get a kick out of it, but old enough to go ahead by himself.*

Much love, my dear, S'Mae

No. 49
Mount Vernon, Iowa
April 2, 1945        Monday morning
Dearest Gerald,

Just a note this morning, to let you know we're thinking of you. It is colder today, and snow is prophesied for the western part of the state. That's not unexpected tho', and we're thankful for what warm weather we've had.

We had a lovely time at Johnsons' last eve, and even Mother enjoyed it, in spite of the fact that she goes out so seldom, and finds it difficult to visit with "strangers." They had a little gift for each of us, with a verse, and it made it seem very much like a birthday party. Doug Van Metre told Al that Packy MacFarland is in Washington, D.C., and will be there for some time. We can't figure it all out, but it's probably just as well. I guess we were lucky to have seen him at all, for no one else seems to have.†

Tommy is all enthused about baseball now, altho his first love is still football. Al said he heard an Easter broadcast form Cologne cathedral yesterday, with the RX having a part in it, and he swears he heard a voice that sounded like yours. And now to work. Take care of yourself.

Much love, 'S'Mae

No. 50
April 2, 1945        Monday evening
Dearest Gerald,

It is much colder today, and frost is prophesied, but I surely hope not, for fruit trees are almost in blossom – many of the actually are. We had a really a delightful time calling in Lisbon tonight. Rev. Arnold says they had a very fine Easter service. He practically idolizes you. The smell of paint is surely strong in here tonight, but each day brings the job that much nearer to the end. Wonder how much longer before your job will be at an end. And what experiences you must be having. Are you keeping any kind of a diary?

Very weary tonight, so to bed. Hope you are warm.

Much love, 'S'Mae

No. 51
April 4, 1945        Wednesday
Dearest Gerald,

The postman gave me two V-mail letters today up town, but he is almost here, so just a note. I have been writing Marc Pitts story, and have it ready to send to Marc Rose, Senior Editor of the *Reader's Digest*. With a letter of explanation. Also typing script for Al – to send to producers who clamor. Terribly cold this morning with snow flurries. We have to file our intended quota of coal for next winter. More wartime read tape!

The V-mail "Greeting" with love was swell. The other which came today was No. 25. You are only about 20 letters behind (ones that I have written that you have not yet rec'd). It seems strange that it should take so long, but I'm glad they're coming thru. You know by now that we have had lots of letters from you, and that they "go the round to all the family."

Hastily, but heaps of love, 'S'Mae

---

* GLH earned his Second Class Scout badge, but his Troop then lost its Scoutmaster and it disbanded.
† Lt. Col. Lanning "Packy" MacFarland was flown to consult with MG William Donovan about Operation Dogwood, which he headed in Istanbul. See: Richard Breitman, et al. *U.S. Intelligence and the Nazis* (Cambridge University Press, 2005), 52-3.

[Enclosure: EMH to Marc A. Rose / Reader's Digest, 4 April 1945, enclosing the "Floozy" story about Lt. Marc Pitts (see Prologue to this book). She wrote to Rose, "Three of the boys, that we know of, have been killed … we'll never forget the boy who 'could not break a promise' to his country, even tho' it meant his life, or to a little boy in Iowa whom he never expected to see again (and never did).")]

No. 52
Mount Vernon, Iowa
April 5, 1945        Thursday
Dearest Gerald,

Clear and snappy this morning, and I'm afraid some of these early gardeners are going to be discouraged this morning, for it was below freezing last night. I am trying an experiment, which I hope will work out all right. The Lion's Club had copies of the show script made for all you fellows in the service. I told Al Morrissey, I would see to sending yours – so this is the first installment – as much as I can send by air-mail. The others will follow day by day, and I believe you will have it all, faster than if I sent it by regular mail. I think it was very nice of the club to do it – it'll give you some entertainment some evening.

Your letters are very tantalizing – giving us just hints of what you're are doing. Wish you could have gotten a job as correspondent – if only for the RX, for you write so well, when you don't have censorship hanging over your head. Does your tent have a floor in it? And are you still sleeping in a sleeping bag?

And now to work. Much love from all of us.
'S'Mae

No. 53
April 5, 1945 Lion's Script – Am mailing 4 letters today – Hope they all arrive at once – Love 'S'Mae
"Lion's Club Script" (7 pp.), typed, in African-American dialect, with the "n" word used once
No. 54
April 5, 1945 More Lion's Script – Save them & read 'em all together – if you can wait!
"Lion's Club Script" (pp. 8-12) typed in dialect, but without the "n" word
No. 55
April 5, 1945 The last of the script! Suggest you write Al Morrissey your thanks – Tell him I sent it "piecemeal by air"
"Lion's Club Script" (pp. 13-16) typed, in dialect, but without the "n" word

No. 56
April 6, 1945                Friday
Dearest Gerald,

Just a word of explanation about the big "jump" in numbering my letters – just in case you don't receive them in consecutive order. No. 52, 53, 54, and 55 went yesterday in three big envelopes – instead of four. They contained the script of the Lion's show, which I wanted you to get by airmail, rather than regular mail. Originally, I thought they would have to go in 4 envelopes, but when I weighed them at the P.O I found they could go as three.

And now to answer your wonderful letter of March 24, which came yesterday. Was it ever appreciated! You really did a grand job of describing your work, and I loved every word of it. I'm looking forward to my "gifts" from France – Boy! Will I be proud! There is a great clothing drive on all over the U.S., organized by Kaiser of Victory ship fame, for the people of Europe. After reading your letter about the desolation of the people over there, I am moved to be generous to the point of real "sacrifice" for I know some of them would be glad to wear things that we have. The trouble is, we just wear patched stuff ourselves. Living in our "isolation" here in the middle west, I'm sure we can't possibly realize what the rest of the world are suffering.

Do you still try to keep all my letters? I can't get over what an advantage it is to have carbons here to refer to, as your answers come. It seems like each time I get to feeling low because mail gets delayed, THEN comes a wonderful letter like the one yesterday, and I feel ashamed that I was impatient. Bear with me, please. Many delays in getting this letter written. Seems like it takes a long time for the kids to get to school today – have had to jump up a million times to see that they have everything they need. Bye, my dear. Blessings on us all.
Much love, Essie Mae

No. 57
Mount Vernon, Iowa
April 8, 1945          Sunday
Dearest Gerald,

We have been enjoying the letter of March 24, which came two days ago (Friday, April 6) – did you realize that it was close to 3000 words (I am wondering how long it takes you to write a manuscript like that). It was all so wonderful – I picked up the copy of the *Geographic* you mentioned, and it made it very real to read about Dieppe and Rouen, from the pictures and your description. Will be anxious to see the pictures you took. We got up about six o'clock yesterday and did a great multitude of things – from the week's ironing to making a blouse for myself. As a result, I didn't get a letter off to you, and I'm sorry, for I like to send some word every day. Nothing has ever been censored out of your letters – in fact, the ones sent air-mail are not even opened. George is getting ready to go on a Boy Scout hike, wearing your old knapsack – which fits him quite well now. He weighs 95 pounds – a gain of nearly 15 pounds since we came to MV. A whole group of them went "double" to the college swimming show and "eats" afterwards. You should see the way he dolls up for special occasions now, and he gets quite disgusted with Tommy because "he doesn't seem to care anything about his appearance." He did a wonderful job of collecting yesterday, and painted the hardware in the kitchen with aluminum paint like we had in Lisbon. It looks very nice.

Will dash out to the depot with this now, and write more tomorrow. Much love from us all.

Essie Mae

No. 58
April 8, 1945          Sunday evening
Dearest Gerald,

I sent out two letters to you today, one containing nothing but clippings from the Sunday paper today. The letter was short, and I did not feel that I "did right by you" at all, but believe it or not, I've been doing "homework" for you all evening. I made six carbon copies of a "digest" of those last two long letters of yours written March 24 and 25, and included a letter of explanation with each one – sent them to Barkers, Adelia, Rev. Arnold, Harry Sizer, Manly, and Mrs. Thomas. I was very thrilled to do it, for they were such grand letters, and I know all those people will enjoy reading about your experiences. I realize that if you weren't so swell about writing to me, you would have time to write more letters to other people, so I try to give them the benefit of your letters too. I edited them, so that I didn't include anything that would not be of "general interest."

Your description of the trips to Paris and Dieppe and Rouen was most graphic. You told it most interestingly, and I am glad you told about your seeing the famous sights as well as the details of the RX work and your accommodations. That is just the sort of thing which we, here at home "eat up." We loved your telling about the children in the schoolyard in Dieppe – did they look pretty well fed, or "did they need food and clothes"? How do the Germans look and act? Glad to know you have been getting pretty good food – sounds good to us. We have no trouble getting the "necessities" but it's all very high. Have bananas now, more often than earlier in the war. Never see any pineapple any more, tho', and canned fruit, what there is of it, is very high in points as well as price. I bought my first can of pears the other day (nothing to brag about in quality) cost 80 blue points and 45 cents in cash. We're going to appreciate our garden very much. Have you seen or tasted any of the famous French wines or champagne?

The papers today told of the 90th finding that tremendous cache of German gold and art treasures. I'll be interested in hearing what you have heard about it. Surely hope you see Gaylord [Andre] – what experiences he has had! Must be getting to bed now – I've been at the machine now for 3½ hours, and it's time to quit. Much love, and hopes that you are safe, warm, and content.[*]

Essie Mae

Enclosure: Map of Europe from *Des Moines Sunday Register* (8 April 1945) [see Photo Album]

---

[*] *The Monuments Men* (2014), a fictionalized film version of this story, was said to be "episodic and never entirely cohering."

On April 9, several prisoners were hanged at the Flossenbürg concentration camp, including Admiral Wilhelm Canaris and Pastor Dietrich Bonhoeffer. "At the place of execution [Bonhoeffer] said a short prayer and then climbed the steps to the gallows, brave and composed. His death ensued after a few seconds … Two weeks later, on April 23, the Allies marched into Flossenbürg. In another week, Hitler committed suicide and the war was over." — Metaxas, *Bonhoeffer*, 532

No. 59
Mount Vernon, Iowa
April 10, 1945      Tuesday
Dearest Gerald,

     Good thing I wrote to you Sunday night, for I was quite "incapacitated" yesterday. When I was getting out of bed, I twisted my neck and threw something out of joint. Went to the osteopath in the afternoon, and he turned on "deep heat" and massaged and jerked and pounded until I guess it is back in place again – feels better today, but still sore. That's only natural, I guess, but I surely was "done in." The men are finishing up the kitchen sink installment this morning, so things can be moved back to place soon. Am also sorting out old clothes for European sufferers. Nice and warm outdoors – the kids are fine. This kind of khaki handkerchiefs [enclosed] were all that I could get.

     Much love, 'S'Mae

No. 60
April 11, 1945      Wednesday
Dearest Gerald,

     The chapel bell rang long and loudly for Palisades Day this morning, but George and I both jumped out of bed and ran for the radio, thinking it might be the signal for V-E Day. The papers are so full of the tremendous progress all the armies are making toward Berlin, that it seems as if the big day may come any time now. I am feeling very well this morning, after not doing much by lying around for the last two days. Guess I just needed a little enforced vacation. We got a big box of clothes for European sufferers sorted out yesterday.

     The country is beautiful now – all fruit trees in blossom, and the grass very green. We had a little rain last night, but it is nice and balmy this morning. The sink is in place, and the kitchen is unbelievably convenient and nice. We should have taken some "before and after" pictures. No mail since your letter of March 25. I know you must have done many interesting and exciting things since then – waiting anxiously to hear all about them.

     Much love from all of us, 'S'Mae

No. 61
April 12, 1945      Thursday morning
Dearest Gerald,

     Your No. 27 letter, written on Easter Eve came yesterday, and confirmed my guess that you were in Germany on Easter Sunday. It was a wonderful letter, and I could read much between the lines, as to your feelings on that night, although you wrote beautifully. It hardly seems right that we should have had the peace and quiet of that day, here, celebrating Mother's birthday, but we are very conscious that we owe it to the sacrifices that you and the other men over there are making for our security.

     These last two weeks must have been terrific ones for you. I imagine you can say now that the training which the men get ahead of time is none too much. How far back from the front lines is the RX? I'll bet you get as close to everything as you possibly can. No time for shaving and clean clothes now!

     Hope that mail is coming thru to you now – but when it does, you'll know that you have at least one letter every day. Everyone listens to the radio, and combs the newspapers for news – the news this morning is that the 9th is 55 miles from Berlin – by the time this reaches you, it will probably be all over! What a desolation you'll see!

     The kids' grade cards came yesterday – Tommy got A in Art and Music, B in Reading, Spelling, History, English, Geography, Science, and Conduct, and C in Writing and Arithmetic (fractions). George got on the Honor Roll at last, thanks to a B in conduct, but his grade average was not as high as it has been other times – B in most everything except A's in Arithmetic (!) and History. His grades were very good, and I am certainly happy that he made the Honor Roll – which he did just to please me. Our nice day of yesterday, changed to storm in the PM, and tornado east of Lisbon. Took the roof off of a farmer's house near here. Better than bombing tho' I should say. Had some hail here in town, and high wind, but no damage, I guess.

          Love, 'S'Mae


"Washington, April 12 – Franklin Delano Roosevelt, War President of the United States and the only Chief Executive who was chosen for more than two terms, died suddenly and unexpectedly at 4:35 P.M. today at Warm Springs, Ga. ... He was 63."

          – Arthur Krock, *The New York Times: Complete World War II*, 516

No. 62
Mount Vernon, Iowa
April 13, 1945     Friday morning
Dearest Gerald,
        Seems like we can't think of much else but Roosevelt's death this morning. All regular radio programs have been cancelled, and we hear only news, fine music and comments on Roosevelt. We have been thinking and wondering how you heard about it, and what the reaction was amount the people there. I was painting kitchen accessories out on the back porch, George was reading the *Gazette*, when Tommy dashed in about 5:30 and said, "Have you heard the news?" I said, "What news?" "The President is dead!" "What did you say?" I asked. When Tommy repeated it, I thought he was mistaken, but George dashed to the radio, and of course, then we heard it. As a commentator said this morning, "The news that the war was over would have been accepted – that Tokyo was invaded would have been believed, but this was something that people just couldn't believe.
        We are keeping the papers, so you can read about it when you get home, if you care to. I told T. that he would be telling his children about it, when they came to study history. George has commissioned me to find some black cloth to put on the flag, a la picture in the Boy Scout manual. But I guess that will have to do, for this brief account – after all, I can't possibly do more than suggest the shock that the whole country – world – feels, and by the time you get this, it will all be past history. The war is so awful! The pictures of the German prisoners (Americans held by the Nazis) in this week's *Time* are simply ghastly. I wonder if you have seen any. The RX seems to have been the one bright spot in their existence. George just came in from town with the *Chicago Sun* – to read and keep as a memento. He had tried to buy black crepe up town unsuccessfully, so I found an old black dress belt, which he is now ripping apart to drape the flag with. He is looking forward to Civics and History classes today.
        Wish I knew how things are going with you, and what you are doing. It doesn't seem right that we can maintain our lives here so uneventfully, but that is just what you are "fighting for," I guess.
        Much love, and trusting that you are safe, Essie Mae


No. 62A April 13, 1945     Friday morning
Dearest Gerald – In case No. 62 & 62A get "separated," I sent "62" this morning – telling of Roosevelt's death! – and reactions here. This is just a "clean hankie" [enclosed] for you. Imagine it's pretty difficult to get washing done nowdays. Wish I could help. Thinking of you & sending <u>much</u> love. Your – Essie Mae


No. 63
April 14, 1945     Saturday morning
Dearest Gerald,
        I doubt whether there was ever a time when people listened to their radios more constantly than these days. All regular programs were cancelled yesterday and programs of music and news were on all the networks. We listened to the descriptions of Roosevelt's "entourage" leaving "Warm Springs" yesterday morning and it was most dramatic and moving. All stores and movie theatres are closed today all over the country, from three to five PM, and

memorial services were held yesterday in schools everywhere – school children of course can't remember any other president. The trend of thought in papers and private conversations seems to indicate a "unifying" tendency, which is a good thing. Truman seems to be starting out in a way that is gratifying, in spite of everyone's previous qualms. Hope so, anyway, for the war must go on! I'll be so interested to know how the news was received where you are, and what the reactions were. The radio says that news blackout from the Western front still continues, and that the end may be "any minute." No wonder we don't leave our radios for any long time!

The cards you mailed from Paris came yesterday, and were especially appreciated, for they gave an "extra angle" on your trip, and bridged over this gap in our current letters. The booklet is very tantalizing, and we are going to ask Bertha to read it to us when they come for Anne's birthday dinner tomorrow night.

I am taking eight of the Boy Scouts to CR today to get uniforms. The organization is working out better now that the kids are "hitting their stride" and I think it will be especially good for them this summer.

Tommy again scored a hit, with Al Johnson. Al wanted to make a wagon for Anne for her birthday, and I, in a sudden burst of enthusiasm, volunteered the information that we had some wagon wheels. When I asked Tommy about them, it developed that he had been treasuring them to build a wagon himself, when he got some lumber for his birthday. He had a hard struggle with himself, but finally decided to give them up, so he presented Al with them. Al hadn't realized how impossible it is to buy things like that, and when it really soaked in, he was so touched by Tommy's self-sacrifice that the Johnsons decided to buy her one of these "war-time" models that won't last any time at all – but Tommy got his wheels back, and a great deal of credit for unselfishness!

It is raw and chilly this morning but the country is beautiful with blossoms. This has been a freakish spring with warm weather and tornadoes. The kids are getting up for breakfast now, so must sign off, and get to work.

Much love, from all of us, 'S'Mae

No. 64
Mount Vernon, Iowa
April 16, 1945     Monday morning
Dearest Gerald,

I am wondering and thinking about you this morning, for it has been three weeks and two days since you wrote the last letter we have received. What kind of shelter have you had? Have there been tragedies among your friends that have "racked your soul"? Are you all right? Have you had enough food? How have you stood the "baptism of fire"? Has mail been coming thru? What kind of work and service are you doing now? Have you met anyone whom you knew before you got to Europe?[*]

And now, since Time and Patience will answer all those questions and the many more that I have in my mind, I guess I'll turn back to the "day by day" report on the home front. George got his Scout uniform (shorts, shirt, neckerchief, hat, compass, and socks) on Saturday, and he looks grand in it. He takes to a uniform just like his Dad, I guess, and you would be proud of his "manly" appearance. He is so anxious to be "every inch a soldier" that he and Tommy both stand at salute whenever they even hear the National Anthem on the radio. They practice folding the flag for long intervals and study regulations by the hour.[†]

I got the famous, precious Dictionary when we were in CR, and we are pouring over it with great delight. If you ever find a misspelled word from now on, you will know that it is "simply a typographical error." It is a real treasure, and a very touching gift. Because of the long delay – it is now my Mother's Day present, which make it very nice, too. George finally wrote to Mr. Snook yesterday, thanking him for his autograph. I insisted on it, for there's no telling when the "good opinion" of some "recognized Chicago personage" might be of value to him – and Mr. Snook certainly had a high opinion of him at the time of the play.

Must "brave the elements" now, and go uptown, to make sure the postage on your mail is correct. Thank goodness, there's enough chicken and noodles left for last night to furnish us with lunch. Hoping for mail – but I know it will come eventually.

Much love for all of us, Essie Mae

---

[*] For "racked my soul": Balzac, "The lily of the valley" (1899), and in a play, *The Distrest Mother* (1804); paraphrased "rack my soul" is in a song from Yeomen of the Guard (1888). For "baptism of fire" – John the Baptist (Matt. 3:11).
[†] The poem "Every Inch a Soldier" by John Strange Winter (1894) was popular in World War I.

No. 65
Mount Vernon, Iowa
April 17, 1945     Tuesday morning
Dearest Gerald,

I was relieved and happy to get 2 letters from you, written March 29 and April 5. The latter came thru in 11 days, which I think is very good. Your letters suggested enough to set our imaginations running riot, but I don't – we can't – really picture what you have seen and done – no one can, who hasn't been on the ground! I was trying to picture the Rhine valley in my mind's eye as I read *The Seventh Cross* last night, which as you know is a war story of Germany – the concentration camps for the Germans themselves! It has been made into a movie, with Spencer Tracy as the leading man. I found a 50¢ edition of it in the dime store Sat. but it is very satisfactory.*

Wish the censorship would lift so that we could know what Army you are with. The papers this morning say that Ger. is almost "cut in two" – Russians only 17 miles from Berlin! The political situation here at home seems to be stabilizing itself – Truman made a good impression in his speech to Congress yesterday, and everyone seems willing and anxious to pull together to get the war won as quickly as possible. Our flag seems to be the only one (besides the school) which is still flying – at half mast – but the kids are proud to put it out each morning and take it in. George and Bobby Gaston collected another 115 pounds of paper on Saturday. And so it goes. At best, there doesn't seem much that we can do, except "keep the home fires burning."†

Much love from us all, 'S'Mae

No. 66
April 18, 1945     Wednesday morning
Dearest Gerald,

9:30 AM – Have just finished the ironing, and now "to the typewriter" before I start on the morning dishes. Was thrilled to get two more grand letters from you yesterday morning – written April 7 and 8 – the latter came thru in 9 days, which is about the best time so far. Was much interested in the description of your "billet" with the electric generator outside. Hope the weather soon warms up, so you are nice and warm again INCLUDING YOUR FEET! You are very philosophical about the inconveniences, and that is a wonderful attitude and point of view.

Your description of riding up to the OP in a jeep going full speed was most interesting, and I'm surely glad no sniper was around! I am confident that you are giving wonderful service to your men, and are a grand example of morale. Tommy is pleased and proud that you wear and use his lanyard. Jacques Jolas told me yesterday that he'd "give ten years of his life to be over there where you are now." He simply goes into raptures! I got a big kick out of your supplying beer for the men – what a variety of things the RX "do do"!

Am so glad you are getting mail regularly. Far from being a "chore" as you say – these daily visits with you are a "pleasure" indeed. Life is very uneventful but I'm glad you like this "rehash" of our household activities. We may be wrong about trying to "read" anything into the Packy and Eke [MacFarland] situation – hope so.‡ Your saying "my needs are very few and I really don't know of a thing at this time that I really need" moves me to comment that I think one of the good things that may come out of the war experiences of lots of folks (I hope) is a sort of reevaluation of what is important. I know that is true of me – this business of "keeping up with the Joneses" is a snare and a delusion and it really is surprising how much more satisfying it is to keep living simple and vital. It's nice to have hot water on tap, but any one knows that a great deal of our "civilized social life" is the bunk! That's my opinion, at any rate.

I stayed up pretty late last eve, writing the story of George and Admiral Leahy – rewriting it, I mean – for "Life in These United States." Good practice for me in "self expression," even if it doesn't get the cash in hand – and I can still be hopeful, can't I? George is in a great period of "system." He has lists of things to do, and goes according to the clock, practically down to the split second! 6:30, get up, come downstairs, put the tea kettle on, wash, brush

---

* Anna Seghers, *Das siebte Kreuz* (1942) was translated into English and published by Little Brown; the movie, *The Seventh Cross* (1944) starred Spencer Tracy. The title refers to the escape of seven prisoners from a Gestapo camp, and the mission to capture and crucify them. Only George Heisler (Tracy) eludes capture. Both book and movie were highly praised.
† Ivor Novello, *Keep the Home Fires Burning* (1914) was a popular patriotic poem in World War I.
‡ Packy probably divorced Eke. He married again, at an unknown date. His second wife already had a child.

teeth. 6:40 go upstairs, and study. 7:30 come down for the paper. 7:35 breakfast, etc. He has been rearranging his shoulder patches, and was happy to get an "airborne division" at Armstrong Hall on Sat. Tommy is practicing the Boy Scout salute, and gives commands to himself, while he marches. He thinks two years to wait is an AWFUL long time. He is very mysterious about a Mother's Day present he is making me at school.

I think you must know by now, that your letters are not even opened by a censor, and nothing was cut out of the V-mail. No stamp of any kind on them – except your own.

Johnsons are having a time trying to decide on a Commencement play. They have decided to submit *Cry Havoc*, which is a story about the nurses on Bataan, to Mrs. Cole – it has an all-girl cast, and is a powerful play, but they don't want criticism from the administration afterwards, so they will let her pass on it first. There's some pretty hard language in it, I guess, but it is a very moving play, and has had wonderful success on B'way.*

Lots of love, Essie Mae


No. 67†
Mount Vernon, Iowa
April 19, 1945      Thursday morning
Copy of a story I sent to "Life in these United States" – *Reader's Digest*

It was eleven-year old George's first experience at a formal tea. He was panic-stricken at the sight of the gold braid and Phi Beta Kappa bedecked dignitaries. The faculty and officers of the Naval Flight Preparatory School were all there in "full dress" to do honor to the distinguished guest. Among them was one little boy. "Gee, Mom, just look at all those service ribbons," George had exclaimed as he had studied the newspaper pictures of the man, and he had joyously accepted his Mother's invitation to be her escort to the affair. Going through the receiving line, George did not realize the haste with which he was "passed along," but his Mother knew. She yearned desperately to shield the lad from the embarrassment which her effort to compensate for the disruption the war had brought their home life would cost him.

She needn't have worried!

"Hello, George, how are you?" the guest of honor said, smiling with genuine warmth and kindliness, as he shook hands. Later, seeing the boy still looking at him with worshipful eyes, he asked, "Anything I can do for you?" and without waiting for an answer he modestly signed the proffered autograph book: William D. Leahy, United States Navy

George thinks formal teas for five-star Admirals are wonderful!

By Mrs. G. L. Hill
Mount Vernon, Iowa


No. 68
April 19, 1945      Thursday morning
Dearest Gerald,

Your letter written April 10 came today, and seems to me to mark "another" turning point in your experiences, in telling of your observation of conditions in Germany, and the casualties that are coming to your men. It must be very soul-wracking for you, and I am very proud of the way you are carrying on with your job, and putting your whole self into it. I like the bits of description of the country that you put in, too.

The main feature of this letter, however, is the one from Mrs. Thomas, which I am enclosing. I feel quite certain that you will be moved to write to her personally – I suggest that when you do, you make a carbon for me, and then "we'll both have one." I feel sure it is with people like her that you will particularly like to visit, for they can appreciate so well what you have seen and done, especially when they appreciate the work you are doing now. Evidently hearing from us in that way, put her into a very mellow and touching mood, and I think her letter is

---

* Nearly forgotten now, *Cry Havoc* (c.1942) told the wrenching story of nurses trapped on Bataan as the Japanese surrounded them. The *Cry Havoc* movie (1943) starred Margaret Sullivan. The title comes from Shakespeare's *Julius Caesar*.
† *Reader's Digest* did not accept her story for publication.

terribly sweet. George is out with the rest of the HS collecting clothes for the Europeans this afternoon. We had nearly 90 pounds ourselves. Don't worry, you'll still have some clothes when you get home, but none of us will have all the things we had before.

Much love, 'S'Mae

Enclosed: Letter from Eloise (Stuckslager) Thomas (Mrs. Seth), Fort Dodge, Ia., to EMH, 17 Apr 45; mentions their trips to Europe before the war and details of their visits to Paris, Rouen, and Dieppe. "It is surely a thrilling work that Gerald is doing and I am so glad he is a part of it and he is having this rich experience. We surely need men like him to look after our boys so far away from home."

No. 69
Mount Vernon, Iowa
April 21, 1945         Saturday 9:30 P.M.
Dearest Gerald,

It has been a long time since I've sent as little mail to you, as I have the last two days – but it's been a long time since Lester was here! Got a letter from him yesterday morning (Friday) saying he'd decided to come to Iowa this weekend. Of course, I was plenty busy from then on. Tommy & I got away early in the eve & went to a show in CR (*National Velvet* with Mickey Rooney) and then met the *Rocket* & it was about 2 A.M. when we quit talking for the night. It surely reminded me of the time you were taking the *Rocket* for St. L. Made me "nostalgic" – very!*

It's been 11 days since you wrote the last letter we've rec'd – which isn't "too" long – but with the papers so full of news from Germany, I am constantly wondering about you. My! Such awful stories about the conditions of prisoners in the concentration camps! How can the Germans have been so inhuman! The news we near, puts all armies closer & closer to Berlin, but the cost of lives, lives, lives!

[later] April 23, 8:30 A.M. Monday

And now it is Monday morning – I don't know when I've been so lax about my letter writing, and I do feel very guilty. I hope you haven't been worried about us. But you can imagine how it has been, while Lester was here – an additional factor, which I didn't mention in the Sat. night part of this letter, was the fact that George's slumber party was too much for him, and he has been in bed since Saturday PM. Just a little temp. and sore throat, but mostly just tiredness. He was awfully good, but of course, it meant delivering papers for him on Saturday and Sunday morning, running in and out of the bedroom to wait on him, etc. He feels all right this morning, but I didn't urge him to go to school, so he has his ear glued to the radio. He is also anxious to hear the announcement of the joining of the American and Russian armies, that he doesn't leave the radio for an instant. There is a tremendous air of expectancy, and in addition to that, there is news of the coming conference at San Francisco. These are surely momentous times! I keep wondering all the time about you, and how you are located in the whole picture.

Lester was in fine form, and we were on the go all the time. I had Frank and Ruby [Runkle] here for dinner yesterday, besides the Highs and Mother. In all our good "fellowship" I was very conscious of the fact that probably here in America was the only place where such a gathering would be possible these days. I guess that's what you're fighting for – the security and happiness of the folks back home – but I just want to tell you that I just had in the back of my mind all the time, the sounds of the guns along the front and the hardships and the sacrifice they are making.

I am going to get my first taste of "reading proof" today – the "copy" of *Love Your Neighbor* came Sat. and it surely looks mighty nice to see George Hill's name leading the "cast of the original production." I surely hope and trust and pray that you are all right. So much must have happened in the 13 days since you wrote the last letter we have received. We just eagerly await direct news – radio news is terrific! Must get started on the morning's work, altho' I'm slow moving this morning. George will be OK, and Tommy is thrilled with the new baseball equipment which Lester brought. Last night was the first time I've left them alone in the eve for ages, but they were touchingly sweet about my going. I guess I felt more reluctant than they did, for I found them peacefully sleeping when I got back. I tried to imagine what the European mothers must feel as they see their children destitute of even enough food to eat, and kids as big as George out doing a man's work in all sense of the word.

Bye, dear. Much love from all of us, 'S'Mae

---

* *National Velvet* (1944), starred Mickey Rooney and a young Elizabeth Taylor.

No. 70
Mount Vernon, Iowa
April 24, 1945       Tuesday morning
Darling,

I am very conscious of you this morning, but also conscious of the fact that I am not going to have time to write as much as I would like to again today. I have been typing for more than three hours this morning, making a complete "excerpt" copy of your letterers from shipboard days until the last written April 14. The completed "story" in your letters, making a wonderful record, now goes to the friends who I know you will want to have contacted.

We are all fine this morning. George is still loafing around the house, but he feels all right – just a little weak and lazy. I think he had a "vacation" coming to him, for the kids both worked at home and school like troopers all year long. It is a long stretch without any spring vacation, like they used to have. Must dash for town to mail all the correspondence now, for it will be "heavy" postage. Good bye dear, trusting that you are all right.

Heaps of love, Essie Mae


No. 71
April 25, 1945       Wednesday evening
Dearest Gerald,

I sent copies of the six-page transcript of your letters to Marie Hill, Mary White, and Judge Littell yesterday, and a shorter one (bringing her up-to-day) to Mrs. Thomas. It was grand to reread them all myself, and it helped to make this "waiting" time, until the next one comes, pass a little more quickly.

George went to school this morning, but Tommy is taking his turn with sore throat, and "laziness." He is growing tall, and has a cute new crop of tiny gold freckles over his nose. He was practicing an "oral composition" last night at home, on his trip thru a B-17. He remembered it very well. We have been reminiscing about our trip to Montana, too, and he remembers that very well, also. George is so thrilled with the "Librarian" sleeve insignia, which was delivered to him last eve. The "investment" service for the Scouts is tomorrow evening, starting with a picnic supper for the Scouts and parents at the church. Mrs. Cooper called me last night about it, and we all got a laugh out of the fact that she absent-mindedly asked "if my husband would be there"? Then I could hear Joe's exclamation of disgust at "such a break. My gosh, you're talking to Mrs. TOOT Hill." She was much embarrassed. I told her, that if he were here, he'd surely be there, and added comments of our appreciation of Scout work.

The news from Europe is tremendous – I keep wondering what it means as far as you are concerned. The *Register* has a detailed map of Berlin, which will "locate" you when you write about it. I wonder if your mail comes thru to you now. Word has come that Harold Beach died a prisoner in Germany! Certainly is awful! I have been thinking about accepting Mary White's invitation and going to Montana this summer – there are many angles: How to get there, what to do with the apartment, whether by any chance you will be coming home, and whether there would be things that the kids and I could do that would really be a help there.

Today the big conference in SF begins. It is surely momentous, and every "intelligent" person is wondering what will transpire and hoping that the decision will be wise ones. George read last night in his History about Coolidge's taking his first oath of office – he was fascinated!

Much love from all of us, 'S'Mae


No. 72
April 26, 1945       Thursday morning
Dearest Gerald,

I was SO glad to get your letter yesterday (No. 32). I surely hadn't expected to hear that you were so close to the front tho' – the house where you were being shelled, etc.! Gosh! Your letter was so graphic, it gave us a wonderful picture of what conditions are like. Sleeping on a concrete floor, and all the rest. You're wonderful, honey. I dreamed about it last night, the whole darned night – the house was being shelled, I'd wake up in a cold sweat, or smothering. I feel for you in losing your close friends, too. Terrible! Every word of your letter is "gone over" again and again, and I surely appreciate the time and thought you put into them.

I have been so interested in your comments on what to do after you come back. I agree that it is nothing to worry about now – that will take care of itself when the time comes. Whatever comes will be all right.[*]

We have been listening to the opening of the SF conference, and the clipping of the view of the city you sent was most interesting. I know, it has extra significance for you. Tommy said naively last night, as we listened to Truman, "That just doesn't sound like the President." Naturally, it wouldn't. He uses a typical mid-western way of talking, and sounds very much "like one of us."

I wrote Mrs. Pitts yesterday as you requested. A letter from Marc Rose, Editor of *Reader's Digest*, came and was very appreciative of "my letting him read the manuscript, but 'It is America's salvation that she has thousands of such fine boys; her tragedy is that they are dying thus'." In other words, there are so many stories dealing with fine young Americans and the war!

George is all pep and smiles this morning – he is on a debate at school today, and then this big Scout meeting tonight, when he is officially "invested." He can just hardly wait! He was so glad to get the information about your Scouting experience. And now to work – I feel like "pitching in" after being very lazy all day yesterday. Take care of yourself. Thinking of you,

> Much love, 'S'Mae

The San Francisco Conference at which the United Nations Charter was drafted, lasted from 25 April to 26 June 1945. It was the largest international conference ever held. "President Roosevelt had been working on his speech to the conference before he died. That never-delivered address contains the often-quoted words: 'The work, my friends, is peace; more than an end of this war—an end to the beginning of all wars; … as we go forward toward the greatest contribution that any generation of human beings can make in this world—the contribution of lasting peace—I ask you to keep up your faith'."[†]

No. 73
Mount Vernon, Iowa
April 27, 1945       Friday morning
Dearest Gerald,

The Boy Scout meeting last night was especially fine – but Gosh, how I missed you. Joe Cooper looked very nice in his new wool Scoutmaster uniform – the boys and parents, Troop committee and wives were all there. Tables decorated, boys very gallant. Afterwards, a candle-lighting service, when the boys were presented with their Tenderfoot badges, then the mothers were called up, and each boy pinned a miniature badge on his mother. The boys' pins were put on upside down – to be reversed after their mothers had been assured that they had "done their good deed." I kept thinking how much you would have enjoyed it, but I knew also that you would say, "I sure would, but that's what I'm out here fighting for!" Am I not right?

Had to smile at George when he said, "This is the best church dinner we ever had, 'cause there weren't a lot of little kids running around!" I guess that shows how fast kids grow up. My cold has gone up into my head – and I am grateful for the Kleenex. I'm so grateful too for your letters. I guess I'm about the most fortunate person I know of, in that regard – you are most faithful, and I do appreciate it.

> Thanks for being so darned sweet and good,
> Heaps of love, Essie Mae

April 28, 1945. "First Link Made Wednesday by Four Americans on Patrol … The United States and Russian armies have met on the Elbe. The Western and Eastern fronts are at last linked up and Germany is cut in two. First contact was made two days ago – at 4:40 P.M., April 25."
> – Harold Denny, *New York Times: Complete World War II*, 526

---

[*] This attitude of acceptance was commonplace in WWII. It was exemplified by Doris Day (1922-2019) in her signature song, "Que sera, sera," (whatever will be, will be) in the movie *The Man Who Knew Too Much* (1956).
[†] https://www.nationsencyclopedia.com/United-Nations/The-Making-of-the-United-Nations-THE-SAN-FRANCISCO-CONFERENCE-25-APRIL-26-JUNE-1945.html

No. 74
Mount Vernon, Iowa
April 28, 1945      Saturday morning
Dearest Gerald,

Getting an early start this morning – it is only a little after 8, but George is already out collecting, we have had our waffle breakfast (no one was very hungry tho') and even Tommy is up and dressed. G. wants to get his collecting done (for two weeks) so he can pitch into paper collecting again, with the Scouts. He is trying to persuade his patrons to pay a month at a time – which will save trouble for them – and him.

In another week we'll be in the midst of May Festival and Tommy's birthday will be over. All he wants is lumber for building – hope I can get him some. Hard to realize that he is ten years old.

Lester said that he talked to Commander Heffelfinger at Blake Homecoming last fall, and that he particularly remembered George. Margaret Dilley's husband has been in Europe more than three years now, and I hear that she has a terrific fore-boding that after being wounded several times, that any time now he will be a "fatality." Haven't heard from him since back in March. It must be an awful suspense. These are trying times for you at the front, and for us at home too, but I surely do appreciate your letters.

Much love – now to build up the furnace fire.
        Much love, 'S'Mae

No. 76 [and 75]
April 29, 1945      Sunday morning
Dearest Gerald,

I am sending V-mail and airmail both today, to try out again, which is faster. Dilleys are so worried about their son-in-law: Capt. Lynn Morrow / O-1012995 / 41st Armored Inf. Reg. /APO 252 c/o Postmaster New York.

He is with the 2nd Armored of the 9th Army. He had his feet frozen in the "Belgium Bulge" – refused to go to the hospital, and went back into action with his feet still draining. His specific group had trouble along the Elbe on April 14, so Dilleys read in the papers. They haven't heard from him since the middle of March, and Margaret is nearly at her wit's end. Mrs. D. wrote to him, suggesting that he have his RX man write them, if he couldn't, but I offered to send this information to you, just on the bare chance that you might be near.

As a result of the Scouts' work yesterday, every boy in the Troop is eligible for the Eisenhauer [sic] award, which is given to each boy who collects 1000 pounds of paper. Each boy is also eligible for a gold bar for 25 hours of "civic service." George worked early and late, but he feels all right today, thank goodness. He was awfully disappointed that I couldn't allow him to stay all night with Stanley Grant again. I went on to bed, feeling pretty sad about the "blow-up" myself, while he flounced off upstairs to his room. After a while, he came down again, and we had a very touching teary scene, getting back to a mutual understanding basis of love and appreciation, and he finally fell asleep downstairs with me, after I had rubbed his back to get the tenseness and tiredness out.

Took the Geology book over to Nelsons' yesterday afternoon, and they were much touched over the memorial gift. The primary thing in all our minds is the hope that the news that it is all over in Europe will come soon. Like millions of others, I keep wondering what that will mean as far as "reuniting our family" is concerned.

Time to get ready for church now. Blessings to you, and much love. Essie Mae

No. 77
April 30, 1945      Monday   0900
Dearest Gerald,

The thought just occurred to me, that some housewives don't rest in the mornings until their breakfast dishes are done, and the beds made – not ME! I just seem to gravitate toward the typewriter, as soon as the kids are off to school, and get the day started right, with a letter off to you.

Mrs. Dilley called me last eve, and said the dreaded message that Lynn Morrow is "missing in action" came yesterday PM. I am so glad I got the letters to you, about it, off yesterday. It was a comfort to them – a "straw to clutch at" that they had a personal friend in you, over there. A cheering coincidence, however, was the fact that Grace McGaw got a V-mail letter from Brad saying that he was a prisoner of the Germans. It must have been

143

smuggled out – for that is really unprecedented. I heard a rumor that it had been done thru a German guard, who had once gone to school at Ames. Sounds fantastic – but it was wonderful for her to have gotten direct word from him. Roy and Florence Nelson called in person last eve, to bring back the memorial book, which I left at their house for them to examine. I am sure you will be hearing from them. I am sure they appreciate it.

My cold is better today – and I forgot my appointment at the beauty parlor this morning! Yes, people do still patronize them – even I, every couple of months or so "whether I need it or not." You can see it isn't on my mind very much tho' – not as much as making pancakes for breakfast this morning. Started last eve on what was supposed to a birthday picnic for Tommy with the Johnsons, but it started to sprinkle and turned cold, so we ate our sandwiches at their house. It was a great disappointment to the kids tho', and I have had to assure T. over and over again, that we will have a "celebration" of our own. Just think! Ten years old!

Headline news today is Mussolini's ignominious death. Constantly listening to the radio for the official announcement that war in Europe is over. AND most of all, waiting for the mailman.

Bye for the time, my dear. Heaps of love,

Essie Mae

## May 1945
## The war in Europe is over, and Gerald is safe
## Essie Mae Writes "My thoughts were of you" at the Celebration on V-E Day

"The instrument of total, unconditional surrender was signed by General Bedell Smith and General Jodl, with French and Russian officers as witnesses, at 2:41 A.M. on May 7. Thereby all hostilities ceased at midnight on May 8. The formal ratification by the German High Command took place in Berlin, under Russian arrangement, in the early hours of May 9."

– Churchill, *Triumph and Tragedy*, 540

No. 78
Mount Vernon, Iowa
May 1, 1945        Tuesday morning
Dearest Gerald,

In combing the papers for Air Corps news about Marc Pitts, George discovered that the 97th is with Patton's Third Army. We had missed the announcement, when it came out in the paper on Sunday, April 29 – and it was surely a big thrill to discover it. George was so proud and happy. I have been rereading *Time,* and all the recent newspapers, in the light of that knowledge, and Oh! it helps so much. No mention has been made specifically of the 303rd (that we have seen) but this morning's paper told that the 97th took the air field at Eger. This puts you (we now realize) a long way from the 9th (Capt. Lynn Morrow – whom I wrote about yesterday) and Bremen (Marc).

I am wondering whether you have seen any of the ghastly prison-liberations which we have been reading about. Where were you when the Americans and Russians "joined up" – and most of all – how are you standing up under the grueling experiences you are having? Has your mail been reaching you in good season? Handkerchiefs and all? So much can happen – and <u>has</u> no doubt, since you wrote the last letter we have received. Altho' I realize that I am very fortunate as far as mail is concerned.

And now to work – thinking of you,

Much love, Essie Mae

No. 79
Mount Vernon, Iowa
May 2, 1945          Wednesday morning
Dearest Gerald,

Just letting you know I'm thinking of you & hoping you are safe. Ruby is working as a volunteer nurse/helper at the Clarion hospital. She tells of members of the Hill family: "All are well," and of Jessie's honor in Rainbow girls. She mentions reading about Ernie Pyle's death in combat, but, "I do trust tho' that Gerald will have no harm come to him, only the thrilling experiences that he writes about."

Very much love – Essie Mae


No. 80
May 3, 1945          Thursday morning
Dearest Gerald,

Well, ten years ago, you were a little late getting to work, because of the sleepless night before "getting your new baby borned." It doesn't seem possible! Tommy was a happy boy this morning and looked so nice – he is a child to be proud of. And I know that you are thinking of us, as we are of you. The only thing he wanted for his birthday was lumber for building, which is practically unobtainable in "these times." However, I talked the lumber yard here out of some scraps, and I am going to Lisbon (to the bank) and will visit the feed store to see if I can't get some more. I also got him a small plane and a hack saw, which pleased him mightily. With the plane he can spend a lot of time smoothing up these boards into good shape. It is raw and chill this morning, but both kids looked nice – George in a white shirt and blue sweater. He gives an oral composition this morning in English on his insignia collection, and he took the most interesting ones to school. Papers are full of the alleged death of Hitler this morning. Got a nice note from June DeNio yesterday, thanking me for my letter after Denny's father died, and wanting me to come up some weekend, for a talk about you and the kids, and all.

A report from the "home front." Was lucky enough to get a pound of bacon this week – very scarce – and we had toasted peanut butter, bacon, and tomato sandwiches last night, with a "store cake" with vanilla pudding over it for dessert. Very filling and good. The latest "shortage" is toilet paper – altho strangely enough, paper towels are not so scarce. Everyone uses margarine now, and the kids like it better than butter, even when it's uncolored. I suppose your supply of "salt and soda" toothpowder has been used up long ago. What do you use now? Have you been able to get a haircut? Do you live in tents now, or houses? Have you seen any of the liberated prisoners?

I am having one of Tommy's pals here for supper tonight, and he thinks that will be a fine birthday party. He stayed in bed all day yesterday, but was very contented, and seems to feel fine today. We played checkers last eve, and he was delighted to win a game from me finally – and he really did, too – he's sharp!

Bye, my dear, hoping and trusting you are well, and thinking of you always, with much love,
Essie Mae


No. 81
May 4, 1945          Friday morning
Dearest Gerald,

I'll start this letter, and then if I get mail from you, put an addition on it. Here's hoping! On the way to Lisbon yesterday morning, I suddenly decided to stop and see Mrs. Thomas – had a nice visit with her while she dressed to go to a Trustee meeting at the bank, and IMAGINE, she invited me to dinner last eve. It was rather complicated, for I had told Tommy he could invite a guest for birthday dinner here, but we had the children eat at 5 o'clock, so everything was squared away. I went over to Lisbon with the Van Metres. The guests included Eke McFarland. We ate in the dining room. I sat between two Chicago men, near Mrs. Thomas. It was very casual and pleasant, and I am sure it was your letter to Mrs. T. (which I sent her) which was responsible for the invitation. She said to tell you that "I was doing a good job while you are away" – whatever that is worth to you. My Festival ticket was at the opposite end of the seat where we usually sit – across the "divider."

I left at intermission, to come home to put Tommy to bed on his birthday. He was touched to tears, to think I hadn't forgotten him on that very important day. His birthday wish was that "Daddy would soon come home."

Absolutely no mention was made of Packy, but I missed his not being there – he is the only one of those Chicago men who seems to me to have much of any personality.

George had a date with Eloise Littell again last eve, and he is so darned cute about telling me everything about it afterwards – more like a girl than most boys would do with their Moms. He got an A- on his speech about insignia – he had only about three minutes or so, and that is too short a time to do the subject justice, when he knows so much about it. The 97th was one of the few patches he chose to discuss, of course. Quote – "This one with the trident, I'm especially interested in, for that's the one my Daddy wears." (Correct us, if we're wrong about that.)

And now to wait for the mail (meantime, ironing, getting lunch, and generally keeping busy, to make the time go faster). Much love, from all of us, Essie Mae

No. 82
Mount Vernon, Iowa
May 5, 1945          Saturday morning
Dearest Gerald,

Your No. 33 letter (April 21) DID come yesterday, and were we ever glad! I am glad to think of you as having a good place to sleep, for a change, and I surely would love to have been there. It doesn't seem possible that the official announcement of V-E Day will be far away, but I'm surely relieved to know that you are safe. I'll be it seemed good to get bathed and shaved and rested after the life in the open for so long. I trust that you get your typewriter fixed promptly – you would be lost without it – and so would I – you write such darned good letters!

The big news for MV is that word came over the radio yesterday, and is in the paper this morning, that CAPT. LYNN MORROW has been liberated from prison. As I wrote you, Margaret has been SO worried for fear he was killed, so we are all terribly relieved. The postman was having a wonderful time yesterday, for he told us the news, and brought me a letter from you, which I had been pestering him for – he loves to be the "bearer of good tidings," you know. Have you seen much evidence of "looting"? How do the Germans where you are react to Americans? This week's *Life* was simply horrible – pictures of the murder of slave laborers in Nazi prisons.[*]

Are you using your camera? Wish I could meet you in Chicago or NY when you come home, so that we could have a week or so together, before you get out here where I'll have to "share" your company with all your friends. How does that appeal to you? A note from Rev. Arnold yesterday says that he wrote to you – I think he has a great personal interest in you – and probably feels that you are doing the kind of work he would like to do. Bertha said that Al gets very low, because he thinks and realizes that there is so little he can do to help in these times.

Hope you can contact Gaylord Andre. And now to the morning's work – George is out collecting and T. is getting set to "build." Much love from all of us. 'S'Mae

No. 83
May 7, 1945          Monday morning
Dearest Gerald,

Once more I am writing to the "accompaniment" of the radio giving the AP flashes about the signing of unconditional surrender. None of the other news agencies are carrying it yet, and it is not official – but it is exciting. How George did hate to leave for school this morning! Personal news (very important to us!) is that I have two letters from you to answer. No. 34 and 35. We love to read about your travels, trying to identify where they might be – it helps to know that it is 3d Army, at least. I am glad that you weren't burned when the stove exploded. You can imagine how I used to lie in bed this winter and wonder whether the furnace fire was fixed all right, or would "explode." Coal gas can be very tricky – and now I'm glad that you have good headquarters.

I love your Mother's Day card – it is beautiful. I notice that it was printed in Luxembourg. The pineapple and other good food sound wonderful, and I am glad they are feeding you well. It will be grand to eat pineapple again, but we are really well fed, too, and doing without some of the "luxuries" we used to enjoy is really a very small item in the whole picture – there is so little that most of us can do to actively help, that it is all part of the game to cook in "these times." (Radio says London is getting excited about the peace rumors and paper is begin to fill the air in NY.) Was much interested in your comments on the clothing donations. Of course, it has all gone by this time,

_____

[*] EMH rarely used the word "Nazi." She often spelled it as "Naxi" but I have corrected this misspelling.

but if it is not needed, and is not used to advantage, the US people have certainly been sold a "Bill of goods," for it undoubtedly was the most organized and publicized "drive" so far. We have plenty to wear, I assure you, but I was much interested in your comment. I suppose you have been getting the handkerchiefs – glad to know that you have plenty now. ---- The radio says that the news has not been announced officially, but that this is undoubtedly The Day. Millions are undoubtedly saying, "Thank God!" Radio – Yelling in "Times Square"!!

   I get very lonesome for you, and think how grand it will be for you to be home – My <u>mind</u> – if not my emotions – says that I hope you have an opportunity to see all you can while you are there, and while we are at home are "geared" to you being away. I think it is wonderful, the way you can and do throw yourself into your work of caring for your men, and it is a great satisfaction to know that you are doing such a darned good job, and that the men appreciate it. You're seeing sights and doing the war work for all of us, you know – I'm sure we're of the same mind. I'll sign off now, and hope that the war will be officially over some time very soon.

     Much love from all of us, Essie Mae

No. 84
Mount Vernon, Iowa
<u>May 8, 1945</u>  V-E Day   Tuesday
Dearest Gerald,

   As I sat in the chapel this morning in the service of "celebration" my thoughts were of you, and I am hoping that you are writing, telling us how you are spending the day, and what is going on where ever you are. I sat on the back seat and I wondered whether there would be another "peace day" by the time OUR grandchildren came along. The service was very dignified, with Judge Littell giving the opening prayer, and talks by the Navy and Marine commanders here on the campus. College classes go on as usual today, but the public schools are dismissed.

   For the record: It is bright and sunny today, chilly wind, temp. 45°.

   George was the first one up this morning – came down stairs dressed in his Boy Scout uniform about seven o'clock. He got more and more tense and excited as 8 o'clock approached, and phoned for the correct time at 7:58, then phoned Bobby Gaston, who was still in bed, "ordering" him to get up and listen to Truman's proclamation. We listened, and then listened to the recording of Churchill's proclamation. By that time, the fire siren was blowing and the chapel bell ringing, and George was very high-pitched. He took off for school, saying "Goodbye," then hung around the door, and then said again, "Did I say Goodbye?" and dashed out. I saw him at the chapel and he said 17 of the Boy Scouts had been there in uniform. Stores and business houses are closed for the day, but the town is very quiet. Mother and I plan to go ahead with the washing. I think people are conscious of families like the Nelsons, and realizing that peace is not really here until the boys are back home. I wonder what changes this will bring in the nature of your work. CBS on the radio is giving "reactions all over the country." Just now, San Francisco is on – and apparently things are very much the same out there. Everything turns toward the Pacific now. Quote: "Everything is entirely normal out here." Hope you are close to a radio, but I imagine you are very busy.

   Will "sign off now" – hoping to hear from you soon,[*]

     Much love from all of us, Essie Mae

No. 85
May 9, 1945  Wednesday evening
Dearest Gerald,

   Your No. 37 letter came this morning, and I have located the Wagnerian Opera House as being at Bayreuth – am I right? Ever since we read in the paper that the 97th was with Patton's 3rd, we have been wondering whether you weren't getting toward Czechoslovakia, and I am glad you got to see "one more country." I hate to think that the Germans are still holding out there though. It was interesting – very – to hear that you were near Gaylord Andre, and probably you have seen him by this time. Surely hope so. It must be wonderful to meet people you know, when you are so far from home! The papers tonight tell of Goering's capture. Wish they could get hold of Hitler.

   It has been so cold and disagreeable here the last couple of days – I am mighty sick of shoveling coal – I am nearly down to the bottom of the pile and there doesn't seem to be much heat in it – Oh, we'll get by all right – we

---

[*] EMH knows that GLH will remember Edward R. Morrow's signature "sign off" from London: "Good night, and good luck."

were just spoiled with nice warm weather in April, I guess. I notice in your letter today, that you have been cold too – so we're both in the same boat. Things were very quiet here yesterday – V-E Day. I think people all over the country (with the exception of NY) just leaned over backwards, not to be accused of forgetting that the Japs still have to be licked. I wonder whether the censorship rules will be relaxed for you now that fighting is supposed to be at an end. And I am wondering what the plans for you and your men will be now. Do the men talk much about going to the Pacific? Have you had many RX messages to deliver from the men's families here at home? I appreciate the letter writing that you do for us here at home so much, that I know how much your other "interested people" would love to get a direct message from you, even just a card – Just thought that you might have time now – sometime.

        Must get Tommy started bedward now. Thinking of you, and so glad the "shooting's over."

              Essie Mae


No. 86
Mount Vernon, Iowa
May 11, 1945       Friday morning
Dearest Gerald,

        Enclosures will make up the bulk of this letter, for life "on the home front" is certainly very calm and uneventful, now that V-E Day is over. I just keep wondering how far into Czechoslovakia you have gotten and what you are doing these days. It still stays cold and chilly, with frost most every night. I am going to take Mother to Lisbon this PM to work around, and then bring her back here to sleep. School kids are thinking about Commencement – they are going to have very nice "exercises" for the Eighth Grade. George is on the committee to draft the Class Prophecy. He has been drifting along as far as studying is concerned, but he has enough "background" to get along all right. We celebrated (I don't know why) by going to the movie last night – saw *Objective, Burma!* – a very good show. Are you able to get movies for your men now?[*]

        I am glad you don't think I have to do anything more with the "Collector of Internal Revenue." I haven't done anything – but it has been on my conscience. I wrote to Ruby night before last. I was shocked to learn that Adelia will probably teach again next fall. Hope your Dad's cold is better.

        Have heard nothing more from the Whites, so I'm letting that Montana proposition drift along – I doubt if we go out there this summer. It is 8:15 now, and I must get the kids up to eat breakfast and get ready for school.

        Much love from all of us, and hoping that we get some more mail soon.

          'S'Mae


No. 87
May 12, 1945       Saturday  7:15 PM
Dearest Gerald,

        Again tonight, the postmaster proved to be a "friend indeed" by calling and telling me to come over for some mail. Was I ever glad! No. 37 and 38, and the pony edition of *Time*, April 2! They did me a world of good. They have all been read and reread and passed around, maps looked up to find Siegen and Cologne, and old issues of *Time* recombed. Tommy is lying on the davenport now, reading the pony *Time*, while Mother does the evening dishes and I write. I have been very neglectful in my writing this week, for no particular reason, except that since V-E Day there has been a terrific falling off of news in the papers from Europe, and there just hasn't been much to "put my teeth into."

        Now that I know you have been transferred back to your previous Army, I'll know what to look for in the news. We are going to church in Lisbon tomorrow, and then on the McVille for dinner. Mother finally got us cranked up to washing the winter's dirt off the car (and it was terrible), so we will really be proud to be on the road. Tommy was a great help, and personally beat the floor rug and did the polishing. He has simply slaved over my Mother's Day present too – with great secrecy – and paint! I shall thank Mr. Arnold for you tomorrow when I see him. He was so interested in your description of the church service you attended – "armed." Mr. Arnold has recently gotten a robe to wear in the pulpit, which I think is a very good idea. Tommy's comment over the transfer to

---

[*] *Objective, Burma!* (1945), starring Errol Flynn, was based on the six-month campaign in 1944 of a U.S. Army forces unit, Merrill's Marauders. It got a D- in History from *The Guardian* in England because it neglected the other Allied forces.

another Army – "Mother I'll bet you're glad." "Why, that means the Army of Occupation, and he won't be home for a long time," answered I. "Well," Tommy said, "He won't be going to the Pacific, anyway!" Good old Tommy – always sees something to be glad about!

You answered all my questions in grand style, and I mull over everything you write about your comings and goings. I almost can "see" you in your session about "over buying for the GI's" – and I'll bet you win out! We are glad to know that you can wear the ETO ribbon. George was especially happy about that – the great "decoration guy, you know." What you say about the prisoners, and the contrast between them and the Germans, certainly checks with all we hear, and I am glad to know that it is really authentic. The guerilla war, too – you just can't be sure for a minute that you won't get shot – darn it! They just can't be trusted for a minute, and I think that they will be a problem for years to come. I have been dreaming up a nice dream, that involves your getting a more or less permanent job in some capacity over there – maybe with the UNRRA – if not the RX, and then we'll all come over, and "headquarter" somewhere in Europe. I just let my imagination work over time, and build the grandest air castle, about, about a "European" education for the kids for a year or so, and a job for me in some school room or office. Isn't that a grand air castle? There'll certainly be lots of work to be done over there by Americans, for years to come.

Tommy went with me to a style show (Home Economics Dept.) in the chapel last night. He was the only male for quite a while, and then a couple of middle-aged husbands came in. T. looked at them, and then said, "Those women look like they'd say, 'You come on, or else'." Which I thought was quite an observation for a ten-year-old. He then said (at my questioning) that I didn't look like that and that I wouldn't be able to get away with it with Daddy even if I did. George certainly takes his Scout work seriously. They had inspection last night, and his uniform had to be pressed, shoes shined, hair combed, etc., as if the "general" himself were to be there. He is Librarian, and takes great pride in his filing system, and "book keeping."

I am very grateful that I have the kids' "confidence." At least, I am very sure that they tell me more than lots of kids do their mothers. For instance, Tommy said after supper last night, "Mother, may I go out tonight?"
MOTHER. Why of course, where are you going?
TOMMY. Over to the school house.
MOTHER. That's all right, just be a good boy. Do you want to tell me what you're going to do?
(Tommy looks serious and rather mysterious)
Then it comes out, gradually, that three of the kids (including himself) had put their newly painted Mother's Day presents in the basement window to dry, and had left the window unlocked, so they could open it, and get out the gifts. This being Friday, they were afraid they wouldn't be able to get them in time for Mother's Day, otherwise.

I didn't preach to him, but I told him, that if by any chance someone did break into the school house and do some damage, that they would be involved in it, even if they did not do any damage themselves. I told him I would much rather wait, than to have him get my present that way, but if he felt like going ahead, then it was his decision. He decided not to! And went with me to the style show instead. The payoff was that the Art teacher was at the school today (Saturday). He worked there all afternoon, so everything turned our fine. I am very glad, and so is he.

Your letters are a great morale builder for us at home – and we need it too. We are thrilled over the long ones, but the short ones are greatly appreciated too.

And now, G'nite – Heaps of love, 'S'Mae

No. 88
Mount Vernon, Iowa
May 14, 1945        Monday morning
Dearest Gerald,

Ahhh – Whew – Brrr! That describes Iowa weather the last twenty-four hours. You can expect – and get everything! Yesterday (Mother's Day) started out as the most beautiful day you ever saw. The kids and I went to SS and church, here in MV, for Mother wasn't feeling very well, and didn't care to go to Lisbon after all. We went to Rachie's, stopping in Lisbon to pick up a nice looking young private from the S. Pacific who was hitch hiking to Schick Hosp. at Clinton. We had a very nice relaxed time on the farm, and didn't realize that it had started to rain. By the time we started for home, the road was so slippery, that we came home the back way and just more than skidded around. It poured all night, and is still at it, and so we're thankful we have enough coal to "see us thru."

Mrs. Dilley called me last night to say that they had gotten a message from the Gov't, saying that Lynn Morrow was liberated, and then last eve, they got a message from him personally, saying "I'll be seeing you soon." It made a wonderful Mother's Day gift for them, and make one's heart ache for Mother's like Mrs. Beach and Florence Nelson. The gold star mothers of the town have been honored on several occasions lately, which is only very right, but I don't see how they stand it – it would keep the "wound" open, it seems to me![15]

George took a great deal of pride in repainting the Highs' mail box yesterday with aluminum paint, a black post, and red letters. They want him to come down after school is out (it is all over this week) and do some more painting – a hog house, etc., and he is delighted to think he can really have a "job." Wish you could be here for his Eighth grade graduation. It is to be a very nice occasion I think, with a dance, and everything.

Tommy's big present to me was a "smoking stand." Isn't that the modern viewpoint tho'! He really put lots of work into it, and it is all painted black with great painstaking labor. He also gave me a wooden bracelet, which he decorated with my name, at school. I gave the kids each a new shirt – Tommy a dress shirt, and G. a khaki colored sport shirt to wear on Scout hikes. He is very much delighted!

Another question – Is the scope of your work to look after the men in a <u>Company</u> or a <u>Regiment</u> or what? I think it is wonderful that your men are eligible for a decoration for their work.

And this is all for this morning – Heaps of love, 'S'Mae

No. 89
Mount Vernon, Iowa
May 15, 1945        Tuesday
Dearest Gerald,

I just finished making a big batch of cottage cheese, and just as you say when you have pineapple – "Wish we could share it with you." V-E Day is a week "gone by" and I am wondering whether you still go armed and are still having to watch out for "guerillas" – news in the papers is very, very scarce indeed. Evidently the Germans do not in any way repudiate their leaders, as the Italians did Mussolini. Have you seen or had any contacts with the Russians? This seems to be a period of "marking time" for the MV "home front," at least. Held up primarily because of this wretched weather – when it was so nice and warm back in March, we might have known what to expect – but the thermometer was near freezing again last night with a raw, damp, chilly rain, and the ground is sodden this morning. Mother is cleaning out the cob bin down cellar, and is patiently waiting for a chance to get home. George has been reorganizing the military collection, and is looking forward to that Nazi banner. He wore a couple of dog tags around his neck to school this morning.

Tommy came home giggling yesterday about the plans which the sixth grade have for their "graduation." Quote – "Why they've even made up a song about how the hate to leave the dear old Ward school." He is plenty sore to think that the fifth grade only get to go to Ash park for their final picnic, instead of going somewhere exciting where there's <u>water</u>. Do you ever see anything that looks like fresh rhubarb or asparagus, or are all such things canned when they come to you? I sent a box of a dozen rolls of toilet paper, and a pound of bacon to the Runkles last week. Both are among the "next to impossible" to get in Mpls – the former – "one roll to a customer" once a week. We can get plenty of meat in general, but bacon is scarce. We don't really have anything to complain of tho'.

Everyone except Tommy – including the Highs – thinks my European air castle is the bunk, so don't take it too seriously. I feel like I'm getting into an awful rut tho', and I must get reorganized with something stimulating to do. Are the German shops open, so you can get haircuts and shoes shined? Do you sleep in a <u>bed</u> these days?

Bye for this time, Much love,
'S'Mae

No. 91
May 17, 1945        Thursday   7:45 AM
Dearest Gerald,

We're up early for a change – I have to go up to the office and work on the thesis which I am typing for a college girl – it's quite a job! Went to an AAUW picnic supper last night and came home very much thrilled over what George's teachers had to say about him. His History teacher, Miss Ralston, said she was sorry that "the outstanding history student" had to be chosen from the Junior and Senior classes," for in her opinion George was the outstanding History student of the school. He got the highest grade of any one in his final exam, and just has a wonderful concept of history in general. Then Mrs. Davis, his math. teacher (with whom he has scrapped all year) told me that he got the highest grade in the final test (100) and that his paper was <u>very</u> neat and nice besides. That is an achievement too, for she has fussed about the appearance of his papers a good deal. Then, before I left, Miss West, the science teacher, told me how much she had enjoyed having him as a student the last two years. Said he was always asking questions out ahead of the assignment. So, you can imagine, I felt pretty darn good! He was thrilled with the bond which I gave him, and Grandma gave him a dollar this morning.[*]

I've been meaning to ask you how often you have "mail call" – not every day, I would judge.

George says to tell you that he can tie 15 different kinds of knots. He is scheduled to help load the paper which the Scouts collected – about 15 tons. Got Jessie and Junior's graduation invitation yesterday – I'll have to pick out presents for them. I think Jessie plans to come to Cornell next year. Got the new Blue Cross insurance policies the other day. We'll be very much interested to receive *Yank* magazine.[†]

I wonder how much news and comment you hear about the SF conference. It is quite confusing to me – haven't had enough experience with political science to be able to read the future in the "present" and it is difficult to sift out the prejudice and propaganda from the reports and editorials about it. From the garbled conditions in Europe   what to do with Germany – the Big Shots – and all that – I surely hope that something can be decided ahead of time about Japan, and not leave everything until after they are licked. It seems pretty sad to me to fight a war, and then not know what to do with the peace after it is won! You're the Political Science student in the family – what is your opinion in the light of what you see and know? And now to work – eagerly looking forward to the mail.

Much love from all of us.          Essie Mae


No. 92
Mount Vernon, Iowa
May 18, 1945       Friday    8:45 AM
Dearest Gerald,

This is one of those mornings when we get up and do a day's work before breakfast – Mother's idea, not mine! She is determined to go home, but she wanted to help with one more washing and ironing before she left – which we haven't done all week, because it was so rainy – it is bright this morning, but still chilly!

This is Palisades Day for the HS and I am waiting for George to bring home some supplies for his lunch. He went with a bunch of kids to Lisbon this morning to get some flowers for a gift to the teacher (Mrs. Davis). His graduation from Eighth grade yesterday afternoon was very nice. He looked especially fine I thought, with a pair of dark brown pants, and light tan coat, white shirt, with brown necktie and hankie in his coat pocket. He was very jittery – and solemn – Oh, the kids all wore white carnations, too. The valedictorian was chosen from among those who had gone to school here in MV from kindergarten – that was Martha Osgood. The top honors for this year's grades went to Martha and Bobby Gaston, with George and Beverly Nation just one A apiece less. Considering the fact that George had his play in addition to what the other kids learned, I think that is doing very well.

*Time* yesterday says that censorship has tightened as a result of V-E Day. Have you had new instructions about it? That must account for the shortage of news from Europe in the papers. Ruth Dean says Judd is staying on in Europe. The folks who live upstairs have gone to New Jersey for a two weeks "leave" – they paid the rent in advance. One of the kids in Tommy's class brought his grade card – he has a semester average of about B plus. Tommy has a miserable cold, and he is getting so tired of staying in with only Grandma for company. There really isn't much he can do to entertain himself – or to be entertained with. This summer vacation is a <u>problem</u>! He and I played checkers all last eve, but it wasn't very exciting for either of us.

And now to work. Hoping for mail.

Much love, 'S'Mae

---

[*] The Daughters of the American Revolution Prize was awarded to the best student in American History in grades 11 or 12.
[†] Junior is the son of GLH's brother, Myron Hill. Jessie (Cornell College, BA '50) is the daughter of GLH's sister, Ruby (Hill) Woodin. She married her college classmate, Kenneth Kent (BA '50).

151

No. 93
Mount Vernon, Iowa
May 21, 1945      Monday morning
Dearest Gerald,

What has the last three weeks brought to you? It was three weeks ago today that you wrote the last letter we've rec'd, and I know that an infinite amount of "things" must have happened to you since then.

I haven't written for the last two days – (Sat. and Sun.) – but our "over-all" pattern changes little if any. This is the first official day of summer vacation, and summer has come in with a bang – of thunder and lightning. The humidity is so high that the water tower "sweats" a regular shower, and real showers have been spasmodic. It is a relief to have it warm, however! Saturday, I typed in all my spare time, and Tommy was out selling Tags for the "Volunteers of America" – a charitable organization founded by the sister of the founder of the Salvation Army. I wasn't too sure of it myself but it was sponsored by the town, and the school kids sold the tags. Tommy worked into third place, and got a $1 for his efforts, which thrilled him tremendously. He is a complete extrovert about selling, and thoroughly enjoyed his day "on the street."

Yesterday the kids both went to the Pal in the P.M. and played "jungle commando" all afternoon. They came home tired and dirty, but thrilled to death with crawling over the cliffs and in and among the trees. I spent a very quiet and uneventful day, reading most of the time – I got out William Shirer's *Berlin Diary* to reread, as I do every so often, to re-evaluate it in the light of present events. It is always interesting, too. The Arnold family called in the evening, and we had a nice visit. Their kids were entranced with Tommy's playthings, and the parents were in a very gay mood. Rev. Arnold said he had gotten tired and sick of the Federates slams and digs!*

Letters from Grace Barker and Mary White recently. Grace spoke about your letter, and looked forward to the time when we could "catch up on everything together." Mary wants to know "when we are coming?" I am trying to figure out an "excuse" for enough gas to drive out, for I just don't see going by any other means of transportation. I talked to Neil Miner about his summer Geology camp, maybe something can be worked out about transporting some of his pupils. Their camp is just S. of Teton Nat'l Park – which is quite a way from Twodot, but considerably closer than M.V. I am anxious to hear your reaction to the trip. I know you will be interested in the enclosed clipping about the Honeymead Co. Would like to know the details, and the reason for their selling, etc.[16]

And this brings us up to date on the news from home – will be hoping for mail this morning. Much love from all of us. 'S'Mae

No. 94
May 21, 1945      Monday morning
Dearest Gerald,

Tommy's birthday letter came yesterday, and we were all so pleased and happy over it. It was a lovely letter for him, and I was so interested in the information it gave about where you were on V-E Day. I told the Vodickas about it this morning, and Rudy says that his home was about 15 or 18 miles from the Moravian border. They were all smiles over the anticipation of talking to you about the "home country" when you get home, and are hoping that you are doing an extra good job of "looking" at everything, because you know of people back here who will want to know all about how things look – and that you will be able to tell him, first hand.

Toppy Tull called me this morning about the book we gave the library in Harlan Nelson's memory, and I suggested that he put in print somewhere that you were in CZ, etc. I think there has been all too little publicity about you from Cornell. The upshot of our conversation, which turned out to be quite extensive, was that I gave him a copy of the "excerpt" of your letter to read, and I am impatiently waiting his reaction. He seemed genuinely interested, and I spent the whole morning bringing it up to date. It makes quite a manuscript – close to 12,000 words,

---

* William Shire was famous for *Berlin Diary* (1941) and later *The Rise and Fall of the Third Reich* (1960). Shirer was known to the Hills, because he was a student at Coe College ('25) in Cedar Rapids when they were students at Cornell College, 13 miles away. The Federated Church ("Federates") was the other Protestant church in Lisbon.

I would judge, and goes from your first letter on shipboard to V-E Day. I think it is a wonderful record, and I shall be most interested in what he thinks. I will report to you, of course.[*]

George has been having the pink eye, but is better now. I had to deliver his papers again yesterday, but I've issued an ultimatum on that – he can get a substitute like the other boys! I have done that just about as long as I intend to. They have been very busy with mock battles – handmade weapons, of course. What kind of response did you get from your telling your Red Cross supervisor that you would not stand for having "pipes," etc., you had bought for the men charged to your personal account? Have you been on the move a lot lately, or have you gotten located somewhere, where you will be for a while? Have you given any thought to my "air castle" about all of us coming over to spend some time in Europe? Do you consider that too fanciful for any consideration?

And what about CZ itself – what does the country look like? What is their attitude toward Americans – did you have to get all your money changed into the "coin of the realm" again? Is the countryside pretty much demolished? Do you see anything of the Russians? Are you allowed to contact the native CZs? Do you "see" anything of the famous Czech beer? I expect that a good many people in your travels in CZ would be much interested in the fact that we are so close to Cedar Rapids.[†]

It was really grand to go over all your letters again, as I did in making this new transcription. I realized anew how much "drama" you have packed into the lines that you have written, and in spite of the thousands of words that it totals, how much there is "between the lines." Did you ever hear from or about Marian Chipperfield, since you've been across? What arrangements are there for recreation, or have you and the other men any time for that? I know you will probably be answering most or all of these questions just in the course of your letters, but I just constantly keep wondering. The paper tonight says that the first boatload of troops came into NY today, and we are wondering if Margaret Dilley's husband is among them. It is grand to think that their story has a "happy ending" or so we hope. Supper is over now, and I better do the dishes. George has "flashes" of great inspiration, and Tommy just keeps plodding along on his ideas, never giving up even if he can't work things out right away. He is disappointed that he won't be able to sell poppies next Saturday for a "commission" – for he really goes for this selling game.　　Much love from all of us, 'S'Mae

No. 95
Mount Vernon, Iowa
May 25, 1945　　Friday morning
Dearest Gerald,

Yesterday was a RED LETTER DAY! Finally got a letter – No. 39, dated May 1, arrived May 24. I told the kids that if I didn't hear from you yesterday, that I'd think that something had either happened to you, or that you were on your way home. It was wonderful to hear from you, and I am hoping that the next letters will not be so long delayed. So glad that you sent a carbon of your letter to Mrs. Thomas. It was a very lovely letter, and I am sure she will be very happy to get it. I was glad to read it, too. It must have been very trying to live in that kitchen with the GIs, with all the discomfort, noise, clutter, etc. I hope you have better quarters now. Have you seen or driven thru any mountains on your travels? And how does the Rhine, as you saw it, compare in size with our rivers?

Paper this morning tells of Himmler's suicide – that's one less to have to dispose of some other way!

Saw Irene Andre a minute last night, and she said Gaylord had sent your letter on to Lucille. I told her what you had reported about the difficulties of contacting folks, and that you were sorry not to have been able to see him.

I took George down to the farm last night to stay for a few days, painting the hog houses, mowing lawns, etc. Mother was spading the garden when I got there. The house looked nice, but she had a little cold. This darn weather! Rainy again this morning, so it's no wonder one catches cold. Did I tell you that "we" are giving Bob Runkle a Bible for a graduation present? That is what he wanted, and I am happy that they "allowed" us to get it for him. I guess he is really quite religious, and serious.

---

[*] EMH's 12,000-word excerpt of GLH's letters from "shipboard to V-E Day" has apparently been lost.
[†] The Hills had many Czech friends whose lives were similar to those depicted in Willa Cather's novel, My Ánotonia (1918). The National Czech and Slovak Museum is in Cedar Rapids. The family of Leo Beranek, Ph.D. (1914-2016), founder of the science of acoustics, lived next door to the Hills in 1944-5. He graduated from Mount Vernon H.S. and Cornell College, '36. Leo's father owned a hardware store on the north side of Main Street (aka 1st St. W), on the east side of 1st Ave N.

It was very interesting to hear what you did for those two couples (pregnant) at Camp Cooke, and what a sad ending to the story. That is the tragedy of war, tho', as you said!

You had not told me that you were back with the 1st Army – of course, that may have been changed again by this time. Also, I hadn't known until Ms. Thomas's letter, that Dusseldorf was your first "objective."

There is to be an Art class this summer (4 wks.) for children – tuition free – and I am so glad that Tommy is willing and interested in going. I brought home his pottery pieces yesterday, and they are very "creditable – Art and Music were his two A subjects. Since it has been impossible for him to keep on with his music here in MV, I am so glad to have the opportunity to give him some extra instruction in Art. With it, he is just a normal boy, however, and THANK GOODNESS! He's certainly no sissy.

We have been having lots of fresh asparagus and radishes and lettuce and onions from the garden. Do you get potatoes, and bread? Or is all your food "canned"?

This is all for the morning – Much love, Very, from all of us, 'S'Mae

No. 96
Mount Vernon, Iowa
May 25, 1945        Friday evening    7:20 PM
Dearest Gerald,

I am going to write "tomorrow's letter today, so that it won't be yesterday's if I wrote it tomorrow." How's that for the Dutch of it? But to translate it and put it into relatively plain English: Tommy has gone to the movie, it isn't time to go to the play, so I'll answer the letter I got from you today, instead of waiting until tomorrow like I usually do. It was wonderful to hear from you again today – two days in a row – this one No. 40 – just three weeks enroute. I saw Elsie Meffert on the campus this afternoon and she says Clyde Meffert is in Pilsen in CZ. Wonder if you are anywhere near there.

Hope you will really consider that air castle I wrote to you about – about us all coming over to Europe for a few years. I have an awful bug to travel today. I expect, with all the traveling that you have to do by jeep over terrible roads, that seems like a very crazy bug. We seem to be laying up a little as we go along, even if we are making considerable sacrifice to do it.

So glad you have escaped unharmed thru all of your journeying around over the country by night and day alone. Also, glad that the script (Lion's) finally reached you – that Benedictine made my mouth water! Will try to get to CR the first part of next week, and do the errands you have mentioned as well as some of my own.

I sent Bob Runkle's graduation gift today – a Bible. Lester has been having a little heart disturbance, and the Doc. says he needs rest and a change – it'll be a good thing for both of them to get up to camp. Am waiting to hear your reaction about going to Montana this summer, before I make any more definite plans – and what the peace (if any) in Europe has done to your work. Gen. Hodges of the 1st is home – I see by the paper tonight.*

May 26, 9:30 AM

Got started bright and early this morning – just got back from the office, where I checked over and checked in the thesis. I got $15 for typing it and I am on my way downtown to put it, along with $5 which I got for doing some other typing, and another $5 from the rent from the upstairs apartment to make $25 more to put on that MV bank loan. I expect you will think that is not very high-powered finance, but I am just determined to get that paid off, even if only a little at a time.

The play went very well last night, technically, and this is a nice day for the Alumni who come back for Commencement. Have a lot of cleaning to do around the house so Bye for this time.

Love – 'S'Mae

---

* General Courtney H. Hodges (1887-1966) was the commander of the First U.S. Army in Europe in WWII.

154

No. 97
Mount Vernon, Iowa
May 27, 1945          Sunday
Dearest Gerald,

          Airmail has been so slow lately that I will be glad to know how long it takes for this to reach you. This was Baccalaureate and no church or Sunday School, so it has been a long day for Tommy and me. It seems strange with only Tommy and me here since George is still down on the farm. Wonder what we would have done if you had been here – as it was, I have been very lazy – reading, and sleeping most all day. It has poured rain outside, but Clint was out cleaning the gutters, gathering a few strawberries and asparagus.

          Am sending a lot of clippings from the Sunday papers by air-mail. I think you will be interested in reading about a CR man who is home on leave from the South Pacific (RX) and has been doing some parachute jumping. By the way, I hope that you are having some pictures taken of <u>yourself</u> as "you go along." Iowa newspapers are anxious to get pictures of "Iowans abroad," so give yourself a boast, if you can.*
Do you write to the families of the men who have been killed?
Have heard nothing from the story of George and Admiral Leahy, so I guess it "didn't make the grade."
All is quiet and calm – just wanted you to know that we are thinking of you.
                    Much love from all, Essie Mae


No. 98
EMH to GLH, envelope postmarked May 1945, probably sent 28 May, with two 6¢ airmail stamps, containing:
Father's Day card with verse ending "I love you more each day," signed Essie Mae. Two enclosures:
          "To dad From George, "There is a word to say / It's happy Father's Day / But it isn't quite sufficient / To say what we are wishen' / Every Sunday – EVERY DAY."
          Tommy: "Dear Daddy / I got your Birthday letter this morning. It was surly good to hear from you. Day before yesterday I sold things and got a dollar. I sold More than 11 dollars worth but one of the boys sold 20 Dollars worth. Yesterday I went out to the palisades found out where devils Kitchen is and I think it was the best day of my life.          Tommy Hill          P.S. Happy fathers day"


No. 99
May 31, 1945          Thursday  8:15 AM
Dearest Gerald,

          Another day – Of course, it is another <u>rainy</u> day, another <u>cold</u> day, and another day without mail from you, but nevertheless, it's another DAY, and therefore the possibility of mail. One of these days, I'll get a dozen or so letters, maybe!
                    Much love, Essie Mae


No. 100
May 31, 1945          Thursday  8:30 AM
Dearest Gerald,

          This is a continuation, and I hope you get both of the letters I'm writing this morning at the same time.
          Yesterday was a very nice Memorial Day, with beautiful weather – for a CHANGE. I took advantage of the sunshine, to clean the downstairs closet, and air everything, resort your lockers, and move the file out into the bedroom, behind the door that leads to the living room. George wore his Scout uniform all day, marched in the MV procession in the morning, and I took him and Bobby Gaston and Tommy to the Lisbon ceremonies in the afternoon. I took pictures of G. and T. standing beside the car, as I used to do every Decoration Day, just for the record. Some of

---

* A Red Cross Field Director with the Military Welfare Service is shown in line ready to bail out with paratroopers in November 1943. Another Field Director is shown loading supplies to parachute in Burma in 1944 (*American Red Cross*, 154-5). EMH is paraphrasing the title of Mark Twain's book, *The Innocents Abroad* (1869).

the earliest pictures show Tommy hardly reaching to the handle of the door. Rachie came up in the afternoon, and she and Mother were both here for supper, which made the day "something special." It certainly seemed like a <u>long</u> time ago, that the golf season opened on that day, we had our nice dinner at the Palisades with Manly, etc., with all the other times we have had. Visited with Rev. Baltz a few minutes at the Memorial service yesterday morning. 83 years old, he is, and sat up all the way from California! I asked him whether he was going on to New York to "tie the knot" for Harold, and he replied that he didn't know, "He hadn't gotten over the shock yet."

A letter from Ruby, says everyone is fine out there, including your Dad, whose chief worry is to see a dandelion growing in the yard. He really goes after them. Jessie finished high school, very weary. John Howard is working hard at his school [Harvard] in the East. Our summer plans (tentatively) are, Tommy goes to Art classes in Summer school for four weeks in June and forepart of July; George goes to Scout camp for 2 wks. in July; and then <u>maybe</u> we'll go to Montana for the month of August. Am so anxious to hear what you think about going to Montana, and what your plans are. And this is all for this time. Hoping for mail today.

> Much love from all,
> Essie Mae

## She Wonders What the Future Holds
### June 1945 – August 1945

### June 1945

### Radio says the 97th is coming home this month
### "I know that 'time will tell' and have learned to be patient"

"What had happened to the more than six billion letters which were sent overseas during World War II? … After conducting exhaustive searches, we did not locate any books based on the home-front letters of American women … The letters in our collection are wonderfully compelling."

> – Litoff and Smith, *Since You Went Away*, vii-ix

No. 101
Mount Vernon, Iowa
June 1, 1945       Friday   1:30 PM
Dearest Gerald,

Today was the DAY! Your letter, No. 44, came this AM, leaving No. 41, 42, and 43 yet to come. That accounts for the long delay without mail, and I surely was over joyed to get the letter today. It gave me the answer I was waiting for, in order to answer Whites' invitation. I will tell them not to look for us before August, and by that time, we will know whether or not you are coming home for sure, this summer. If you are going west, it might even work out that we could all go as far as Mont. together. Time will take care of all that – there is no immediate rush about deciding.

NEWS SCRAPS: Capt. Lynn Morrow got home this morning, and is in very good shape "considering." Aunt Grace Stockwell is coming on the afternoon train from Chicago to visit for a few days. Jim McCutcheon is anxious to print some news about you, but I haven't quite decided what information to give him – think I'll wait a few days and see what later developments might be. Bobby Gaston has been with us, as a guest the last 24 hours, while his mother is away. We have been glad for the extra room upstairs, as we will be when Aunt Grace comes, too.

It was quite a shock to me to hear that you probably will not be staying on in Europe, but with George's "steadying" philosophy to help, I am getting accustomed to the idea. We certainly are far better situated here at home than we have been at any time since you left, and we are "salting away" a little, even if my "work" doesn't seem very productive. The record the kids are making has to speak for me, I guess. And this is all for this time. More tomorrow. And "thank the Lord" for your letters – and <u>you</u>. Love,

            Essie Mae

No. 102
Mount Vernon, Iowa
June 3, 1945         Sunday Eve   10:00
Dearest Gerald,

     This has been a wonderful weekend, with your letters No. 47 and 48, and the *Stars and Stripes* arriving yesterday. That was coming thru in wonderful time, for the last one was written May 25, and came June 2, and was sent to Mechanicsville to "boot." The news that you will be coming home this month is simply wonderful!! Harry Sizer told me tonight that he heard on the radio that the 97th was coming home, so it must be official. I shall be looking forward to hearing what happened between you RX men with the 97th, and headquarters (RX) in Paris, and what that outcome is.

     In the meantime, just checking off the days on the calendar, one by one. I got so impatient with having to wait until the mail was delivered at the house, that I got a box for this month, June 1. The post office called me yesterday PM to tell me that "my box was paying dividends, that there were three letters there for me"! We had a delightful time with Aunt Grace. The only drawback was that it has been so very cold, but we kept the oven going in the kitchen, and it was warm enough for her there. I tried to build a furnace fire yesterday, but it just wasn't adequate. I invited several women for tea (Mother, too) and it was very nice. Aunt Grace put on her costume, and told us the dramatic story of how she got out of Burma.

     I hope you are out of the mud and rain and tents by this time, and are enjoying some clean comfortable beds somewhere. I surely appreciate your writing those long letters, under what must have been most trying and difficult conditions. The enclosures were most interesting – the pictures of the Polish women, and the German money and folders. The story of the Polish women must have been in some of the missing letters, but I am so glad you got their pictures, they certainly look pathetic. Will close for tonight and write more tomorrow. Am so happy to think that each day brings you closer home – I hope.

            Much love, 'S'Mae

No. 103
June 4, 1945         Monday  9:30 P.M.
Dearest Gerald,

     As I sit in the kitchen tonight, typing this letter, I am thinking about the time when you were in Czechoslovakia, living in the kitchen, writing to me, and you told the commander "that there was a good furnace in the house, if there was some fuel put into it." A very parallel case – but I want you to know it was 34° in CR last night, and it would have been very nice to have had a "bed warmer." The sun shone today, however, and by the time you get home, I am sure the weather – and everything else – will be quite perfect.

     I've been reading the new Literary Guild book which just came – and it's wonderful. You may never have time to read it – *The Townsman* – until we retire to California in our old age, but I shall insist upon it then, for I am sure you would enjoy it – by having it read to you, at least. I was asked to be vice-president of the PTA for next year (which means chairman of the program committee), but I think I shall "decline with thanks" – I like to be busy, but I don't think I need to let myself in for "headaches." Right? I won't dare to tell Tommy tho' for he was disappointed this year, when he wasn't able to "bask in the reflected glory" of his Mother being an officer in the PTA.*

     Was so glad to get your reports on conditions as you have seen them, about refugees, prisoners, etc., and the attitudes of the Germans. We'll want to mark a map of all your travels when you get home. The *Geographic* has a

---

* *The Townsman* (1945) was written by Pearl S. Buck. It was one of four novels that she wrote using the pseudonym John Sedges. It was soon re-released under her name. Buck was the first woman to win the Nobel Prize for Literature.

157

very good map of Germany and surrounding countries.  Angle on Capt. Morrow:  <u>After</u> he got home, Margaret got a letter from Col. Parson of his outfit, saying that his <u>grave</u> had been located in Germany.  You can imagine their reaction to that, especially with him "there in the flesh with them" when they got the letter.  I am wondering what you found out from headquarters in Paris, but I'll probably know in a few days.

        Much love, 'S'Mae

No. 104
Mount Vernon, Iowa
June 5, 1945        Tuesday evening
Dearest Gerald,

        Your letter of May 27 came today, <u>wonderful</u> service.  I suppose that means you are nearer the "point of departure."  I splurged, and bought some new clothes, with which to "greet my husband in proper style," including some "night time wear" as well as day time!  It was practically like buying a trousseau.  I've been saving my money for some special occasion and this is IT.  Used the money Johnsons gave me for a new purse, very plain, tailored, but as good leather as I could buy.  Even so, they said at the store it wouldn't wear like the one I got when I was teaching at Coe, and have carried every day since then – and it cost twice as much!

        Was amused at G.'s telling of a discussion they had at Scout meeting.  Joe Cooper suggested that they give some of their money to some worthy cause.  G. immediately suggested the RX.  Stanley Grant suggested the church.  At which Joe said, "Well, if I were a prisoner of war, the church might send me a Bible, but the RX would send me food and cigarettes and I think I'd like it better."  They had quite a discussion about it, some of it quite funny.

        We didn't get home from CR until about seven o'clock, but G. went up to the Post Office, and again I was glad I had a box, for he brought home your letter.  It is good to think that you are in more comfortable living quarters now.  I hope you get a chance to see more of Paris before you leave.  Too bad about your lost films.

        Big ironing to do tomorrow – so to bed now, to try to "warm up the bed, alone" for a few more nights.

        Much love, 'S'Mae

No. 105
June 7, 1945        Thursday  11:15 A.M.
Dearest Gerald,

        Your letter of May 10 (No. 41) came this morning.  Altho' we have had several later ones, it was grand to get this one, in this "interval" when I know you are on the road, and told me, in the letter of May 27, that you would not be able to mail any for a while, while you were on the road to Paris.  This one filled in details of your last days in CZ which were most interesting.  I was glad to hear about the refugees, and the slave workers which you had seen.  I am wondering if you are not in Paris right now.  So many questions to be answered, but it shouldn't be long now!

        I finally broke down yesterday and started up the furnace fire again, and I have felt well repaid, for it is nice and warm in the house.  I stand guard at the doors, to keep them shut, as the kids tear in and out – "can't warm up all out doors," as I keep telling them.  Tommy is at Art class, and George is reading the new *Life*.  Lunch is about ready, so 'Bye – heaps of love.

        Essie Mae

No. 106
June 9, 1945        Saturday morning
Dearest Gerald,

        No mail, either from you or to you yesterday, so I am starting this out bright an early, so I won't get "sidetracked" like I did yesterday.  I am busy sewing – two dresses nearly done, and a sort of negligee.  I have been using the lavatory for a sewing room, and having a wonderful time.

        Yesterday was a red letter day for George.  He started on a full time job, and ended up with an over night Scout hike.  His job is to tend the boiler for Dick Stoltz's dry cleaning and pressing establishment.  I think it is fine, if Dick thinks he can do it – and he does.  He is supposed to get down there at 7:30 AM and build the fire in the tiny fire pot under the boiler in the basement of the building beside Bauman's store. He then just watches the steam gauge and keeps the fire going so that the pressure remains approximately the same. He gets terribly dirty, for the basement hasn't been cleaned of the coal dust of years, but Dick pays him 25¢ an hour, so G. is quite the envy of his pals. He will get bored with it, for there really isn't much to do, but it's good while it lasts. He has been wanting to drop his paper route, and awfully sore at me because I wouldn't OK it, but now Tommy and another boy are acting as substitutes on the paper route, and George is content.

This overnight hike is Joe Cooper's last gesture toward the Scouts. They were going down to Whitman's quarry, and thank goodness it was a little warmer and drier last night. G. took three blankets, canteen, cooking kit, flashlight, heat tabs, his breakfast, and I don't know what else. He was certainly loaded down, but I know they'll have a wonderful time.

-----------

It is now 7:30 and George just came in, tired but happy. He said he didn't get to sleep until 12:30 last night, so he went right upstairs to bed now. Joe brought them in to town this morning in his big red hearse – that wasn't so bad either, for I think they were nearly <u>dead</u>.

And this, I guess, brings us up to date on the home front. Will be looking forward to your next letter, as well as two more written from CZ which have not come yet.

Much love from all of us, 'S'Mae

No. 107
Mount Vernon, Iowa
June 11, 1945      Monday   0945
Dearest Gerald,

This was indeed a memorable day, with your letters No. 42, 43, and 46, all coming at once. During that interval when you were writing them, I was anxiously watching for mail, which as so long delayed. I would have loved to get them in the right order, but since "I lived thru that time" I am more than grateful to have them now. You did give me "warning" about going to the Pacific in these letters, so you know that by not getting them until now, the news that was in the plans did come as quite a shock, when I got it in your later letters.

It is all right, whatever happens, and I know that whatever you decide after you get home will work out all right, too. I suppose that by this time, you yourself are much more certain about what the immediate future would be than you were when you wrote those letters.

This is just a note to tell you that I love you very much, and that we are all fine. You see, I have a new job. It really isn't much, but I can work at it enough to say I am secretary to the Dean of the College." I helped Harold Baltz get out some Conservatory correspondence (I still can't spell)* and Jay McGregor happened to overhear him telling about it up at the College office. So, he called me this morning to do some work for him. There will be about a hundred letters all together, quite long, dictated. I just got home from the office with a notebook full, and must get to it, before my shorthand gets cold. You can see my fingers are stiff, and I'll have to go slower than I'm writing this! It will be very good experience for me, and "no telling" it might lead to something else. Al has had very little or nothing for me to do lately.

Also had a very successful singing experience at the Presbyterian church yesterday, judging from the comments. I sang "The Lord is My Shepherd," which is a favorite of most people anyway, but I don't know when so many have called or mentioned it in person – very nice. I got my sewing done just in time, I guess, and I have two very pretty new dresses, a lovely lace trimmed nighty, some silk PJ's, a negligee, some new slips, shoes, etc. George is still enthusiastic about his job, and trying hard to make a success of it. He found some extra things to do around the shop today, which I am sure Stoltz appreciates in a boy. He swept the sidewalk in front of the shop and he reports, "I said good morning, very spritely to everyone who went past." I can just picture it, for he was so happy to be working on Main Street. And now to dash up town to the mail box.

Much love from all of us, 'S'Mae

---

* I have silently corrected her mis-spellings in this sentence, and many of the others elsewhere in her letters.

No. 108
Mount Vernon, Iowa
June 12, 1945          Tuesday
Dearest Gerald,

I surely have been neglecting you of late, but I hope you won't mind too much. I have been working at the typewriter in all of my extra time – if any. I took dictation from Jay MacGregor for over two hours this afternoon, and I have a notebook full of letters to transcribe. I asked him for a college machine, to have at home while I was doing this work, and I just got this machine home. It is one of the new standard Royals, and it is a wonderful typewriter. I have worked on the old Underwood at the Theatre and our little portable at home so long, I'll have to get used to this one, but it does run so much more dependably and easily.

I am wondering, of course, where you are, and what new news about "our future" you may have by this time. I shan't be surprised to get a phone call from N.Y. any time now, but I am not getting <u>Too</u> impatient, I hope. Tommy has just finished a remarkable little "car" concocted out of his old wagon wheels, a two by six which he dug up somewhere, and pulley, and everything else. He had some holes drilled in an axle which he found, and I am really amazed at the result. He is such a persistent little cuss, and really has imagination, a quite a lot of skill. Your letter of May 14 (No. 42) telling of the mines in German fields, make me think of an article in *Life* not long ago along that same line. It certainly makes one's blood boil to think of the destruction that those darned Germans have brought about. The newspapers are filled with conflicting reports about controls over there, and one just wonders what the future is going to be, and whether Germany will find some way to arm itself again in a few years, and start all over again. Your description of the farm houses with the manure and all was most interesting, and I was particularly interested to know that they do actually exist that way. My, the stories you will have to tell us when you get home. Surely hope that somehow you will be able to wear that ETO ribbon.

And now to dash up to the PO to mail this and see if I have any mail. Also, to get some salad dressing – we're having potato salad for supper, and the Lord knows what else. Lots of garden lettuce which you would enjoy, I think, but which the kids are not fond of. George goes on another overnight hike tomorrow, but he spent more than ten hours yesterday at the shop, which is a long day for anyone.

Much love from all of us,
Essie Mae


No. 109
June 13, 1945          Wednesday evening
Dearest Gerald,

Another day gone by, and the score is one letter from you, and none written – that's bad for you, but very nice for me. The one I received from you was another "long delayed" one, telling of taking the "dirty blonde" German girl on her way toward home. That must have been an interesting episode. No doubt she knows how to "get around." I keep wondering what the newest developments are, but I know that "time will tell" and have learned to be patient. Dick Stoltz said he never saw a boy like George! He is so pleased with him, and of course, G. just falls over backward to make his work a success. I guess they find plenty to kid him about, and he takes it with good spirit. For instance, today, Dick had him putting on a screen door. He was reaching up so high, he lost his balance and fell over into a pail of water. He yelled, "Blankety, blank, blank!" (I mean he really yelled that – didn't swear.) Another time, he was sweeping, and Dick said, "Oh, your steam pressure is up to 95!" George tore down the stairway, and then Dick said he was just kidding. George said he was so scared and relieved that he just hung onto the broom and it "swept itself" – he was shaking so. But they have good fun, along with the work, and that makes it interesting. He and his gang are going on another overnight hike tomorrow night. It requires great preparation and planning, and they are deep in the midst of it now.

They were interested in your telling of sleeping in the pup tent, with the ditching around the outside. You should be quite an authority on this overnight business, by the time you come home.

But now, to wash the supper dishes, and get the kids rounded up for bed.
Much love from all of us, 'S'Mae

## July-August 1945
### Home Again – Planning for the Post-War World
### It's "in the lap of the gods" now

> "Women war workers never forgot the job experience they had for the duration of World War II. They never forgot the thrill of getting a chance to do a war job and doing it … They never forgot the excitement of being independent. They never forgot that once there was a time in America when women were told that they could do anything. And they did."
>
> – Colman, *Rosie the Riveter*, 103

Gerald Hill departed with the 97th Division on June 16, 1945, on the *USAT Brazil* (formerly *SS Brazil*) from Le Havre, France. The ship arrived in New York City on June 24, and the men proceeded to Camp Shanks, N.Y., a few miles from the city. After the Division had assembled at Camp Shanks, they were released and allowed to travel to their homes for one month of leave. Gerald rode on a troop train to Camp Grant, Illinois, where he was met by Essie Mae and the boys. They drove home together, and then spent the next month together as a family. They visited friends in Mount Vernon and Lisbon, Essie Mae's sister at her farm in Mechanicsville, and Gerald's family at their homes in Clarion. They accepted Mary White's invitation and drove to Montana for a week's vacation at the MacFarland-White Ranch. After they returned to Mount Vernon, Gerald returned to Camp Grant. He traveled by troop train to Fort Bragg, N.C., to join the re-assembled 97th Division as it trained for action in the Pacific. During his month of home leave, Gerald discussed taking a position with the First National Bank in Perry, Iowa, and they visited Perry. That potential position was pending when Essie Mae's correspondence with Gerald resumed on August 1.

No. 1
Mount Vernon, Iowa
August 1, 1945     Wednesday Eve
Dearest Gerald,

Starting a new "series" – it seemed strange to be buying airmail stamps again! I'm sitting here at the west window thinking of you and your hot and wearisome trip to N.C. I do hope you got acceptable accommodations, but I know how you will welcome a bath when you finally arrive.

We had a pleasant and very congenial trip home, stopping several times, and it didn't seem unduly hot until we got about to Maquoketa, so we made it very well. We got a big kick out of looking forward to, and then finally seeing the five numbers turn over to 50,000 miles, just as we reached Wyoming.

George had worked out the mileage, and prophesied the place correctly. We were pretty well pooed by the time we got here, but we sat around with little or nothing on, reading the accumulated papers, and drinking cool water, until we got up ambition to take baths and unload the car. I am all set to sing tomorrow eve at church.

I plan to write to the folks at Clarion and send out the pictures. It seemed very lonely and the house seems empty without you. Got badly spoiled while you were home. It was a wonderful vacation month, and I loved every minute of it. It will be grand to look back on it, even if we don't have another long time like that together with nothing much to do, for a long time. It was wonderful! Again – I surely miss you. There is a big "emptiness" here without you.

My left arm got sunburned enough so you can see a white streak where my watch protected it. It is mighty hot here tonight, but I'm thinking about the grand time we had last eve on the picnic and afterwards. Tommy has been doping his mosquito bites, that he got from playing in the park, but agrees that it was lots of fun, anyway. We stopped at Mother's in Lisbon on the way home to let her know we were here. Didn't stay long tho' – too hot. I am

161

so glad we had a chance to go with you to Camp Grant this morning and meet the men. I see now what you mean when you say they are so "young." I see too, how very fond they are of you.

Well, Honey, this is all for tonight. I am thinking of you, and with all my confidence and love.

Essie Mae

Thursday AM        August 2

Dearest Gerald,

Mr. Risser called from Perry about 8:30 – said he had sent you a night letter, but thought I might be in more direct contact with you, so wanted to report directly. He said that one of the directors was still out of town, so they had not been able to iron out the difficulties on the board, but that he would keep in touch with us, and that the board, as he had "canvassed them," seemed entirely favorable to you. I thought it was very nice of him to call here, and he seemed very much in earnest. I told him "we appreciated his hospitality very much, enjoyed the hotel accommodations," etc., etc.

It seems to me that that job is "in the lap of the gods," and I shall be much surprised if you are not offered the position in Perry – if it works out that you don't feel that there is rush about deciding. You know that we are entirely satisfied to leave it up to you to decide what to do – we will be happy wherever you are.

It was very warm last night, but cooled off with a nice shower, and is overcast today. I have water hot for washing now, and am ready to start in.

Will be happy to hear from you, and know how things seem there at Fort Bragg.

Much love,
'S'Mae

Essie Mae's World War II correspondence ends at this point, without revealing what happened over the next few days. An offer was soon made and it was accepted. Gerald left Fort Bragg and returned home, and the family moved to Perry, Iowa. He began work on September 1 as cashier of the First National Bank in Perry. Essie Mae and the boys moved to Perry and they started the school year there in September.

Gerald and Essie Mae's World War II letters, photographs, and other documents were carefully arranged and placed in his footlockers. They remained there, unseen, until 2017. They rarely mentioned their World War II experiences.

# Chapter Four

# Peace Again

## Problems, Success, and Retirement

"Women war workers never forgot the job experience that they had for the duration of World War II. They never forgot the thrill of a chance to do a war job and doing it. They never forgot the thrill of earning good wages. They never forgot the excitement of being independent. They never forgot that once there was a time in America when women were told that they could do anything. And they did."

*– Rosie the River*, 102-3

The Hill family never paused as it moved into life after the war. Gerald decided to resign from the Lisbon Bank, and take a chance on the future. In the month of August 1945, Gerald was like a whirlwind. In July, the first month after he returned from Europe, he found a potential opening in a bank in Perry, Iowa. He was interviewed there, and continued negotiations by mail after he returned to duty and was assigned to Fort Bragg, N.C. The job in Perry was to be his. Writing and telephoning from his base with the Red Cross in North Carolina, he made plans to move his family to Perry, many miles away – where they knew no one. His relief arrived at Fort Bragg on 14 August, and he went immediately to Washington, D.C., to resign from the Red Cross, and return to Mount Vernon. From there, the family would have to move quickly. They pack up what they could, put the rest of their belongings into storage somewhere, and move to Perry in time for him to begin work on September 1. Before they moved, they would also have to find a place to live, and after they arrived, the boys would soon start the fall term in school. He prepared to leave Linn County, Iowa, where he had spent the last two decades, and where he had many friends. For Essie Mae, at age 42, it would be an even more disruptive move. For as long as she could remember, she had lived in the adjacent towns of Mount Vernon and Lisbon. And now, she would be leaving her mother, her sister, and many friends. What could she do? Well, she had learned new skills – Morse code, typing, and shorthand – and she later learned to read and write Braille. She taught junior high school students, and then students who were both blind and deaf.

The Hill family spent the next nine months in Perry. The boys were happy, and Essie Mae found new friends. But things didn't go well for Gerald at that bank, and by the end of the school year, it was over. He decided to look for work somewhere else. He was making a little money as a life insurance salesman, but he had little saved, and the future was now uncertain. He decided to move back to Mount Vernon, to begin the search for another job. Perhaps it would be at the bank in Mount Vernon or in Lisbon. His sister Ruby had stored some of their furniture when they left Mount Vernon to move to Perry, and now she loaned him enough to get by on – for the time being. Once again, the boys were unaware of the problems that their parents faced; they were happy to be with their old friends again. But that soon ended. There would be no opening for him to return to the local banks, and commissions on his insurance sales wouldn't be enough for them to live on. However, he located a job as cashier of a bank in Sac City, Iowa, in the northwest part of the state. Before Labor Day in 1946, he moved his family there, in time for the boys to enter school – George in tenth grade, and Tommy in seventh. It was a good move, and they all were happy. After a year in a rented house, they moved into their own house. It was a small house, newly built, but it was theirs. For the next twenty-five years, Gerald's career had an upward trajectory, and they had a good life together. Like many others who returned from the war, he found it difficult to re-enter civilian life – to adjust to the post-war world. But he finally did.

One of the central characters in the movie *The Best Years of Our Lives* (1946) is "Al Stephenson" (played by Frederic March), who had been a banker in a small town in the Mid-West before World War II. He returned to his job after the war, but found the head of the bank to be unsympathetic to veterans' problems. Myrna Loy played his supportive wife "Milly." This immensely successful movie was based on a novella by Mackinlay Kantor, who was born in Webster City, Iowa, 25 miles from Gerald's home town of Clarion. "Fred Derry" (played by Dana Andrews) was a bombardier on a B-17. With its Iowa-born writer, a small-town banker, and a B-17 bombardier (think Marc Pitts of "Floozy"), *Best Years of Our Lives* is a haunting story that reprises many of the events of the wartime and post-war experiences of Gerald and Essie Mae Hill. Myrna Loy was born in 1905, the same year that Gerald was born.[17]

In Sac City, Gerald resumed his activities in the Lions Club and the Masons, and he was a member of the local Boy Scout committee. He and Essie Mae enjoyed the local country club and they were active in the Methodist Church. George graduated with honors from Sac City High School in 1949, and he left home to attend Yale and the Harvard Medical School on scholarships. He would later marry Helene Zimmermann, and they would have four children. In 1951, Gerald accepted a position in a larger bank, in Sioux Falls, S.D. He and Essie Mae found many more opportunities in Sioux Falls – the largest city in South Dakota – than they had in the small town of Sac City. They both decided to be confirmed in the Episcopal church, and they became leaders in the cathedral in Sioux Falls. Gerald enjoyed being the treasurer of organizations, rather than to be president. Both of them resumed their activities as officers in Civil Air Patrol, and they enjoyed flying with the CAP. Gerald was commander of the Sioux Falls Squadron, with the rank of major, and Essie Mae was a first lieutenant, commanding the CAP cadets in Sioux Falls. Tom was a member of her CAP cadet group, and he graduated from high school in Sioux Falls in 1952. He went to the University of Colorado on a U.S. Air Force ROTC scholarship. He had a career as a navigator in the Air Force, and later was a team leader for aeronautical engineering projects. Tom was awarded the Distinguished Flying Cross for his service in Viet Nam and he retired after his final tour of duty at the Pentagon. In 1959, he married Keiko Nambara, daughter of Dr. Shigeru Nambara, president of Tokyo University. Keiko had studied in the U.S. after graduating from college in Japan, and she and Tom met when he was on a visit to Japan.

In 1955, Gerald and Essie Mae moved to Aberdeen, S.D., when Gerald accepted an invitation to become the chief executive officer of a bank that was being formed there. As vice president, and later as president, he led the Farmers and Merchants Bank to become the flagship of the Dakotah Bank Holding Company. As the DBHC acquired banks other towns in northern South Dakota, Gerald supervised the operations of the F&M Bank and the other banks in the chain. DBHC became the Master Card franchise for South Dakota, and his stock holdings in DBHC enabled him to retire in 1972 at the age of 67. By that time, he had served on the South Dakota Board of Blue Cross-Blue Shield, and as chairman of the Small Bankers Commission of the Bank Institute of America. Essie Mae and Gerald enjoyed opportunities to travel to bank officers' meetings, and to see and do many things that were beyond their expectations as a young married couple. In 1970, they traveled around the world, and were thrilled to spend some time with Tom when he was stationed in Thailand. Gerald would have known that in combat – as Tom was then – one never knows what may happen. Tom completed his year of duty in South East Asia, and in that year, the entire Hill family got together in Aberdeen for Christmas. Tom and Keiko and their two children, Vicki and Tommy; George and his wife Helene, known as "Lanie," and their children Jim, Dave, Sarah, and Lana. It was the last time the entire family was together, for Keiko died in 1977.

As he looked toward retirement, Gerald and Essie Mae planned to move to a warmer location. They visited friends in Sun City, Arizona, near Phoenix, and they liked what they saw. More of his classmates from Clarion High School were living in that area than still lived in Iowa. They bought a two-bedroom condominium in Sun City, one of several in a complex that surrounded a courtyard with orange trees and bushes of fragrant herbs. They enjoyed their new neighbors, and they hosted many others who came to visit – especially during the winter. They became members of All Saints of the Desert Episcopal

Church, and they also were members of the Sun City Rockhound Club (amateur geologists) and the Cyclemates (bicyclists). Essie Mae took poetry lessons and she began writing her first book. (She eventually would publish three more.) She was a frequent speaker at meetings of clubs and church groups, on subjects as diverse as "Gems and Minerals of the Bible" and poetry about women of the Bible, in costume. Essie Mae was delighted when she was invited to become a member of the P.E.O. sisterhood, and she was a member of the Arizona Poetry Club. Gerald and Essie Mae returned to Iowa in 1974 for a last reunion with her brothers Manly and Harris, and with the Runkles and her nephew Jim High, at the time that Cornell College presented Gerald with the Alumni Achievement Award.

Gerald and Essie Mae bought a two-bedroom cabin in the mountain village of Payson, Arizona, as a retreat from the heat of summer in Phoenix. They called it "Jerry and Essie Mae's Hillsite." It was there that Gerald, working in the garden, had a heart attack and died in 1979. He was only 73 years old. Essie Mae continued to write, to play the electric keyboard – she especially enjoyed Methodist hymns – and to entertain her friends. She was always impeccably dressed, perfectly coiffed. She broke first one hip, and then the other, and for a time, she had a part-time helper at her home. When she needed more help, around the clock, Tom arranged for her to have a room at Sun City's Brighton Gardens by Marriott. She continued to host visits from her neighbors and fellow members of her clubs and the church, and to talk on the phone with old friends from all over the country. She was given a plaque as "Brighton Gardens Resident of the Month" in February 1994 and she slipped away peacefully in the following month at age 90.[*] Both Gerald and Essie Mae arranged to be cremated. Their ashes were interred in the Graceland Cemetery in Rowan, Iowa, beside his parents and grandparents.[18]

---

[*] Her obituary is in the Arizona Obituary Archive (http://obits.arizonagravestones.org/view.php?id=41227)

# Chapter Five

# Epilogue

Time, like an ever-rolling stream,
bears all its sons away;
they fly forgotten, as a dream
dies at the op'ning day.[*]

After Essie Mae died, George and Tom arranged for a memorial service to be held at All Saints of the Desert, and they then sold the condominium in Sun City. George sent Gerald and Essie Mae's papers to his home in New Jersey, and Tom arranged for the transfer of her other possessions to his home in Buffalo, N.Y. After Tom's wife Keiko died, Tom married a family physician, Dr. Suzanne "Suzy" Eppley. He earned a Ph.D. in mathematics at the University of Buffalo and he taught there until he retired again. He and Suzy then moved to a small acreage in Salem, N.Y., on the Vermont border. Suzy practiced medicine there, and Tom worked to transform their property into a farm, which they called "Pentameadows." He died in a tractor roll-over accident in 2003. Tom's daughter Vicki married Mark Norfleet; they live in Ann Arbor, Michigan, where Mark, a luteist, has a workshop in which he repairs stringed instruments. Tom's son, Lt. Col. Thomas D. Hill, Jr., was a U.S. Air Force pilot; after retiring from the USAF, he is a test pilot at Alamogordo, N.M. He and Julia Sheehy had a son, Conor Sheehy.

George and his wife Helene had four children: Jim, David, Sarah, and Helena. Jim was a public defender; now retired, he and his wife Uma Narayan, Ph.D., the Mellon Professor of Philosophy at Vassar, live in Poughkeepsie, N.Y. David, a poet and composer of music, married Shari Davison; both of them have died. Their daughter, Heather, of Parkersburg, W.Va., married Jason Haught; before they were divorced, they had three children: Marcina, Landon, and Christian. George and Lanie's third child, Sarah, has a Ph.D. in anthropology. She teaches at Western Michigan University in Kalamazoo, where she lives with her wife Megan Reynolds, J.D., and their two daughters, Georgia and Rosalie, who are half-sisters. George and Lanie's fourth child, Lana, is an educator; she lives in Baltimore. After George retired from his career as a surgeon, he earned a doctorate in history. He now writes books on genealogy and other non-fiction subjects. George's wife, Helene, known as Lanie, was a graduate of Smith College and she received a Ph.D. from Brandeis. She was a professor of radiology at Rutgers-New Jersey Medical School. Her book, *Hidden Data*, tells of her career and how it led her to become a whistle blower.

George recently edited and republished Essie Mae's four books in one volume. *Prairie Daughter*, 2d edition, is now available for Heritage Books (2018).

Could Gerald and Essie Mae be eligible for any service medals or ribbons from the Civil Air Patrol? George went to the CAP website in search of the answer to that question, because he wanted to photograph all of their CAP badges and then put them into shadow boxes. He was astounded to read that a Congressional Gold Medal had been awarded in 2014 to the CAP for its service in World War II, and that replicas of the medal could be presented to CAP veterans of the war, and to their families. Could they be eligible for it? George sent a query to the Civil Air Patrol about this at 6:01 p.m. on June 20. Three hours later, he received an affirmative reply: "The evidence provided is sufficient to verify the World War II CAP service of your mother and father and thus your eligibility to receive the CAP Congressional Gold Medal on their behalf."[19]

---

[*]Isaac Watts, from "O God Our Help in Ages Past" (1719).

# THE PHOTO ALBUM

*Gerald Hill and Essie Mae Thompson - Wedding, December 25, 1930*
*Methodist Church, Mount Vernon, Iowa*
*Attendants (left to right): Lester Runkle, Helene Runkle, Judd Dean (Best Man),*
*Harris Thompson          Flower Girl: Kathleen Thompson*

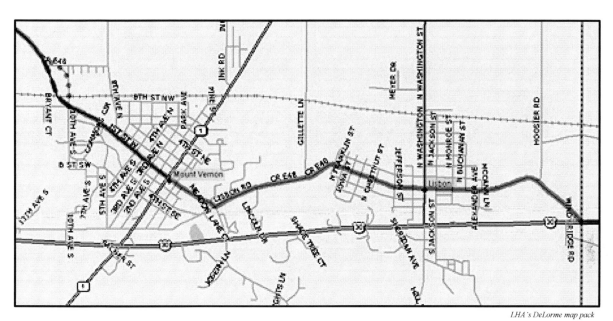

**Mount Vernon and Lisbon, Iowa**

# Views of Lisbon's Main Street
## It was then the Lincoln Highway, U.S. Route 30

*Photos by Thomas D. Hill, Jr.*

*South Side of Main Street at the intersection of Washington Street in 2012*
*Hills Bank (no connection to Gerald Hill) was then the Lisbon Bank and Trust Co.*
*Gerald Hill's desk was at the window in front, facing inward*
*The building at right was Fouse's General Store*

*Google street view*

*Main Street, view to West,*
*Toward Mount Vernon, with Opera House at right*

# Cornell College

*Photos by Thomas D. Hill, Jr.*

*Clockwise from upper Left:*
*View to East on Main Street, with the hilltop campus on right.*
*Science building with King Chapel behind it.*
*"Old Main" building in the 1940s.*
*Closeup of King Chapel.*

171

# Cornell College

### Buildings that were on campus when Essie Mae and Gerald were students there

*From top to bottom:*

*Carnegie Library*

*"Old Sem" – Science Building (L)*
*Gymnasium (R)*

*Bowman Hall residence*

# Cornell College buildings that were used by the Navy in WWII

*Merner Hall was a men's dormitory. It was used by the US Navy and renamed "The Wasp" for the aircraft carrier, USS Wasp*

*Armstrong Hall - the Fine Arts building - was used by the Navy for classrooms in WWII. The Cornell Little Theatre was here*

*The Cornell College football stadium at Ash Park. It was renamed the Van Metre Stadium on September 8, 2018. As an undergraduate and later as an alumnus, Gerald typed in the press box above the field. George's junior high schoolmate, David Van Metre, made a $1M donation on behalf of the family. His father, Doug Van Metre, was president of the Mount Vernon Bank.*

**Gerald and Essie Mae Hill lived in Mount Vernon, Iowa from 1930 until 1936**

*Gerald became the assistant cashier of the Mount Vernon Bank in 1931.*

*Bauman's was then <u>the</u> haberdashery for men in Mount Vernon. Stoltz's Cleaners was adjacent at the left, where George worked in 1945*

**The Hills moved to Lisbon in 1936**

*The Hills' house was at 310 East Market Street. The boys' room was 2d floor front on this side.*

*They sat in front of the fireplace for their Christmas picture in 1938*

*Gerald and Essie Mae and the boys visit his nephew Paul Hill in Des Moines in 1943, as Paul prepares to join the Navy*

*The Hills had this photograph taken in October for their 1943 Christmas card. Tommy (age 8) and George (11) are with Essie Mae and Gerald, in CAP uniforms. Essie Mae is wearing no badge of rank; her cap emblem, left sleeve patch, and collar pins are basic CAP insignia. Gerald is wearing sleeve insignia showing his rank as 1st Sgt., and his left collar shows that he is a pilot. He wears the one-wing Observer badge.*

# Civil Air Patrol Insignia of Gerald Hill

*Civil Air Patrol World War II*
*Service Ribbons (above)*

*Gerald's Observer Wings and*
*Pilot's collar badges*

*Coldwell Banker photo*

*312 3rd St., NW, Mount Vernon, Iowa*
*House rented by the Hills from 1943-1945*

*Mount Vernon High School as it was in 1943*
*"Old High School" for Grades 7-12*
*George attended 7th and 8th grades here*

### Women Fly, Too, in the CAP

TWO FLYING ENTHUSIASTS . . . and members of the local squadron of the civil air patrol are Miss Margaret Ann Twogood, left, and Mrs. Nadine Forey, pictured above. Miss Twogood, a junior student at Coe college, is majoring in aeronautics. She has her student pilot's license. Mrs. Forey has a private pilot's license.

IT MAY LOOK . . . like a choice sample of impressionistic art, but that conglomeration of symbols on the blackboard is a weather station model map to Civil Air Patrol Students Amelie Faymon, left, 125 Bowling street SW, and Eleanor Gunderson, 1865 Ellis boulevard NW. Instruction in navigation, weather and dozens of other subjects is given the prospective flyers in ground school now being held at the Y.M.C.A.

Instructor in civil air regulations, at right, is Mrs. G. L. Hill of Mt. Vernon. Mrs. Hill was instructor in aerology at the navy flight preparatory school at Cornell college and she taught civil air regulations to the Aircrew at Coe college and to the Lisbon CAP.

...tions, at right, is Mrs. G. L. Hill of Mt. Vernon. Mrs. Hill was ...vy flight preparatory school at Cornell college and she taught civil ...t Coe college and to the Lisbon CAP.

★ ★ ★

A REAL opportunity is open to women who are interested in learning to fly, and aiding their country at the same time, in the Civil Air Patrol courses now under way in Cedar Rapids. Approximately eight women and 75 men are now in the local squadron. Their goal is a girls' squadron, which requires at least 24 girls, 18 years of age or over.

Wearing approved army uniforms, the students must complete a 25-hour course in ground work before flying. The course, which is free, is being given at the Y.M.C.A. once a week with Mrs. G. L. Hill of Mt. Vernon the instructor.

The Civil Air Patrol offers basic flight training for women, who later may enter one of the various phases of flying.

Besides Miss Twogood and Mrs. Forey, pictured here, other local future women flyers include: Mrs. Maxine Weed, who has obtained her observer's wings for participating in a re-

quired number of missions; and Miss Eleanor Gunderson, who has made application to enter the ferry command and is awaiting her orders from Washington, D. C.

Anyone interested in further information may contact Lt. Truman F. Hanson, commander of the Cedar Rapids squadron.

oOo

### Quasqueton

Mr. and Mrs. Elmer Glass celebrated their golden wedding anniversary Jan. 1 and among the 40 persons present at their reception was Mrs. Alma Foster, who served as an attendant at their wedding and was a guest at all their anniversary celebrations except two.

Mr. and Mrs. Glass were married at the Baptist parsonage in Vinton and farmed in Buchanan county until four years ago, when they retired and moved to Quasqueton. They have a son, Amon Glass, who lives on the home farm; five grandchildren and two great-grandchildren. A daughter, Marie, died seven years ago.

*"Instructor in civil air regulations, at right, is Mrs. G. L. Hill of Mt. Vernon. Mrs. Hill was Instructor in aerology at the navy flight preparatory school at Cornell college and she taught civil air regulations to the Aircrew at Coe college and to the Lisbon CAP."*

*Cedar Rapids* Gazette *(9 Jan 1944)*

*Gerald L. Hill by Lasswell*

*Abbé Creek School near Mount Vernon, with Abbé Creek in background. It is Iowa's oldest one-room brick school building. George swam in the creek without permission on May 14, 1944. Essie Mae helped Tommy launch a "raft" there on May 29 & 30.*

*The Methodist Church*
*Lisbon, Iowa*
*Rev. Charles S. Arnold, Pastor*

*Ward School     Mount Vernon*

*Facing 3d Avenue N, between 3rd and 4th Sts., NE*
*View of SW corner*
*For grades K-6 in 1944-45*

*Tommy Hill attended grades 4 and 5, and played football here*
*The school has since been torn down*

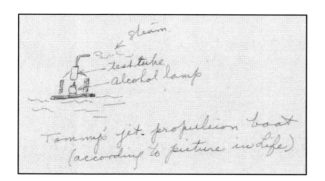

*Essie Mae's sketch of Tommy's jet propulsion boat - 27 November 1944*

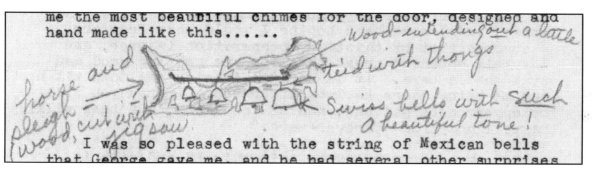

*Essie Mae's sketch of her Christmas present from the Runkles, 27 December 1944*

**Mt. Vernon, Iowa - 8th-Grade Class - Spring 1945**

| | | | |
|---|---|---|---|
| 1. Stan Grant | 6. Joan Blinks | 11. Dick Winsor | 16. Jack Stanton | 21. Bev Nation |
| 2. Maynard Barrett | 7. Jeanie Baldwin | 12. Eloise Littell | 17. Dick Franta | 22. Martha Osgood |
| 3. Elwin Wooff | 8. Larry Nutt | 13. Becky Current | 18. Eric Anderson | 23. Nancy Ink |
| 4. George Hill | 9. Clarence Smith | 14. Nancy Dean | 19. Mary Thompson | 24. Dorothy Wright |
| 5. Bob Gaston | 10. Donald Biggs | 15. Mary Baldwin | 20. Ardis Kirkpatrick | |

*Mount Vernon, Iowa - 8th Grade Class - Spring 1945*
*George Hill in front row, center*

179

## George's Story about Red Cross "Field Director Bob Trent" (26 January 1945)

Bob Trent had been a lawyer. Now as he sat in his tent thinking over his past experience it seemed almost unreal. That Order of the Purple Heart he received in World War 1 for receiving a piece of shrapnel that kept him out of this one. Then he became a successful lawyer and settled down. He got married and has two children. Then--

He was suddenly interrupted when a bedraggled Captain puffed into his tent-office. "Bob, my men are just back from the front. Where's the donut wagon?"

"It's over at A company, I'll phone for it."

Okay, we're over at CP."

The captain left and FD Trent told Mary Anderson to drive over. Now he heaved a sigh of relief and settled down. He thought back again. When the war broke out he tried to get in to the army but was turned down because of his wounds. The same with the Navy and Marines. He became a member of the local Civilian Defense organization and was learning to fly. Then he found out about the Red Cross. He went to St.Luis and enlisted. There he was sent to Washington. Boy, that was a place that was. Lost in the pentagon and--

"Major, which way is out?"

"Go around that corner over to your left, when you come to the second corridor turn right and down the stairs. Go one corridor right and one left to---"Oh, ~~[illegible]~~ haven't I seen you some place before?"

"Are you Bill Nelson?" : I and I saw Washington from the point of view of an ex-judge friend of mine.

Then shipped to California to San Luis Obispo and Hunter Liggitt MR. Boy, seeing tycoon Hearst's castle from a Piper Cub was really good. At Camp Roberts he went into training with the 97th Division, now his assignment. Then he had seaduty. "Boy, was I sea-sick," he thought back. "But that wasn't anything compared to the real thing."

His division moved from that camp to Camp Miller but on the way an accident laid him in the hospital. The ABC regimental Infantry Combat Team was ready to ship and he was released and flown to the port of emberation just in time for the gang plank was being drawn up.

Now in his tent he had to live on the bare necessities of life. "Quite a change, wasn't it Bob?" As he was pondering over his last thought, the regimental commander, Colonel Benton came into say that the men at hospital 8 wanted cigarettes and that he should get some in LaRoux.

"O.K."

Another day in the "uneventful" life of a Red Cross Field Director.

## Love Your Neighbor"
## or
## "A Short Cut to a Sharp Point"
## By
## Essie Mae Hill
## (31 January 1945)

LOVE YOUR NEIGHBORS

or

"A Short Cut to a Sharp Point"

A ONE ACT DRAMA OF EVERYDAY LIFE

ACT I

CAST OF CHARACTERS:

TESSYMAE, "An attractive matron in her early forties"

WINDY, a tousel-headed twelve year old boy

TJommy, a rather serious-minded nine year old

DISCOVERED: Tessymae, slouched in an easy chair of a wartime apartment living room. She is dressed in faded corduroy slacks, and has her hair tied up in a kerchief. A dustmop and vacuum cleaner stand in the middle of the room, indicating that she has had good intentions of cleaning up the place, but she sits now, oblivious to the clutter around her. On the floor is a conglomeration of discarded newspapers, small boy's overshoes, unrolled typewriter ribbons, model airplanes, ice-skates, etc.

Windy, is lying out at full length on the floor on his stomach, pouring over a war map, while

Tjommy, sits at a table with colored crayons and drawing paper spread out in front of him.

Windy: Say, Mom it sure keeps me busy nowdays, moving these Russian flags.....

"Love Your Neighbors"

1 - 2

Tessymae: (rather absent mindedly) Yes, I s'pose so---- Say, do you boys know what day tomorrow is?

Windy: Why.. Tuesday, I guess--- This is Monday.

Tessymae: Oh, I didn't mean that--- What SPECIAL day?

Tjommy: I betcha I know --- Last saturday night at the show Greer Garson told about the March of Dimes for the president's birthday.. and isn't his birthday tomorrow?

WINDY: Oh sure, I forgot about that. Score 1 for you, Tjomm.

TESSYMAE: Yes, you're right, but something else--- that we talked about a long time ago. Give up?

BOTH BOYS: Guess we'll have to --- I can't think what you mean.

TESSYMAE: It's a wedding anniversary, Now do you get it.

BOTH BOYS TOGETHER: Bertha and Al! Is it really? What do you know about that. Why, when we talked about it, it seemed a LONG time away!

TJOMMY : (excitedly) And did you get them what I thought up.

TESSYMAE: Yes, I did - surprised YOU that time, didn't I?

WINDY; What're ya goin' to tell them about it - isn't that a kinda funny wedding present?

TESSYMAE: Well--- there's no doubt about THAT, but they've got everything that we could wish for them, like home and happiness, and Anne, and each other.

TJOMMY: Yes, I just can't think of a thing they don't have... except a PENCIL SHARPENER. .... why, they've got just everything!

WINDY: (triumphantly) Well, that will help them "get the point" anyway.

TESSYMAE: We might suggest that they call it "Friends"

ALL: And we do wish them happiness, and Congratulations, and we want to tell them how glad we are they had that "merger" thirteen years ago.

CAST OF CHARACTERS [paraphrasing the descriptions in Al Johnson's next play, *Love your Neighbor*]
TESSYMAE, "An attractive matron in her early forties" WINDY, a tousle-headed twelve-year old boy
TJOMMY, a rather serious-minded nine-year old

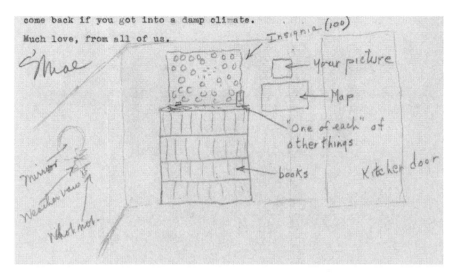

*EMH's bookshelf with George's collection of military insignia*
*3 February 1945*

*Card enclosed with EMH's letter of 14 February 1945*

*George as Wingy Vashki in* Love Your Neighbor *with letter of 3 March 1945*

*Toot Hill on his motorcycle with EMH letter of 18 March 1945*

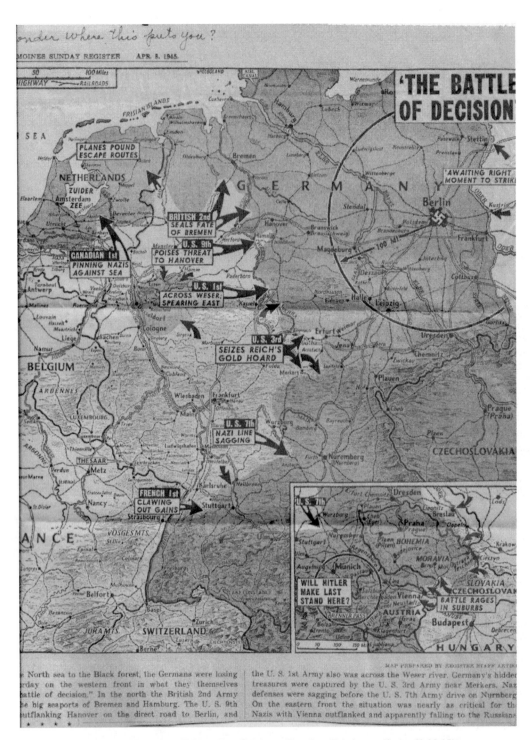

*"Battle of Decision" from* Des Moines Sunday Register *(8 April 1945).*
*The Ruhr Pocket is still in German hands in this map.*

182

*George and Tom in Scout uniforms – 1945 Perry, Iowa*

*The Hills in Sac City, Iowa - 1947*

*Gerald and Essie Mae Hill (front row, center) and their family in Aberdeen, S.D., in 1970    Left: Tom and his wife, Keiko, with their children, Vicki and Tom, Jr.*
*Right: George and his wife, Helene, with their children (left to right): Jim, David, Sarah, Helena (in front, beside Gerald)*

# Afterword

No members of "Greatest Generation" who appear in the letters of Gerald and Essie Mae Hill are still alive, and also only a few of the next generation are alive who appear in these letters. The next generation was once known as the "Depression Babies" although it is usually called "The Silent Generation." It is easy for us to look back, though it is hard to look ahead – "into the dim future," as Essie Mae would say. I am glad to have had the chance to do this project, trying to see the world as my parents saw it, and telling the story that they might have told.

I would add only what I believe my parents would have wanted to say in conclusion – that throughout their lives, they tried to live by the principles that are expressed in Paul's letter to the Galatians: to avoid such things as enmities, jealousy, anger, envy, and dissensions, but rather to seek to find joy, peace, patience, kindness, generosity, faithfulness, self-control, and love.[*]

---

[*] From Galatians 5:1, 13-25.

# Notes

[1] He was known to be fond of telling jokes on himself. Two of the most famous were of events in December 1937 and March 1939. The stories appeared in many papers, viz.:

> Lisbon, Iowa – Dec. 29 (AP) – As he had done many times before with meticulous care, Gerald (Toot) Hill, town bank cashier, drew his pistol and fired toward the skylight, ending the first half of a Cornell College basketball game. To the floor, almost at his feet, feathers following in its wake, dropped the carcass of a pigeon. Students, concealed in the rafters above, chortled loudly (Sent by his friend, Burton F. Tarr, a clipping from *The Binghamton Press of Binghamton, N.Y.* Many other clippings with the same story, or variations on this "practical joke," are in his scrapbook).

> G. L. "Toot" Hill of Lisbon had a lasting lesson in modern speed and transportation during his recent trip to a bankers' meeting in Minneapolis. At La Crosse, Wis., the Zephyr, by which Toot and his friends were traveling, had an accident. The group left the train to get the details. When Toot had satisfied his curiosity, he looked up and saw no tail lights. The train had slipped noiselessly away. There he stood in near zero weather with no overcoat, no hat, no gloves. At Prairie du Chien the Zephyr pulled to an unscheduled stop and a wire was delivered to D. U. Van Metre of Mount Vernon, who had supposed Toot was in the diner. The wire was an S.O.S. from the stranded Lisbon man. The hat and coat were left with the station agent at East Dubuque, while Toot borrowed clothing from a La Crosse agent and arrived home the next morning, just in time to receive the heaviest razzing of his life (From an Iowa newspaper, probably the *Mount Vernon Hawkeye-Record*, 5 March 1939).

[2] More about my chemistry set in Hill, *Edison's Environment*, xiv-xv: "Like many other youngsters since Edison's time, I followed the same route to obtain pyrotechnic chemicals. Sulfur and powdered charcoal (two of Edison's favorite chemicals) were in my Gilbert Chemistry set, and the formula for black powder (gunpowder) was in my high school's *Encyclopedia Americana.*"

[3] Rowena "Rowdy" Stuckslager's mother went to Vassar and Rowena went to Smith College. Her family was wealthy, and she traveled widely when she was young. Rowena married (1) to Ward McConologue in 1924, but she returned to Lisbon in 1932 and was divorced in 1939. She lived in New York in 1945. She married (2) in 1953 to Jens Friedrich, who fled from Nazi Germany and did broadcasts from New York for several years for the Voice of America. He died in 1968 and she returned to Iowa. For more on Essie Mae and her connection with the Stuckslager family, see *Prairie Daughter*, pp. 10, 11, 20-1, 23, 32-3, 46, 52, 61, 70, 72, 74. Dr. Gazda is later identified as a Navy doctor at Cornell College.

[4] Hartzell Spence was the son of the Methodist minister in Clarion, and he was a student at S.U.I. in Iowa City at the same time GLH and EMH were nearby in Mount Vernon. During WWII he was the founding editor of the Army publication *Yank* and coined the term "pinup." I recall that Methodists' behavior and custom were unchanged in my own childhood.

[5] The book by Gen. Robert L. Scott, *God Is My Co-Pilot* (1943), tells of his service in China in the Flying Tigers. It became the subject of a film in 1945, starring Dennis Morgan, with Raymond Massey playing Gen. Claire Chennault, commander of the Flying Tigers. Harry W. Flannery, *Assignment to Berlin* (1943) continues the story started by William Shirer, who was famous for *Berlin Diary* (1941) and later *The Rise and Fall of the Third Reich* (1960). Shirer was known to the Hills, because he was a student at Coe College ('25) in Cedar Rapids when they were students at Cornell College, 13 miles away.

[6] Her talk was an imaginary conversation with those who were away in service – as was Dr. Gordon Andre, who was President of the Alumni Association. The theme was Virgil's *Forsan haec olim meminisse juvabit* ("Someday you will be glad to remember these things."). EMH was the permanent President of the Class of 1920. Her Address was first published by her in *Flapper Fun* and was republished in *Prairie Daughter* (2d edition), 152-5.

[7] It was commonly believed in Mount Vernon that Admiral Leahy was in Iowa on 3-4 June as part of the deception to keep the Germans from believing that the landings in Normandy on 6 June were really the start of the expected invasion of France. FADM Leahy was Chief of Staff for FDR. Presumably the Germans would think he'd not be in Iowa when Operation Overlord was launched. But Overlord was indeed underway on June 6. The phony Army that Patton commanded was still in England, as another deception.

[8] A retyped story which Virginia [Thompson] sent from the *Denver Post*:

> "DENVER PILOT BRINGS IN SHRAPNEL-PIERCED PLANE FROM MISSION

> "Green Island in the South Pacific. June 8 (A.P.)

"Returning from a mission over Borpop airdrome, New Ireland, Marine First Lieut. John P. Thompson of 1271 Downing Street, Denver, discovered he had twenty-eight shrapnel holes in his Dauntless dive-bomber. 'I was in my dive and about half-way down when a shell exploded in my right wing,' he said. 'My gunner yelled over the radio that we were on fire, but at the moment I couldn't worry about that. As I pulled out of the dive, I could see we weren't on fire. The plane was working nicely, so I headed for home.' One large piece of shrapnel was imbedded in the fuselage just a few feet behind the gunner's cockpit. Lt. Thompson was commissioned in May 1943."

[9] Ed.: "Tommy Takes a Telegram" (6pp.) is "Dedicated to Daddy." Essie Mae never mentioned this story to Tommy or me. It was never published, and I regret that I didn't discover it when I was editing her four books for *Prairie Daughter* (2nd ed.). It appears that Al Johnson's "suggestions" on the evening of 19 July were so discouraging that she never continued with the story.

[9] She probably sang the Navy Hymn. It begins with "Eternal Father, Strong to Save."

[10] There are some strange coincidences in this story. It is believed that Harlan Nelson was on a mission to deliver an air drop to the OSS in Yugoslavia. By coincidence, the Chief of OSS mission in that country was Lt. Col. Charles Thayer. He had previously been in Kabul, Afghanistan, where he worked with LT Al Zimmermann, a U.S. Naval Intelligence officer in Karachi, India. In 1960, George Hill married Zimmermann's daughter Helene, who had been a school mate with Thayer's niece. The information about Zimmermann, Thayer, and the OSS is told in books written by Thayer, and in Hill's books, *Proceed to Peshawar* and *"Dearest Barb" from Karachi, 1943-1945.* In another air drop, Tex McCrary – later a radio and television personality – flew into Yugoslavia to see Thayer; many years later, the Hills had lunch with McCrary. And Lt. Col. Lanning "Packy" MacFarland, who was married to Elizabeth "Eke" Stuckslager, was the OSS chief in Istanbul. He was in charge of "Operation Dogwood," an undercover operation in Yugoslavia, which may have been compromised by a double agent.

[11] *Since You Went Away* starred Claudette Colbert (1903-1996) as "Anne Hilton," with Jennifer Jones and Shirley Temple playing her daughters; Robert Walker as Jennifer's doomed fiancé; Monty Wooley as an old colonel, the fiancé's grandfather; LCDR Joseph Cotten as Hilton's best man; Agnes Moorhead as a catty neighbor; Hattie McDaniel as the loyal African-American maid, and Lionel Barrymore as a minister. The mood changes when Anne receives a telegram saying that her husband, Tim, is missing in action. The last scene is set in December 1943, when word is received that Tim is safe, but it is a bittersweet ending because several men have died in service, including Jennifer's fiancé. The movie depicts many of the effects of the war in America, as it shows people coping with shortages of many things and taking on new jobs, while worrying about those in service. The movie is said to have been the fourth most popular that was made in 1944. However, I doubt that it played well on the Home Front, because many – including the Hills – worried every day about what might happen to their men who "went away."

[12] Ed.: The comment suggesting racist views came as a surprise to me. The minstrel shows in Mount Vernon of the Lion's Club in blackface were typical of the 1940s, although we now consider them to be racist. It was shocking to read about outspoken opposition from one of the women in the Lisbon Methodist Church to provide meals and lodging for the Rust College singers.

[13] Synopsis of Albert Johnson's *Days without Daddy*, a farce-comedy in three acts, for ten men and eleven women.

SCENE: The combination living room and study of the Day family, in a sizable city in the midlands, U.S.A.

Time: The present

ACT I: Late morning.

ACT II, Scene 1: About 5:3, the following afternoon.

ACT II, Scene 2: About 11:30, that evening.

ACT III: A few moments later

Characters (partial list):

Mrs. David Day (Dorothy) [played by Mary Stevenson at Cornell College]

David Day (Dorothy's husband "Daddy")

Betty Day (twenty)

Professor Frank Fud

p.5: "the Day family is not a regulation family – as you will soon find out"

p.29: "Mrs. Day. My husband is a good many thousand miles away; and as long as you're here, Lieutenant, let's just call it a military encounter and let nature take its course."

p.65: "Mr. Day. I fly six thousand miles just to have a few quiet days with my family. I arrive in time to see my wife stepping out with an overnight bag and a professor."

p.92: "I'm not home to stay. There's a little mess over there that still has to be cleaned up."

[14] Enclosed: a carbon copy of a humorous "order" supposedly from a commanding officer to "All Officers, Department heads, Civilian Supervisors": "It has been brought to the attention of this office that many civilians are dying and refusing to fall after they are dead. This must be stopped. On or after January 1945, any Civilian caught sitting up after he has died will be off the payroll immediately (i.e., within 90 days) … To complete the case, push the body aside and make room for the next civilian. By order of the Commanding Officer, Rigor Mortis, Captain, U.S. Army."

[15] The movie, *Since You Went Away* (1944), based on a novel (1943) with the same name, tells the story of a family from a suburb of Chicago whose father is missing in action. Several service men are killed in accidents in the U.S. and in battle, including the boyfriend of one of the daughters, but at the climactic ending, a telegram is received saying that Father is safe. The viewer/reader shares joy at the end, but can't forget those who never return alive. The movie was popular in New York City, but it was not as popular elsewhere in America.

[16] R. P. Andreas was a director of the Lisbon Bank when GLH was cashier. His food commodity firm, R. P. Andreas Co., changed its name to Honeymead Products. His son, Dwayne (1918-2016), lived across the street from the Hills in Lisbon. He sold 60 percent of Honeymead to Cargill in 1945. In 1966, he began purchasing ADM, which became a giant firm. He was involved in price-fixing of lysine, as depicted in the movie *The Informant* (2009). Long before that time, GLH said, "I'd never trust him."

[17] Myrna Loy (1905-1993) put her acting career aside during World War II. As an outspoken opponent of Hitler, her films were blacklisted in Germany. After the U.S. entered the war, she became an active Red Cross volunteer. She ran a canteen in New York City and was Assistant to the Director of Military and Naval Welfare Service – Gerald Hill's branch of the ARC. Her third husband was the movie producer, Gene Markey, and she was his third wife. Markey had recently returned from India, where he

was chief of Naval Intelligence in the South East Asia Theatre. Captain (later Rear Admiral) Markey was decorated for service in World War I, and he was decorated again for service with Admiral "Bull" Halsey in the Pacific. He was a philanderer, and Loy, who was raised as a Methodist, soon found that his eyes were wandering again. Markey was the supervisor of LT Albert Zimmermann in India (see Hill, *Proceed to Peshawar*, 66-70).

[18] Arizona Obituary Archive (http://obits.arizonagravestones.org/view.php?id=41227)

[Cedar Rapids-Iowa City, Iowa] *Register* (17 March 1994), posted 2011-01-01:

Essie Mae Thompson Hill, 91, of Sun City, Ariz., formerly of Linn County, died Tuesday, March 15, 1994, in Brighton Gardens nursing center, Sun City, after a lingering illness. Burial: Hill family cemetery, Wright County, Rowan. Survivors include two sons, Dr. George Hill of West Orange, N.J., and Dr. Thomas Hill of Buffalo, N.Y.; six grandchildren; and a great-grandchild. Born June 29, 1903, in Linn County, Essie was the fourth of five children of William Henry Thompson, a creamery operator, and Sadie D. Rundall, a Methodist laywoman and weaver. After graduation from Lisbon High School, she attended Cornell College in Mount Vernon, where she graduated with a B.A. degree in 1926. She was elected to Phi Beta Kappa and was a member of the geology faculty at Cornell from 1926 to 1930. In 1930, she married Gerald Leslie Hill of Clarion, a Cornell classmate. In 1972, they moved to Sun City, Ariz., from Aberdeen, S.D., after Gerald retired as president of the Dakotah Bank Holding Co. He died in 1972. During the years her husband was in the banking profession, Essie was active as a teacher. She taught vocal music to private students in Lisbon and Mount Vernon, and held Iowa and South Dakota teacher's certificates. She was certified as an instructor in navigation by the Civil Aeronautics Administration and was a teacher in the South Dakota System for the Visually Handicapped. After moving to Arizona, she became a member of the PEO Sisterhood and All Saints of the Desert Episcopal Church. She was a member of Sun City Rockhound Club, Sun City Poetry Club and Arizona State Poetry Club. She was the author of four books, including "Prairie Daughter" (1978) and "Let Thy Handmaidens Speak" (1983). Her latest book, "Flapper Fun: Other Poems and Stories," was published in 1988. Memorials may be made to All Saints of the Desert Episcopal Church, Sun City, Ariz.; Cornell College Geology Department, Mount Vernon; or Pickerel Lake United Sunday School, c/o Mrs. Harold Webb, 1316 S. Main St., Aberdeen, S.D. 57401.

[19] June 20, 2019     6:01 p.m.

To: Civil Air Patrol, National Office (Attention: John Swain, at dcoffice.cap@verizon.net and cgm@capnhq.gov)

Subject: Application for CAP CGM replicas for Gerald L. Hill and Essie M. Thompson Hill

re:(https://web.archive.org/web/20151124115122/http://www.capmembers.com/cap_national_hq/goldmedal

I believe my parents, named above, may qualify for the Congressional Gold Medal authorized for service in World War II. Both of my parents joined the Civil Air Patrol in the summer or early autumn of 1942. They continued in membership until the end of World War II, and thereafter until about 1952. They began in the Iowa Wing, as members of the Lisbon Flight of the Cedar Rapids Squadron. My father was the Flight Leader of the Lisbon Flight, with the rank of 1st Sgt. My mother was a certified instructor in Civil Air Regulations for the Civil Aeronautics Administration. She taught Meteorology (Aerology), C.A.R. Regulations, and Navigation to the Cedar Rapids Squadron. She was presented with the chevrons of a M/Sgt. on 23 December 1943. My father went on active duty with the American Red Cross (Military Welfare Service) in November 1943. He was a Field Director (simulated rank of captain) with the 303rd Infantry Regiment/Regimental Combat Team, 97th Division, in the European Theatre of Operations. His service medals include the American Theatre, European Theatre (with two bronze battle stars), and WWII Victory, and Red Cross ETO ribbon. He resigned as a CAP Flight Leader when he joined the Red Cross, but he continued to be a member of the CAP through the rest of the war. The Cedar Rapids Squadron became dormant due to lack of membership and leadership in 1944-45, and the Lisbon Flight was discontinued. Nevertheless, my mother continued to be a CAP member. After the war, they were active in the Sioux City Squadron (Sac City Flight) in 1946-50, and in the Sioux Falls, S.D. Squadron from 1950-55. My father rose through the ranks to become a Major and was Commander of the Squadron. His CAP ID card number 3092, issued on 18 January 1952, shows him as a major, with CAP Serial Number 7-2-1732. He originally wore CAP Observer Wings, but I believe he later qualified for Pilot wings. My mother was appointed First Lieutenant and Commander of the Civil Air Patrol Cadet Squadron in Sioux Falls in 1952.

Documents and photographs supporting this letter follow on additional pages. If the information about their post-war activities leads you to finding information about their wartime experiences, I would appreciate having a copy of your files on that subject. With thanks for your consideration, I remain, / Very truly yours, / George J. Hill

---------------

Col Frank Blazich, Jr., CAP fblazich@cap.gov

To: George Hill / Jun 20 at 9:04 PM

Good Evening Sir,

The evidence provided is sufficient to verify the World War II CAP service of your mother and father and thus your eligibility to receive the CAP Congressional Gold Medal on their behalf. In terms of a presentation ceremony, would you prefer such an event to take place in Maryland or elsewhere?

Very Respectfully, Frank / Col Frank A. Blazich, Jr., CAP

Director, Col Louisa S. Morse Center for CAP History / National Historian Emeritus

PhD, History / 202-750-1943 (Morse Center) / U.S. Air Force Auxiliary gocivilairpatrol.com / history.cap.gov

# Acknowledgements

I am pleased and honored to thank my parents, Gerald and Essie Mae Hill, for saving their letters and for encouraging me in my work in family history and genealogy. I also thank my brother, the late Thomas David Hill, for his friendship and support, and Keiko, the deceased mother of Vicki and Tom, Jr.; and his second wife Suzy, who survives and remembers him with "Spirit o' Tom." I thank our children and their spouses: Jim and Uma, Sarah and Megan, Lana; and the memory of David; our grandchildren, Georgia, Rosie, and Heather; and Heather's children: Marcina, Landon, and Christian. I also thank Helen Lucille "Hona" Frink, and many other friends – most of whom are now long gone – in Lisbon, Mt. Vernon, Perry, Sac City (especially Howard Kuske and Tudy Irwin); and the memory of Gerald and Essie Mae's friends in Sioux Falls and Aberdeen, South Dakota, and Sun City and Payson, Arizona. I thank many others in the Hill and Thompson families who preserved family records and helped me to understand the history of their families – especially Paul Hill, Charles Hill, Avis (Boyington) Hill, Lela (Hill) Odland, Jessie (Woodin) Kent, Jeanine (Humbert) Johnson, Sally (Hill) Elliott, Dr. Margaret Thompson, Priscilla Thompson, and Kevin Corwin.

I thank the Civil Air Patrol for the opportunity that the CAP provided for my parents to contribute to our effort in World War II, and for acknowledging this with the Congressional Gold Medal. I thank the American Red Cross for all of the good work that this organization – its professional staff and volunteers – has done for our family, and for so many others.

I also thank Leslie Wolfinger and Debbie Riley of Heritage Books for their continuing support.

# Bibliography

[Anon.] *The Story of the 97th Infantry Division.* Washington, D.C.: Orientation Branch, Information and Education Services. ACPL Call Number D107.2: In 3/97th div. Govt. Docs., n.d.

Adams, Henry H. *Witness to Power: The Life of Fleet Admiral William D. Leahy.* Naval Institute Press, 1985.

Adler, Bill, ed., with Tracy Quinn McLennan. *World War II Letters.* New York: St. Martin's Press, 2002.

Bernstein, Roberta Lesner, and Judy Lesner Holstein, eds. *Somewhere in Europe: The World War II Letters of Sam Lesner.* Bernstein and Holstein, 2016.

Breitman, Richard, Norman J. W. Goda, Timothy Naftali, and Robert Wolfe. *U.S. Intelligence and the Nazis.* Cambridge: Cambridge University Press, 2005.

Brokaw, Tom. *The Greatest Generation.* New York: Random House, 1998.

Blumenson, Martin. *Patton: The Man Behind the Legend, 1885-1945.* New York: William Morrow and Co., 1985.

Carroll, Andrew, ed. *War Letters: Extraordinary Correspondence from American Wars.* New York: Scribners, 2005.

Cather, Willa. *My Ántonia.* Boston: Houghton Mifflin, 1918.

D'Este, Carlo. *Patton: A Genius for War.* New York: HarperPerennial, [1995] 1996.

Dulles, Foster Rhea. *The American Red Cross.* New York: Harper and Brothers, 1950.

Egan, Timothy. *The Worst Hard Time: The Untold Story of Those Who Survived the Great American Dust Bowl.* New York: Houghton Mifflin Harcourt, 2006.

Gilbo, Patrick F. *The American Red Cross: The First Century.* New York: Harper and Row, 1981.

Colman, Penny. *Women Working on the Home Front in World War II.* New York: Crown Publishers, 1995.

Hill, Essie Mae Thompson. *Prairie Daughter.* Sun City, Ariz.: C.O.L. Publishing, 1978.

_____. *Flapper Fun: Other Poems and Stories.* Sun City, Ariz.: Privately printed, 1988.

_____. *Prairie Daughter: Stories and Poems from Iowa.* 2d ed. Edited by George J. Hill. Berwyn Heights, Md.: Heritage Books, 2019.

Hill, George J. *Four Families: A Tetralogy. Reader's Guide to Western Pilgrims, Quakers and Puritans, Fundy to Chesapeake, and American Dreams; Synopsis of 481 Immigrants and First Known Ancestors in America from Northern Europe in the Families of George J. Hill and Jessie F. Stockwell, William T. Shoemaker and Mabel Warren, William H. Thompson and Sarah D. Rundall, John Zimmermann and Eva K. Kellenbenz, with Outlines of Their Descent from the Immigrants.* Berwyn Heights, Md.: Heritage Books, 2017.

_____. *Fundy to Chesapeake: The Thompson, Rundall and Allied Families; Ancestors and Descendants of William Henry Thompson and Sarah D. Rundall, Who Were Married in Linn County, Iowa, in 1889.* Berwyn Heights, Md.: Heritage Books, 2016.

_____. *Hill: The Ferry Keeper's Family, Luke Hill and Mary Hout, Who Were Married in Windsor, Connecticut, in 1651 and Fourteen Generations of Their Known and Possible Descendants.* Westminster, Md.: Heritage Books, 2011.

_____. *John Saxe, Loyalist (1732–1808) and His Descendants for Five Generations.* Westminster, Md.: Heritage Books, 2010.

_____. *Western Pilgrims: The Hill, Stockwell and Allied Families; Ancestors and Descendants of George J. Hill and Jessie Fidelia Stockwell, Who Were Married in Wright County, Iowa, in 1882.* Westminster, Md.: Heritage Books, 2014.

_____, ed. *Prairie Daughter: Stories and Poems from Iowa by Essie Mae Thompson Hill.* 2d ed. Berwyn Heights, Md.: Heritage Books, 2019.

Kays, William M. *Letters from a Soldier: A Memoir of World War II.* Wimke Press, 2010.

Litoff, Judy Barrett, and David C. Smith, eds. *Since You Went Away: World War II Letters from American Women on the Home Front.* Lawrence, Kansas: University Press of Kansas, 1991.

Overy, Richard, ed. *The New York Times Complete World War II 1939-1945: The Coverage from the Battlefields to the Home Front.* New York: Black Dog & Leventhal, 2013

Styron, Emery. "Prisoners of War." *The Iowan* 68, no. 1 (2019): 18-27. [Algona POW Museum]

Villard, Henry Serrano and James Nagle. *Hemingway, In Love and War: The Lost Diary of Agnes von Kurowsky.* 1989; London: Sceptre, 1997.

Wilder, Margaret Buell. *Since You Went Away: Letters to a Soldier from His Wife.* New York: Whittlesey House, McGraw-Hill Book Co., 1943.

Zelman, Laura Cantor. *In My Father's Words: The World War II Letters of an Army Doctor.* Potomac Falls, Va.: Laura Cantor Zelman, 2016.

# ESSIE MAE THOMPSON HILL
## Curriculum Vitae

Occupation: Housewife and mother; geologist; vocalist and music teacher; school teacher; lecturer; narrative writer and poet

Birth:    June 29, 1903, at Paris (Linn County), Iowa. The fourth of five children, and the second daughter, of William Henry Thompson, a creamery operator, and Sadie D. Rundall, a Methodist laywoman and weaver.

Death:    March 15, 1994, at Sun City (Maricopa County), Arizona. Burial: July 30, 1994, Graceland Cemetery, Rowan, Iowa

Education: 1909-1920  Lisbon, Iowa, public schools. Graduated from Lisbon High School, 1920. President of the Class of '20.
　　　　　　　1920-1926  Cornell College, Mount Vernon, Iowa.  B.A., 1926.
　　　　　　　1927　　　　Graduate study in Geology, University of Iowa, Black Hills, South Dakota
　　　　　　　1928　　　　Field and graduate studies in Geology, University of Colorado, Boulder, Colorado
　　　　　　　1929　　　　Graduate study in Geology, University of Iowa
　　　　　　　1930　　　　Graduate study in Geology, University of Iowa
　　　　　　　1944-45　　Classes in Morse code, shorthand, typing, and art, Cornell College, Mount Vernon, Iowa
　　　　　　　1953　　　　Graduate study, University of South Dakota, Extension Division
　　　　　　　1969　　　　Classes in Braille, Aberdeen, South Dakota
　　　　　　　1980-1989  Poetry classes at Arizona State University, Sun City, Ariz.

Marriage:  December 25, 1930, in Mount Vernon, Iowa, to Gerald Leslie Hill of Clarion, Iowa; publicity director of Cornell College, and later President, Dacotah Bank Holding Company, Aberdeen, South Dakota. Died, June 14, 1979 at Payson, Arizona. Burial, Hill Family Cemetery, Rowan, Iowa

Employment:
　1918　　Teacher, Second Grade, Lisbon School
　1921-22 Teacher, Valley Chapel School, near Lisbon, Iowa (one room, all grades)
　1923-24 Teacher, DeWitt, Iowa, Public School (third grade)
　1924-26  Assistant in Geology and Physical Geography, Cornell College, Mt. Vernon, Iowa
　1926-30  Instructor in Geology, and Physical Geography, Cornell College, Mt. Vernon, Iowa
　1926-43  Self-employed (part time) alto soloist and teacher of vocal music.
　　　　　　 Cornell College Baccalaureate soloist, 1926 and 1927.
　　　　　　 National radio soloist for American Legion Auxiliary.
　1939-43  Choir Director, Methodist Church, Lisbon, Iowa.
　1944　　Instructor in Civil Air Regulations, U.S. Army Air Corps School, Coe College, Cedar Rapids, Iowa; and Instructor in Meteorology, Civil Air Patrol, Cedar Rapids; appointed to rank of Master Sergeant, CAP, on 23 December 1943.
　1944-45  Instructor in Navigation, Aerology and Engines, U.S. Naval Flight Preparatory School, Cornell College, Mt. Vernon, Iowa
　　　　　　　　With appointment at Cornell College as Instructor in Mathematics and Physics
　1945　　Executive Secretary for Prof. Albert Johnson and for the Dean of the College, Cornell College, Mt. Vernon, Ia.
　1946-50  Instructor, CAA Ground School and CAP Flight, Sac City, Iowa
　1950-52  Teacher, Sioux Falls, South Dakota, Junior High School
　1950-52  First Lieutenant, Sioux Falls Flight, South Dakota Wing, CAP; Commandant of Sioux Falls CAP Cadets, July-Nov 1952
　1969-73  Teacher, South Dakota School for the Visually Handicapped, Aberdeen, South Dakota
　1973-94  Author and lecturer, Sun City, Arizona. Topics include "Gems and Minerals of the Bible," "Women of the Bible," and poetry readings.

Honors and Certificates:
　　　　　Permanent President, Class of 1920, Lisbon, Iowa, High School
　　　　　President, Lisbon High School Alumni Association, 1939
　　　　　Linn County, Iowa, Teachers Certificate, by examination, 1922
　　　　　Iowa State Teachers Certificate, 1926
　　　　　Scholarship awarded for graduate study in geology at Clark University,
　　　　　　 Worcester, Mass., 1930 (award declined)
　　　　　President, Mt. Vernon, Iowa, Chapter, American Association of University Women, 1934-35
　　　　　Instructor rating in Navigation, Meteorology, and Civil Air Regulations, by
　　　　　　 Civil Aeronautics Administration (now F.A.A.), 1944
　　　　　First Lieutenant, Civil Air Patrol; and Commander, C.A.P. Cadet Program, Sioux Falls, S.D., 1951-52
　　　　　South Dakota State Teachers Certificate, 1953; renewed and effective until July 1, 1960

190

"Ambassador of the Diplomatic Corps of South Dakota," 1968
Vice President, Sun City (Arizona) Rockhound Club, 1973-74
Resident of the Month, Brighton Gardens, Sun City, Arizona, March 1994

Memberships:
American Association of University Women
Phi Beta Kappa
P.E.O. Sisterhood
The Sac City [Iowa] Woman's Club, 1946-50; Chairman, Music Department, 1947-48
Sun City [Arizona] Rockhound Club, Vice President, 1973; Historian, 1974-84
Sun City Poetry Club
Arizona State Poetry Club
University Club, Sun City, Arizona
All Saints of the Desert Episcopal Church, Sun City, Arizona

Publications:
Hill, E. M. T., *Prairie Daughter* (Phoenix: O'Sullivan, Woodside and Company, 1978)
Hill, E. M. T., *Let Thy Handmaidens Speak* (Chatham, N.J.: Minuteman Press, 1983)
Hill, E. M. T., *Flapper Fun: Other Poems and Stories* (Phoenix: O'Sullivan, Woodside and Company, 1988)
Hill, E. M. T., *Essie Mae's Cook Book, with Recipes from Family and Friends*
(privately printed, n.d., c. 1990)

Personal:
Her grandmother, Rachel (Manly) Rundall, is said to have been a teacher at Cornell College prior to her marriage in 1856. Her mother, Sadie Rundall held a Teacher's Certificate by examination at age 19 from Linn County, Iowa. Her husband, Gerald, received the annual Alumni Award from Cornell College's Alumni Association in 1974. She was the first female faculty member in Cornell College's history to be permitted to continue teaching after she was married, except for the wife of the head of the geology department, a decade earlier.

Her two sons, her daughters-in-law, and her six grandchildren and their spouses have earned twenty-eight college and university degrees, including nine doctorates and six master's degrees.

Many careers – She has been a teacher, in grade school, in junior high school, in the South Dakota school for the deaf and blind, and in college; a geologist and lecturer; a performing artist as vocalist and character actress; a wife and mother; and a writer of poetry and family history.

References (cited 6/2/19): obits.arizonagravestones.org/view.php?id=41227
https://www.amazon.com/Prairie-daughter-Essie-Thompson-Hill/dp/B0006CZZL6
https://books.google.com/books/about/Let_Thy_Handmaidens_Speak.html?id...

# Abbreviations

4-F = Draft category: failed; ineligible
AAUW = American Association of University
    Women
A.F.D. or AFD = Assistant Field Director
aka = also known as
Ames, Iowa = Iowa State College (now University)
A.R.C. or ARC = American Red Cross
"ammunition" = alcoholic beverages
A.U. = Aviation Unit
AWOL = Absent without leave
Batt. = Battalion
B.B. = Basketball
BB gun = Long barrel, uses compressed air
C.A.A. or CAA = Civil Aviation Authority
Callan = Camp Callan, California
C.A.P. or CAP = Civil Air Patrol
C.A.R. or CAR = Civil Air Regulations
C.C. = Mount Vernon Country Club
CO = Commanding Officer
Cooke = Camp Cooke, California
Coe = Coe College, Iowa
Cornell = Cornell College, Iowa
C.R. or CR = Cedar Rapids, Iowa
CZ = Czechoslovakia
D.M. or DM = Des Moines, Iowa
DS = Methodist District Superintendent
EMH = Essie Mae (Thompson) Hill
F.D. or FD = Field Director
FDR = Franklin Delano Roosevelt
GI = Government Issue, or US soldier
GJH = George J. Hill
GLH = Gerald L. Hill
H.L. or HL = Hunter Liggett Training Camp
H.Q. or HQ or Hq. = Headquarters
H.S. or HS = High School
I.Q. = Intelligence Quotient
Iowa City, Iowa = University of Iowa
KIA = Killed in action

L.A. or LA = Los Angeles
La. = Louisiana
lav. or Lav. = Lavatory
MC = Master of Ceremonies
McVille = Mechanicsville, Iowa
M.E. = Methodist Episcopal (United Methodist)
MG = Major General
Mpls. = Minneapolis, Minn.
M/Sgt. = Master Sergeant
M.V. or MV = Mount Vernon
Nav. = Navigation
N.F.P.S. = Naval Flight Preparatory School
N.W. Nat'l = Northwestern National Life Insurance
N.Y. or NY = New York
O.E.S. or OES = Order of the Eastern Star
OP = Observation Post
PBK (also Phi Bete) = Phi Beta Kappa
PBY = PBY-5 "Catalina" Navy flying boat
P.O. = Post Office
PT = Physical Training
PTA = Parent and Teachers Association
R.C. or Red C. = Red Cross
Roberts = Camp Roberts, California
RX = Red Cross
R.R. = Railroad
S.F. or SF = San Francisco
SLO = San Luis Obispo
SS = Sunday School
S/Sgt. = Staff Sergeant
SUI = State University of Iowa (University of Iowa)
T.B. = Tuberculosis
TDH = Thomas "Tommy" D. Hill
UNRRA = United Nations Relief and Rehabilitation
    Administration
USES = United States Employment Services
USO = United Services Organization
X-Day = Day 1 of EMH's menstrual period

# Names and Places

## Families
### With years of birth and death shown for those who are mentioned in this book

**Gerald Leslie Hill** (1905-1979) was the son of George J. Hill (1857-1952) and Jessie Fidelia Stockwell of Wright County, Iowa. Their children and grandchildren were: 1. William Benjamin "Ben"; children: Howard, Paul (1911-1997) m. Marie Johnson (1912-2000); children: Sharon, James; Leola, Genevieve, Ruth, Charles. 2. Harland: child: Prof. Charles Eugene. 3. LeRoy; children: Velda, Max, Marion, La Vonne, Minnie. 4. Myron (1888-1955) m. Julia Woodin (1881-1984); children: Dale m. Avis, Myron Jr. "Junior" (1927-2016), Lela (1930-2015). 5. Nellie. 6. Grace. 7. Ruby (1896-1995) m. Howard Woodin (1892-1942); children: John Howard (1924-2012) m. 1948 Betti Gray (1927-2009), Jessie (1927- ) m. Ken Kent (1927-2016), Mildred (1932-1997). 8. Adelia (1898-1984) m. Edward Hemenway; child: Edward (1927-1993). 9. Gerald Leslie "Toot" or "Jerry" or "Gerry" (1905-1979) m. Essie Mae Thompson (1903-1994); children: George (1932- ), Thomas "Tommy" (1935-2003).

Birthdays: Gerald, 18 September. Essie Mae, 29 June. George, 7 October. Tommy, 3 May.

Jessie Stockwell had 6 siblings, including Emma (Stockwell) Lum (b. 1874) and Grace Stockwell (b. 1877), both of whom were Methodist missionaries in India and Burma; and Eugene, whose son, Rev. Olin Stockwell, was a missionary in China.

Two of the children of George and Jessie (Stockwell) Hill married children of John and Elizabeth (Peters) Woodin: Myron Hill married Julia Woodin, and Ruby Hill married Howard Woodin, who was a soldier in World War I. In World War II, three of George and Jessie's grandchildren were in service: Paul Hill and John Howard Woodin were Naval officers (Paul was in combat, and John was sent by the Navy to Harvard Business School), and Edward Hemenway was in the Army ASTP program.

**Essie Mae Thompson** (1903-1994) was the daughter of William Henry Thompson and Sarah D. Rundall (1865-1949), of Linn County, Iowa. Their children and grandchildren were: 1. James Everett (1890-1974) m. Mae Hoover (1888-1986); children: Harriet (1918-2010) m. 1944 Rev. Albert Ronander (1914-2007), Kathleen (1926- ). 2. Manly Grant (1892-1975) m. Marie Simonton (1892-1952); children: William "Bill" (1915-c. 2000), John Paul "Johnny" (1920-2002) m. Virginia White (1922-2011), Elizabeth. 3. Rachel Edith "Rachie" (1894-1961) m. & div. James High; child: James "Jim" (1917-2001). 4. Essie Mae m. Gerald L. Hill; children: George "Toot II" (1932- ) m. Helene Zimmermann (1929- ); children: James (1954- ), David (1955-2004), Sarah (1962- ), Helena (1965- ); Thomas "Tommy" (1935-2003) m. (1) Keiko Nambara (1928-1977); children: Thomas Jr. (1960- );Victoria (1962-); he m. (2) Suzanne Eppley (1947- ). 5. William Harris "Harris" (1904-1984) m. Helen McKune (1904-1991); children: Martha (1930- ), Sally (1933- ).

Sarah D. ("Sadie") Rundall was the sister of Martha "Mattie" Rundall (1867-1934); she m. Frank Runkle (1873-1949); child: Robert Lester, called Lester or "Runk," Runkle (1904-1975) m. Helene Black (1903-1996), a great-niece of Robert Koch, the Nobel-prize winning microbiologist; children: 1. Robert Lester "Bob" (1927-2010); 2. Dorothy "Dottie" (1929- ). Bob enlisted as a seaman in the Navy in April 1945. After Mattie (Rundall) Runkle died, Frank married (2) Ruby___..

Will and Sadie Thompson's son Manly served in World War I as a captain in the U.S. Army Military Police, and he served again at the same rank and organization in World War II. Three of Will and Sadie's grandchildren served in World War II: Harriet Thompson was a Naval officer in the WAVES; William "Bill" Thompson was a Naval officer who served in combat, and then was sent by the Navy to Harvard Business School; and John Paul "Johnny" Thompson was a Marine Corps pilot. He was entitled to wear the Asia-Pacific Theatre Medal with three battle stars, and his unit received two awards of the Presidential Unit Citation.

# Other People

Anderson, Byron = Red Cross FD from Cedar Rapids, Iowa; with 89th Division in ETO.

Andre = Dr. Gordon, m. wife Vera (née Dyson), Cornell College '27; many other Andre family members in Lisbon, including Norman, Irene, Bertha, and Lucille. Gordon was the 90th Division Surgeon in the ETO.

Andreas, Dwayne = Owned Archer Daniels Midland (ADM); lived near the Hills in Lisbon.
>   R. P.'s son, Dwayne (1918-2016), sold 60 percent of Honeymead to Cargill in 1945. In 1966, Dwayne began purchasing ADM, and became CEO; he was portrayed by Tom Smothers in the film *The Informant* (2009) about lysine price-fixing. Enormously wealthy and had great political power by the time he died.

Andreas, Rueben P. ("R. P.") = Director of Mt. Vernon Bank. Had 4 sons: Lowell, Albert, Glenn, and Dwayne. The R. P. Andreas Co., a food commodity firm in Cedar Rapids, Ia., changed its name to Honeymead Products.

Andreas, Albert = son of R. P. Andreas; offered GLH a job in May 1942; he declined it by letter of 18 May 1942.

Andrist, Karl and Alice = science teacher at Cornell College, taught Navigation to Navy students.

Arnold, Rev. Charles S., and wife Mary = Minister, Lisbon Methodist Church.

Baltz, Harold W. = Cornell '26, Music Professor; Phi Beta Kappa with EMH; m. Manette Marble.

Barker, Richard "Dick" and Grace, and their children, Ann and William "Bill" = friends from Cornell College; he was coach at Franklin and Marshall in 1943-4, and later at Pennsylvania State College (now University).

Bauman's = The finest (and only) haberdashery in Mt. Vernon, Iowa.

Beach, Harold "Mutt" (aka Chuck) = Mount Vernon man, died as prisoner in Europe shortly before war's end.

Beranek, Leo (1914-2016) = World famous acoustical engineer; his father lived next door to the Hills in 1944-45.

Blinks, David = a cadet in the Lisbon Flight of CAP; killed in action, 4 Feb 45.

Bostrom, Rev. ___ = Methodist Minister in Lisbon, Iowa. Had a son, Eddy, who was George's age.

Bourke-White, Margaret = Brave woman, photojournalist in WWII; lectured at Cornell College.

Brackett, Charles = Hollywood script writer and producer, visited Al Johnson; Oscar winner.

Chipperfield, Miriam = Cornell College '27; GLH's classmate. In ARC, SAF, in WWII.

Cole, Russell = President of Cornell College in 1944; wife Betty; daughters Arolla & Nancy.

Cooper, Joe = Scoutmaster of Troop 40, Mount Vernon; owner/operator of gas station near MV High School.

Cummings, Tait = Cedar Rapids *Gazette* columnist; friend of the Hills.

Dailey, Lt. ___ = unpopular Commanding Officer in the Navy program at Cornell College.

Davis, Watson and Mrs. = Cornell faculty member. Mrs. Davis was a math teacher at Mount Vernon High School.

Dean, Lloyd C. "Judd" & Ruth = Cornell College '26; EMH's class; coach; Lt. Col., USAAF.

Dean, Rex & Helen = She contracted with GJH for Naval Cadets' laundry; parents of Judd.

DeNio, Edward W. "Denny" and June (Jen) = N.W. National Life insurance agent in C.R., supervised GLH.

Dilley, Margaret D. = Cornell '41; father Harry owned Mt. Vernon grocery store; m. Cpt. Lynn Morrow.

Ebersole, Dr. William S. (1862-1952). = Family doctor and physician for Cornell College.

Eisel, Mr. and Mrs. = A Marine stationed at Cornell College, and his wife; rented a room.

Eisenhower, Dwight D., General = His name was twice mis-spelled as Eisenhauer by EMH in April 1945

Ennis, Harold = Red Cross Home Service worker in MV.

Fisher [aka Fischer], Albert = leader of the Cedar Rapids CAP after GLH joined ARC.

Fisher, Mrs. Charles = Mathematics teacher at Mount Vernon High School.

Forbes, Capt. Robert "Bob" = USAAF officer; pilot of "Floozy" the B-17; later KIA.

Ford, Elizabeth Smith = Cornell College '15, author of two books about her childhood in Mount Vernon.

Franks, Ed and Mary = Friends of the Hills in Lisbon, with daughter Lib. Ed died October 1944.

Frink, Gale & Helen; and children Marilyn, Peggy (Cornell College '44), Lynn, Rich, Helen ("Hona") '56 = Neighbors of the Hills in Lisbon.

Gardner, Dr. J. R. = "Doc" was family doctor for the Hills in Lisbon.

Gaston, Robert "Bobby" = A classmate of GJH in Mount Vernon; father Sam; sister, Nancy.

Gazda, Dr. ___ = a U.S. Navy physician, stationed at Cornell College.

Gordon, Max = Broadway producer, corresponded with Al Johnson.

Grant, Rev. Dr. ___ = Methodist District Superintendent in Mount Vernon; father of GJH's classmate, Stanley.

Gray, Betti = Cornell College '49, married GLH's nephew, John Howard Woodin, '47.

Halsey, Milton B., Brigadier General = Commanding General, 97th Division, WWII; later was Major General

"Hanna" = The Hills' springer spaniel, named for Tommy's friend, Helen Lucille "Hona" Frink

Hartong, Rev. and Mrs. Robert = Methodist minister and his wife who were in Lisbon before Rev. Arnold.

Heffelfinger, LCDR Totten P., USNR = CO, Naval Flight Preparatory School, Cornell

High, Rachie and Jim = EMH's sister and nephew, lived on a farm S of Mechanicsville. See Family (above).

Hisatomi, Y. Charles = Cornell College '30, was student of EMH; was interned in a relocation camp in WWII.

Hoover, Ben and Betty = Hills' friends in Mt.V.; Marine captain in the Pacific.

Hunter, Dan = owned Hunter Airport, Cedar Rapids, IA; called "Iowa's Mr. Aviation" (*Citizen Times* [1Feb67])

Johnson, Albert "Al" and Bertha (née French) = He was a playwright and head of the Drama Department of Cornell College in the 1940s; in the 1950s, head of Drama Department at Redlands University (Calif.) He was blind. His wife, Bertha, was his invaluable helper. They adopted a daughter, Anne.

Johnson, Dorothy "Dode" = Cornell College '30; Naval officer at San Diego Naval Hospital, probably a nurse.

Jolas, Jacques = a friend of the Hills in Iowa, who knew Paris before the war; wife Libby. Must have been French.

Keubler, Frank (aka "Clint") = Roomed on the 3d floor of the house rented by the Hills in Mt. V.

Kharas, Ralph and Elizabeth "Min" (née Mohn) = friends of the Hills from Lisbon and Cornell; Ralph was Dean of the Law School at Syracuse University.

Killian's = Clothing store in Cedar Rapids, Iowa.

King, (Dean) Albion = a dean at Cornell College in 1944-45.

Large, Alice May (m. Horr) = Cornell College '24; classmate of EMH.

Lasswell's = Professional photography studio in Cedar Rapids, Iowa

Leahy, Fleet Admiral William D. = Chief of Staff to FDR; George met him and obtained his autograph.

Leigh, Elda = lived at 312 3rd St. NW, 2nd floor, front. Her brother, Earl, owned the house.

Littell, Claire F. "Judge" = Professor of History and Political Science at Cornell College. Son, Franklin Littell, Cornell '37, was a scholar of the Holocaust; daughter Eloise Cornell '53 was GJH's classmate.

Luecke, William "Bill" = SAFD at Camp SLO, FD in Europe with 97th Div. HQ, then 387th RCT.

Lum, Emma (Stockwell) = GLH's aunt; Methodist missionary in India; returned to U.S. shortly before the war.

McConologue, Ward, Jr. = son of Rowena Stuckslager by her first husband; probably related to Ray McConologue.

McConologue, Ray = perhaps husband of Mrs. June (Mathison) McConologue, Cornell '39.

McCutcheon, James "Jim" = Editor of the *[Mount Vernon] Hawkeye-Record*.

McFarland, Lt. Col. Lanning "Packy" (1898-1971); m. (1) Elizabeth "Eke" Stuckslager; m. (2) Virginia Nordstrom; Director, Mt. Vernon Bank; was head of OSS operations in Istanbul, in charge of Operation Dogwood.

McGaw, Brad and Grace = friends and neighbors of the Hills in M.V. He was captured in Europe, but was freed.

McGregor, Jay = Dean of Cornell College.

McKibben, Rev. ___ = Minister, Mount Vernon Presbyterian Church.

Meffert, Clyde B., MD = Cornell College '24, with EMH; MD, U. of Ia.; near GLH in ETO.

Meffert, Elsie B. Schule (m. Clyde) = Cornell College '24.

Meredith, Tom = Pharmacist in Mount Vernon, Iowa; handled Western Union wires in M.V.

Meyers, Gordon & Elizabeth = Cornell '41; at Julliard when entered the Army; his papers are now at U. Colo.

Miner, Neil = Cornell College Navy teaching coordinator; also at Coe College.

Moffatt, Toy "Dutch"; wife Margaret = CAP officer, Lisbon.

Mohn, Elizabeth "Min" = In EMH's class in Lisbon & Cornell; m. Ralph Kharas; her mother was Lena Mohn.

Morrissey, Al = Lions' Club script writer, Mount Vernon, Iowa.

Morrow, Lynn, Esq. = Cornell College '38; in Waukon, Ia., in 1981; m. Margaret Dilley '41.
    He was reported MIA and his colonel wrote that his grave had been located; but he returned alive.

Mortonson, Robert S. = EMH's Navy student in the NFPS at Cornell College; m. Margaret.

Nelson, Roy A. and Florence = Business Manager, Cornell College; son Harlan m. Katherine, was KIA in Europe, 21 June 44; son Charles m. Audrey Jean; son Richard, who later became an interior designer in Newport, R.I., was a classmate of George's; daughter Doris was a friend of George's.

Ostergaard, ___ = Mount Vernon High School Principal.

Patton, Gen. George S., Jr. (1885-1945) = Commander of the U.S. Third Army, killed in post-war auto accident.

Pillsbury boys = descendants of Charles Pillsbury, Hefflefingers; founded Pillsbury Co. in Minneapolis.

Pinkerton, Ruth ("Pinky") = Cornell, Honorary degree; vocalist, former student of EMH; singer in NYC.

Pitts, Marc = USAAF bombardier. His B-17 had a forced landing in Linn Co., Iowa. Later KIA in Europe.

Pitts, Zazu (aka Zasu) (1894-1963) = Silent film actress; "almost bought" film rights from Al Johnson.

Prall, Dr. E. C. = Dentist and Councilman in Mount Vernon; was the dentist for GLH and his sons.

Ralston, Betty L. = George's 8th grade teacher of American history; Cornell College '45; m. Arthur W. Anderson.

Reed, ___ = In C.R. CAP. Began to assemble a high school book on science, to which EMH contributed.

Roosevelt, Col. James = lectured on amphibious operations to the 97th Division at Camp San Luis Obispo, 2Aug44.

Rowe, Robert (Bobby) = Naval officer; wife, Elaine, a flyer, they rented a room in EMH's house in 1944.

Rowley, Rev. Glenn = Methodist Minister, Mount Vernon, Iowa.

Shackelford, Ruth "Shack" = Cornell College '27, from Clarion, Iowa.

Shirer, William = Coe College graduate, a contemporary of the Hills at Cornell. Author of *Berlin Diary.*

Sizer, Harry and Faye = Banker in Lisbon, Iowa. Succeeded GLH when he went in service.

Slaght, Col. Morley = Cornell College '34, MBA Harvard '36; in Clearwater, FL in 1981.

Snook, Lee Owen = Agent for the publishers, Row, Peterson. Autographed playbill for GJH.

Spence, Hartzell = Successful writer, born in Clarion, Iowa; a contemporary of GLH.

Stahl, Eldon "Bish" = Florist and grocer in Lisbon, Iowa; friend and neighbor of the Hills.

Stevenson, Mary S. = Cornell College '45; m. William G. Whitehead; in *Days without Daddy & Minstrel Show.*

Stimson, Col. Henry L. = Secretary of War in WWII; a relative may have been at Cornell College.

Stockwell, Grace = GLH's aunt; Methodist missionary in Burma; escaped when Japanese invaded.

Stoltz, Dick = Dry cleaner, Mount Vernon; employed George in 1945.

Stuckslager, Mary = Married (1) Van Metre; (2) Frank Shaw; was Dean of Women at Oberlin.

Stuckslager, Rowena = Rowena "Rowdy" (Stuckslager) (1896-1989); twice m. and divorced; m. (1) Ward McConologue. m. (2) Jens Friedrich. She was a contemporary of EMH in Lisbon.

Thomas, Mrs. Eloise (Stuckslager) ["Madam"], Director, M.V. Bank; m. (2) "Judge" Seth Thomas.

Tull, Clyde C. "Toppy" and wife Jewell = Professor at Cornell College. Tull co-edited *Prophesies of Hope* (1943), which is still available from Amazon.

Van Etten, Benny = a friend and colleague of GLH in Iowa Manufacturing Co.

Van Etten = Winifred (Wayne), Cornell College '25 married Ben Van Etten '28. She was a Professor of English at Cornell; author of the prize-winning novel, *I Am the Fox* (1936).

Van Metre, Douglas U. and Mary = A Mount Vernon banker and his wife, associates of the Hills; their son, David, was a school mate of George's.

Vodicka, Rudy = A Czech friend of the Hills; his farm was near Lisbon.

Von Larkum = Physician in Mount Vernon, Iowa.

Weber, Karl = Cornell College '37; actor and producer; worked with Al Johnson on film project.

West, Ken and Bertha (aka Eva) = Members of C.A.P. unit in Cedar Rapids.

White = Wilbur "Pete" White, Cornell College '30, GLH's fraternity brother; and his wife Mary (McFarland) White, heir to a ranch in Two Dot, Montana. He was in the U.S. Army in WWII.

Woodin, Julia = m. Myron Hill, Sr., brother of Gerald L. Hill; sister of Howard Woodin who married Ruby Hill.

Woodin, Jessie = Cornell College '50; GLH's niece, daughter of Ruby (Hill) Woodin; married Kenneth Kent '50.

© *JanPressPhotomedia*

# About the Author

George J. Hill is a fifth-generation Iowan. He graduated from high school in Sac City, Iowa, and then attended Yale University, where he majored in history. He received the M.D. from Harvard Medical School, and after forty years as a surgeon, he is now Professor Emeritus at Rutgers University. He served in the U.S. Marine Corps and the U.S. Public Health Service, and he was awarded the Meritorious Service Medal upon retirement as a Captain, Medical Corps, in the U.S. Navy. Dr. Hill also earned an M.A. in history at Rutgers University and a D.Litt. in history from Drew University. He has written or edited 17 books on medicine and surgery, genealogy, and history.

## Other Books by the Author

### Medicine and Science

*Leprosy in Five Young Men*
*Outpatient Surgery* (3 editions; 2 translated into Spanish)
*Clinical Oncology*, with John Horton

### Genealogy and Family History

*John Saxe, Loyalist*
*Hill: The Ferry Keeper's Family*
*Western Pilgrims*
*Quakers and Puritans*
*Fundy to Chesapeake*
*American Dreams*
*Prairie Daughter*
*Four Families*
*Prairie Daughter*

### History

*Edison's Environment* (3 editions)
*Intimate Relationships* (2 editions)
*Proceed to Peshawar*
*"Dearest Barb" from Karachi*
*Three Men in a Jeep*

## Heritage Books by George J. Hill:

*American Dreams: Ancestors and Descendants of John Zimmermann and Eva Katherine Kellenbenz, Who Were Married in Philadelphia in 1885*

*"Dearest Barb": From Karachi, 1943–1945, Letters and Photographs in the World War II Papers of a Naval Intelligence Officer, Lieutenant Albert Zimmermann, USNR*

*Edison's Environment: The Great Inventor Was Also a Great Polluter*

*Four Families: A Tetralogy Reader's Guide to* Western Pilgrims, Quakers and Puritans, Fundy to Chesapeake, *and* American Dreams; *Synopsis of 481 Immigrants and First Known Ancestors in America from Northern Europe in the Families of George J. Hill and Jessie F. Stockwell, William T. Shoemaker and Mabel Warren, William H. Thompson and Sarah D. Rundall, John Zimmermann and Eva K. Kellenbenz, with Outlines of Their Descent from the Immigrants*

*Fundy to Chesapeake: The Thompson, Rundall and Allied Families; Ancestors and Descendants of William Henry Thompson and Sarah D. Rundall, Who Were Married in Linn County, Iowa, in 1889*

*Hill: The Ferry Keeper's Family, Luke Hill and Mary Hout, Who Were Married in Windsor, Connecticut, in 1651 and Fourteen Generations of Their Known and Possible Descendants*

*John Saxe, Loyalist (1732–1808) and His Descendants for Five Generations*

*Prairie Daughter: Stories and Poems from Iowa by Essie Mae Thompson Hill*

*Quakers and Puritans: The Shoemaker, Warren and Allied Families; Ancestors and Descendants of William Toy Shoemaker and Mabel Warren, Who Were Married in Philadelphia in 1895*

*Rolling with Patton: The Letters and Photographs of Field Director Gerald L. Hill, 303rd Infantry Regiment, 97th "Trident" Division, 1943–1945*

*The Home Front in World War II: From the Letters of Essie Mae Hill to Field Director Gerald L. Hill*

*War Letters, 1917–1918: From Dr. William T. Shoemaker, A.E.F., in France, and His Family in Philadelphia*

*Three Men in a Jeep Called "Ma Kabul," Script for a Movie: A True Story of High Adventure by Three Allied Intelligence Officers in World War II*

*Western Pilgrims: The Hill, Stockwell and Allied Families; Ancestors and Descendants of George J. Hill and Jessie Fidelia Stockwell, Who Were Married in Wright County, Iowa, in 1882*